DRAVYA-SAṂGRAHA

LALA SUNDAR LAL JAIN

RESEARCH SERIES

Volume III

General Editor

PROF. DAYANAND BHARGAVA

Vahuvali Gommatesvara

DRAVYA-SAṂGRAHA

OF

NEMICHANDRA SIDDHÂNTA-CHAKRAVARTTÎ

[English Translation with Prakrit Gâthâs (Text) and Sanskrit Chhâyâs (renderings) and Padapâṭha]

Edited by

S. C. GHOSHAL

MOTILAL BANARSIDASS

Delhi Varanasi Patna Bangalore Madras

First Published : Arrah, 1917
(As Volume 1 of the Sacred Books of the Jainas Series)
Reprinted: Delhi, 1989

MOTILAL BANARSIDASS
Bungalow Road, Jawahar Nagar, Delhi 110 007

Branches
Chowk, Varanasi 221 001
Ashok Rajpath, Patna 800 004
24 Race Course Road, Bangalore 560 001
120 Royapettah High Road, Mylapore, Madras 600 004

ISBN : 81–208–0634–4

PRINTED IN INDIA
BY JAINENDRA PRAKASH JAIN AT SHRI JAINENDRA PRESS, A-45 NARAINA INDUSTRIAL AREA, PHASE I, NEW DELHI 110 028 AND PUBLISHED BY NARENDRA PRAKASH JAIN FOR MOTILAL BANARSIDASS, DELHI 110 007.

TABLE OF CONTENTS

APPENDICES

LIST OF ILLUSTRATIONS

LIST OF CHARTS

PREFACE

THIS is perhaps the first systematic attempt in India to publish the sacred and secular works of the Jainas with translation in English, so that not only the Jainas scattered over different parts of India, speaking different languages, but also the savants of Europe and America, may be enabled to explore the fountain-head of Jainism and derive a first-hand knowledge of the hitherto sealed literature of the Jainas. At the outset, we acknowledge gratefully the help derived from the works published and researches made by the orientalists with reference to Jainism without which it would have been impossible for us to launch into this great undertaking. It is not too much to say that, without the epoch-making researches of scholars like Weber, Hoernle, Jacobi, Leumann, Guerinot, Lewis Rice, Bhandarkar, etc., and the publication of original works by various societies in India, the literature of the Jainas would not have attracted even the slight attention which the modern orientalists deem fit to bestow on it.

Though Jainism is one of the oldest religions of India whose votaries in the past ranked from the prince to the peasant, exercising a noble influence in placing all beings on the same sacred status by unfurling the banner of peace and universal brotherhood, under which they were called to assemble, it is at the present day understood to consist of some customs and practices, the relics of a noble system, at which the other religionists continually fling their weapons of ridicule. The true principles and tenets of Jainism are as little known to these antagonists of the present day as to the Jainas themselves, and, consequently, we find a thickening of the gloom of ill-feeling in the minds of the friends and foes of Jainism which would have been easily dispelled by the light of knowledge, if they studied the original works of the Jaina Âchâryas. It is also a pity that the different sects of the Jainas waste their time and labour in finding faults of one another, each endeavouring to belittle the other sects and with well-meant, but ill-advised ways make the breach between them wider and wider every day. A study of their own canons, with the history of the great schisms in their order, would certainly dispel the deep-rooted aversion against the sects which profess to hold different doctrines; for all will then understand that the different sects are like different branches of a river which have sprung from a single source, but, under stress of varying causes, were led to wander in different ways, always having in view the ultimate end of joining the ocean. The schisms in Jainism were in like manner, caused by circumstances of time and place, and the varying angles of vision of Jain Âchâryas, Sâdhus, and Srâvakas, the preceptors and the initiates, though the ultimate goal of liberation is the same to all.

We intend to include in this series all the sacred works of the Jainas—those accepted by all the sects and those the authority of which is accepted by only a particular sect of the Jainas. By this course, we hope to open a field of impartial investigation, by which each sect of the Jainas can find out what are the actual points of difference of opinion, and without suffering any depreciation of their own, will be enabled to appreciate what is good in the views of others.

It would not have been necessary to dilate upon this point at the very beginning, had it not been for the fact that in India, at the present day, with a very few notable exceptions, every undertaking to promote the cause of Jainism is very often suspected as a sectarian propaganda. It is therefore necessary to emphasise that in the present series the sacred works of all sects of the Jainas will receive equal and impartial attention.

The difficulties which we shall have to overcome in our undertaking are many. The valuable manuscripts of the sacred works on Jainism are kept so very concealed and neglected in temples and private libraries that they may be said to be almost inaccessible. Fortunately for us, there is a band of enlightened scions of different sects of the Jainas gradually increasing in number who have nobly sacrificed their time and money in propagating the tenets of Jainism, irrespective of minor differences of opinion. It is only with the help of friends like these that it has been possible for us to gain access to the rare manuscripts, which will be published in the subsequent volumes of this series.

Our aim, therefore, is to publish the sacred books of the Jainas in original, together with old commentaries; and, in order to make the sacred works written in languages little understood at the present day, accessible to all, to add translation, elucidation and notes. In the opening volumes of the series we shall take up simpler treatises on Jainism and proceed to add exhaustive original commentaries, so that even a reader with little or no knowledge of Jainism may without difficulty prepare himself by gradual stages to grasp the abstruse tenets of Jainism embodied in works to be published in the subsequent volumes.

Our series opens with Davva-Saṃgaha (Dravya-Saṃgraha) by Nemichandra Siddhânta-chakravarttî, a brief, but exhaustive, work very useful to a beginner in his study of Jainism. This work is written by a Jaina sage, belonging to the Digambara sect, and it may not be out of place to mention that the Digambara sect of the Jainas arranges their sacred works into four classes, according to the subject-matter; and these four classes consist of (i) works which lay down rules of conduct, (ii) works in which an exposition of numerical sciences are given, (iii) works which by means of allegories and fables expound the tenets of Jainism, (iv) and works which treat of Dravyas (substances) existing in and composing the universe. The exposition of the principles of Jainism, as contained in the sacred books of the Jainas, is technically called Anuyoga, and the exposition of these four kinds of works mentioned above are respectively called (i) Charaṇânuyoga, *i.e.*, exposition of what one ought to do, (ii) Gaṇitânuyoga, *i.e.*, exposition of sciences, like mathematics, etc., (iii) Dharmakathânuyoga, *i.e.*, exposition of parables and stories, and (iv) Dravyânuyoga or exposition of substances existing in this universe. Charaṇânuyoga is also known as Prathamânuyoga, because it heads the list. Among the Aṅgas, the canonical works of the Jainas according to the Svetâmbara school, Âchârâṅga belongs to the first, Chandra-prajñapti to the second, Jñâtri-dharmakathâṅga to the third, and Sûtrakritâṅga to the fourth class of works mentioned before.*

Though Dravyânuyoga is mentioned last, it must not be

* "अनुयोगो हि सूत्रार्थयोर्व्याख्यानम्। तस्य चत्वारो भेदास्तत्र प्रथमश्चरणानुयोग आचारवचनमाचाराङ्गादिसूत्राणि। द्वितीयो गणितानुयोगः संख्याशास्त्रं चन्द्रप्रज्ञप्त्यादिसूत्राणि। तृतीयो धर्मकथानुयोग आख्यायिकावचनं ज्ञातृधर्मकथाङ्गादिसूत्राणि। चतुर्थो द्रव्यानुयोगः षड्द्रव्यविचारः सूत्रकृताङ्गादिसूत्राणि, सम्मतितत्त्वार्थप्रमुखप्रकरणानि च महाशास्त्राणि।"

[द्रव्यानुयोगतर्कणा। प्रथमसूत्रव्याख्या।

supposed that, in studying the scriptures, the exposition of Dravya should be sought last of all. On the contrary, without Dravyânuyoga, the first and the most important exposition, of Charaṇânuyoga becomes ineffectual.* For, first of all, a person must have knowledge of substances existing in this universe and then proceed to regulate his conduct accordingly.† Therefore, though the exposition of the rules of conduct (Charaṇânuyoga) is, from the religio-secular point of view of more importance than the exposition of substances (Dravyânuyoga), the first step to be taken in comprehending the scripture of the Jainas must be the study of works which expound the theory of substances.

This is the reason why we open our series with a work on Dravya. The other authoritative works on Dravya are Sûtrakritâṅga, Tattvârthâdhigama Sûtra by Umâsvâmi, Sammati Prakaraṇa, etc. The exposition of Dravya is also found in later works like Pravachanasâra and Pañchâstikâya-samaya-sâra by Kundakundâchârya, Dravyânuyogatarkaṇâ by Bhojadeva, etc. In the first volume of our series, while expounding Dravya, we have quoted parallel passages from these works to enable the reader to refer to many authorities on a single point.

Besides these works, we have also quoted from works like Jaina epics, passages illustrative of Dravya, so that the reader may judge how, even in the secular literature of the Jainas, the subject of Dravya has been treated by different writers.

In conclusion, we beg to thank the authorities of institutions like Deva Kumar's Central Jaina Oriental Library, Arrah, and Hemchandra Jaina Library, Benares, for kindly placing many rare and

* "विना द्रव्यानुयेागेाहं चरणकरणाख्ययेाः ।
सारं नेति कृतिप्रेष्ठं निर्दिष्टं सम्मतै स्फुटम् ॥"

[द्रव्यानुयेागतर्कणा ॥ २ ॥]

† "चरणकरण प्पहाणा ससमयपरसमय मुक्कवावारा ।
चरणकरणस्स सारं णिच्छयसुद्धं ण जाणंति ॥"

[सम्मतिप्रकरणम् ।]

‡ "तत्त्वार्थ सम्मतिमुखेषु महाश्रुतेषु ।
द्रव्यानुयेागमहिमा कथिता विशेषात् ॥"

[द्रव्यानुयेागतर्कणा ॥ १ ।]

valuable works and manuscripts at our disposal, and we also acknowledge our indebtedness to Mr. Ajita Prasad, M.A., LL.B., of Lucknow, Mr. Champat Rai Jain, Bar-at-Law of Hardoi, for their valuable help and to our loved friend, Kumar Devendra Prasad Jaina of Arrah, without whose untiring zeal this volume would never have seen the light of day.

Admitting many imperfections, we beg to ask the co-operation of all scholars interested in the study of Jainism, so that the future volumes may be worthier than the present one and more suited to the noble object which we have set before us in this great undertaking.

Śrutapanchami :

26th May, 1917. S. C. GHOSHAL.

ALPHABETICAL LIST OF WORKS CONSULTED.

Âchârânga Sûtra (H. Jacobi) S. B. E. Series.
Adhyâtma-kalpa-druma. *Ahmedabad.* Vikram Samvat 1971.
Alphabetical Index of MSS. in the Government Oriental MSS. Library, Madras. *Madras*, 1893.
Amarakośa. Nirṇaya Sâgara Press, *Bombay.*
Anekânta-jaya-patâkâ, *Ahmedabad.*
Âpta-mîmamsâ (Pandit Gajadharlâl) *Benares*, 1914.
Âpta-parîkṣâ (Pandit Gajadharlâl), *Benares*, 1913.
Arthaprakaśikâ (Pannalal Jain), *Calcutta*, 1916.
Asiatic Researches, Vol. IX. *London*, 1809.
Astaka-prakaraṇa, *Ahmedabad.*
Bhâṣârahasya, *Ahmedabad.*
Chandraprabhâ-charitam, (Pandit Durgaprasad and V. L. Śâstrî), *Bombay*, 1912.
Dharmaśarmâbhyudayaṃ (Pandit Durgaprasad), *Bombay*, 1894.
Dravya Samgrah Marathi Hindi Edition, Kolhâpur, 1900.
Dravya Samgrah (Pandit Suraj Bhan, Vakil) Deoband, 1909.
Dravya-samgraha (Pannalal Jain) *Bombay*, 1910.
Dravya-samgraha, *Benares*, 1909.
Dravyânuyôga-tarkaṇâ (Râyachandra Series), *Bombay*, Vîr Nirvâṇa Samvat 2432.
Dvisandhânam (Pandit Sivadatta and K. P. Parab), *Bombay*, 1895.
Epigraphia Carnatica, Vols. II, III and VIII, *Bangalore*, 1889.
Epigraphia Indica, Vols. V. and VII.
Essai de bibliographie Jaina (M. A. Guerinot), *Paris*, 1906.
First Principles of Jaina Philosophy (J. L. Jhaveri) *Bombay*, 1912.
Fraser's Magazine, May, 1875.
Gommata-sâra, Jîva-kâṇda (Râyachandra Series), *Bombay*, 1911.
Gommata-sâra Karma-kâṇda (Râyachandra Series), *Bombay*, Vikram Samvat 1969.
Heart of Jainism, The (Mrs. S. Stevenson), *Oxford*, 1915.
History and Literature of Jainism (U. D. Barodia), *Bombay*, 1909.
History of Indian Architecture (Fergusson).
History of Fine Art in India and Ceylon (Vincent Smith).
Imperial Gazetteer of India.
Indian Antiquary Vols. II, V and XII.
Introduction to Jainism (A. B. Latthe) *Bombay*, 1905.
Inscriptions at Srâvaṇâ Belgola (Lewis Rice), *Bangalore*, 1889.
Insight into Jainism (R. D. Jain) Meerut.
Jainendra Prakriyâ (Srilâl Jain), *Benares*, 1914.
Jainism (Herbert Wârren) *Madras*, 1912; Arrah, 1916
Jaina-siddhânta-praveśikâ (Gopâl Dâs Baraia) *Bombay*, 1912.
Jaina-tattva-digdarśana (Vijaya Dharma Suri) *Benares*. Vîr Nirvaṇa Samvat 2437.
Jîvandhara-champû (T. S. K. Sâstri), *Tanjore*, 1905.
Jñânârṇava (Râyachandra Series), *Bombay*, 1907.
Jñâtridharmakathâṅga (Rai Dhanpat Singh Bahadur), *Calcutta.*,
Karma Philosophy (V. R. Gandhi), *Bombay*, 1913.
Kathâ-kośa (C. H. Tawney).
Key of knowledge (C. R. Jain), Arrah, 1915.
List of the Strassburg Collection of Digambara MSS. (E. Leuman).
Lieut.-Col. Mackenzie's Collection (H. H. Wilson), Vol. I.
Mahâvîra-stavanaṃ, *Ahmedabad.*
Manual of Salem District (Rev. T. Foulkes).
Manual of South Canara (Slurrock).
Mokṣa-śâstra (Pannalal Jain), *Bombay*, 1917.
Mysore and Coorg (Lewis Rice).
Nâgânanda, *Calcutta.*,
Nemi-nirvâṇa (Pandit Sivadatta), *Bombay*, 1896.
Notes on Modern Jainism (Mrs. S. Stevenson), *Oxford*, 1910.
Notices of Sanskrit MSS. (Rajendralal Mitra) Vols. VI. and IX.
Notices of Sanskrit Mss. (Haraprasâd Sastrî).
Nyâya-karṇikâ (M. D. Desai) *Arrah*, 1915.
Nyâyâloka. *Ahmedabad.*
Nyâvatâra (S. C. Vidyabhusana), *Arrah*, 1915.
Nyâya-dîpika (Srîlâl Jaina), *Calcutta*, 1915.

Outlines of Jainism (J. L. Jaini), Oxford 1916.
Pañchâdhyâyî. *Kolhâpur.* Saka 1828.
Pañchâstikâya Samayasâra (Râyachandra Series), 1904.
Paṇhâ-vâgaraṇa (Rai Dhanpat Singh Bahadur), *Calcutta.*
Parîkṣâ-mukha. *Kolhâpur.* Saka 1826.
Pârsvâbhyudayam, *Bombay.* Vîr Nirvâṇa 1933.
Paramâtma-prakâsa (R. D. Jain), *Arrah,* 1915.
Patraparîkṣâ (Pandit Gajadharlal) *Benares,* 1913.
Pramâlakṣma. *Ahmedabad,* Vîr Nirvâṇa Samvat 1967.
Pramâṇa-mîmâṃsâ, *Ahmedabad.*
Pramâṇa-nayatattvâlokâlankâra, *Benares.*
Pramâṇa-parîkṣa (Pandit Gajadharlal), *Benares* 1914.
Prameya-kamala-mârttaṇḍa, *Bombay.*
Ratnâkarâvatârikâ, *Benares.*
Report on the Search for Sanskrit MSS. (R. G. Bhandarkar), *Bombay,* 1887.
Sabdârnava-chandrikâ (Srîlâl Jain), *Benares,* 1915.
Sâgâra-dharmâmrita (Lâlârâm Jain), *Surat.* Vîr Nirvâṇa Samvat 2442.
Sâkatâyana Vyâkaraṇa, *Benares.*
Samaya-prâbhrita (Pandit Gajadharlal), *Benares,* 1914.
Sammati-tarka, *Benares* (Yaśovijaya Series).
Sanâtana-Jaina-granthamâla (Pannalal Bansidhar) *Bombay,* 1905.
Sapta-bhaṅgi-taraṅginî, *Bombay.* (Râyachandra Series).
Sarva-Darsana-saṃgraha (Cowell).
Sarvârtha-siddhi (Kalâpa Sarmâ) *Kolhâpur,* 1903.
Sthânâṅga (Rai Dhanpat Singh Bahadur) *Calcutta.*
Sûtra kritaṅga (Rai Dhanpat Sing Bahadur). *Calcutta.*
Svâmikarttikeyânuprekṣa (Râyachandra Series), *Bombay,* 1904.
Syâdvâdamañjarî (Yaśovijaya Series), *Benares.*
Tattvârthâdhigama-sûtra } (Pandit Gajadharlal), *Benares* 1915.
Tattvârtha-râja-vârttika } (Pandit Gajadharlal), *Benares* 1915.
Tattvârtha-sâra. (Sanâtana-Jainagranthamâla Vol. I), *Bombay,* 1905.
Upadeśa-rahasya, *Ahmedabad.*
Vedânta Sûtra. Nirnaya Sagar Press, *Bombay.*
Vipâka sûtra (Rai Dhanpat Singh Bahadur) *Calcutta.*
Vrihad-dravya-saṃgraha (Râyachandra Series), *Bombay.* Vîr Nirvaṇa Samvat 2433.
Wiener Zeits chrift für die kunde des Mongenlardes Vol. XI. *Wien,* 1897.
Yaśastilaka-champû (Pandit Sivadatta and K. P. Parab), *Bombay.* Vol. I, 1901. Vol. II, 1903.

MANUSCRIPTS.

Gommata-sâra-vritti by Abhayachandra Traividya Chakravarttî.
Gommata-sâra-vritti by Keśava-varnî.
Harivamśa-purâṇa by Jinasena.
Kṣapaṇa-sâra by Nemichandra Siddhânta-Chakravarttî.
Labdhi-sâra by Nemichandra Siddhânta-Chakravarttî.
Pândava-purâṇa by Subha-Chandra.
Pratiṣṭhâpâṭha by Nemichandra Siddhanta-Chakravarttî.
Pravachana-sâra by Kundakundâchârya.
Râjâvalî-kathe.
Sthala-purâṇa.
Svâmi-kârttikeyânuprekṣâ-tîkâ by Śubha-Chandra.
Triloka-sâra by Nemichandra Siddhanta-Chakravarttî.
Triloka-sâra-tîkâ by Mâdhava-Chandra.
Vâhuvali-charitra.
Vardha-mâṇa Purâṇa by Sakalakîrti.
Viśeṣâvaśyaka-bhâṣya.

PERIODICALS.

Digambara Jain, Edited by M. K. Kapadia Esq., *Surat.*
Jaina Gazette, Edited by Ajit Prasad M. A., LL B., *Lucknow.*
Jaina Hitaisi, Edited by Nathuram Premi, *Bombay.*
Jaina Mitra-Edited by Brahmchari Sital Prasad, Surat.
Jaina Siddhanta Bhâskara, Published by Deva Kumar's Central Jaina Oriental Library *Arrah.*
Jaina Svetambara Conference Herald, Edited by M. D. Desai B. A., LL.B., Bombay.

BIBLIOGRAPHY

Besides the works mentioned in the preceding list we mention the following:—

Alaṅkâra-chintâmaṇi, *Bombay*.
Antagaḍa-dasâo and Anuttarova-vâiya-dasâo (L. D. Barnett), *London*, 1907.
Annual Address. Asiatic Society of Bengal (A. F. R. Hoernle), *Calcutta*, 1898.
Atma-khyâti-samaya-sâra, *Bombay*.
Bhadrabahu-samhitâ, *Bombay*, Arrah 1916.
Bhasabatyaṅga (Rai Dhanpat Singh Bahadur) *Calcutta*.
Bhaktâmara-stôtra, *Bombay*.
Bombay Gazeteer, Vol. IX Part I.
Cave Temples (J. Fergusson and J. Burgess), *London*, 1880.
Daśa-vaikâlika-sûtra, *Bombay*.
Dharma-mahôdaya.
Die Lehre vom karman in der Philosophie der Jainas, (Helmuth von Glasenapp), *Leipzig*, 1915.
Digambara Jaina Iconography (J. Burgess), 1903.
Encyclopædia of Religion and Ethics. (Hastings.)
Essai sur la religion des Jains (De Millone) Le Musion, *Louvain*, 1884.
Early History of India, the (A. Vincent Smith) *Oxford*, 1914.
Guruguṇaratnakara kâvya (Yaśovijaya Series), *Benares*.
Haima-liṅgânuśâsana, *Benares*.
Hîra-saubhâgya. Nirṇaya Sâgar Press, *Bombay*.
Indian Religions (W. Crooke) in the Imperial Gazetteer of India, Vol. I. *Oxford*, 1909.
Jagadguru-kâvya (Yaśovijaya Series), *Benares*.
Jaina-nitya-pâṭha-saṅgraha. Nirṇaya Sâgar Press, *Bombay*.
Jaina-stotra-ratnâkara. Nirṇaya Sâgar Press, *Bombay*.
Jaina-stotra-saṅgraha. Nirṇaya Sâgar Press, *Bombay*.
Kavi-kalpa-druma (Yaśovijaya series), *Benares*.
Kalyâṇa-mandira stotra, *Bombay*.
Kalpa-sûtra, *Bombay*.
Kâvya-mâla. Part VII. Nirṇaya Sagar Press, *Bombay*.
Kâvyânuśâsana (Nâgbhata) Nirṇaya Sâgar Press, *Bombay*.
Kâvyânuśâsana (Hemachandra) Nirṇaya Sâgar Press, *Bombay*.
Kriyâratna-samuchchaya (Yaśovijaya Series) *Benares*.
Lecture on Jainism (Lâla Banârsi Das), *Agra*, 1902.
Life of Mahâvîra (Manak Chand Jaini) *Allahabad*, 1908.
Mallinâtha-mahâkâvya. (Yośovijaya Series), *Benares*.
Metaphysics and Ethics of the Jainas, The (Transactions of the Congress for the History of Religion), *Oxford*, 1908.
Miscellaneous Essays (H. T. Colebrooke) Vol. II.. *London*, 1873.
Mudrita-kumuda-chandra-prakaraṇa (Yaśovijaya Series), *Benares*.
Nava-tatva (Rev. J. Stevenson), *London*, 1848.
Nirvaya-bhîma-vyâyoga (Yaśovijaya Series) *Benares*.
Notes on the Sthânakwasi or the non-Idolatrous Śvetâmbara Jains (Seeker) *India*, 1911.
Nyâyârtha-mañjûṣâ (Yaśovijaya Series) *Benares*.
Nyâya-sâra, *Calcutta*.
On the Indian Sect of the Jainas (J. G. Buhler, Ed. by J. Burgess), *London*, 1903.
Pariśiṣṭaparva, *Calcutta*, 1891.
Parvakathâsaṅgraha (Yaśovijaya Series) *Benares*.
Pârśvanâtha-charitra (Yaśovijaya Series), *Benares*.
Pravandha-chintamaṇi, *Calcutta*.
Prâkrita Lakṣaṇa, *Calcutta*.
Prâkrita Paiṅgala, *Calcutta*.
Religions of India, The (E. W. Hopkins) *Boston*, 1895.
Sacred literature of the Jainas (A. Weber) Translated in the Indian Antiquary Vols. XVII—XXI, 1888-1892.
Saḍdarśana-samuchchaya (Yaśovijaya Series), *Benares*.
Sâlibhadra-charitra (Yaśovijaya Series), *Benares*.
Samarâichchakahâ, *Calcutta*.
Śântinâtha-charitra (Yaśovijaya Series), *Benares*.
Siddha-hema Sabdânuśâsana (Yaśovijaya series) *Benares*.
Sîla-dûta-kâvya (Yaśovijaya series) *Benares*.
Specimens of Jaina sculptures from Mathura (J. G. Buhler) Epigrapica Indica Vol. I., 1892, Vol. II, 1894.

Stôtra-saṅgraha (Yaśovijaya Series), *Benares.*
Subhaṣita-ratna-sandoha, Nirṇaya Sâgar Press, *Bombay.*
Tilaka-mañjari, Nirṇaya Sagar Press, *Bombay.*
Uber Des, Leben Des Jaina-mönches Hemachandra, Vienna, 1889.
Upadesâ-taraṅgini (Yaśovijaya series) *Benares.*
Upamiti-bhava-prapañchâ-kathâ, *Calcutta.*
Uvâsaga-dasao, *Calcutta*, 1890.
Vâgbhatâlaṅkâra, Nirṇaya Sâgar Press, *Bombay.*

[*N.B.*—The reader may also refer to the following works for further lists of works and articles concerning Jainism :—

Essai de Bibliographie Jaina (in Annales du Musée Guimet, Bibliotheque d' Études, tome XXII) *Paris*, 1906.
Répertoire d'Epigraphie Jaina (Publications de l' E'cole Francaise d'Extrème Orient, Vol., X), *Paris*, 1908.]

A GUIDE TO TRANSLITERATION

VOWELS.

अ = A	उ = U	ऌ = Li	ओ = O
आ = Â	ऊ = Û	ॡ = Lli	औ = Au
इ = I	ऋ = Ṛi	ए = E	ं = Ṃ
ई = Î	ॠ = Ṛî	ऐ = Ai	ः = Ḥ

CONSONANTS.

क = Ka	ट = Ṭa	प = Pa	ष = Ṣa
ख = Kha	ठ = Tḥa	फ = Pha	स = Sa
ग = Ga	ड = Ḍa	ब = Ba	ह = Ha
घ = Gha	ढ = Dḥa	भ = Bha	
ङ = Ṅa	ण = Ṇa	म = Ma	
च = Cha	त = Ta	य = Ya	
छ = Chha	थ = Tha	र = Ra	
ज = Ja	द = Da	ल = La	
झ = Jha	ध = Dha	व = Va	
ञ = Ña	न = Na	श = Śa	

INTRODUCTION.

The Gaṅga Dynasty.

AMONG the ancient royal dynasties of India, the Gaṅgas of the West were devoted followers of Jainism. There is a tradition that a Jaina Âchârya, named Siṃhanandî, belonging to the Nandigaṇa, helped Śivamâra, the first king of the Gaṅga dynasty, to rise to the throne. In one inscription we find a mention of the fact that Śivamâra Koṅguṇivarmâ was the disciple of Siṃhanandî,* and in another that the race of the Gaṅgas prospered through the sage Siṃhanandî.† It is therefore no wonder that we shall find in Jaina works verses to the effect that the Gaṅga kings worship the feet of Siṃhanandî,‡ or that a dynasty which owed its origin to the help of a Jaina Âchârya should be staunch to

---

* *Vide* Repertoire d'epigraphie Jaina (A. A. Guerinot) Inscriptions Nos. 213 and 214. Also—

"योऽसौ घातिमलद्विषद्बलशिला-स्तम्भावली-खण्डन—
ध्यानासिः पतुरर्हतो भगवतः सोऽस्य प्रसादीकृतः ।
छात्रस्यापि स सिंहनन्दिमुनिना नो चेत् कथम् वा शिला-
स्तम्भो राज्यरमागमाध्वपरिघस्तेनासिखण्डो घनः" ॥

[Inscription in Pârśvanâtha Basti on Chandragiri Hill, Śravaṇa Belgola, Mysore. (Inscription No. 54—' Inscriptions at Śravaṇa Belgola' by Lewis Rice, page 42.)]

† "यस्याभवत् प्रवरकाश्यपवंशजोऽग्रे
कण्वो महामुनिरनल्पतपःप्रभावः ।
यः सिंहनन्दिमुनिपप्रतिलब्धवृद्धि—
र्गंगान्वयो विजयतां जयतां वरः सः ॥"

[Manual of the Salem District—Revd. T. Foulkes, II, 369.] The reading मुनिप instead of नृप in the above verse is according to Lewis Rice.

‡ "श्रीदेशीयगणाब्धिपूर्णमृगभृच्छ्रीसिंहनन्दिव्रति—
श्रीपादाम्बुजयुग्ममत्तमधुपः सम्यक्त्वचूडामणिः ।
श्रीमज्जैनमताब्धिवर्द्धनसुधासूतिर्महीमण्डले
रेजे श्रीगुणभूषणो बुधनुतः श्रीराजमल्लो नृपः ॥"

[Vâhuvali Charitra, Verse 6.]

the Jaina religion. There are records which establish beyond doubt that the kings of the Gaṅga dynasty were the promoters and protectors of Jainism. Numerous inscriptions, dating from the fourth to the twelfth century A. D., testify to the building of Jaina temples, consecration of Jaina images of worship, hollowing out caves for Jaina ascetics and grants to Jaina Âchâryas by the rulers of the Gaṅga dynasty.

Mârasiṃha II.

In this dynasty there was a king, named Mârasiṃha II, mentioned in the inscriptions as Dharma-Mahârâjâ-dhirâja Satyavâkya Koṅguṇivarmâ-Parmânaḍi Mârasiṃha. The reign of this king was conspicuous by great and decisive victories over the Cheras, the Cholas, the Pândyas and the Pallavas of the Nolambâdi country. The most notable success of Mârasiṃha II against his enemies was that against Vajjala-deva, and his most terrible fights were fought at Gonûr and Uchchaṅgi. Faithful to the doctrines of Jainism, this great king, after a glorious reign, abdicated his throne and gave up his life by a three days' fast, in the presence of his spiritual preceptor, the great Ajitasena, at Bânkâpur, in the Dhârwâr district. The epitaph of Mârasiṃha II is contained in the inscription engraved on the four sides of the base of the pillar known as Kûge Brahmadeva Khambha, near the entrance to the temples on Chandragiri hill, at Śravaṇa Belgola (Mysore) §. Though this inscription is without date, the year of the death of Mârasiṃha II is inferred from another inscription to be 975 A. D. ||

Châmuṇḍarâya.

Châmuṇḍarâya or Châmuṇḍarâja was the worthy minister of this great king. It is the heroism of this minister that enabled Mârasiṃha II to win his great battles against Vajjala and those fought at Gonûr and Uchchaṅgi. In an inscription at Śravaṇa Belgola, we have an eulogy of Châmuṇḍarâya in the following terms :

Châmuṇḍarâja, the sun adorning, like a jewel, the head of the eastern mountain of the Brahma-kṣatra race, the moon increasing by the rays of fame the waters of the Brahma-kṣatra race, a jewel in the garland sprung from the mountain containing the mine of the

§ *Vide* Inscription No. 38. 'Inscriptions at Śravaṇa Belgola' by Lewis Rice.

|| *Vide* Inscription at Melâgâni, quoted in the footnote to the 'Introduction to the Inscriptions at Śravaṇa Belgola (Lewis Rice), page 18. *Vide* also, Epigraphia Indica,' Vol. V, Inscription No. 18.

Brahma-kṣatra race, and a fierce wind to raise the fire of the Brahma-kṣatra race, was born.

Where the array of the enemy was broken like that of a herd of deer before a pursuing elephant, in front of the victorious elephant of his lord, the king Jagadekavîra (the one hero in the world), when at the order of king Indra* he raised his arm to conquer Vajjala-deva, of terrible power, like the ocean disturbed at the end of age, and who was the younger brother of Pâtâla-malla.

He who was thus praised by his lord in the fight with the king of Nolambas : " Which king among my foes will not fall as food to the black snake of my arrow when you sitting always in the front of the bravest heroes—an elephant by whose tusks, resembling a thunderbolt, the rock of the temples of the elephants of the enemy are split, and a goad to the wild animals—the enemy—are present?"

Who fiercely roared thus in the fight with king Raṇa-siṃha, " O king Jagadekavîra! By your prowess I can conquer in a moment (an enemy), even if he be Râvaṇa, his city, Laṅkâ, the citadel, Trikûta, and the moat, the briny ocean."

To whom the celestial damsels bestowed the blessing—" We were thirsted in many battles of this hero by our eagerness to embrace his neck, but now we have been satiated with the water of the edge of his sword. O victor of Raṇa-raṅga-siṃha! live to the end of age."

Who, formerly frustrated the desire of king Chaladaṅka-gaṅga, who wished to snatch by power of arms the fortune of the empire of the Gaṅgas, and who satisfied the desire of the Râkṣasas, who were eager to drink blood, by holding the blood of his brave enemies in skulls of heroes resembling cups made of jewels.†

---

* Indra IV, grandson of Kriṣṇa III. [*Vide* Inscription No. 18. Vol. V, Epigraphia Indica.]

† "ब्रह्मक्षत्रकुलोदयाचलशिरोभूषामणिर्भानुमान्
ब्रह्मक्षत्रकुलाब्धिवर्द्धनयशोरोचिः सुधादीधितिः ।
ब्रह्मक्षत्रकुलाकराचलभवश्रीहारवल्लीमणिः
ब्रह्मक्षत्रकुलाग्निचण्डपवनश्चामुण्डराजोऽजनि ॥
कल्पान्तक्षुभिताब्धिभीषणबलं पातालमल्लानुजम्
जेतुम् वज्जलदेवमुद्यतभुजस्येन्द्रक्षितीन्द्राज्ञया ।
पत्युः श्रीजगदेकवीरनृपतेर्ज्जैत्रद्विपस्याग्रतो
धावद्दन्तिनि यत्र भग्नमहितानीकं मृगानीकवत् ॥

The above inscription is Châmuṇḍarâja's own information about himself. But the greater part of this inscription seems to have been lost. "Heggaḍe Kanna, in order to have only two lines and-a-half inscribed regarding himself, appears to have caused three sides of Châmuṇḍarâya's originnal inscription to be entirely effaced, leaving only the one side" * a translation of which we have given above.

"Châmuṇḍarâya composed a work called Châmuṇḍa Râya Purâṇa, containing an epitome of the history of the 24 Tîrthaṅkaras, and at the end its date is given as Śaka 900, the year Iśvara (A. D. 978)."† The statements found in the verses of the inscription quoted above "accord with those given in the Châmuṇḍa Râya Purâṇa. It is there said, in the opening chapter, that his lord was the Gaṅga-kula-chûḍâmaṇi Jagadekavîra Nolambakulântaka-deva; and that he was born in the Brahma-kṣatra vaṃśa. In the concluding chapter

---

अस्मिन् दन्तिनि दन्तवज्रदलितद्वित्कुम्भिकुम्भोपले
वीरोत्तंसपुरोनिषादिनि रिपुव्यालाङ्कुशे च त्वयि ।
स्यात् को नाम न गोचरः प्रतिनृपो मद्बाणकृष्णोरग—
ग्रासस्येति नोलम्बराजसमरे यः श्लाघितः स्वामिना ॥
खातः क्षारपयोधिरस्तु परिधिश्चास्तु त्रिकूटः पुरी—
लङ्कास्तु प्रतिनायकोस्तु च सुरारातिस्तथापि क्षमे ।
तं जेतुं जगदेकवीरनृपते त्वत्तेजसीति क्षणान्
निर्व्यूढं रणसिंहपार्थिवरणे येनोर्ज्जितं गर्ज्जितम् ॥
वीरस्यास्य रणेषु भूरिषु वयं कण्ठग्रहोत्कण्ठया
तप्ताः सम्प्रति लब्धनिर्वृतिरसास्तत्-खड्गधाराम्भसा ।
कल्पान्तं रणरङ्गसिंहविजयि जीवेति नाकाङ्गना
गीर्वाणीकृतराजगन्धकरिणे यस्मै वितीर्णाशिषः ॥
आक्रष्टुं भुजविक्रमादभिलषन् गङ्गाधिराज्यश्रियं
येनादौ चलदङ्कगङ्गनृपतिर्व्यर्थाभिलाषीकृतः ।
कृत्वा वीरकपालरत्नचषके वीरद्विषः शोणितम्
पातुं कौतुकिनश्च कोणपगणाः पूर्णाभिलाषीकृताः ॥"

[Inscription on the Tyâgada Brahma Deva Khambha. Size 1′ 9″ × 1′ 6″. *Circa* A. D. 983. *Vide* Lewis Rice Inscrip. at S. B., p. 85.]

* Lewis Rice—'Inscriptions at Śravaṇa Belgola.' Introduction, page 33.

† Lewis Rice—'Inscriptions at Śravaṇa Belgola.' Introduction, page 22. *Vide* also Lieut.-Col. Mackenzie's Collections, Edited by H. H. Wilson, Vol. I, p. 146, where it is said that Châmuṇḍa Râya Purâṇa gives "an account of the sixty-three celebrated personages of the Jainas."

it is said that he was the disciple of Ajita-sena; also that in the Krita Yuga he was Ṣaṇmukha, in the Treta Yuga Râma, in the Dvâpara Yuga Gâṇḍîvi, and in the Kali Yuga Vîra-mârttaṇḍa. The origin of his various titles is then related. From his defeat of Vajjala Deva, in the Khedaga war, he obtained the title *Samara-Dhurandhara*; from the valour he displayed on the plains of Gonûr in the Nolamba war, the title *Vîra-mârttaṇḍa*; from his fight in the fort of Uchchaṅgi, the title *Raṇa-raṅga-siṃha*; from his killing Tribhuvana Vîra, and others, in the fort of Bâgalûr and enabling Govinda to enter it, the title of *Vairikula-kâladaṇḍa*; from his defeat of Râja and others in the fort of king Kâma, the title of *Bhuja-vikrama*; from his killing his younger brother, Nâga-varmma, on account of his hatred, the title of *Chhaladaṅka Gaṅga*; from his killing the Gaṅga warrior (bhaṭa) Mudu Râchayya, the titles of *Samara-paraśurâma* and *Pratipakṣa-râkṣasa*; from his destroying the fort of the warrior (bhaṭa) Vîra, the title of *Bhaṭa-mâri*; from upholding the brave qualities of himself and others, the title of *Guṇavaṃ Kâva*; from his virtue, liberality, etc., the title of *Samyaktva-ratnâkara*; from his not coveting the wealth or wives of others, the title of *Śauchâbharaṇa*; from his never telling an untruth even in jest, the title of *Satya-yudhiṣṭhira*; from his being the head of the bravest, the title of *Subhaṭa-chûḍâmaṇi*. Finally, in his composition, he calls himself *Kavijana-śekhara*, the head of the poets.

Of most of these allusions we have no other information; but it is remarkable that among so many distinguished actions no mention is made of a single work of religious merit......On the contrary, there is little more than a record of warfare and bloodshed from beginning to end.".†

But there are authentic records to show that, with the advance of his age, Châmuṇḍarâja devoted himself mostly to religion, under his spiritual teacher, Ajitasena, and became immortal as one of the greatest promoters of Jaina religion, by erecting the colossal images of Gomateśvara and Neminâtha in Vindhyagiri and Chandragiri at Śravaṇa Belgola, (Mysore,) and devoting the greater part of his wealth to the maintenance of worship of these images.

Râchamalla II or Râjamalla II.

After the death of Mârasiṃha II of the Gaṅga dynasty, Pañchaladeva, fully known as Dharma-mahârâjâdhirâja Satyavâkya Koṅguṇivarmâ Pañchaladeva, ascended the throne, and he was succeeded by

* Lewis Rice—'Inscriptions at Śravaṇa Belgola.' Introduction, page 34.

king Râchamalla or Râjamalla II *, fully known a Dharma-mahârâjâdhirâja Satya-vâkya Koṅguṇivarma Parmanaḍi Râchamalla. Châmuṇḍa Râja was also the minister of Râchamalla or Râjamalla II. In one inscription we read "Râya (*i.e.*, Châmuṇḍa-Râya), the excellent minister of the king Râchamalla," † and in another "Châmuṇḍa Râya, second in glory to king Râcha-malla." ‡ In a Jaina work, named Vâhuvali-Charitra, we find that there was a king named Râjamalla, the worshipper of the feet of the sage Siṃhanandî. Châmuṇḍa Bhûpa (or Râja) was his minister.§ In a manuscript we read "Châmuṇḍa Râya, having the titles of *Raṇaraṅga-malla, Asahâya-parâkrama, Guṇa-ratna-bhûṣaṇa, Samyaktva-ratna-nilaya,* etc., the *Mahâmâtya* (highest minister) of Râjamalla of the Gaṅga dynasty, graced by the great sage Siṃhanandî."‖

---

* Mr. Fleet has accepted the name Râcha-malla to be the correct one (Epigraphia Indica, Vol. V, Inscription No. 18), and, though we find this name in some inscriptions, the name Râjamalla is also used by Jaina writers whom we have quoted in this Introduction and in inscriptions like No. 107 MD. Vol. III, Epigraphia Carnatica.

† "राचमल्लभूवर-वरमन्त्रि-रायने" Inscription at Bhaṇḍâri Basti. Śravaṇa Belgola, Mysore. [*Vide* Lewis Rice—'Inscriptions at Śravaṇa Belgola,' p. 108.]

‡ "राचमल्लं जगन् नुतन् आ भूमिपण द्वितीयविभवं चामुण्डरायम्" Inscription to the left of the Dvârapâlaka doorway. [*Vide* Lewis Rice—'Inscriptions at Śravaṇa Belgola,' p. 67.]

§ "श्रीदेशीयगणाब्धिपूर्णमृगभृच्छ्रीसिंहनन्दिव्रति—
श्रीपादाम्बुजयुग्ममत्तमधुपः सम्यक्त्वचूडामणिः ।
श्रीमज्जैनमताब्धिवर्द्धनसुधासूतिर्महीमण्डले
रेजे श्रीगुणभूषणो बुधनुतः श्रीराजमल्लो नृपः ॥........
तस्यामात्यशिखामणिः सकलवित् सम्यक्त्वचूडामणि—
र्भव्याम्भोजवियन्मणिः सुजनवन्दिव्रातचूडामणिः ।
ब्रह्मक्षत्रियवैश्यशुक्तिसुमणिः कीर्त्यौघमुक्तामणिः
पादन्यस्तमहीशमस्तकमणिश्चामुण्डभूपोऽग्रणीः ॥"

[Vâhuvali-Charitra, Verses 6 and 11.]

‖ "सिंहनन्दिमुनीन्द्राभिनन्दितगङ्गवंशललाम........श्रीमद्राजमल्लदेव—महीवल्लभमहामात्यपदविराजमान—रणरङ्गमल्ल—सहायपराक्रम—गुणरत्नभूषण—सम्यक्त्वरत्ननिलयादिविविधगुणग्रामनामसमासादितकीर्त्ति ... श्रीमच्चामुण्डराय—भव्यपुण्डरीक—द्रव्यानुयोगप्रश्नानुरूपं......"

[Commentary on Gommata-sâra by Abhayachandra Traividya-chakravarttî. The MS. from which we quote the above passage is in the Central Jaina Oriental Library, Arrah.]

PLATE I Chandragiri at Sravana Belgola in Mysore

PLATE II The Temple of Neminâtha by Châmundaraya on Chandragiri (Southern Side)

Before we proceed to describe the images and buildings established by Châmuṇḍa Râya, it will be better to give a brief description of the places which bear these monuments of piety and which have now become some of the holiest places of pilgrimage resorted to by the Jainas.

Sravaṇa Belgola.

Śravaṇa Belgola or Belgola of the Śramaṇas (Jainas) is a village in the Channarayapaṭṇa Taluq of the Hassan district in Mysore. The word 'Śravana' is used before Belgola to distinguish it from two other Belgolas which are known as Hale Belgola and Koḍi Belgola. Belgola in Canarese indicates "white lake;" and in many inscriptions we have references to "Dhavala-sarovara," * "Dhavala-sarasa" and "Śveta-sarovara," † all signifying the "white lake;" and the place must have derived this name from the beautiful lake situated on the spot. There are two hills, one on the north and the other on the south of the village, which are respectively known as Chandragiri (see Plate I) and Vindhya giri (see Plate IV), on which there are temples and images established by the Jainas and numerous inscriptions throwing a flood of light on the ancient history of this faith. Chandragiri according to a tradition derives its name from Chandragupta, who followed his spiritual teacher, Bhadrabâhu, when the latter with twelve thousand disciples, at the approach of a terrible famine, left Pâtaliputra and moved towards the south. It was on Chandragiri that Bhadrabâhu left his mortal body, and in his last moments there was only one disciple, the above-mentioned Chandragupta, who was present. If we accept the tradition of the Jainas we shall have to come to the conclusion that this Chandragupta, the disciple of the sage Bhadrabâhu, was none other than the celebrated Maurya emperor of the same name.‡

Chandragiri and Vindhyagiri.

It was on Chandragiri that Châmuṇḍa Râya erected a magnificent temple containing the image of the twenty-second Jaina Tirthaṅkara, Neminâtha. [See Plate II.] Subsequently, the upper storey of the building was added by the son of Châmuṇḍa Râya, and an image of the twenty-third Tîrthaṅkara, Pârśvanâtha, was placed in it. Both

* Inscription No. 108. Lewis Rice—Inscriptions at Ś. B.

† Inscription No 54. Lewis Rice—Inscriptions at Ś. B.

‡ For a detailed discussion on this point, the reader may refer to Epigraphia Carnatica, Vol. II. Introduction, pages 1-14. *Vide* also 'The Heart of Jainism' by Mrs. Sinclair Stevenson, page 10.

these storeys were built in the tenth century A. D. and give a fine idea of the beautiful architecture of that age. [See Plates II and III.]

Gommateśvara.

On Vindhyagiri, Châmuṇḍa Râya erected a colossal image of Vâhuvali or Bhujabali, more commonly known as Gommat Svâmi or Gommateśvara. [See frontispiece]. Later on, imitating Châmuṇḍa Râya, the chief Vîra-Pâṇdya erected another statue of Gommateśvara at Karkala (South Canara), in A. D. 1432; and afterwards a similar figure of Gommateśvara was established by the chief Timmarâja at Yenur (South Canara), in A. D. 1604.*

These "colossal monolithic nude Jain statues......are among the wonders of the world." † These are "undoubtedly the most remarkable of the Jain statues and the largest free-standing statues in Asia .....All three being set on the top of eminences, are visible for miles around, and, in spite of their formalism, command respectful attention by their enormous mass and expression of dignified serenity. The biggest, that at Śravaṇa Belgola, stands about 56½ feet in height, with a width of 13 feet across the hips, and is cut out of a solid block of gneiss, apparently wrought *in situ*. That at Karkala, of the same material, but some 15 feet less in height, is estimated to weigh 80 tons. The smallest of the giants, that at Yenur, is 35 feet high. The three images are almost identical, but the one at Yenur has the 'special peculiarity of the cheeks being dimpled, with a deep grave smile,' which is considered to detract from the impressive effect. The extreme conventionalism of Jain art is well-illustrated by the fact that, whereas all the three colossi are substantially identical, save for the smile at Yenur, the dates vary widely." ‡

The image erected by Châmuṇḍa Râya "is not only the most ancient in date and considerably the highest of the three, but from its striking position on the top of the very steep hill and the conse-

* References for Śravaṇa Begola statue: Indian Antiquary, Vol. II, page 129; Epigraphia Indica, Vol. VII, page 108; Lewis Rice—'Mysore and Coorg,' page 47.

References for Karkala statue: Indian Antiquary, Vol. II, page 358; Epigraphia Indica, Vol. VII, page 112.

References for Yenur statue: Indian Antiquary, Vol. V, page 37; Epigraphia Indica, Vol. VII, page 112.

† Imperial Gazetteer of India, page 121.

‡ Vincent Smith—'A History of Fine Art in India and Ceylon,' page 268.

Further references to these statues will be found in Slurrock—'Manual of South Canara,' page 85; Fergusson—'History of Indian Architecture,' page 267; 'Fraser's Magazine,' May, 1875 (Mr. Walhouse's article).

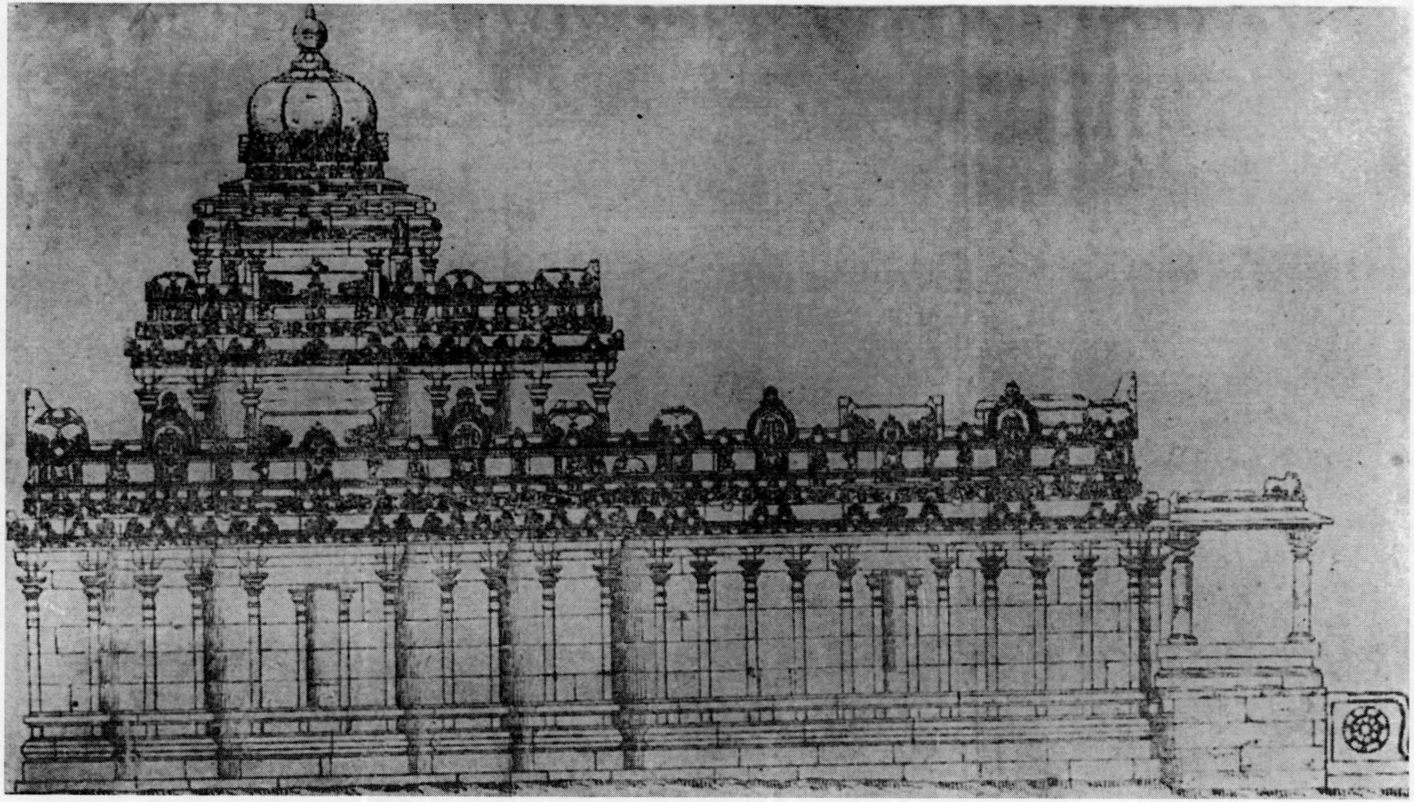

PLATE III The Temple of Neminâtha by Châmundaraya (lengthwise)

PLATE IV The Temple of Vâhuvali Gomateśwara by Châmundaraya on Vindhyagiri at Sravana Belgola

quently greater difficulty involved in its execution, is by far the most interesting. The image is nude and stands erect facing the north...... The figure has no support above the thighs. Up to that point it is represented as surrounded by ant-hills, from which emerge serpents: a climbing plant twines itself round both legs and both arms, terminating at the upper part of the arm in a clustre of fruit or berries. The pedestal on which the feet stand is carved to represent an open lotus." *

The Inscriptions below the image of Gommateśvara at Sravaṇa Belgola.

There are inscriptions on the slabs near the right and left foot of the image of Gommateśvara at Śravaṇa Belgola. [See Plate V]. The inscription on the right-hand slab is as follows:—

Śrî-Châmuṇḍarâjaṃ mâḍisidaṃ;
Śrî-Châmuṇḍarâjan [śe] Yv [v] ittâṇ;
Śrî-Gaṃgarâja suttâlayavaṃ mâḍisida;

that is to say—

Śrî Châmuṇḍarâja caused to be made.
Śrî Châmuṇḍarâja caused to be made.
Śrî Gaṃgarâja caused the Chaityâlaya (enclosure) to be made.

"The alphabet and language of the first and third lines are Canarese. The second line is a Tamil translation of line 1, and consists of two words, of which the first is written in the Grantha and the second in the Vaṭṭeluttu alphabet. The first two lines record that Châmuṇḍarâja caused to be made the image, at the foot of which the inscription is engraved, and the third line that Gaṃgarâja caused to be made the buildings which surround the image."†

The inscription on the slab on the left-hand is as follows:—

Śrî-Châmuṇḍarâjeṃ karaviyaleṃ
Śrî-Gaṃgarâje suttâle karaviyale;

that is to say—

Śrî Châmuṇḍarâja caused to be made.
Śrî Gaṃgarâja caused the Chaityâlaya (enclosure) to be made.

"The alphabet is Nâgarî, and the language is Marâthi......The Marâthi language was perhaps adopted for the benefit of Jain pilgrims from the Marâthâ country."†

In Plate VI we have given a facsimile reprint of the inscriptions mentioned above, beginning with that on the left. From the

* Epigraphia Carnatica, Vol. II, Introduction, page 29.

† E. Hultzsch—'Inscriptions on the Three Jain Colossi of Southern India' (Epigraphia Indica, Vol. VII, pages 108-109.)

identical type used in both the lines, the inscription on the left-hand slab is supposed to be engraved during the reign of Gaṅga-râja, when he erected the building round the image of Gommateśvara established by Châmuṇḍa-Râya. It is all the more probable, as the inscription on the left is nothing but a repetition of that on the right in a different language.

Gaṅga-râja.

Gaṅga-râja was the minister of Viṣṇuvardhana, a king of the Hoysala dynasty, who ruled in the 12th Century A. D. In an inscription dated about 1160 A. D., we find the praise of Gaṅga-râja and Châmuṇḍa-Râya, together with that of Hulla, as follows :—

"If it be asked who in the beginning were firm promoters of of the Jina doctrine (*i.e.*, in Śravaṇa Belgola)—(they were) Râya, the minister of king Râchamalla ; after him, Gaṅga, the minister of king Viṣṇu ; and after him, Hulla, the minister of king Nṛisiṃha-deva : if any others could claim as much, would they not be mentioned ?"*

Besides the inscription at the foot of the image announcing that Châmuṇḍa Râya established the same, we find reference to this in another inscription, dated about 1180 A. D., in the following manner :—

"Combining in himself wisdom, religion, glory, high character and valour, the moon of the Gaṅga race was Râchamalla, famed in all the world. That king's second in glory (his minister Châmuṇḍa Râya), equal to Manu, was it not he that had this Gommata made by his own effort?"†

The legendary account of Bhujavali.

The three statues represent Vâhuvali or Bhujavali, also known as Gommateśvara, who was the son of Âdijina Ṛiṣabhanâtha, the first Tîrthaṅkara of the Jainas. Ṛiṣabhadeva, according to tradition, was a king, and had two wives, Nandâ (some say Sumaṅgalâ) and Sunandâ. Nandâ or Sumaṅgalâ gave birth to the twins, Bharata and Brâhmî, a boy and a girl, the former of whom was placed on the throne by Ṛiṣabhadeva, when he retired to seek absolute knowledge. Vâhuvali and his sister, Sundari, were born of Sunandâ, and the former ascended the throne of Takṣa-śila (modern Taxila), when his father distributed his

* *Vide* Epigraphia Carnatica, Vol. II, Introduction, page 34. Hulla was the minister of Narasiṃha I, of the Hoysala dynasty, who ruled in the 12th century A.D.

† *Vide* Epigraphia Carnatica, Vol. II, page 154. The line speakin of the construction of the image is—

"चामुण्डरायं मनुप्रतिमं गोम्मटं अल्ते माडिसिदन् इनती देवनं यत्नदिम् "

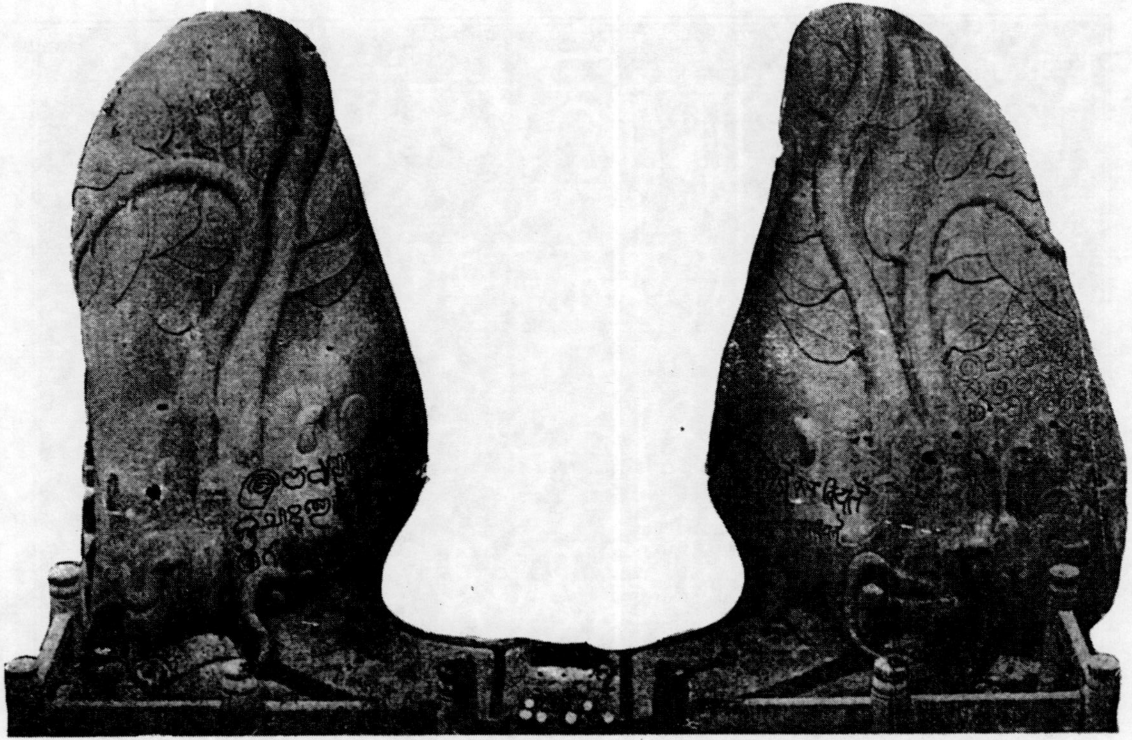

PLATE V Inscribed slabs below the image of Vâhuvali in Gommateśvara temple on Vindhyagiri

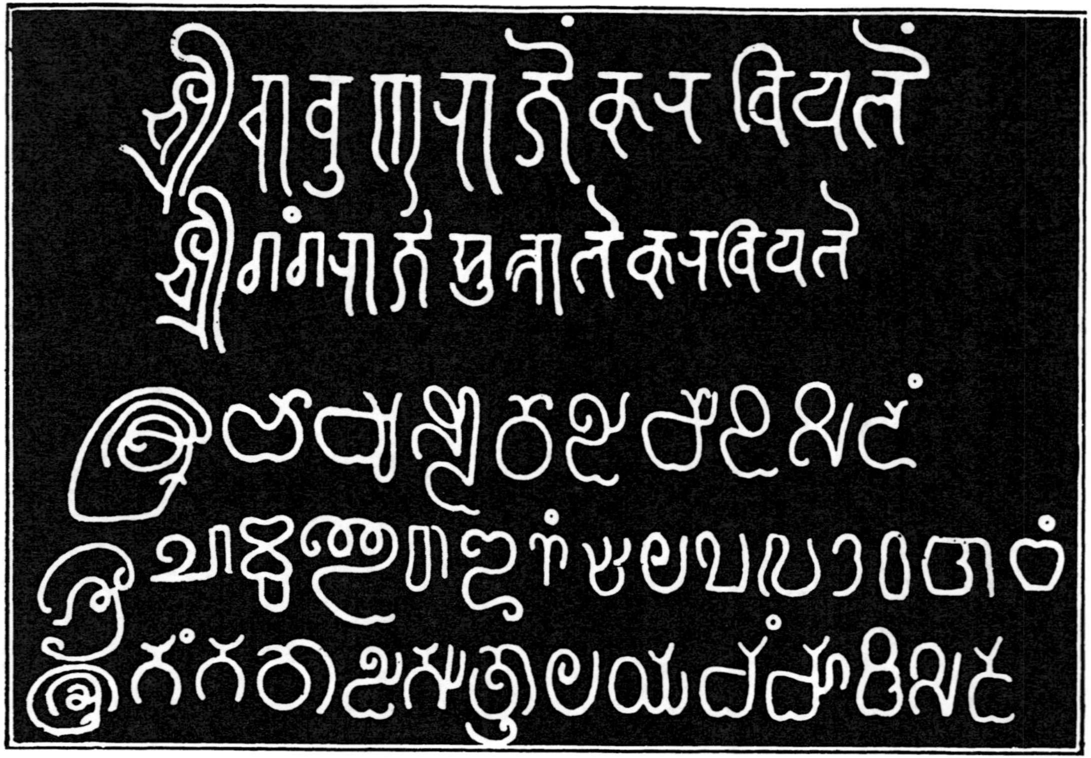

PLATE VI Inscription at the foot of the image of Vâhuvali in Gommateśvara temple on Vindhyagiri

kingdom among his sons. Bharata had possession of a wonderful Chakra (discus), which could not be withstood by any warrior in fight. With the help of this Chakra, Bharata conquered the earth and returned to his capital. But the discus would not enter the capital (or, according to another account, the armoury). Bharata then took this as a sign that there was still another territory on earth which had not been conquered by him, and, after reflection, came to the conclusion that there was only the kingdom of Takṣa-śila, ruled by his brother, Bhujavali, which had not been subdued by him. Bharata then declared war on his brother, Bhujavali, and in the terrible fight that followed, Bhujavali was victorious. Even the discus of Bharata could do no harm to Bhujavali. But Bhujavali, though victorious, suddenly became lost in meditation, thinking of the vanity of this world. Bharata made obeisance to Bhujavali and returned to his place; but Bhujavali went to the summit of Kailâsa mountain, remained standing there (or, according to another account, stood on the very field of battle) in a statuesque posture for one year* and "the creepers, wreathing round the boughs of the trees on the bank clung to his neck and crowned his head with their canopy and the blades of kuśa-grass grew between his feet, and he became in appearance like an ant-hill."† Subsequently, Bhujavali obtained absolute knowledge and became one of the Kevalîs.

In an inscription, however, we read that Puru was the father of Vâhuvali or Bhujavali and Bharata.‡ Then the inscription goes on to say that "Bharata, the son of Puru Deva, surrounded by all the kings conquered by him, erected, in glee, an image, representing the victorious Vâhuvali Kevali, which was 525 bows in height, near Podanapura. After a long time, innumerable Kukkuta-sarpa (dragons having the body of a fowl and the head and neck of a snake), terrifying the world, grew up in the place surrounding (the image of) that Jina, for which the image became known as Kukkuteśvara."§

* *Vide* Harivaṃśapurâṇa by Jinasena, Chapter XI. For a slightly different account, see Kathâkôśa, translated by C. H. Tawney, pages 192-195.

† *Vide* The Kathâ-kośa or Treasury of Stories, translated by C. H. Tawney, pages 192-195.

‡ "पुरु-सूनु-बाहुबलि वोल्" Inscription No. 85, Epigraphia Carnatica, Vol. II, page 67.

§ "धृत—जयबाहु—बाहुबलिकेवलि—रूपसमान—पञ्चविंशति—समुपेत-

In the light of these traditions, we shall be able to understand the significance of the sculptured anthills, from which serpents are issuing, and the climbing plant which twines round the legs and arms of the images of Gommateśvara at Śravaṇa Belgola, Karkala and Yenur. "These details are identical in all three, and supposed to represent so rigid and complete an absorption in penance that ant-hills had been raised around his feet and plants had grown over his body, without disturbing the profoundness of the ascetic's abstraction from mundane affairs." *

The legendary accounts of the establishment of the image by Châmuṇḍa Râya.

The story of the establishing of the image of Gommateśvara by Châmuṇḍa Râya is thus described in a work, composed in Sanskrit verses, named Vâhuvali Charitra.

The story in Vâhuvali Charitra.

In the city of Madhurâ (now known as Madura) in the Drâviḍa country there was a king, named Râjamalla, who encouraged the spread of Jaina tenets, and was the worshipper of Sîṃhanandi, belonging to the Deśîya Gaṇa † His minister was called Châmuṇḍa Râja. One day, when the king sat with his minister in the royal court, a travelling merchant came there and told them that in the north there is a town called Paudanapurî, where there is an image of Vâhuvali, also called Gommata, established by Bharata. Hearing this, the devout Châmuṇḍarâja resolved to visit the shrine of the image, and going home narrated the tale to his mother, Kâlikâ Devî whereupon she also wished to go with him to that sacred spot. Châmuṇḍarâja then went to his spiritual preceptor,

---

पञ्चशतचापसमुन्नतियुक्तम् अप्प तत्—प्रतिकृतियं मनोमुदवे माडिसिदं भरतं जिताखिलक्षितिपतिचक्रि पौदनपुरान्तिकदोल् पुरुदेव-नन्दनम् । चिरकालं सले तज्जिनान्तिक—धरित्री—देशादोल् लोकभीकरणं कुक्कुटसर्पसंकुलं असंख्यं पुट्टि दल् कुक्कुटेश्वरनामन्……" Inscription No. 85, Epigraphia Carnatica, Vol. II, page 67.

* Lewis Rice—Inscriptions at Śravaṇa Belgola : Introduction, page 33.

† When the Âchâryas of the Nandi-saṅgha of the Jainas spread themselves over the country (Deśa), their saṅgha came to be known as Deśîya-Gaṇa, *vide* :—

"पूर्वं जैनमतागमाब्धिविधुवच्छ्रीनन्दिसंघेऽभवन्
सुज्ञानर्द्धितपोधनाः कुवलयानन्दा मयूखा इव ।
सत्सङ्घे भुवि देशदेशनिकरे श्रीसुप्रसिद्धे सति
श्रीदेशीयगणो द्वितीयविलसन्नाम्ना मिथः कथ्यते ॥"

[Vâhuvali Charitra, verse 87.]

Ajitasena, who revered Siṃhanandi and made a vow before the latter that he will not drink milk till he sees the image of Vâhuvali. Accompanied by Nemichandra, his mother and numerous soldiers and attendants, Châmuṇḍarâja started on his pilgrimage and reached the Vindhyagiri (in Śravaṇa Belgola). In the night, the Jaina Goddess Kuṣmâṇḍî (the Yakṣinî attendant on Neminâtha, the twenty-second Tîrthaṅkara) appeared in a dream to Châmuṇḍarâja, Nemichandra and Kâlikâ, and told them that it was very difficult to go to Paudanapurî but on that very hill there is an image of Vâhuvali, formerly established by Râvaṇa, which will be visible if the hill be cleft by a golden arrow. According to the dream, on the next morning, Châmuṇḍarâja stood on the hill with his face towards the south and let loose a golden arrow from his bow. Immediately the mountain was cleft in twain, and an image of Vâhuvali became visible. Châmuṇḍarâja then established and consecrated the image and granted lands for the worship of this image. When king Râjamalla heard of this affair, he conferred the title of "Râya" on Châmuṇḍa râja and granted further lands for the regular worship of the image.

The story in Râjâvalî-kathe.

In a very recent work, named Râjâvalî-kathe, written by Deva Chandra in the Kannâḍa language, the same story is repeated, with variations in details. It is there written that Châmuṇḍa Râya was a feudatory chief of king Râjamalla. His mother learnt from Âdi-purâṇa, when this work was being read to her, that in Podanpura there was an image of Vâhuvali. Thereupon she set out with her son to see this image, but on her way on the hill where Bhadrabâhu Svâmi died, she dreamt one night that Padmâvatî Devî appeared to her and said that there is an image of Vâhuvali on that very hill, covered by stones, which was formerly worshipped by Râma, Râvaṇa and Mandodarî. On the next morning an arrow was shot and the image of Vâhuvali became visible.

Thus, in the legendary accounts of the Jainas, we find that Châmuṇḍa Râya was not the person who caused the image to be made, but that there was already an image on the hill which he established and consecrated in the proper way. The high priest at Śravaṇa Belgola had also stated, according to these traditions, that "in ancient times, an image was at this place, self-formed from earth, under the shape of Gomat Îśvara Svâmi which Râvaṇa, the monarch of the Râkṣasas, worshipped to obtain happiness."

Châmuṇḍarâja discovered it and "made the workmen cut it into a regular shape, with the utmost accuracy of proportion in all its parts; the several proportions of the body resembling the original likeness of Gomat Iśvara Svâmî in profound contemplation to obtain Mokṣa. He also caused several buildings to be constructed as temples and other edifices round the God (?). On their completion, he established the worship of the image...with great ceremony and devotion."* In an extract taken from Sthala-purâṇa, we find the following passage which agrees with the above story:

The story in Sthala-purâṇa.

"Châmuṇḍarâja ...... set out with his family ... with a view of visiting the God Gommateśvara ... at Padanapura and the 1,254 other gods scattered throughout the surrounding country. *En route* he came to Śravaṇa Belgola Kṣetra, having heard a good deal about the God Gommateśvara ... He repaired the ruined temples and, among other ceremonies, had that of sprinkling the god performed. He appointed Siddhântâchârya as Guru of the Maṭh to conduct the daily, monthly, annual and other processions. He established in the Maṭh a Chattram, where food, medicine and education were provided for pilgrims. He appointed men of his caste to receive with due respect the devotees and pilgrims of all three castes who should resort to the place from Delhi, Kanakâdri, Svitpura, Sudhâpura, Pâpâpuri, Champâpuri, Sammida-giri, Ujjayanta-giri, Jayanagara, etc. For this purpose, certain villages ... were made over to the temple. He fixed Śilâ-śasanas in the four directions ... This endowment was maintained by his descendants for 109 years."†

Now let us attempt to find out how far these statements to the effect that Châmuṇḍa Râya was merely the discoverer of the image of Gommateśvara at Śravaṇa Belgola are true. The work, Bhujabali Charitra or Vâhuvali Charitra, is composed in Sanskrit verses, and in it we find only a collection of traditions handed down from mouth to mouth, with variations arising from such a course. The date of the work cannot be definitely ascertained, but, from its style, it can be inferred that it was composed long after the establishment of the image of Gommateśvara. Râjâvalîkathe

* Historical and Legendary account of Belliagola (Asiatic Researches, Vol. IX, page 263).

† "Sthalapurâṇa" Extract taken by Capt. I. S. F. Mackenzie (Indian Antiquary, Vol. II, page 130).

is "a compendium of Jaina history, legends and chronology, drawn up early in the present century for Devîramma, a lady of the Mysore royal family, by Devachandra of the Jaina establishment at Maleyûr"* This work also cannot, therefore, be called to be an authority for determining the question in hand. In Râjâvalî-kathe and in Sthala-purâṇa, the authors made no attempt to be accurate on historical points, for the subject-matter in their hands was merely a collection of legends and fables. It is true that there are historical materials underlying these stories, but these should not be taken on trust as they are, but we should test the accuracy of the same by comparing these with other and more trustworthy records before we could accept them as matters of history. To mention one among many inaccuracies in Sthala-purâṇa, we may quote the line "Châmuṇḍa Râya, king of Dakṣina Madura and the descendant of Jaina Kṣatri Pându,"† from which we shall understand how in the legendary accounts Châmuṇḍa Râya, the minister, came to be described as the king of Madura.

Further, if there had not been any contemporary and authentic records to prove who caused the image to be constructed, we might have doubted, on the basis of these traditionary accounts, that Châmuṇḍa Râya erected this statue. But, fortunately for us, there are records to prove that it was Châmuṇḍa Râya and no other who had the image of Gommateśvara constructed.

First, there is the inscription which we have already quoted under the feet of the image in which it is distinctly stated that Châmuṇḍa Râja "made" the image. Next, in an inscription, dated about 1180 A. D. (see page X), we have seen that Châmuṇḍa Râya had this image made by his own effort. These are supported by a work, named Gommata-sâra, composed by Nemichandra, the

---

* Lewis Rice—Inscriptions at Śravaṇa Belgola : Introduction, page 3 (1889).

† Extract taken from "Sthala-purâṇa" by Capt. Mackenzie (Indian Antiquary, Vol. II, page 130). It may also be mentioned that in the Pattâvali of Sena-gaṇa, we have "Châmuṇḍarâya, the king of the Southern Tailaṅga and Karnâṭaka, the crest jewel of the Kṣatriya race, a resident of the city of Dakṣina Madhurâ, for whose awakening of soul) the image of Vâhuvali Gommata Svâmi (was efficacious) and consecrated by Ajîta-sena Bhaṭṭâraka." ["दक्षिणमधुरानगरनिवासि—क्षत्रियवंशशिरोमणिदक्षिणतैलङ्गकर्णाटकदेशाधिपतिचामुण्डराय—प्रतिबोधक—बाहुबलिप्रतिबिम्बगोमट्टस्वामिप्रतिष्ठाचार्य्य—श्रीअजितसेनभट्टारकाणाम्"] [Jain Siddhânta Bhâskara, Part 1, No. I (1912), page 38.

preceptor, and therefere contemporary, of Châmuṇda Râja, in which we have the following verses:

"Let the aphorisms consisting of the Gommata compendium, the Gommata Jina, on the summit of Gommata Hill and the Dakṣiṇa Kukkuta Jina (the Southern Kukkuta Jina) *constructed* by Gommata Râya, be victorious.

"Let that Gommata by whom the face of the image was *constructed* which was seen ... by the gods ... and sages, be victorious."*

The image of Gommateśvara caused the hill on which it was situated to be called Gommata hill, and Nemichandra uses the words "constructed (**विणिम्मिय**) by Châmuṇḍa Râya." We have already mentioned that the image of Gommateśvara, which was established by Bharata in Paudanapura, came to be known as Kukkuteśvara, when dragons sprung up around it. The image established by Châmuṇḍa Râya came to be called the Southern Kukkuta Jina to distinguish it from the other one which was in the north. Châmuṇḍa Râya, by having this image constructed came to be called Gommata Râya.

From these facts we have not the least doubt that it was Châmuṇḍa Râya who had this image constructed. For such a great act he himself came to be known as Gommata Râya, which would have been hardly possible, had it been the fact that he merely discovered the image. Nemichandra, the preceptor of Châmuṇḍa Râya, must have been present at the time of the establishment of this image (for even in Vâhuvali Charitra we find that Nemichandra was present on this occasion), and consequently the words of Nemichandra, supported as they are by the inscription, must be accepted to be conclusive on this point.

The reason why in the works like Vâhuvali Charitra, Râjâvalîkathe, etc., we find that Châmuṇḍa Râya was merely the discoverer of the image, may probably be that the writers of these works desired to ascribe to the image a greater antiquity, causing the image to be considered an object of deeper veneration.

---

* "गोम्मटसंगहसुत्तं गोम्मटसिहरुवरि गोम्मटजिणो य ।
गोम्मटरायविणिम्मियदक्खिणकुक्कुडजिणो जयउ ॥
जेण विणिम्मिय—पड़िमा—वयणं सव्वट्टसिद्धिदेवेहिं ॥
सव्वपरमोहिजोगिहिं दिट्ठं सो गोम्मठो जयउ ॥

[Gommata-sâra. Karma-Kâṇda, verses 968 and 969].

PLATE VII. The anointing ceremony of Vâhuvali Gommatesvara

There is one more legend connected with the image of Gommateśvara which describes how the pride of Châmuṇḍa Râya for establishing such a figure was humbled. The story is as follows :—

"Châmuṇḍa Râya, after having established the worship of this image, became proud and elated, at placing this God by his own authority at so vast an expense of money and labour. Soon after this, when he performed in honour of the God the ceremony of *Pañchâmrita snâna* (or washing the image with five liquids—milk, curds, butter, honey and sugar), vast quantities of these things were expended in many hundred pots ; but, through the wonderful power of the God, the liquor descended not lower than the navel, to check the pride and vanity of the worshipper. Châmuṇḍa Râya, not knowing the cause, was filled with grief that his intention was frustrated of cleaning the image completely with this ablution. While he was in this situation, the celestial nymph, Padmâvatî, by order of the God, having transformed herself into the likeness of an aged poor woman, appeared, holding in her hand the five *amritas* in a *Beliya Gola* (or small silver pot) for washing the statue : and signified her intention to Châmuṇḍa Râya, who laughed at the absurdity of this proposal, of accomplishing what it had not been in his power to effect. Out of curiosity, however, he permitted her to attempt it ; when, to the great surprise of the beholders, she washed the image with the liquor brought in the little silver vase. Châmuṇḍa Râya, repenting his sinful arrogance, performed a second time, with profound respect, his ablution, on which they formerly wasted so much valuable liquids, and washed completely the body of the image. From that time this place is named after the silver vase (or *Beliya Gola*), which was held in Padmâvatî's hand." *

The date of the construction of the image.

We shall now try to ascertain the probable date on which the image of Gommateśvara was erected by Châmuṇḍa Râya. We have already seen that Châmuṇḍa Râya was the minister of Mârasiṃha II and Râchamalla or Râjamalla II. It was during the reign of Râjamalla that the tradition ascribes the establishment of the image of Gommateśvara. We have found that during the reign of Mârasiṃha II, Châmuṇḍa Râya distinguished himself as a valiant warrior, and in an inscription in

* Asiatic Researches, Vol. IX, page 266. In the above account a quite different explanation of the name of Śravaṇa Belgola has been given. Recently the Jainas performed an anointing ceremony of Gommateśvara, a picture of which with the scaffoldings erected, is reproduced here. [See the illustration facing this page].

which he gives an account of himself he only makes mention of the victories which he had won. There is no mention of any religious work done by him, and had it been the fact that he erected the colossal image during the reign of Mârasiṃha II, he must have mentioned the same, it being a monumental work which has immortalised his name. Mârasiṃha II died in 975 A. D. Châmuṇḍa Râya, in his work, named Châmuṇḍa Râya Purâṇa, gives a detailed account of all his exploits and mentions all his titles and how he derived the same, but there is not the slightest mention of the erection of the image of Gommateśvara by him. At the end of this work the date of its completion is mentioned to be Śaka 900 (A. D. 978). It must have been, therefore, after A. D. 978 and before the last year of the reign of Râchamalla or Râjamalla II that the image of Gommateśvara was erected. The reign of Râjamalla II ended in A. D. 984. We therefore come to a limited period, *viz.*, 978—984 A. D. within which the statue must have been established.

There is a verse in Vâhuvalî Charitra which purports to give the exact date of the establishment of the image. That verse is as follows:—

> "कल्क्यब्दे षट्शताख्ये विनुतविभवसंवत्सरे मासि चैत्रे,
> पञ्चम्यां शुक्लपक्षे दिनमणिदिवसे कुम्भलग्ने सुयोगे ।
> सौभाग्ये मस्तनाम्नि प्रकटितभगणे सुप्रशस्तां चकार
> श्रीमच्चामुण्डराजो वेल्गुलनगरे गोमटेश-प्रतिष्ठाम् ॥"

i.e., Śrî Châmuṇḍarâya established the image of Gomateśa in the city of Belgula, in Kumbha Lagna, on a Sunday, the fifth day of the bright lunar fortnight, in the month of Chaitra, in the praised year Vibhava, in the Kalki age, known as 600, when the auspicious Mrigaśirâ star was visible.

If we accept that the date mentioned above is the true one, as it indicates an auspicious day on which such a great work might have been performed, we shall have to find out on what date in the years between 978 and 984 A. D. (for we cannot go beyond this period, as has been already shown) was such a combination possible. We have carefully tested all the possible dates according to the methods adopted in astronomy and found out that on Sunday, the 2nd of April 980 A. D., there was Mrigaśirâ Nakṣatra, and that from the previous day (the 20th Chaitra) there was Pañchami Tithi (Sukla Pakṣa) and that there was also Kumbha Lagna on Sunday. This, therefore, may be accepted to be the date on which Châmuṇḍa Râya established the image.

But there is one point in the above verse which at the first sight is in discrepancy with the accepted period derived from history. In the above verse, it is stated that in the Kalki age 600, in the praised year Vibhava, the statue of Gommateśvara was established. The Śaka Samvat begins after 605 years five months elapse from the Nirvâṇa of Mahâvîra* and the Kalki era begins 394 years and seven months after the Śaka era, or, in other words, 1000 years after the Vîranirvâṇa. The Kalki era therefore begins from 472 A. D. The year 600 of the Kalki would therefore be 472+600=1072 A. D., which does not accord at all with history, for Râchamalla II's reign ended in 984 A. D. Further, even by astronomical calculation we find that the Pañchamî Tithi in Śukla Pakṣa in Chaitra of the Kalki year 600 falls on Friday, the 23rd Chaitra, a fact which is opposed to that laid down in the verse itself, *viz.*, that the Śukla Pañchamí in Chaitra was a Sunday in that year.

It is, therefore, necessary to interpret "the Kalki era 600" as the sixth century of the Kalki. The Vibhava year should be the eighth in order, so that it may accord with historical facts. By "the Kalki era 600 in the praised year Vibhava," therefore, we should mean the eighth year in the sixth century of the Kalki, *viz.*, the year 508 of the Kalki era; and, if we accept this, it exactly accords with the year 980 A. D. and corresponds in every astronomical detail with the facts mentioned in the verse.

There are, therefore, two courses open for us to adopt; first, to reject the verse contained in the Vâhubali Charitra as opposed to the historical records, or to interpret it in the way we have done, so that it may accord with the data obtained from the inscriptions; and we think that the latter course would be the best to adopt.

Nemichandra Siddhânta-chakravarti, the author of Dravya-saṃgraha.

We shall now try to collect all available information about the author of *Davva-saṃgaha* (*Dravya-saṃgraha*) or compendium of the substances. From the last verse of this work, it appears that it was

---

* *Vide*:—

"पणछ सयवस पणमासजुदं

गमिय वीरणिव्वुइदो सगराजो ।"—[Triloka-sâra by Nemichandra.

i.e., six hundred and five years, joined to five months, having passed away, since the Nirvâṇa of Vîra, the Śaka king (was born)]. [See *Indian Antiquary*, Vol. XII, page 21 (1883).

composed by Muni Nemichandra.* In Vâhuvali Charitra we read that Nemichandra, belonging to the Deśîya Gaṇa, accompanied Châmuṇda Râya and his mother when they started to see the image of Gommateśvara at Paudanapura. Further, that Nemichandra also dreamt that there was an image of Gommateśvara on the Vindhyagiri, and that Châmuṇḍa Râya, after establishing the image, offered villages yielding a revenue of ninety-six thousand coins at the feet of Nemichandra for the daily worship and festivals of Gommateśvara.†

That Nemichandra was revered by Châmuṇḍa Râya appears from the following verse in an inscription dated about 1530 A. D., engraved in the enclosure of Padmâvatî temple in Nagar Taluq, Shimoga District, Mysore :—

"त्रिलोकसार-प्रमुख............
.... भुवि नेमिचन्द्रः ।
विभाति सैद्धान्तिक-सार्वभौमः
चामुण्डराजार्चित-पादपद्मः ॥"

i. e., "(The author of) Trilokasâra and other (works).........Nemichandra, the Saiddhântika Sârvabhauma (the Paramount Lord of those versed in the Siddhântas) shines in this world, his lotus-feet worshipped by Châmuṇḍa-râja."‡ Though a fragment of this verse is effaced, the meaning is quite clear. The Saiddhântika Sârvabhauma is a synonym of the epithet 'Siddhânta-chakravarttî," generally applied to Nemichandra.

Nemichandra himself, in his work entitled Gommatasâra, has praised Gommata Râya or simply Râya which, as we have shown before (see page xxxiv), is but another name of Châmuṇḍa Râya. In the eulogistic verses, Nemichandra has mentioned that Ajitasena was the

---

* "दव्वसंगहमिणं मुणिणाहा दोससंचयचुदा सुदपुण्णा ।
सोधयंतु तणुसुत्तधरेण णेमिचंदमुणिणा भणियं जं ॥"
[Dravya-saṃgraha, verse 58.]

† *Vide* :—
"भास्वद्देशीगणाग्रेसररुचिरसिद्धान्तविन्नेमिचन्द्र—
श्रीपादाग्रे सदा षण्णवतिदशशतद्रव्यभूग्रामवर्य्यान् ।
दत्वा श्रीगोमटेशोत्सवसवननित्यार्चनावैभवाय
श्रीमच्चामुण्डराजो निजपुरमथुरां संजगाम क्षितीशः ॥"
[Vâhuvali Charitra, verse 61.]

‡ Epigraphia Carnatica, Vol. VIII, Nagar Taluq, Inscription No. 46.

PLATE VIII Nemichandra Siddhânta-chakravarttî explaining the scriptures to Châmuṇḍâraya

spiritual preceptor of Châmuṇḍa Râya, who erected the image of Gommateśvara.*

In the introduction to the commentary on Gommatasâra by Abhayachandra, we find that this work was composed according to the desire of Châmuṇḍa Râya, who wished to learn the exposition of substances as enumerated in the canonical works of the Jainas. In a very old illuminated manuscript of Trilokasâra, composed by Nemichandra, we have a picture representing Châmuṇḍa Râya, with several courtiers hearing the tenets of Jainism as expounded by Nemichandra. (See picture facsimile reprint of this, facing this page).

The works of Nemichandra.

Nemichandra Siddhânta-chakravarttî is the author of (1) Dravya-saṃgraha, (2) Gommatasâra, (3) Labdhi-sâra, (4) Kṣapaṇasâra and (5) Trilokasâra. In Vâhuvali Charitra we have "Nemichandra, the author of Gommatasâra, Labdhisâra and Trilokasâra."† In the last verse of Dravya-saṃgraha, Nemichandra has mentioned his name.‡ Similarly, from a verse in

---

* "गोम्मट संगहसुत्तं गोम्मटसिहरुवरि गोम्मटजिणो य ।
गोम्मटरायविणिम्मियदक्खिणकुक्कुडजिणो जयउ ॥
जेण विणिम्मियपडिमावयणं सव्वट्ठसिद्धिदेवेहिं ।
सव्वपरमोहिजोगिहिं दिट्ठं सो गोम्मटो जयउ ॥
वज्जयणं जिणभवणं ईसिपभारं सुवण्णकलसं तु ।
तिहुवणपडिमाणिक्कं जेण कयं जयउ सो राओ ॥
जेणुव्भियथंभुवरिमजक्ख—किरीटग्गकिरणजलधोया ।
सिद्धाण सुद्धपाया सो राओ गोम्मटो जयउ ॥
जम्हि गुणा विस्संता गणहरदेवादि—इड्ढिपत्ताणं ।
सो अजियसेणणाहो जस्स गुरु जयउ सो राओ ॥"

[Gommatasâra Karmakâṇḍa, verses 968—971 and 966.]

† *Vide*:—

"सिद्धान्तामृतसागरं स्वमतिमन्थक्ष्माभृदालोड्य मध्ये
लेभेऽभीष्टफलप्रदानपि सदा देशीगणाग्रेसरः ।
श्रीमद्गोमटलब्धिसारविलसत्त्रैलोक्यसारामर—
क्ष्माजश्रीसुरधेनुचिन्तितमणीन् श्रीनेमिचन्द्रो मुनिः ॥"

[Vâhuvali Charitra, verse 63.]

‡ "णेमिचन्दमुणिणा भणियं जम् ।"

[Dravya-saṃgraha, verse 58].

Gommatasâra we know that it was composed by Nemichandra.* It may be well to give a brief account of the works of Nemichandra at this place.

Gommatasâra.

Gommatasâra is so named, as it was composed for the reading of Châmuṇḍa Râya who, as we have already shown, was also known as Gommata Râya. This work is also known as Pañcha-saṃgraha† [the compendium of five things], the significance of which will be understood when we mention that in it the following five subjects have been thoroughly treated: (1) Bandha (bondage), (2) Badhyamâna (that which is bound), (3) Bandhasvâmi (that which binds), (4) Bandha-hetu (the cause of bondage) and (5) Bandha-bheda (the varieties of bondage).

The work consists of 1705 verses in Prâkrit, and is divided into two parts Jîvakâṇḍa and Karmakâṇḍa, containing 733 and 972 verses respectively. In Jîvakâṇḍa, there is an enumeration of Mârgaṇâs, Guṇasthânas, Jîva, Paryâpti, Prâṇa, Saṅga and Upayôga.‡ In Karmakâṇḍa, there are nine sections, called Prakritisamutkîrtana, Bandhodayasatva, Sattvasthânabhaṅga, Trichûlikâ, Sthânasamutkîrtana, Pratyaya, Bhavachûlikâ, Trikaraṇa-chûlikâ and Karma-sthiti-rachanâ. The eight varieties of Karma and the bondage of Karma, with respect to its Prakriti, Sthiti, Anubhâga and Pradeśa, are also treated in detail. There are also various other subjects connected with Karma which are elaborated in this part. To be brief, the first part of Gommatasâra gives an idea of the natural characteristics of Jîvas and the means and stages of their development, while the second part describes the obstacles producing bondage of Karma which must be removed, in order that Jîvas might attain liberation. The advancement of the soul is the end which the author always keeps in view; and it is in this light that he has summarised the precepts of Jaina Âchâryas on this point in Gommatasâra. The work, in very brief limits, comprises most of the important tenets of Jaina philosophy,

---

* "सिद्धंतुदयतडुग्गयणिम्मलवरणेमिचंदकरकलिया ।
गुणरयणभूसणंबुहिमइवेला भरउ भुवणयलं ॥"
[Gommatasâra, Karmakânda, verse 967.]

† *Vide*:—
"श्रीमच्चामुण्डरायप्रश्नानुरूपं गोम्मटसारनामधेयपञ्चसंग्रहशास्त्रं प्रारभमानः।"
[Commentary on Gommatasâra by Abhayachandra. From a MSS. in the Central Jaina Oriental Library, Arrah.]

‡ What these mean will appear from Dravya-saṃgraha, pages 39, 37, 33, 7 and 8 respectively.

and proceeds to lay down the ways and means to liberation, warning us against the hindrances and obstacles to the same.

Commentaries on Gommatasâra.

Châmuṇḍa Râya himself wrote a commentary on Gommatasâra in Canarese language. In the last verse of Gommatasâra there is a reference to the fact that Châmuṇḍa Râya wrote in the popular language a commentary, named Vîra-mârttaṇḍî.* [Gommatasâra, Karmakâṇḍa, verse 972.] One of the titles of Châmuṇḍa Râya being Vîramârttaṇḍa, he named his commentary "Vîra-mârttaṇḍî," meaning "composed by Vîra-mârttaṇḍa." This commentary of Châmuṇḍa Râya seems to have been lost, and we only have a reference to it in another commentary, named Keśavavarṇîyâ Vṛitti, by Keśavavarṇî, in the opening verse of which the author says: "I write the Vṛitti on Gommatasâra from the Karnâtaka Vṛitti."† There is another commentary on Gommatasâra, named Mandaprabodhikâ, written by Abhayachandra‡. Following these commentaries, Todarmalla has written a commentary in the Hindi language which is widely read by the Jaina Pandits of the present day.§

Labdhisâra.

Labdhisâra|| is a treatise on Labdhi, which literally means "attainment." The sense in which it is used in Jaina philosophy is "the attainment of those things which will lead to perfect conduct." Labdhi is said to be of five kinds,

---

* *Vide*:—

गोम्मटसुत्तल्लिहणे गोम्मटरायेण या कया देसी ।
सो राओ चिरं कालं णामेण य वीरमत्तण्डी ॥"

[Gommatasára, Karmakâṇḍa, verse 972.]

† *Vide*:—

"नेमिचन्द्रं जिनं नत्वा सिद्धं श्रीज्ञानभूषणम् ।
वृत्तिं गोम्मटसारस्य कुर्वे कर्णाट-वृत्तितः ॥"

[Vṛitti by Keśavavarṇî.]

‡ *Vide*:—

"मुनिं सिद्धं प्रणम्याहं नेमिचन्द्रं जिनेश्वरम् ।
टीकां गोम्मटसारस्य कुर्वे मन्द-प्रबोधिकाम् ॥"

[Commentary by Abhayadeva.]

§ The editions of Gommata-sâra are:—

1. Jîva-Kâṇḍa (Ed. by Pandit Manoharlal) Bombay, 1914.
2. Karmakâṇḍa (Râya Chandra Series) Bombay, 1912.

|| Labdhisâra has not yet been printed, and we give the above account from a manuscript in the Central Jaina Oriental Library, Arrah. A notice of another manuscript of Labdhisâra, where a brief summary of the work has also been given, may be found in Notices of Sanskrit Manuscripts, by Rajendralal Mitra, Vol. IX Part I, page 86. The manuscript is there numbered 2980.

Kṣâyopaśamika, Viśuddhi, Deśanâ, Prâyôgya and Karaṇa.* The first four kinds of Labdhi appear without distinction to Bhavya and Abhavya individuals, but the fifth one appears only to a Bhavya individual who is advanced towards perfect conduct. The opening verse of Labdhisâra is as follows :—

सिद्धे जिणिंदचन्दे आयरिय उवज्झाय सब्बसाहुगणे ।
वंदिय सम्मद्दंसण चरित्तलद्धिं परूवेमो ॥

i.e., "Bowing to Siddhas, Jinendras, Âchâryas, Upâdhyâyas and Sâdhus,† I shall relate the attainment of perfect faith and conduct."

Kṣapaṇasâra.

Kṣapaṇasâra‡ by Nemichandra should not be confounded with another work of the same name written by Mâdhavachandra, the latter being composed in Sanskrit prose and the former in Prâkrit verse. The subject-matter of both these works is the same, for each of them treats of Bandha, Kaṣâya, Leśyâ, etc., and lays down the means by which Kaṣâyas may be removed. Kṣapaṇa literally means 'destruction' and Kṣapaṇasâra deals with the destruction of Kaṣâyas. The opening verse of the work is as follows :—

कसायखवणो हाणे परिणामो केरिसो हवे ।
कसाए उवजोगो लेस्सा वेदो य को हवे ॥"

This work may be considered to be a continuation of Labdhisâra, and both Labdhisâra and Kṣapaṇasâra are so related to Gommatasâra that these may be said to be a sequel to it. The number of verses in Jîvakâṇḍa of Gommata-sâra is 733, that in Karmakâṇḍa 972, that in Labdhisâra 380 and that in Kṣapaṇasâra 270.

Trilokasâra.

Trilokasâra§ contains a description of the three Lokas (regions of the universe). In it is found a description of the countries of the earth, with oceans, mountains, etc., together with a description of the abodes of heavenly beings and

---

* *Vide* :—

"खयउवसमियविसोही देसणपाउग्गकरणलद्धी य ।
चत्तारि वि सामण्णा करणं पुण होदि सम्मत्ते ॥"

[Gommatasâra, Jîvakâṇḍa, verse 650.]

† For an explanation of these terms, see Dravya-saṃgraha, page 112.

‡ The account given here is from a manuscript in the Deva Kumar's Central Jaina Oriental Library, Arrah.

§ This work has not yet been printed. We give an account of it from Notices of Sanskrit Manuscripts by Rajendaralal Mitra, Vol. VI, page 97. Manuscript No. 2041. There is a manuscript of this work in the Arrah Library.

the inmates of hell. The stars and planets, with their orbits, are described, and there is a mention how night and day are caused by the motion of the earth. Besides these, there are other subjects, such as the various kinds of measurements, methods of reckoning, etc.

The opening verses are as follows :—

"बलगोविंद सिहामणि किरणकलावरुणचरणणहकिरणं ।
विमलयरणेमिचंदं तिहुवणचंदं णमंसामि ॥
भवणवेंतरजोइसविमाणणरतिरियलोयजिणभवणे ।
सव्वामरिंद णरवइ संपूजिय वंदिए वंदे ॥"

The last verse, similar to that of Dravya-saṃgraha, is as follows :—

"इदि णेमिचंदमुणिणा अप्पस्सुदेणभयणंदिवच्छेण ।
रयिओ तिलोयसारो खमं तु तं बहु सुदाइरिया ॥"

There is a commentary on Trilokasâra, written by Mâdhavachandra Traividya, in the introduction of which we find that the work was obviously written by Nemichandra for imparting knowledge to Châmuṇḍa Râya.* It is curious to note, however, that at the end of the commentary, Mâdhavachandra says that he himself wrote some verses which have been incorporated in this work, according to the instructions of his preceptor Nemichandra.† The commentary begins with the following verse :—

"त्रिभुवनचन्द्रं जिनेन्द्रं भक्त्या नत्वा त्रिलोकसारस्य ।
वृत्तिरियं किञ्चिज्ज्ञ—प्रबोधनाय प्रकाश्यते विधिना ॥"

Pratiṣṭhâpâṭha. We further hear that there is a work, named Pratiṣṭhâpâṭha, by Nemichandra, which was written in imitation of another work of the same name written by Indranandi, to whom Nemichandra makes obeisance in Gommatasâra.‡ This work is said

---

* "श्रीमदप्रतिहताप्रतिमनिःप्रतिपक्षनिष्करण—भगवन्नेमिचन्द्रसैद्धान्तदेवश्चतुरनुयोगचतुरुदधिपारगश्चामुण्डरायप्रतिबोधनव्याजेन अशेषविनेयजनप्रतिबोधनार्थं त्रिलोकसारनामानं ग्रन्थमारचयन् तत्रादौ निर्विघ्नतः शास्त्रपरिसमाप्त्यादिकफलकुलमवलोक्य विशिष्टदेवतामभिष्टौति ।"

[Introduction to the Commentary by Mâdhavachandra.]

† "गुरुणेमिचंदसम्मद—कदिमयगाहा तहिं तहिं रइदा ।
माधवचंदतिविज्जे णिणमणुसरणिज्ज मज्झेहिं ॥"

[Commentary by Mâdhavachandra.]

‡ "णमह गुणरयणभूसणसिद्धंतामियमहद्धिभवभावं ।
वरवीरणंदिचंदं णिम्मलगुणमिंदणंदिगुरुं ॥"

[Gommatasâra, Karmakâṇḍa, verse 896.]

to consist of directions for the establishment and consecration of images. Pandit Javâharlal Shâstrî has written that he has seen an incomplete manuscript of this work.* We are at present unable to give any further information about the same.

The Gurus of Nemichandra.

In Gommatasâra, we have a mention of several sages to whom Nemichandra makes obeisance as his preceptors. These sages are Abhayanandi, Indranandi, Vîranandi and Kanakanandi.† There is an epic, named Chandra-prabha Charitaṃ (which we have often quoted in our commentary on Dravya-saṃgraha) composed by Vîranandi, at the end of which it is written that Vîranandi was the disciple of Abhayanandi ‡ and that Abhayanandi was the disciple of Guṇanandi. In Gommatasâra itself we find that Kanakanandi was the disciple of Indranandi.§

---

* *Vide* Introduction to Vrihad-dravya-saṃgraha, page 9, footnote No. 2.

† "णमिऊण अभयणंदिं सुदसायरपारगिंदणंदिगुरुं ।
वरवीरणंदिणाहं पयडीणं पच्चयं वोच्छं ॥"

Also :—

"वरइंदणंदिगुरुणो पासे सोऊण सयलसिद्धंतं ।
सिरिकणयणंदिगुरुणा सत्तट्ठाणं समुद्दिट्ठं ॥"

[Gommatasâra, Karmakâṇḍa, verses 785 and 396.]

‡ "बभूव भव्याम्बुजपद्मबन्धुः पतुर्मुनीनां गणभृत्समानः ।
सदग्रणीर्देशिगणाग्रगण्यो गुणाकरः श्रीगुणनन्दिनामा ॥
मुनिजननुतपादः प्रास्तमिथ्याप्रवादः
सकलगुणसमृद्धस्तस्य शिष्यः प्रसिद्धः ।
अभवदभयनन्दी जैनधर्माभिनन्दी—
स्वमहिमजितसिन्धुर्भव्यलोकैकबन्धुः ॥
भव्याम्भोजविबोधनोद्यतमतेर्भास्वत् समानत्विषः
शिष्यस्तस्य गुणाकरस्य सुधियः श्रीवीरनन्दीत्यभूत् ।
स्वाधीनाखिलवाङ्मयस्य भुवनप्रख्यातकीर्त्तेः सतां
संसत्सु व्यजयन्त यस्य जयिनो वाचः कुतर्काङ्कुशाः ॥"

[चन्द्रप्रभचरितप्रशस्तिः । श्लोकाः १, ३, ४,]

§ "वरइंदणंदिगुरुणो पासे सोऊण सयलसिद्धंतं ।
सिरिकणयणंदिगुरुणा सत्तट्ठाणं समुद्दिट्ठं ॥"

[Gommatasâra, Karmakâṇḍa, verse 396.]

Davva-saṃgaha or Dravya-saṃgraha,* the work which we are publishing as the first volume of our series, may be conveniently divided into three parts. The first part deals with the six Dravyas (substances) including the five Asti-Kâyas existing in and comprising this universe. This part extends from verse 1 to verse 27. The second part, comprising verses 28-39, deals with the seven Tattvas and nine Padârthas. The third part, consisting of verses 40-57, describes the way to attain liberation.

Dravya-saṃgraha.

In the opening verse, along with the usual Maṅgalâcharaṇa, it is mentioned that Dravya consists of Jîva and Ajîva. In the second verse, Jîva is defined; and the several characteristics of Jîva mentioned in this definition are taken up one by one in verses 3-14, and a detailed consideration of the same is embodied therein. After this detailed description of Jîva, the author proceeds to describe Ajîva in verse 15 which consists of Pudgala, Dharma, Adharma, Âkâśâ and Kâla, each of which is defined in verses 16-22. These five classes of Ajîva with Jîva make up the six Dravyas existing in this universe.

Among these, Jîva, Pudgala, Dharma, Adharma and Âkâśa are called Astikâyas (verse 23), the definition of which is given in the next verse. The first part ends after two more verses.

The second part deals with the seven Tattvas, *viz.*, Âsrava, Bandhana, Samvara, Nirjarâ Mokṣa, Jîva and Ajîva. These seven, together with Puṇya and Pâpa are known as the nine Padârthas. Some again regard all these nine as Tattvas. The different verieties of Âsrava, Samvara, etc., are treated in detail in verses 29-38.

The third part begins with verse 39, in which and the next verse the means to attain liberation are stated, according to the ordinary and realistic points of view. Perfect faith, perfect knowledge and perfect conduct which are essential to obtain liberation are then defined, and

* Manuscripts of Dravya-samgraha are: Dravya-saṃgraha par Nemichandra [E. Leumann. A list of the Strassburg collection of Digambara manuscripts. (Wiener Zeitschrift für die kunde des Morgenlandes, Vol. XI, page 297-312), Wien. 1897]. There is also a MSS. of Dravya-saṃgraha with Dravya-samgraha-sûtra-vritti in the Govt. Oriental MSS. Library, Madras [*Vide* Alphabetical Index of MSS. in the Govt. Oriental MSS. Library, Madras, 1893.] *Vide* also notices of MSS. of Dravya-saṃgraha and its commentary in Notices of Sanskrit MSS. by Haraprasad Śâstrî, Vol. X, Nos. 3292 and 3293, the latter being a copy of the commentary by Brahmadeva. The printed editions are Vrihad-dravya-saṃgraha, edited by Javaharlal Śâstrî (Raychandra Jaina Śâstramâla No. 10) (Bombay) Dravya-saṃgraha published by Jaina Grantha-Ratnâkara Office (Bombay). and Dravya-samgraha (Benares) 1900.

in this connection the importance of Dhyâna (meditation) is emphasised. In verse 49 we are introduced to the prayers of the Jainas by which one should attempt to concentrate the mind upon the Arhats, Siddhas, Âchâryas, Upâdhyâyas and Sâdhus. These five classes of beings are known as the five Parameṣṭhis, and their characteristics are described in verses 50-54. The work ends with a mention of the efficacy of Dhyâna (meditation).

Brhmadeva's commentary.

The commentary on Dravya-saṃgraha which we publish herewith is composed by Brahmadeva.‡ Portions of this commentary have been quoted by Śubhachandra in his commentary on a work entitled, Svâmi-kârtikeyâ nuprekṣâ.* There is, therefore, no doubt that Bramhadeva must have lived before, or at least was the contemporary of, Śubhachandra. The commentary on Svâmi-kârtikêyâ-nupreksâ by Śubhachandra was finished on the 10th of Magh, in the Vikrama year 1613† Śubhachandra wrote another work, named Pândava-Purâṇa, at the end of which it is mentioned§

‡ "द्रव्यसंग्रहसूत्राणां वृत्तिं वक्ष्ये समासतः ।" [ब्रह्मदेववृत्तिः]
Also श्रीनेमिचन्द्रसिद्धान्तिदेवैर्विरचितस्य द्रव्यसंग्रहाभिधानग्रन्थस्य सम्बन्धिनी श्रीब्रह्मदेवकृतवृत्तिः समाप्ता ।

* We mention this on the authority of a passage written by Pandit Javaharlal Śâstrî in his Introduction to Vrihad-dravya-saṃgraha, page 11. There is evidence that Śubhachandra was well-versed in the works of Nemichandra.

cf. त्रैलोक्यसार-गोमट्टसार-लब्धिसार-क्षपणासारादिशास्त्र-सरित्पतिपारप्राप्तानां"

[Pattâvali printed in Jain Śiddhânta-Bhâskar, a Part I, No. 4., page 45.]

†Vide: "श्रीमद्विक्रमभूपतेः परिमिते वर्षे शते षोडशे ।
श्रीमच्छ्रीशुभचन्द्रदेव-रचिता टीका सदा नन्दतु" ॥

[Praśasti of the commentary on Svâmîkârtikeyâ-nuprekṣâ by Śubhachandra as quoted in Jaina Siddhânta Bhâskaraa Part I, No. 4 page 67]

Dr. Bhandarkar, however, in his Report on Sanskrit Mss. page 113 (Bombay), says "Śubhachandra finished his work on the 10th of Mâgha in the year 1613 of Vikrama"

§ "श्रीमद्विक्रमभूपतेर्द्विकहते स्पष्टाष्टसंख्ये शते
रम्येऽष्टाधिकवत्सरे सुखकरे भाद्रे द्वितीयान्तिथौ ।
श्रीमद्वाग्वरनिर्वृतीदमतुले श्रीशाकवाटे पुरे
श्रीमच्छ्रीपुरुषाभिधे विरचितं स्थेयात् पुराणं चिरम् ॥"

[Pândava-Purâṇa Praśasti verse 86. From a Mss. in Jaina Library, Arrah.]

The place, Śâkabâta Pura, where the work Pândava Purâṇa was finished, is Sangbârâ, where Subhachandra succeeded his guru in the Patta established in that place. The order of succession of Gurus of Śubhachandra is as follows; Padmanandi, Sakala-kîrti, Bhubana-kîrti, Jñânabhûṣana, Vijayakîrti, Subhachandra. For a further account of Śubhachandra, the reader may refer to an article in Jaina Siddhânta Bhâskara, Part I, No. 4 pages 65-68.

that it was finished in the Vikrama year 1608. Manuscripts of the commentary on Svâmi-kârtikeyâ-nuprekṣâ and Pândava-Purâṇa have been discovered from which we quote the above dates. This Śubhachandra seems to be different from an author of the same name who composed Jñânârṇava, etc.

Thus it is clear that the commentator, Brahmadeva, was born several centuries after Nemichandra. Consequently, the statements which he makes about the composition of works by Nemichandra must be read with caution and accepted only when the same are confirmed by other proofs. Keeping this fact in view, we are not inclined to accept, without any further evidence, the statement made by Brahmadeva, namely, that Nemichandra first wrote a small treatise, in twenty-six verses, entitled Laghu-dravya-saṃgraha, for a merchant named Soma, in the temple of the Tîrthaṅkara Muni Subrata, in the town Âśrama of the ruler Srîpâla, under the King Bhoja of Dhârâ, in Mâlwa, and that subsequently Nemichandra enlarged the work and named it Vrihad-dravya-saṃgraha.† We do not find any indication of such a fact in the work itself, and in the last verse, Nemichandra has named his work to be "Davva-saṃgaha (or Dravya-saṃgraha and not "Vrihad-dravya-saṃgraha)," as it would have been the case according to the statement of the commentator. Further, the supposition that Nemichandra flourished during the reign of Bhoja of Malwa makes his date later than what has been proved by inscriptions and authorities quoted before. For this reason we do not feel ourselves justified in agreeing with Pandit Javâharlal Śâstrî in holding that Nemichandra resided for a time in Malwa and then went to other places, especially as there is no certainty as to the Bhoja (for there are several kings of this name) mentioned in the commentary.

---

†"अथ मालवदेशे धारानामनगराधिपति-राजभोजदेवाभिधानकलिकालचक्रवर्त्तिसम्बन्धिनः श्रीपालमण्डलेश्वरस्य सम्बन्धिन्याश्रमनामनगरे श्रीमुनिसुव्रततीर्थकरचैत्यालये...सोमाभिधानराजश्रेष्ठिनो निमित्तं श्रीनेमिचन्द्रसिद्धान्तिदेवैः पूर्वं षड्विंशतिगाथाभिर्लघुद्रव्यसंग्रहं कृत्वा पश्चाद्विशेषतत्त्वपरिज्ञानार्थं विरचितस्य बृहद्द्रव्यसंग्रहस्याधिकारशुद्धिपूर्वकत्वेन वृत्तिः प्रारभ्यते ।"

[Introduction to the commentary by Brahma-deva.]

In the Mss. of Dravyasaṃgraha-sûtra-Vritti preserved in the Govt. Oriental Mss.. Library, Madras, the name of the merchant given is मोम instead of सोम,

With these words as a preliminary, we leave the reader to peruse the following pages, hoping that the subject matter and the method of treatment adopted by the celebrated Jaina Âchârya will meet with due justice in his hands according to the intrinsic merits underlying the same.

द्रव्य-संग्रहः

DRAVYA-SAMGRAHA

जीवमजीवं दव्वं जिणवरवसहेण जेण णिद्दिट्ठं ।
देविंदविंदवंदं वंदे तं सव्वदा सिरसा ॥ १ ॥*

Jîvamajîvaṃ Davvaṃ jiṇavaravasaheṇa jeṇa ṇiddiṭṭhaṃ
Devinda-vinda-vandaṃ vande taṃ savvadâ sirasâ—(1).

Padâpâtha.—जेण Jeṇa, by whom. जिणवरवसहेण Jiṇavaravasaheṇa, the greatest of the great Jinas. जीवमजीवं Jîvamajîvaṃ, Jîva and Ajîva. दव्वं Davvaṃ, the Dravya. णिद्दिट्ठं Nidditṭhaṃ, has been described. देविंदविंदवंदं Devindavindavandaṃ, worshipped by the host of Indras. तं Taṃ, him. सव्वदा Savvadâ, always. सिरसा Sirasâ, with the head. वंदे Vande, salute.

1. I always salute with my head that eminent one among the great Jinas, who is worshipped by the host of Indras and who has described the Dravyas (substances), Jîva and Ajîva.

COMMENTARY.

The title of this work 'Dravya-Saṃgraha' being interpreted literally means "A compendium of Dravyas." According to the Jaina philosophy, the component factor of the universe is Dravya (substance), which is subdivided into Jîva (living) and Ajîva (non-living) substances. Everything in this universe is either Jîva or

---

* *Sanskrit rendering* :

जीवमजीवं द्रव्यं जिनवरवृषभेण येन निर्दिष्टम् ।
देवेन्द्रवृन्दवन्द्यं वन्दे तं सर्वदा शिरसा ॥१॥
Jîvamajîvaṃ dravyaṃ Jinavaravrişabheṇa yena nirddiṣṭaṃ
Devendravrindavandyaṃ vande taṃ sarvvadâ sirasâ—(1.)

Ajîva or a resultant of these. The author of Dravya-Saṃgraha has fully described Dravya with its classes and sub-classes in verses 1-38 of this work. Jîva, the first variety of Dravya, is defined in verse 2 and a detailed explanation of this definition is given in verses 3-14. Ajîva, the second variety of Dravya, is next described with its subdivisions in verses 15-27.

The first verse of this work is nothing but the usual Maṅgalâcharaṇa, in which the author salutes Mahâvîra, the twenty-fourth Tîrthaṅkara of the Jainas. He is called here the Eminent One among the great Jinas. The word Jina literally means "the Victor". One who has freed himself from the bondage of Karma by conquering Râga (attachment) and Dveṣa (Aversion) is called a Jina by the Jainas. In Buddhist scripture the word Jina is often used as a synonym to Buddha. In the lexicon called Amarakoṣa* and in popular Sanskrit literature, the use of the word Jina to signify Buddha is too common.† The Buddhists take the word Jina to mean one who has conquered Mâra. ‡ But the word Jina is used in a special sense by the Jainas. The Gaṇadharas or disciples of the Tîrthaṅkaras and the Tîrthaṇkaras themselves are known as Jinas, Jinendras, Jineśvaras, etc. [See Appendix A.]

Lord Mahâvîra has been saluted at the beginning of almost all the later works of the Jainas. Here it is said that he is worshipped by the Indras. Indras are Gods who possess special excellent powers [" परमैश्वर्यादिन्द्र-व्यपदेशः । Tattvârtha-râja-vârttika by Akalaṅka Deva. IV. 4. 1.] According to Jaina eschatology there are four kinds of Gods, dwelling in four different spheres, known respectively as Bhavana, Vyantara, Jyotiṣa and Vaimânika. [See Appendix B.] The Vaimânika region is again subdivided into Kalpa and Kalpâtîta spheres. Indras are a higher order of Gods who dwell in Bhavana, Vyantara and Jyotiṣa regions and the Kalpa sphere only of the Vaimânika region. There are no Indras in the Kalpâtîta sphere.

* " सर्वज्ञः सुगतो बुद्धो धर्मराजस्तथागतः ।
समन्तभद्रो भगवान् मारजिल्लोकजिज्जिनः॥"—Amarakoṣa. I. lines 25, 26.

† We quote only one instance among many :—
"सोऽयं मारवधूभिरित्यभिहितो बुद्धो जिनः पातु वः ।"
[Nâgânanda by Śrîharṣa. नान्दी]

‡ In the Jaina work on Nyâya called Parîkṣâmukha, Jina is used in the same sense, e.g.,—
"नमो जिनाय दुर्वार-मार-वीर-मदच्छिदे ।"

Besides these Indras among Gods, there are also others among men and among the lower animals.

There is a difference of opinion between the two principal sects of the Jainas as to the number of Indras. "The Svetâmbaras assert that there are twelve heavens and sixty-four Indras;" but "the Digambaras maintain that there are sixteen heavens and one hundred Olympian monarchs (Indras)."* From a verse † found in most of the commentaries on Digambara Jaina works, we learn that "there are forty Indras among the Gods who dwell in Bhavana (sphere), thirty-two among the Gods (who live in) Vyantara (sphere), twenty-four among the Gods (living in) Kalpa (sphere), two among the Jyotiṣa or planetary Gods, the sun and the moon, (one among) men and (one among) the Tiryaks ‡ (*i.e.*, all creatures excluding Gods, men and inmates of hell)."

Mahâvîra is said to have been the propounder of all the Jaina Canonical works. The wrong theory that Mahâvîra is the founder of Jainism and that Jainism is an offshoot of Buddhism, has long ago been exploded; and when we say that there is a tradition that Mahâvîra spoke to his disciples what has been embodied in the Canonical works of the Jainas, it must be understood that, though the fundamental truths of Jainism were preached long before Mahâvîra, it was after the Nirvâṇa of this last Tîrthaṅkara that the teachings of Jainism were reduced to writing which formed the basis of the Jaina Canonical works now extant.

The Aṅgas which are the Canonical works of the Svetâmbara sect of the Jainas are said to have been dictated by the fifth Gaṇadhara Sudharmâ Svâmi to his disciple, Jambu Svâmi, when the latter asked the former to explain the tenets of Jainism as laid down by Mahâvîra. In the Aṅgas we find questions like this: "What has been laid down by Lord Mahâvîra, the Tîrthaṅkara, on such and such a matter?" § put to Sudharmâ Svâmi by his disciple,

* Asiatic Researches, Vol. XVII, p. 289.

† भवणालय चालीसा विंतरदेवाण होंति बत्तीसा ।
कप्पामर चउवीसा चंदो सूरो णरो तिरओ ॥

‡ "औपपादिकमनुष्येभ्यः शेषास्तिर्यग्योनयः ।"

[Tattvârthâdhigama Sûtra by Umâsvâmi, IV. 27.]

§ "समणेणं भगवया महावीरेणं आइगरेणं तित्थगरेणं......के अट्ठे पण्णत्ते।"
—Jñâtridharmakathâṅga. Introduction.

"समणेणं भगवया महावीरेणं...के अट्ठे पण्णत्ते ।"—Vipâka Sutrâṅga. Introduction.

Jambu Svâmi. Further, in the Aṅgas there are sentences spoken by Sudharmâ Svâmi to the effect: "I am telling you such and such a matter, as described by Lord Mahâvîra."* From passages like these, it becomes certain that Mahâvîra is the earliest authority to which the existing Jaina Canonical works refer.

The Digambaras, however, deny the authority of the Aṅgas and say that the original Canonical works have perished during the first century after the Nirvâṇa of Mahâvîra; but they also maintain that the tenets of Jainism were made popular by Lord Mahâvîra. The tradition of both the Jain sects thus agree in attributing to Mahâvîra the popular exposition of the tenets of Jainism. This is the reason why we most frequently find Mahâvîra worshipped by the Jaina writers in the opening verses of their Works as the great propounder of the Truths of their religion. Here also Nemichandra, the author of Dravya-Saṃgraha, seems to have saluted Mahâvîra as the propounder of Dravya, which is the subject-matter of the present work.

The word "Jîva" is usually translated as "Soul," "Living being," "Consciousness," etc., and Ajîva as "things without life," "non-living substance," etc., but we shall use the original words throughout the translation. The accurate meaning of these terms will be understood from the verses which follow, and which deal with the distinguishing characteristics of each of these substances.

जीवो उवओगमओ अमुत्ति कत्ता सदेहपरिमाणो ।
भोत्ता संसारत्थो सिद्धो सो विस्ससोड्ढगई ॥ २ ॥†

Jîvo uvaogamao amutti kattâ sadehaparimâṇo.
Bhottâ saṃsârattho siddho so vissasoḍḍhagaî—(2)

Padapâtha.—जीवो Jîvo, Jiva. उवओगमओ Uvaogamao, characterised by upayoga. अमुत्ति Amutti, formless. कत्ता Kattâ, agent. सदेहपरिमाणो Sadehaparimâṇo, equal in extent to its own body. भोत्ता Bhottâ, enjoyer. संसारत्थो Saṃsârattho, being in the Saṃsâra. सिद्धो Siddho, siddha. सो So, he. विस्ससोड्ढगई Vissasoḍḍhagaî, having a natural upward motion.

2. Jîva is characterised by upayogâ, is formless

* "वोच्छामि आणुपुव्वीए जह भणियाणि भगवया ।"—Praśna-vyâkaraṇâṅga. VI.

† *Sanskrit rendering*:

जीवः उपयोगमयः अमूर्त्तिः कर्त्ता स्वदेहपरिमाणः ।
भोक्ता संसारस्थः सिद्धः स विस्रसा ऊर्द्ध्वगतिः ॥ २ ॥
Jîvaḥ upayogamayaḥ amûrtiḥ kartâ svadehaparimâṇaḥ.
Bhoktâ saṃsârasthaḥ siddhaḥ sa visrasâ ûrddhvagatiḥ—(2.)

and an agent, has the same extent as its own body, is the enjoyer (of the fruits of Karma), exists in saṃsâra, is Siddha and has a characteristic upward motion.

COMMENTARY.

In this verse the author lays down the distinguishing characteristics of Jîva. The nine characteristics of Jîva mentioned in this verse will be taken up one by one in verses 4-14, and a full explanation of them will be given in the notes to the said verses. Brahmadeva in his Commentary on Dravya-Saṃgraha has mentioned in connection with this verse that each of these characteristics of Jîva is mentioned in order to differentiate the Jaina conception of 'Jîva' from that of Sâṅkhya, Nyâya, Mîmâṃsâ, Chârvâka, Sadâsiva and Bauddha systems of philosophy. His words are as follows:

"जीवसिद्धिः चार्वाकं प्रति, ज्ञानदर्शनोपयोगलक्षणं नैयायिकं प्रति, अमूर्त्त-जीवस्थापनं भट्टचार्वाकद्वयं प्रति, कर्म्मकर्तृत्वस्थापनं सांख्यं प्रति, स्वदेह-प्रमिति-स्थापनं नैयायिक-मीमांसक-सांख्य-त्रयं प्रति, कर्म्मभोक्तृत्व-व्याख्यानं बौद्धं प्रति, संसारस्थ-व्याख्यानं सदाशिवं प्रति, सिद्धत्व-व्याख्यानं भट्ट-चार्वाकद्वयं प्रति, ऊर्द्ध्वगति-स्वभावकथनं माण्डलिक-ग्रन्थकारं प्रति इति मतार्थो ज्ञातव्यः।"

i.e., Jîva is established to (refute) Chârvâka, its characteristic of having upayoga consisting of Jñâna and Darśan is said to (refute) the followers of Nyâya, that of Jîva being formless to (refute) Bhaṭṭa (*i.e.*, those who follow Kumârila Bhaṭṭa, the propounder of one branch of Mîmâṃsâ philosophy) and Chârvâka, that of the agency of Karma to (refute the) Sâṅkhya (view), that of having the same extent of its body is expressed to refute the three, *viz.*, the Nyâya, Mîmâṃsâ and Sâṅkhya views, that of the enjoyment of (the fruits of) Karma is said to refute the Buddhistic view, that of being in the Saṃsâra to refute Sadâśiva, that of being Siddha to refute Bhaṭṭa and Chârvâka, and that of having an upward motion to refute views of all other writers."

It should be remembered that, as the Hindu and the Buddhist philosophers omitted no opportunity to refute the views of the Jaina philosophy, so also the Jain philosophers on their part tried to refute the views of their opponents. It is a special feature of nearly every system of Indian philosophy to proceed to maintain its own views after refuting those of other systems. Examples of such refutation by Hindu philosophers may be found in Vedânta Sûtra, Chapter II, Pâdas I and II, and Sâṅkhya Sûtra, Chapter V. The refutation of the views of the Hindu systems of philosophy may, on the other hand, be found in numerous Jaina works, such as Ratnâkarâvatârikâ, Syâdavâdamanjari, Prameyakamalamârtanda, etc., etc.

In this verse also Jîva is recognised as against the Chârvâka view, which recognises no proof but Pratyakṣa which is only derived through the senses. The Nyâya system recognises the difference between a quality and the possessor of a quality (गुणगुणिभेदः) ; but in this verse, by saying that Jîva consists of the quality upayoga which is made up of Jñâna and Darśana, that theory of Nyâya is upset. Similarly, by saying that Jîva is the agent of all actions, the Sâṅkhya theory that Puruṣa is indifferent (उदासीनः), is denied. The other characteristics also deny in this manner the views of Mîmâṃsâ, Buddhistic and other systems of philosophy. These will be further explained in notes to verses 4-14. But it should be remembered that the author does not directly proceed to refute the views of the other systems of philosophy, for that would be entirely impossible in a compendium like this. What the commentator, therefore, suggests, is that by laying down this definition of Jîva, the author has incidentally denied the opposite views of other systems of philosophy.

For a brief account of the tenets of different systems of philosophy, we refer the reader to Sarvadarśansaṅgraha of Mâdhavâchârya (Ed. by Cowell) in which the account of Jaina philosophy, under the head of "Ârhat Darśan," is worthy of notice as being written by a non-Jaina author who, though not very enthusiastic about Jainism, tried his best to be impartial.

The following verse from Pañchâstikâyasamayasâra by Kundakundâchârya, is exactly similar to this verse of Dravya-Saṃgraha :—

जीवोत्ति हवदि चेदा उपयोगविसेसिदो पहू कत्ता ।
भोत्ता य देहमत्तो ण हि मुत्तो कम्मसंजुत्तो ॥

[पञ्चास्तिकायसमयसारः । २७ ।]

i.e., "Jîva is conscious, formless, characterised by upayoga, attached to Karma, the lord, the agent, the enjoyer (of the fruits of Karma), the pervader of bodies (large or small.)"

The only characteristic of Jîva mentioned in Dravya-Saṃgraha but not found in the above verse, is that of having an upward motion ; but this is mentioned in the next verse of Pañchâstikâyasamayasâra :—

"कम्ममलविप्पमुक्को उड्ढं लोगस्स अंतमधिगंता ।"

[पञ्चास्तिकायसमयसारः । २८ ।]

i.e., "That which goes upward to the end of Loka, being freed from the impurity of Karma."

तिक्काले चदुपाणा इंदिय बलमाउ आणपाणो य ।
ववहारा सो जीवो णिच्चयणयदो दु चेदणा जस्स ॥३॥*

Tikkâle chadupâṇâ iṇdiya balamâu âṇapâṇo ya
Vavahârâ so jîvo ṇichchayaṇayado du chedaṇâ jassa—(3).

Padapâtha.—ववहारा Vavahârâ, according to Vyavahâra Naya. तिक्काले Tikkâle, in three kinds of time. इंदिय Iṇdiya, Indriya (the senses). बलं Balaṃ, force. आउ Âu, Life. आणपाणो Âṇapâṇo, respiration. य Ya, also. चदुपाणा Chadupâṇâ, the four Prâṇas. दु Du, but. णिच्चयणयदो Ṇichchayaṇayado, according to Niśchaya Naya जस्स Jassa, whose. चेदणा Chedaṇâ, consciousness. सो So, he. जीवो Jîvo, Jîva.

3. According to Vyavahâra Naya, that is called Jîva, which is possessed of four Prâṇas, *viz.*, Indriya (the senses), Bala (force), Âyu (life) and Âṇa-prâṇa (respiration) in the three periods of time (*viz.*, the present, the past and the future), and according to Niśchaya Naya, that which has consciousness is called Jîva.

COMMENTARY.

Vyavahâra and Niśchaya Naya is thus distinguished in Dravyânuyogatarkaṇâ of Bhoja :

"तेनेदं भाष्यसंदिष्टं गृहीतव्यं विनिश्चयम् ।
तत्त्वार्थं निश्चयो वक्ति व्यवहारो जनोदितम् ॥"

[द्रव्यानुयोगतर्कणा । ८।२१ ।]

i. e., "Therefore, this is to be understood as described in the Bhâṣya (Viśeṣâvaśyaka-bhâṣya, a celebrated Jaina work) that Niśchaya narrates the real thing and Vyavahâra narrates things in the popular way." Vyavahâra Naya, therefore, is the ordinary or common sense point of view in which we speak every day about the things of this world. But Niśchaya Naya is the realistic point of view, which attempts an accurate description of the realities which are over-

* *Sanskrit rendering* :

त्रिकाले चतुः प्राणाः इंद्रियं बलं आयुः आणप्राणः च ।
व्यवहारात् स जीवः निश्चयनयतः तु चेतना यस्य ॥ ३ ॥

Trikâle chatuḥprâṇâḥ indriyaṃ balaṃ âyuḥ âṇaprâṇaḥ cha
Vyavahârât sa jîvaḥ niśchayanayataḥ tu chetanâ yasya—(3).

looked in our everyday parlance. For example, we ordinarily say "a jar of honey;" but to be accurate we must say "a jar of clay or some other substance containing honey." The characteristics of Jîva will be examined from both these points of view in the following verses.

Here it is said that ordinarily we say that Jîva (Living Substance) possesses the five senses, Sight, Hearing, Touch, Taste and Smell, the three forces of thought, word and action, life and respiration. Indriya (the five senses), Bala (the three forces of thought, word and action), Âyu (life) and Ânaprâṇa (respiration)—these four are called the four Prâṇas of Jîvas in the past, present and the future. The following verse from Pañchâstikâyasamayasâra is parallel to this verse of Dravya-Saṃgraha :—

"पाणेहिं चदुहिं जीवदि जीवस्सदि जेा हु जीविदेा पुव्वं ।
सेा जीवेा पाणा पुण बलमिंदियमाउ उस्सासेा ॥"

[पञ्चास्तिकायसमयसार: । ३० ।]

i. e., "That is Jîva which lives, will live or has lived formerly by four Prâṇas. The Prâṇas are Bala (force), Indriya (the senses), Âyu (Life) and Uchchhâsa (Respiration)."

Thus, from the ordinary point of view (Vyavahâra Naya), we regard Jîva to possess a period of life, during which its characteristics are respiration and the employment of the five senses and the three forces of thought, word and action. But from the realistic point of view, Jîva is distinguished by its own great quality, *viz.*, consciousness.

उवओगो दुवियप्पो दंसण णाणं च दंसणं चदुधा ।
चक्खु अचक्खू ओही दंसणमध केवलं णेयं ॥ ४ ॥*

Uvaogo duviyappo daṃsaṇa ṇâṇaṃ cha daṃsaṇaṃ chadudhâ,
Chakkhu achakkhû ohî daṃsaṇamadha kevalaṃ ṇeyaṃ—(4).

Padapâtha.—उवओगेा Uvaogo, Upayoga. दुवियप्पो Duviyappo, of two varieties. दंसणं Daṃsaṇaṃ, Darśana. च Cha, and. णाणं Ṇâṇaṃ, jñâna. दंसणं Daṃsaṇaṃ, Darśana. चदुधा Chadudhâ, of four kinds. णेयम् Ṇeyaṃ, is to be known. चक्खु-अचक्खू-ओहीदंसणं Chakkhu-achakkhu-ohî-Daṃsaṇaṃ, the Darśana like Chakṣu,

---

* *Sanskrit rendering:*

उपयेागः द्विविकल्पः दर्शनं ज्ञानं च दर्शनं चतुर्द्धा ।
चक्षुः अचक्षुः अवधिः दर्शनं अथ केवलं ज्ञेयम् ॥ ४ ॥

Upayogaḥ dvivikalpaḥ darśanaṃ jñânaṃ cha darśanaṃ chaturddhâ
Chakṣuḥ achakṣuḥ avadhiḥ darśanaṃ atha kevalaṃ jñeyaṃ—(4).

Achakṣu and Avadhi. अथ Adha, then. केवलं Kevalaṃ, Kevala. दंसणं Daṃsaṇaṃ, Darśana.

4. Upayoga is of two kinds, Darśana and Jñâna. Darśana is of four kinds. Darśana is known to be (divided into) Chakṣu, Achakṣu, Avadhi and Kevala.

COMMENTARY.

Verses parallel to these are found in Pañchâstikâyasamayasâra, as follows:—

"उवओगो खलु दुविहो णाणेण य दंसणेण संजुत्तो ।
जीवस्स सव्वकालं अणण्णभूदं वियाणीहि ॥
दंसणमवि चक्खुजुदं अचक्खुजुदमवि य ओहिणा सहियं ।
अणिधणमणंतविसयं केवलियं चावि पण्णत्तं ॥"

[पञ्चास्तिकायसमयसारः । ४०, ४२]

i.e.,—"Upayoga is of two kinds, being connected with Jñâna and Darśana: know that this Upayoga is at all times inseparable from Jîva. Darśana also is said to be with Chakṣu, Achakṣu, Avadhi and the endless and eternal Kevala."

Upayoga is the resultant of consciousness which, according to Niśchaya Naya or realistic point of view, is the sole characteristic of Jîva. Roughly, Upayoga may be said to be a sort of inclination which arises from consciousness. This inclination is either towards Darśana or towards Jñâna. The difference between Darśana and Jñâna consists in this, that in the former the details are not perceived, while in the latter the details are also known. "Before we know things in a detailed way, there is the stage where we simply see, hear, or otherwise become conscious of it in a general way, without going into its ins and outs. We simply know it as belonging to a class, we may know it as a horse, for instance, without going into any further details as to its individual characteristics. This is the first stage of knowledge; it may be called detail-less knowledge or indefinite cognition (Darśana). If this stage is not experienced, there can be no knowledge of the thing."* Cognition of the details consists in Jñâna (knowledge).

Darśana is thus understood to be "cognition in an undifferentiated way......you see a picture, for instance, but you do not go into the details of it; you just know in a general way that it is a picture."†

* 'Jainism' by Herbert Warren, p. 29.

† 'The Karma Philosophy' by V. R. Gandhi, pp. 5-6.

Jîva, according to Jaina philosophy, consists of infinite Jñâna and Darśana, but certain classes of Karma tend to obscure these. Darśana is of four kinds, Chakṣu, Achakṣu, Avadhi and Kevala; so there are also four kinds of Karma which obscure each of these varieties. When there is a cessation or mitigation (**क्षयोपशम**) of one or more of these varieties of Karma, the corresponding class or classes of Darśana is or are evolved. Thus, by the removal of these Karmas, which obscure the Darśana which is received through the eye, a Jîva can see through the eyes. This is Chakṣu Darśana (Darśana through the eye). Again, by the removal of that Karma which obscure the Darśana through any sense other than the eye, or mind, a Jîva can cognise through the four organs of sense—ear, nose, tongue or skin, and through the mind. This is called Achakṣu Darśana (Darśana not through the eye). Similarly, when Karmas obscuring Avadhi Darśana are removed, a Jîva can have Avadhi Darśana (psychic knowledge, limited by space and time and obtained directly by the soul, *e.g.*, clairvoyance). Lastly, by the removal of the Karmas which obscure Kevala Darśana, a Jîva can have Kevala (or perfect) Darśana (in which everything in the three worlds existent in the present, past and the future is at once cognised).

[Besides the four varieties of Karmas obscuring Darśana already mentioned, there are also five others mentioned by Umâsvâmi, *e.g.*, Nidrâ (sleep), Nidrânidrâ (Deep sleep), Prachalâ (Trance), Prachalâ prachalâ (Drowsiness) and Styânagriddhi (Somnambulistic state) *. These, together with the Karmas obscuring Chakṣu, Achakṣu, Avadhi and Kevala Darśana already mentioned, make up nine Darśanâvaraṇîya Karmas.]

णाणं अट्ठवियप्पं मदिसुदओही अणाणणाणाणि ।
मणपज्जय केवलमवि पच्चक्खपरोक्खभेयं च ॥ ५ ॥†

Ṇâṇaṃ aṭṭhaviyappaṃ madisudaohî aṇâṇaṇâṇâṇi

* "चक्षुरचक्षुरवधिकेवलानां निद्रा-निद्रानिद्रा-प्रचला-प्रचलाप्रचला-स्त्यानगृद्धयश्च ।"—[Tattârthâdhigama Sûtra, VIII. 7.]

† *Sanskrit rendering:*

ज्ञानं अष्टविकल्पं मतिश्रुत-अवधयः अज्ञानज्ञानानि ।
मनःपर्ययः केवलम् अपि प्रत्यक्षपरोक्षभेदं च ॥ ५ ॥

Jñânaṃ aṣṭavikalpaṃ mati-śruta-avadhayaḥ ajñânajñânâni,
Manaḥ-paryayaḥ kevalaṃ api pratyakṣa-parokṣa-bhedaṃ cha—(5).

Maṇapajjaya kevalamavi pachchakkha-parokkha-
vheyaṃ cha (5).

Padapâtha.—मदिसुदओही अणाणणाणाणि Matisuda-ohi aṇâṇaṇâṇâṇi, the Jñâna and Ajñâna of Mati, Sruta and Avadhi. अवि Avi, also. मणपज्जय Maṇapajjaya, Maṇaḥ paryaya. केवलं Kevalaṃ, kevala. णाणं Nâṇaṃ, Jñâna. अट्ठवियप्पं Aṭṭhaviyappaṃ, of eight varieties. च Cha, also. पच्चक्ख-परोक्ख-भेयं Pachchakkha-parokkha-vheyaṃ, has the varieties Pratyakṣa and Parokṣa.

5. Jñâna is of eight kinds, *viz.*, Jñâna and Ajñânâ of Mati, Śruta and Avadhi, Manaḥ-paryaya and Kevala. (It is) also divided into Pratyakṣa and Parokṣa (from another point of view).

COMMENTARY.

In the previous verse, the first stage of cognition, *viz.*, Darśana (undifferentiated knowledge) has been described. In this verse the next stage, Jñâna detailed knowledge), with its varieties, is being described.

The eight kinds of Jñana are (1) Mati Jñâna, (2) Śruta Jñâna, (3) Avadhi Jñâna, (4) Manaḥ-paryaya Jñâna, (5) Kevala Jñâna, (6) Kumati or Ajñâna of Mati, (7) Ku-śruta or Ajñâna of Śruta and (8) Vibhangâvadhi or Ajñâna of Avadhi.

Kundakundâchârya has summed up all of them in the following verse :—

"आभिणिवोधिसुदोधिमणकेवलाणि णाणाणि पंचभेयाणि ।
कुमदिसुद-विभंगाणि य तिण्णि वि णाणेहिं संजुत्ते ॥"

[पञ्चास्तिकायसमयसार: । ४१ ।]

i.e., "Âbhiṇibodhika or Mati, Śruta, Avadhi, Manaḥ-paryaya and Kevala—these are the five varieties of Jñâna. Kumati, Ku-śruta and Vibhanga—these three also are connected with Jñâna."

The three last-mentioned are nothing but false knowledge of the first three. It will, therefore, be sufficient to explain the first five varieties only of Jñâna. Umâsvâmi has also mentioned them in Sûtra 9, Chapter I of Tattvârthâdhigama Sûtra. [*e.g.*, "मतिश्रुतावधिमनःपर्ययकेवलानि ज्ञानम् ।"]. It should be remembered that these varieties of Jñâna constitute the two sorts of Pramâṇas recognised in Jaïna Philosophy [" तत् प्रमाणे ।" तत्वार्थसूत्र १ । १०]

Mati Jñâna is knowledge derived through the senses, including the knowledge which arises from the activity of the mind. Śruta Jñâna is knowledge derived through symbols or signs (*e.g.*, words which are symbols of ideas, gestures, etc.). Avadhi Jñâna is the psychic knowledge which is directly acquired by the soul without the medium of the activity of the mind or the senses. Knowledge in the hypnotic state may be cited as an example of Avadhi Jñâna. Manaḥ-paryaya Jñâna is the knowledge of the ideas and thoughts of others. Mind reading is an instance of this kind of knowledge. Kevala Jñâna is omniscience or knowledge unlimited as to space, time or object.

In our everyday life we have Mati Jñâna and Śruta Jñâna, but there are instances, though rare, of persons who, under a hypnotic trance, have knowledge of certain things (Avadhi Jñâna) and of persons who can read the thoughts of others (Manaḥ-paryaya Jñâna). Though the exact nature of the last two kinds of knowledge have not yet been understood, there is no doubt of the possibility of their existence. The mention, therefore, of these kinds of knowledge by ancient Jaina writers proves that at that time there were evidences which led them to believe in these two forms of knowledge. The occult powers attainable by Yogîs which are mentioned in Yoga Philosophy of the Hindus also support the view that in ancient India occult sciences were by no means unknown. The last-mentioned knowledge, Kevala-Jñâna or omniscience, which correspond to the knowledge of the sages called Sarvajñaṣ or Trikâladarśis in the Purâṇas of the Hindus, is, according to the Jaina tradition, only possessed by those who have reached the highest point of elevation. The Tîrthaṅkaras and Gaṇadharas are said to possess such a kind of knowledge.

Though it is not possible to understand the real nature of knowledges called Avadhi Jñâna, Manaḥ-paryaya Jñâna and Kevala Jñâna, we can describe fully the remaining two kinds of knowledge, *viz.*, Śruta Jñâna and Mati Jñâna. Śruta Jñâna is knowledge derived from words spoken by a person, from reading books, from seeing gestures or facial expressions and from all other kinds of symbols or signs. Mati Jñâna requires much detailed consideration; for it gives us an idea of that part of the Jaina psychology which treats of Perception and Memory.

In Jaina psychology four stages in Mati Jñâna are usually recognised. These are called (1) Avagraha,* (2) Îha, (3) Avâya and (4) Dhâraṇâ.

---

*"अर्थस्य।" I. 17. "व्यञ्जनस्यावग्रहः।" I. 18—Tattvârthâdhigama Sûtra.

In works on Jaina Nyâya philosophy, we find that Pramâṇa is of two kinds—Pratyakṣa (independent) and Parokṣa (dependent). Pratyakṣa is clear knowledge or cognition that this object is of such and such a character, without depending upon any other kind of knowledge. That cognition, which is not clear by itself, *i.e.*, that which depends upon some other kind of knowledge is Parokṣa.* Pratyakṣa or independent knowledge is of two kinds, Sâṅvyavahârika and Pâramârthika. Sâṅvyavahârika again is of two kinds, *viz.*, Indriya-nivandhana (caused through the senses) and Anindriya-nivandhana (not caused through the senses.)† The senses recognised in Jaina philosophy are the eye, the ear, the nose, the tongue and the skin. Mind (Manas) is called No-indriya or Anindriya‡ (Not Indriya). This Sâṅvyavahârika variety of Pratyakṣa is what we have in our every-day life. The processes of Perception and Memory are dependent upon this variety of Pratyakṣa only. We shall, therefore, deal with Sâṅvyavahârika Pratyakṣa leaving aside Pâramârthika Pratyakṣa

---

*"प्रमाणं द्विधा ।" I. 1. 9.

"प्रत्यक्षं च परोक्षं च ।" I. 1. 10.

"विशदः प्रत्यक्षं ।" I. 1. 13.

"प्रमाणान्तरानपेक्षेदन्तया प्रतिभासो वा वैशद्यम् ।" I. 1. 14.

"अविशदः परोक्षम् ।" I. 2. 1.—[Pramâṇa Mîmâṃsâ].

"तद्द्वेधा ।" II. 1. "प्रत्यक्षेतरभेदात् ।" II. 2. "विशदं प्रत्यक्षं ।" II. 3. प्रतीत्यन्तराव्यवधानेन विशेषवत्तया वा प्रतिभासनं वैशद्यम् ।" II. 4. "परोक्षमितरत् ।" III. 1.—[Parîkṣâmukha Sûtra.]

"तद् द्विभेदं प्रत्यक्षं च परोक्षं च ।" II. 1. "स्पष्टं प्रत्यक्षम ।" II. 2. "अनुमानाद्याधिक्येन विशेषप्रकाशनं स्पष्टत्वम् ।" II. 3. "अस्पष्टं परोक्षम् ।" III. 1.—[Pramâṇa-Naya-tattvâlokâlaṇkâra].

†"तद् द्विप्रकारं सांव्यवहारिकं पारमार्थिकं च ।"
तत्राद्यं द्विविधमिन्द्रियनिबन्धनमनिन्द्रियनिबन्धनं च ।"
[Pramâṇa-Naya-tattvâlokâlaṇkâra, II. 4, 5].

"इन्द्रियानिन्द्रियनिमित्तं देशतः सांव्यवहारिकम् ।"
[Parîkṣâ-mukha Sûtra, II. 5].

‡"स्पर्शरसगन्धरूपशब्दग्रहणलक्षणानि स्पर्शनरसनघ्राणचक्षुःश्रोत्राणीन्द्रियाणि ।" I. 1. 22.—[Pramâṇa Mimâṃsâ].

"मनोऽनिन्द्रियमिति नो इन्द्रियमिति च उच्यते ।"
[Pramâṇa Mîmaṃsâ Vritti].

which includes the little understood occult knowledges—Avadhi, Manaḥ-paryaya and Kevala mentioned previously.*

Saṅvyabahâra is the act of satisfying a desire to cognize. [**"समीचीनः प्रवृत्तिनिवृत्तिरूपो व्यवहारः संव्यवहारः ।"** Pramâṇa Mimâṃsâ Vritti] This is the essence of Sâṅvyavahârika Pratyakṣa which, according to Jaina philosophers, is of four kinds, *viz.*, Avagraha, Îhâ, Avâya, and Dhâraṇâ.† These four are identical with the four stages of Mati Jñâna already mentioned by us, and we shall now proceed to explain each of these four varieties.

The first stage, Avagraha, consists in the general knowledge of an object when it is brought into contact with a sense organ. First of all, there is an excitation in the sense organ by the stimulus (*viz.*, the object present in the outside world). Then there is an excitation in the consciousness. Thus, in the first stage a person is barely conscious of the existence of an object.‡

The second stage, Îhâ, consists in the desire to know the particulars of the object §, *e.g.*, a desire to know whether it is this or that. Thus, similarities and differences of this object with other objects become the subject of consciousness in this stage.

*** Pâramârthika Pratyakṣa is divided into classes, Sakala (Perfect) and Vikala (Imperfect). Kevala Jnâna comes under Sakala and Avadhi and Manaḥ-Paryaya come under Vikala Pratyakṣa.**

"तद्विकलं सकलं च ।" "तत्र विकलमवधिमनःपर्ययज्ञानरूपतया द्वेधा ।" "सकलं तु... केवलज्ञानम् ।"

[Pramâṇa-Naya-tattvâlokâlaṅkâra. II. 19, 20 and 23].

Hemachandra also mentions Kevala, Avadhi and Manaḥ-paryaya under Pratyakṣa

["तत्-सर्वथावरणविलये चेतनस्य स्वरूपाविर्भावो मुख्यं केवलम् ।"

"तत्तारतम्येऽवधिमनःपर्यायौ च ।"—Pramâṇa Mimâṃsâ. I. 1. 15 and 18].

† एतद्द्वितयमवग्रहेहावायधारणाभेदादेकशश्चतुर्विकल्पम् ।"

[Pramâṇa-Naya-tattvâlokâlaṇkâra. II. 6.]

"इन्द्रियमनोनिमित्तोऽवग्रहेहावायधारणात्मा सांव्यवहारिकम् ।"

[Pramâṇa Mîmâṃsâ I. 1. 21.]

For a detailed account of this part of Jaina philosophy, the reader may refer to my translation of Pramâṇa Mimâṃsâ, published in the *Jaina Gazette*, 1915.

‡ " विषयविषयिसंनिपातानन्तर—समुद्भूत—सत्तामात्र—गोचरदर्शनाज्जातमाद्यमवान्तर—सामान्याकार—विशिष्टवस्तुग्रहणमवग्रहः ।"

[Pramâṇa-Naya-tattvâlokâlaṅkâra II. 7.]

"अक्षार्थयोगे दर्शनानन्तर—मर्थग्रहणमवग्रहः ।"

[Pramâṇa Mimâṃsâ. I. 1. 27]

§ "अवगृहीतार्थविशेषाकाङ्क्षणमीहा ।"

[PramâṇaNayatattvâlokâlaṅkâra. II. 8.]

"अवगृहीतविशेषकाङ्क्षणमीहा ।"—[Pramâṇa-Mîmâṃsa I. 1. 28].

In the first stage (Avagraha), we have for example simply the knowledge of a man, but in the second stage (Îhâ) we desire to know the particulars of this man, *e.g.*, whether he is a resident of Karṇâta or Lâta country, etc.*

In the third stage, Avâya, there is a definite finding of the particulars which we desired to know in the second stage. The second stage is merely an attempt to know the particulars, while the third stage consists of the ascertainment of these particulars.†

The fourth stage, Dhâraṇâ, consists of the lasting impression which results after the object, with its particulars, is definitely ascertained.‡ It is this impression (**संस्कार**) which enables us to remember the object afterwards. Memory, therefore, is the result of these four successive stages of Mati Jnâna.

Now we shall turn to that part of verse 5 of Dravya-Saṃgraha which, after laying down the eight varieties of Jnâna, says that it may also be divided into two classes from another point of view. These two classes are respectively known as Pratyakṣa and Parokṣa.

We have already given a detailed account of Pratyakṣa, and it now remains to narrate briefly Parokṣa knowledge.

Parokṣa knowledge is said to be of five kinds : (1) Smaraṇa, (2) Pratyabhijñâna, (3) Tarka, (4) Anumâna and (5) Âgama. Smaraṇa is simply the remembrance of an object. Pratyabhijñâna is the recognition of an object by noticing similarities and differences. The difference between Smaraṇa and Pratyabhijñâna may be understood from the following examples. We see a certain man. We then remember that we had seen him previously. This is Smaraṇa. We go to a forest and see a strange creature. Then we remember that we have heard or read about such a creature, and we identify it. This is Pratyabhijñâna. This corresponds to Upamâna Pramâṇa recognised in the Hindu philosophies. Tarka or Ûha consists of the knowledge of an universal concomitance of any two things (*e.g.*,

---

* "**अवग्रहेण विषयीकृतो योऽर्थोऽवान्तर—मनुष्यत्वादिजातिविशेषलक्षणस्तस्य विशेषः कर्णाटलाटादिभेदस्तस्याकाङ्क्षणं भवितव्यताप्रत्ययरूपतया ग्रहणाभिमुख्यमीहेत्यभिधीयते ।**"—[Ratnâkarâvatârika. II. 8].

† "**ईहितविशेषनिर्णयोऽवायः ।**"

[Pramâṇa-Naya-tattvâlokâlaṅkâra. II. 9 and Pramâṇa Mîmâṃsâ I. 1. 30].

‡ "**स एव दृढतमावस्थापन्नो धारणा ।**"

[Pramâṇa-naya-tatvâlokâlaṅkâra. II. 9;

"**स्मृति-हेतुर्धारणा ।**"-[Pramâṇa Mîmâṃsâ. I. 1. 29].

wherever there is smoke, there is fire.) This is the same as Vyâpti Jñâna mentioned in the Nyâya philosophy of the Hindus. Anumâna is inference and is either Svârtha (for one's own self) or Parârtha (for others.) There is a detailed treatment of Anumâna in Jaina Nyâya philosophy, similar to that found in the Nyâya philosophy of the Hindus. Âgama is knowledge derived through the words of one who is trustworthy. This also is recognised in different systems of Hindu philosophy, such as Vedânta, Nyâya, Sâṅkhya, Mîmâṃsâ, etc.*

We finish this brief survey of different kinds of knowledge by saying that, as we have mentioned in our notes to verse 4 Dravya-Saṃgraha that there are certain Karmas called Darśanâvaraṇîya Karmas which obscure the different varieties of Darśana, so there are also Karmas which obscure the different varieties of Jñâna. These are known as Jñânâvaranîya Karmas. Umâsvâmi in his Tattvârthâdhigama Sûtra has mentioned that Jñânavaranîya Karmas are of five sorts which obscure Mati, Śruta, Avadhi, Manaḥparyaya and Kevala

---

*"प्रत्यक्षादिनिमित्तं स्मृतिप्रत्यभिज्ञानतर्कानुमानागमभेदम् ।" III. 2.

"संस्कारोद्बोधनिबन्धना तदित्याकारा स्मृतिः ।" III. 3.

दर्शनस्मरणकारणकं सङ्कलनं प्रत्यभिज्ञानम् ।" III. 5.

उपलम्भानुपलम्भनिमित्तं व्याप्तिज्ञानमूहः ।" III. 11.

साधनात् साध्यविज्ञानमनुमानम् ।" III. 14.

"आप्तवचनादिनिबन्धनमर्थज्ञानमागमः ।" III 99.

[Parîkṣâmukha Sûtra.]

"स्मरणप्रत्यभिज्ञानतर्कानुमानागमभेदतस्तत् पञ्चप्रकारम् ।" III. 2.

"तत्र संस्कारप्रबोधसंभूतमनुभूतार्थविषयं तदित्याकारं वेदनं स्मरणम् ।" III. 3.

"अनुभवस्मृतिहेतुकं तिर्यगूर्ध्वतासामान्यादिगोचरं संकलनात्मकं ज्ञानं प्रत्यभिज्ञानम् ।" III. 5.

"उपलम्भानुपलम्भसम्भवं त्रिकालीकलितसाध्यसाधनसंबन्धाद्यालम्बनं इदमस्मिन् सत्येव भवतीत्याद्याकारं संवेदनमूहापरनामा तर्कः ।" III. 7.

"आप्तवचनादाविर्भूतमर्थसंवेदनमागमः" IV. 1.—[Prâmâṇa-Naya-Tattvâlokâlaṅkâra.]

"स्मृतिप्रत्यभिज्ञानोहानुमानागमास्तद्विधयः ।" I. 2. 2.

"वासनोद्बोधहेतुका तदित्याकारा स्मृतिः ।" I. 2. 3.

"दर्शनस्मरणसम्भवं तदेवेदं तत्-सदृशं तद्विलक्षणं तत्प्रतियोगीत्यादिसंकलनं प्रत्यभिज्ञानम् ।" I. 2. 4.

"उपलम्भानुपलम्भनिमित्तं व्याप्तिज्ञानमूहः ।" I. 2. 5.

"साधनात् साध्यविज्ञानमनुमानम् ।" I. 2. 7.—[Pramâṇa Mîmâṃsâ.

knowledge respectively. ["मतिश्रुतावधिमनःपर्ययकेवलानाम् ।" तत्त्वार्थाधिगम-सूत्र, ८।६।]

Now, a doubt is started by the commentator of Dravya-Saṃgraha. He says that in Tark-Śâstra (Nyâya philosophy) of the Jainas we find that Mati Jñâna, with its four varieties, Avagraha, Îhâ, Avâya and Dhâraṇâ, is included under Sâṅvyavahârika Pratyakṣa. But Umâsvâmi in his Tattvârtha Sûtra says plainly that Mati and Śruta Jñânas are not Pratyakṣas, but Parokṣas.* We have the following aphorisms in Tattvârtha Sûtra :—

"मतिश्रुतावधिमनःपर्ययकेवलानि ज्ञानम् ।" I. 9.

"आद्ये परोक्षम् ।" I. 11.

"प्रत्यक्षमन्यत् ।" I. 12.

i.e., "Knowledge is of five kinds : Mati, Śruta, Avadhi, Manaḥparyaya and Kevala. The first two are called Parokṣa and the rest are known as Pratyakṣa."

Now, this is apparently in contradiction with the works on Jaina Nyâya philosophy some of which we have already quoted in our notes. How can this apparent contradiction be explained away?

The commentator says that Umâsvâmi's aphorism is to be regarded as a general ordinance (उत्सर्गः) while the sayings of the writers on Jaina Nyâya philosophy should be taken as a special rule or exception.† (अपवादः)

In special or exceptional cases the general rule should not be followed. In the present instance also, though the general rule as laid down in Tattvârtha Sûtra says that Mati and Śruta Jñânas are Parokṣa knowledge, there are particular exceptional cases, ‡ when

---

* "अत्राह शिष्यः—आद्ये परोक्षमिति तत्त्वार्थसूत्रे मतिश्रुतद्वयं परोक्षं भणितं तिष्ठति, कथं प्रत्यक्षं भवति ?"

† "परिहारमाह । तदुत्सर्गव्याख्यानम्, इदं पुनरपवादव्याख्यानम् । यदि तदुत्सर्गव्याख्यानं न भवति तर्हि मतिज्ञानं कथं तत्त्वार्थे परोक्षं भणितं तिष्ठति ? तर्कशास्त्रे सांव्यवहारिकं प्रत्यक्षं कथं जातं ? यथा अपवादव्याख्यानेन मतिज्ञानं परोक्षमपि प्रत्यक्षज्ञानं तथा स्वात्माभिमुखं भावश्रुतज्ञानमपि परोक्षं सत् प्रत्यक्षं भण्यते ।"

‡ The commentator lays down in the following passage certain cases where Śruta Jñâna is wholly Parokṣa, where it is partially Parokṣa and where it is not at all Parokṣa but Pratyakṣa :—"शब्दात्मकं श्रुतज्ञानं परोक्षमेव तावत् । स्वर्गापवर्गादिबहिर्विषयपरिच्छित्ति-परिज्ञानं विकल्परूपं तदपि परोक्षम् । यत् पुनरभ्यन्तरे सुखदुःखविकल्प-रूपोऽहमनन्तज्ञानादिरूपो-

3

these should be called Pratyakṣa. The commentator further says that we all know that the knowledge of our own happiness and misery is Pratyakṣa, but if we say that, according to Tattvârtha Sûtra, Mati and Śruta Jñânas are always Parokṣa, the knowledge of our happiness or misery should also become Parokṣa, which is absurd. *

The following table of Jñâna can, therefore, be re-arranged from different points of view, in the manner shown in Tables I and II in the accompanying Chart No. I.

Jñâna.

- **Mati.**
  - **Jñâna.**
  - **Ajñâna (Kumati).**
- **Śruta.**
  - **Jñâna.**
  - **Ajñâna (Kuśruta).**
- **Avadhi.**
  - **Jñâna.**
  - **Ajñâna (Vibhangâvadhi.)**
- **Manaḥ-paryaya.**
- **Kevala.**

ऽहमिति वा तत् ईषत्-परोक्षम् । यच्च निश्चयभावश्रुतज्ञानं तच्च शुद्धात्माभिमुखसुखसंवित्तिस्वरूपं स्वसंवित्त्याकारेण सविकल्पमपीन्द्रियमनोजनितरागादिविकल्पजालरहितत्वेन निर्विकल्पम्, अभेदनयेन तदेवात्मशब्दवाच्यं वीतरागसम्यक्चारित्राविनाभूतं केवलज्ञानापेक्षया परोक्षमपि संसारिणां क्षायिकज्ञानाभावात् क्षायोपशमिकमपि प्रत्यक्षमभिधीयते ।"

* "यदि पुनरेकान्तेन परोक्षं भवति तर्हि सुखदुःखादि-संवेदनमपि परोक्षं प्राप्नोति, न च तथा ।"

CHART I.

TABLE I.

[*This table is according to Works on Jaina Nyâya Philosophy.*]

PRAMÂṆA.

- **Pratyakṣa.**
  - **Sâṅvyavahârika.**
    - **Indriya-nivandhana.**
    - **Anindriya-nivandhana.**
      - **Avagraha.**
      - **Îhâ.**
      - **Avâya.**
      - **Dhâraṇâ.**
  - **Pâramârthika.**
    - **Sakala.**
      - **Kevala.**
    - **Vikala.**
      - **Avadhi.**
      - **Manaḥparyaya.**
- **Parokṣa.**
  - **Smaraṇa.**
  - **Pratyabhijñâna.**
  - **Tarka.**
  - **Anumâna.**
    - **Svârtha.**
    - **Parârtha.**
  - **Âgama.**

TABLE II.

[*This table is according to Tattvârthâdhigama Sûtra of Umâsvâmi, but is not exhaustive. Only as much of the details as is treated in Dravya-Saṃgraha has been included in it.*]

JNÂNA.

- **Pratyakṣa.**
  - **Avadhi.**
  - **Manaḥparyaya.**
  - **Kevala.**
    - **Jñâna.**
    - **Ajñâna (Vibhangâvadhi.)**
    - **Jñâna.**
- **Parokṣa.**
  - **Mati.**
    - **Ajñana (Kumati.)**
  - **Śruta.**
    - **Jñâna.**
    - **Ajñâna (Kuśruta.)**

अट्ठचदुणाणदंसण सामण्णं जीवलक्खणं भणियं ।
ववहारा सुद्धणया सुद्धं पुण दंसणं णाणं ॥ ६ ॥*

Aṭṭhachaduṇâṇadaṃsaṇa sâmaṇṇaṃ jîvalakkhaṇaṃ bhaṇiyaṃ.

Vavahârâ suddhaṇayâ suddhaṃ puṇa daṃsaṇaṃ ṇâṇaṃ (6).

Padapâtha.—सामण्णं Sâmaṇṇaṃ, in a general sense. जीवलक्खणं Jîvalakkhaṇaṃ, the characteristic of Jîva. ववहारा Vavahârâ, according to Vyavahâra Naya. अट्ठचदुणाणदंसण Aṭṭhachaduṇâṇadaṃsaṇa, the eight Jñânas and four Darśanas. भणियं Bhaṇiyaṃ, is narrated. पुण Puṇa, again. सुद्धणया Suddhaṇayâ, according to Śuddha Naya. सुद्धं Suddhaṃ, Śuddha (Pure). दंसणं Daṃsaṇaṃ, Darśan (perception). णाणं Ṇâṇaṃ, Jñâna (knowledge).

6. According to Vyavahâra Naya, the general characteristics of Jîva are said to be eight kinds of Jñâna and four kinds of Darśana. But according to Śuddha Naya, (the characteristics of Jîva) are pure Jñâna and Darśana.

COMMENTARY.

The commentator Brahmadeva says that Jîva is said in a general sense to have the characteristics of eight kinds of Jñâna and four kinds of Darśana. By the word "Sâmânya" or "in a general sense" in the original verse we should understand "when we do not desire to distinguish between Saṃsâri (leading a mundane existence) or Mukta (liberated) Jîvas or when we do not distinguish between pure and impure Jñâna and Darśana."† In this verse the author says that really Jîva possesses the characteristics of pure Jñâna and Darśana, but from the ordinary or common sense point of view,

* *Sanskrit rendering:*

अष्टचतुर्ज्ञानदर्शने सामान्यं जीवलक्षणं भणितम् ।
व्यवहारात् शुद्धनयात् शुद्धं पुनः दर्शनं ज्ञानं ॥ ६ ॥

Aṣṭachaturjñânadarśane sâmânyaṃ jîvalakṣaṇaṃ bhaṇitaṃ.
Vyavahârât śuddhanayât śuddhaṃ punaḥ darśanaṃ jñânaṃ.—(6).

† "सामान्यमिति कोऽर्थः ? संसारिजीव—मुक्तजीवविवक्षा नास्ति, अथवा शुद्धाशुद्ध-ज्ञानदर्शनविवक्षा नास्ति ।" Commentary on Dravya—Saṃgraha, Verse 6. By Brahmadeva.

we recognise that Jîva has eight kinds of Jñâna and four kinds of Darśana. Among the eight kinds of Jñâna, varieties of impure or false knowledge are also included, but these can only be said in a general sense to be the characteristics of Jîva, for in Mukta or liberated Jîva, these are not possible. So Jîva in its pure state has only the characteristics of pure Jñâna and Darśana.

The commentator says that verses 4-6 of Dravya Saṃgraha by explaining Upayoga refute the doctrine of Nyâya Philosophy, *viz.*, that a thing and its qualities are permanently distinct.* It should be remembered that in Nyâya Philosophy the identity of a quality and the possessor of that quality is never recognised. Here it is said that Jñâna and Darśana are not only the qualities of Jîva, but are identical with it. Now the question may arise how can this be possible? Can we not conceive of qualities as separated from the possessor of the same? The answer is that Jainism examines everything from different standpoints and though from the realistic point of view Jîva and its qualities are identical, we say from the ordinary or common-sense point of view that these are distinct. That is to say, in Jainism there is no dogmatic assertion as in Nyâya Philosophy that there can be no identity between a quality and the possessor of that qualities. On the contrary, the identity of Jîva and its qualities is recognised. Of course from the ordinary point of view we may recognise qualities as distinct from the possessor of them. That is to say, we can conceive the qualities as distinguishable, but not distinct from their possessor, that is, this separate existence is not real. In Pañchâstikâya-samayasâra also we find the following verse which expresses a similar view:—

" दंसणणाणाणि तहा जीवणिबद्धाणि णण्णभूदाणि ।
ववदेसदो पुधत्तं कुव्वंति हि णो सभावादो ॥"

[Verse No. 52.]

"Darśana and Jñâna, in a similar manner, are identical with Jîva and not separable from it. Only in common parlance we separate (Darśana and Jñâna from Jîva), but in reality there is no such separation."

---

* "एवं नैयायिकं प्रति गुणगुणिभेदैकान्तनिराकरणार्थमुपयोगव्याख्यानेन गाथात्रयं गतम् ।"

Commentary on Dravya-Saṃgraha, Verse 6. By Brahmadeva.

वराण रस पंच गंधा दो फासा अट्ठ णिच्चया जीवे ।
णो संति अमुत्ति तदो ववहारा मुत्ति बंधादो ॥७॥*

Vaṇṇa rasa pañcha gandhâ do phâsâ aṭṭha ṇichchayâ jîve.

Ṇo santi amutti tado vavahârâ mutti bandhâdo—(7).

Padapâṭha.—णिच्चया Ṇichchayâ, according to Niśchaya Naya. जीवे Jîve, in Jîva. वण्ण Vaṇṇa, colour. रस Rasa, taste. पंच Pañcha, five. दो Do, two. गंधा Gandhâ, smells. अट्ठ Aṭṭha, eight. फासा Phâsâ, touch. णो Ṇo, not. संति Santi, are. तदो Tado, therefore. अमुत्ति Amutti, without form. ववहारा Vavahârâ, according to Vyavahâra Naya. बंधादो Bandhâdo, from Bandha (bondage). मुत्ति Mutti, possessed of form.

7. According to Niśchaya Naya, Jîva is without form, because the five kinds of colour and taste, two kinds of smell, and eight kinds of touch are not present in it. But according to Vyavahâra Naya [Jîva] has form through the bondage [of Karma.]

COMMENTARY.

Jîva is naturally invisible, but "when the soul is attacked by the passions...it takes on the Pudgala (material) particles fit for the bondage of the karmas, just as a heated iron-ball takes up water-particles in which it is immersed. This is the bondage of the Karmas." † Thus "the naturally invisible soul is compounded in a very subtle way with visible, tangible matter, and is in a sense thereby rendered visible, as lemon-juice is rendered sweet by the addition of sugar and water. In its pure state the soul [Jîva] is invisible, just as in itself the lemon-juice is sour." ‡

We should therefore remember that, according to the Jaina belief, Jîva, in its natural or real state, is invisible. But it combines with

* Sanskrit rendering :

वर्णाः रसाः पञ्च गन्धौ द्वौ स्पर्शाः अष्टौ निश्चयात् जीवे ।
नो सन्ति अमूर्त्तिः ततः व्यवहारात् मूर्त्तिः बन्धतः ॥

Varṇâḥ rasâḥ pañcha gandhau dvau sparśâḥ aṣṭau niśchayât jîve,
No santi amûrttiḥ tataḥ vyavahârât mûrttiḥ bandhataḥ.

† A. B. Latthe—"An Introduction to Jainism," pages 9-10.

‡ Herbert Warren—"Jainism," pages 10-11.

Pudgala or matter. This combination is the bondage (Bandha) which produces karmas. When Jîva thus combines itself with Pudgala (matter), it leaves its invisible state and becomes visible to us. It is Pudgala (matter) which has form and when Pudgala combines itself with Jîva, the taste, colour, smell and touch of the former which are the requisites of its form, are attributed to the really formless Jîva, and we say that Jîva has form. Every form of mundane life which we see is a Jîva in its impure and visible state in combination with Pudgala. Therefore, according to Vyavahâra Naya, that is to say, from the ordinary or common sense point of view, we may say that Jîvas have form, but we must remember that according to Niśchaya Naya or the realistic point of view, Jîvas are without form.

Brahmadeva in his commentary quotes a verse to support this view:

"बंधं पडि एयत्तं लक्खणदो हवदि तस्स भिण्णत्तं ।
तम्हा अमुत्तिभावो णेगंतो होदि जीवस्स ॥"

i.e. "In bondage [Jîva] is one [with Pudgala], but really according to definition, it is separate [from Pudgala]. Hence formlessness does not always belong to Jîva."

Pudgala is said to possess touch, taste, smell and colour.* Though these qualities are really inseparable from Pudgala, from the ordinary point of view we speak of them as separate from Pudgala.† Colours are of five kinds, *viz.*, Blue (Nîla), Yellow (Pîta), White (Śukla), Black (Kṛiṣna), and Red (Lohita).‡ The varieties of taste are Bitter (Tikta), Sour (Katu), Acid (Amla), Sweet (Madhura) and Astringent (Kaṣâya).§ Smells are of two kinds, fragrance (Surabhi) and its opposite (Asurabhi).|| The eight kinds of touch are Soft (Mṛidu),

---

* "स्पर्शरसगंधवर्णवन्तः पुद्गलाः ।" Tattvârthâdhigama Sûtra V. 23.

† "वण्णरसगंधफासा परमाणुपरूविदा विसेसा हि ।
दव्वादो य अणण्णा अण्णत्तपगासगा होंति ॥"
[पञ्चास्तिकायसमयसारः ॥ ५२ ॥

‡ "वर्णाः पंचधा नीलपीतशुक्लकृष्णलोहितभेदात् ।"
[Tattvârtharâjavârttika No. 10 on Sûtra V. 23.]

§ "तिक्तकटुकाम्लमधुरकषाया रसप्रकाराः ।"
[Tattvârtharâjavârttika No. 8 on Sûtra V. 23.]

|| "गंधः सुरभिरसुरभिश्च ।" [Tattvârtharâjavârttika No. 9 on Sûtra V. 23.]

Hard (Kaṭhina), Heavy (Guru), Light (Laghu), Cold (Śîta), Hot (Uṣṇa), Smooth (Snigdha) and Rough (Rûkṣa).*

The commentator says that the author in this verse establishes the formlessness of Jîva which is contrary to the views held by (Kumarila) Bhatta (and his followers) and Chârvâka. ["इति भट्ट-चार्वाकमतं प्रत्यमूर्त्तजीवस्थापनमुख्यत्वेन सूत्रं गतम्"] Chârvâka recognises nothing but what is capable of being perceived by the senses, hence a formless Jîva is contrary to his doctrine.

पुग्गलकम्मादीणं कत्ता ववहारदो दु णिच्चयदो ।
चेदणकम्माणादा सुद्धणया सुद्धभावाणं ॥ ८ ॥ †

Puggalakammâdîṇaṃ kattâ vavahârado du ṇichchayado.
Chedaṇakammâṇâdâ suddhaṇayâ suddhabhâvâṇaṃ.—(8).

Padapâtha.—ववहारदो Vavahârado, according to Vyavahâra Naya. आदा Âdâ, Jîva. पुग्गलकम्मादीणं Puggalakammâdîṇaṃ, of the Pudgala Karmas. कत्ता Kattâ, doer. दु Du, but. णिच्चयदो Ṇichchayado, according to Niśchaya Naya. चेदणकम्माण Chedaṇakammâṇa, of the thought karmas. सुद्धणया Suddhaṇayâ, according to Śuddha Naya. सुद्धभावाणं Suddhabhâvâṇaṃ, of the Śuddha Bhâvas.

8. According to Vyavahâra Naya, Jîva is the doer of the Pudgala Karmas. According to Niśchaya Naya, [Jîva is the doer of] Thought Karmas. According to Śuddha Naya, [Jîva is the doer] of Śuddha Bhâvas.

COMMENTARY.

In this verse the Jaina doctrine of causation as to the origin of the world is briefly treated. Causes are generally accepted to be of two kinds. Upâdâna (Substantial Cause) and Nimitta (Determining Cause). Take the case of an earthen pot. The Upâdâna or the

* "मृदुकठिनगुरुलघुशीतोष्णस्निग्धरूक्षस्पर्शभेदाः ।"
[Tattvâratharâjavârttika No. 7 on Sûtra 23.]

† Sanskrit rendering:—

पुद्गलकर्म्मादीनां कर्त्ता व्यवहारतः तु निश्चयतः ।
चेतनकर्म्मणां आत्मा शुद्धनयात् शुद्धभावानाम् ॥८॥

Pudgalakarmmâdînâṃ karttâ vyavahârataḥ tu niśchayataḥ
Chetanakarmmaṇâṃ âtmâ śuddhanayât śuddha-bhâvânâṃ.—(8).

Substantial Cause of the earthen pot is the earth, and its Nimitta or Determining Cause is the potter and his implements. First of all, the potter forms an idea of the shape, size, etc., of the pot which he is going to make. This existence of the pot in the idea may be called the resultant in consciousness of the potter. Then follows the existence of the pot which we can perceive by our senses. According to Jaina Metaphysics, Jîvas are only possessed of infinite knowledge, etc., and are not agents. But causation is attributed to Jîvas from different points of view. First, Jîvas are said to be agents of their own resultants, *viz.*, infinite knowledge, bliss, etc. This is according to Śuddha (Pure) Naya. Again, according to Niśchaya Naya, Jîvas are said to be causes of the thought karmas which precede the Pudgala-karmas preceptible by us. According to Vyavahâra Naya, Jîvas are also recognised as agents of even these Pudgala-karmas.

Karmas are generally understood to be of two sorts—Dravya-karmas and Bhâva-karmas. To return to our example of the making of a pot, the existence of a pot in the mind of a potter may be said to be a Bhâva-karma, while the material existence of the pot perceptible by our senses is known to be a Dravya-karma. Now, the potter is directly the cause of the Bhâva-karma, and that Bhâva-karma again is the cause of the Dravya-karma. It should, therefore, be remembered that, according to Niśchaya Naya, the potter is the agent of the Bhâva-karma (the pot existing in idea), and according to Vyavahâra Naya, that of the Dravya-karma (the pot perceptible by us).

Similarly, in the case of Jîvas, they are really possessed of the characteristics, *viz.*, infinite knowledge, bliss, etc. Jîvas, therefore may be said to be the agents of these characteristics according to Śuddha Naya. Next, we may say that the Jîvas are agents of those mental attitudes and conditions which favour the influx of particles of matter. Attachment, aversion, etc., may be mentioned as examples of such states of Jîvas. These are the thought karmas. According to Niśchaya Naya, Jîvas are said to be the agents of these classes of karmas. When the Jîvas cause such thought karmas to be produced, these thought karmas, on the other hand, lead to the generation of the material karmas or Dravya-karmas. The Jîvas are not, therefore, the direct causes of Dravya-karmas. It is according to Vyavahâra Naya only that we can speak of Jîvas as agents of Dravyakarmas. The very essence of Dravya-karmas consists of particles of matter, and these are in no way akin to consciousness—the characteristic

4

of Jîvas. The Upâdâna or substantial cause of a Dravya-karma is therefore Pudgala or matter, and their Nimitta or determining cause is the Bhâva-karma, *viz.*, that condition of the Âtmâ which render it capable of assimilating the particular Dravya-karma. Thus a Jîva is neither the Upâdâna nor the Nimitta cause of Dravyakarmas, according to Niśchaya Naya. It is only from the Vyavahâra point of view that we say that the Jîvas are causes of Dravyakarmas. But, in reality, (according to Niśchaya Naya), Jîva is only the agent of its own attitudes (Bhâvas). In Pañchâstikaya-samaya-sâra, we have : "Âtmâ is the agent of its own Bhâvas, as it causes its own resultants. But it is not the agent of Pudgala-karmas. This should be understood to be the precept of the Jina."*

The universe is therefore made up of Jîvas and Ajîvas. Pudgala or matter is the substantial cause of every material thing, while different Bhâva or thought karmas are the determining cause of these. Jîvas cause these thought karmas to be produced. Thus two sorts of substances, material and spiritual, may be regarded to be the cause of all kinds of manifestations. There are many units of this spiritual substance possessed of qualities which are known as Jîvas, and there are also many units of material substance (Pudgala), which again have their own characteristic qualities. These two kinds of substances act and re-act upon each other, and a constant state of activity is going on in this universe.

The Jaina doctrine of the causation of the world should therefore be remembered as quite distinct from the same of Hindu philosophies, like Vedanta, which asserts that the whole of the universe is one homogeneous spiritual Brahma, or, like Chârvâka, which avers that the universe is made up of matter only.

The commentator, Brahmadeva says that this verse refutes the doctrine of the Sâṅkhya philosophy that Puruṣa (corresponding to Jîva of the Jainas) is always Udâsîna (lit. indifferent, *i.e.*, without activity), for here it is recognised that Jîva is an agent. †

---

* "कुव्वं सगं सहावं अत्ता कत्ता सगस्स भावस्स ।
ण हि पोग्गलकम्माणं इदि जिणवयणं मुणेयव्वं ॥"

[Verse 61.

† "एवं सांख्यमतं प्रत्येकान्ताकर्तृत्वनिराकरण-मुख्यत्वेन गाथा गता"
[Brahmadeva's Commentary on verse 8, Dravya-saṃgraha].

ववहारा सुहदुक्खं पुग्गलकम्मफलं पभुंजेदि ।
आदा णिच्चयणयदो चेदणभावं खु आदस्स ॥९॥*

Vavahârâ suhadukkhaṃ puggalakammaphalaṃ pabhuñjedi.
Âdâ ṇichchayaṇayado chedaṇabhâvaṃ khu âdassa.—(9).

Padapâtha.—आदा *Âdâ, Jîva.* ववहारा *Vavahârâ,* according to Vyavahâra Naya. सुहदुक्खं *Suhadukkhaṃ,* happiness and misery. पुग्गलकम्मफलं *Puggalakammaphalaṃ,* the fruits of Pudgala karma. पभुंजेदि *Pabhuñjedi,* enjoys. णिच्चयणयदो *Ṇichchayaṇayado,* according to Niśchaya Naya. आदस्स *Âdassa,* of Jîva. चेदणभावं *Chedaṇabhâvaṃ,* conscious Bhâva. खु *Khu,* only.

9. According to Vyavahâra Naya, Jîva enjoys happiness and misery, the fruits of Pudgala karmas. According to Niśchaya Naya, Jîva has conscious Bhâvas only.

COMMENTARY.

It has already been laid down that Âtmâ (or soul) is entirely distinct in its characteristics from Pudgala (or matter). The essence of Jîva or Âtma is consciousness which is altogether absent from Pudgala or matter. Hence, as in the previous verse it has been laid down that a spiritual substance (Jîva) cannot be the cause of Pudgala-karmas (*i.e.*, material karmas), so in this verse it is shown that Jîvas from their very nature are unaffected by the fruits of Pudgala-karmas. Really speaking, Jîvas only enjoy eternal bliss which is their essential characteristic. Therefore, according to Niśchaya Naya, a Jîva should only be regarded as an enjoyer of bliss resulting from its characteristic of consciousness. But through the generation of attachment, aversion, etc., Jîvas attain such a condition that they become ready for the assimilation of matter. It is only in such states of Jîvas that there is an influx of matter in them. When there is such an influx of matter, the Jîvas have to enjoy sorrow and delight, happiness and misery, as these are the fruits of Pudgala-karmas.

---

* Sanskrit rendering :—

व्यवहारात् सुखदुःखं पुद्गलकर्मफलं प्रभुङ्क्ते ।
आत्मा निश्चयनयतः चेतनभावं खलु आत्मनः ॥९॥

Vyavahârât sukhaduḥkhaṃ pudgalakarmaphalaṃ prabhuṅkte.
Âtmâ niśchayanayataḥ chetanabhâvaṃ khalu âtmanaḥ.—(9).

Thus, really, a Jîva, through its characteristic consciousness, is incapable of being affected by happiness or misery—the fruits of material karmas. It is only when matter assimilates itself with a Jîva that we see the fruits of material karmas also in that Jîva and say that this Jîva is enjoying happiness or misery the fruits of material karmas. But it should be remembered that this enjoyment of the fruits of karma by a Jîva is only apparent, but not real. Really speaking, Jîvas enjoy bliss only, which is the resultant of its characteristic consciousness.

The commentator says that this verse refutes the doctrine of the Buddhistic philosophy that an agent does never enjoy the the fruits of karma.*

अणुगुरुदेहपमाणो उवसंहारप्पसप्पदो चेदा ।
असमुहदो ववहारा णिच्चयणयदो असंखदेसो वा ॥१०॥†

Aṇugurudehapamâṇo uvasaṃhârappasappado chedâ.
Asamuhado vavahârâ ṇichchayaṇayado asaṅkhadeso vâ.—(10.)

Padapâtha.—ववहारा Vavahârâ, according to Vyavahâra Naya. चेदा Cheda, the conscious Jîva. उवसंहारप्पसप्पदो Uvasaṃhârappasappado, by contraction and expansion. असमुहदो Asamuhado, without Samudghâta. अणुगुरुदेहपमाणो Aṇugurudehapamâṇo, equal in extent to a small or a large body. वा Va, but. णिच्चयणयदो Ṇichchayaṇayado, according to Niśchaya Naya. असंखदेसो Asaṅkhadeso, existent in innumerable Pradeśas.

10. According to Vyavahâra Naya, the conscious Jîva, being without Samudghâta, becomes equal in extent to a small or a large body, by contraction and expansion; but, according to Niśchaya Naya, [it] is existent in innumerable Pradeśas.

---

* "एवं कर्त्ता कर्मफलं न भुङ्क्ते इति बौद्धमतनिषेधार्थं भोक्तृत्वव्याख्यानरूपेण सूत्रं गतम् ।"
[Brahmadeva's Commentary on verse 9, Dravya-saṃgraha.]

† Sanskrit rendering:—
अणुगुरुदेहप्रमाणः उपसंहारप्रसर्पाभ्यां चिदात्मा ।
असमुद्घातात् व्यवहारात् निश्चयनयतः असंख्यदेशः वा ॥१०॥
Aṇugurudehapramâṇaḥ upasaṃhâraprasarpâbhyâm chidâtmâ.
Asamudghâtât vyavahârât niśchayanayataḥ asaṅkhyadeśaḥ va.—(10.)

COMMENTARY.

That portion of Âkâśa, which is obstructed by one indivisible atom, is known as a Pradeśa. [See verse 27 of Dravya-saṃgraha.] That portion of Âkâśa in which Jîva, Pudgala, Dharma, Adharma and Kâla exist, is known as Lokâkâśa, and the Âkâśa beyond it is called Alokâkâśa.* Really speaking, Jîvas fill up innumerable Pradeśas in Lokâkâśa. But, from the ordinary point of view, we speak that a Jîva becomes equal in extent to a small or a large body, by contraction and expansion, when it is without Samudghâta.

Samudghâta has been thus defined : "Samudghâta is the exit of Jîva from the body to another form, without leaving the original body altogether."† Seven kinds of Samudghâta are recognised in Jaina philosophy, *viz.*, Vedanâ, Kaṣâya, Vikriyâ, Maranântika, Teja, Âhâra and Kevali.‡ When the Âtmâ goes out of its restraining body particles through excessive pain, without leaving the original body, we have an illustration of Vedanâ-samudghâta. When, at the rise of excessive anger, etc., the Âtmâ goes out of its material confines without leaving the body to injure others, we have Kaṣâya-samudghâta. The expansion of the Âtmâ from its Pradeśas, without leaving the body, owing to some perturbation due to lust, etc., is called Vikriyâ-samudghâta. The exit of the Âtmâ, without leaving the original body, to that Pradeśa where it has fixed its residence, at the time of death of a being, is Mâranântika-samudghâta. Teja-samudghâta are of two sorts—Śubha and Aśubha. It is said that when a great sage perceives some cause of harm to his mind, he becomes angry, and at that time a red figure, twelve yojanas in length and nine yojanas broad, pointed at the top and broad at the bottom, issues forth from the left shoulder of the sage and, after destroying that cause of evil, consumes itself with the sage. This is Aśubha-samudghâta. There is a Jaina story that such a figure issued forth from the body of the sage, Dvîpâyana, and, destroying Dvârikâ, destroyed itself

* For a detailed description of Lokâkâśa and Alokâkâśa, see verse 20 of Dravya-saṃgraha.

† "मूलसरीरमछंडिय उत्तरदेहस्स जीवपिंडस्स ।
णिग्गमणं देहादो हवदि समुद्धादयं णाम ॥"

‡ "वेयणकसायविउब्वियमारणंतिउसमुद्धादो ।
तेजाहारो छट्ठो सत्तमउ केवलीणं तु ॥"

[Verses quoted in Brahmadeva's Commentary.]

with the sage *. The exit of a white form, having an extent similar to that mentioned in Aśubha-samudghâta, from the right shoulder of a sage who becomes full of commiseration at some calamity of the people, like a famine or an epidemic, is known as Śubha-samudghâta. This, after destroying the calamity, enters its own place. The exit of a white figure, one cubit in length, from the head of a sage, to resolve a doubt by seeing some Kevali (possessed of infinite knowledge), is known as Âhâra-samudghâta. In a certain stage through the rise of all kinds of Karmas, a Kevali's form expands and fills up the whole Lokâkâśa, without leaving the original body. This is called Kevali-samudghâta.

A description of these forms clearly illustrates the belief of various subtle forms by the Jainas. In all cases, when a Jîva does not assume these forms, it fillls up either a large or a small body. This theory of the Jainas is severely criticised in the Vedanta philosophy of the Hindus. Śankarâchârya, in his commentary on Vedanta-sûtra, Adhyâya II, Pâda II, Sûtra 34, had said that if it is admitted that a Jîva is equal in extent to its body, it is impossible that the same Jîva can enter into the bodies of a fly and an elephant. This is not the place to discuss the point in detail. We shall simply mention the view held by the Jainas with respect to this point. The Jainas say that as a lamp, placed respectively in a small pot and a room, illuminates the whole of the space between each of these, so a Jîva contracts and expands, according to the dimensions of different bodies. A better example can be given by mentioning the case of gases like oxygen, which fill up the whole of the space within different vessels, having small or large dimensions. But

---

* Brahmadeva has thus referred to it in his commentary : "द्वीपायनवत्" We find a mention of this story in the following passage quoted from the commentary by Śrutasâgara Sûri on Yaśastilaka Champu by Somadeva Sûri :

"उर्जयनौ गिरौ किल अरिष्टनेमिभगवतः समवसरे नारायणो गणधरदेवेन चापृच्छन् हे भगवन्, एवं समृद्धद्वारवत्या किं कुतोऽपि व्ययो भविष्यति ? इति। वरदत्तः गणधर उवाच, अनया चिन्तया किम् ? इति ब्रुवन्नपि हरिणा कृतनिबन्धो बभाषे, द्वादशवर्षेषु गतेषु द्वैपायनकुमारात् दाहो भविष्यति। तद्वचनं द्वैपायनः श्रुत्वा असत्यं कर्तुमिच्छुः गृहीतव्रतः द्वादशापि वर्षाणि पूर्वदेशे अतिक्रम्य अधिकमासमलक्षयन् द्वारवतीद्वारदेशे कृतकायोत्सर्गः पानविह्वलितमतिना मातङ्गेन विहितस्खलतिमस्तगुञ्जादाघस्र (?) कोपादग्निकुमारो भूत्वा तां नगरीं ददाह।"

this expansion and contraction of Jîvas, according to different bodies, are only recognized from the Vyavahâra point of view. According to Niśchaya Naya, Jîvas can fill up innumerable Pradeśas in Lokâkâsa.

पुढविजलतेउवाऊवणप्फदी विविहथावरे–इंदी ।
विगतिगचदुपंचक्खा तसजीवा होंति संखादी ॥११॥ *

Puḍhavijalateuvâûvaṇapphadî vivihathâvare indî.
Vigatigachadupañchakkhâ tasajîvâ honti saṅkhâdî.—(11.)

Padapâtha.—पुढविजलतेउवाऊवणप्फदी Pudhavijalateuvâûvaṇapphadî, the earth, water, fire, air and plants. विविहथावरे इंदी Viviha-thâvare indî, various kinds of Sthâvara, possessed of one sense. विगतिगचदुपंचक्खा Viga-tiga-chadu-pañchakkhâ, of two, three, four and five senses. संखादी Saṅkhâdî, conches, etc. तसजीवा Tasajîvâ, the Trasa Jîvas. होंति Honti, are.

11. The earth, water, fire, air and plants are various kinds of Sthâvara possessed of one sense. The Trasa Jîvas, conches, etc., are possessed of two, three, four and five senses.

COMMENTARY.

Jîvas are classified under two principal heads—Saṃsâri (leading a wordly existence) and Mukta (liberated). In verses 11—13 of Dravya-saṃgraha the Saṃsâri Jîvas with their sub-divisions are described, and the characteristics of Mukta Jîvas are mentioned in verse 14.

In this verse, two varieties of Saṃsâri Jîvas are enumerated—Saṃsâri, *viz.*, Sthâvara (Immobile) and Trasa (mobile; capable of spontaneous movement.) Earth, water, fire, air and vegetables are Sthâvara Jîvas and possess only one sense, *viz.*, the sense of touch. Those Jîvas which possess more than one sense are called Trasa Jîvas. These might possess two, three, four or five

---

* Sanskrit rendering :—

पृथिवीजलतेजोवायुवनस्पतयः विविधस्थावरैकेन्द्रियाः ।
द्विकत्रिकचतुःपञ्चाक्षाः त्रसजीवाः भवन्ति शङ्खादयः ॥११॥

Prithivîjalatejovâyuvanaspatayaḥ vividhasthâvaraikendriyâḥ.
Dwika-trika-chatuḥ-pañchâ-kṣâḥ trasajîvâḥ bhavanti śaṅkhâdayaḥ.—(11).

senses.* Worms, oysters, conches, etc., are Trasa Jîvas, possessing two senses, taste and touch. Ants, bugs, lice, etc., are Trasa Jîvas having three senses, touch, taste and smell. Mosquitoes, flies, bees, etc., are Trasa Jîvas of four senses, touch, taste, smell and sight. Men, birds, beasts, Gods, inmates of Hell etc., are Trasa Jîvas, possessing all the five senses, *viz.*, touch, taste, smell, sight and hearing.†

It should be remembered that, though really Jîvas have two characteristics, *viz.*, pure Jñâna and Darśana, it is owing to the different karmas that they assume bodies of various kinds possessed of one, two, three, four or five senses. That Jîva which resorts to earth for its body, is called Prithivî-Kâya (*i.e.*, having earth as its body). Stones, etc., are examples of this class of Jîvas. So also there are Jîvas who resort to water, air or fire to have bodies.

---

* "संसारिणो मुक्ताश्च ।"
"संसारिणस्त्रसस्थावराः ।"
"पृथिव्यप्तेजोवायुवनस्पतयः स्थावराः ।"
"द्वीन्द्रियादयस्त्रसाः ।"

Tattvârthâdhigama Sûtra II. 10, 12—14.

† **In the Pañchâstikâya-samaya-sâra, we have the following verses, the sense of which has been summarised in the Commentary :—**

"पुढवी य उदगमगणी वाउवणप्फदि जीव-संसिदा काया ।
देंति खलु मोहबहुलं फासं बहुगा वि ते तेसिं ॥...
एदे जीवनिकाया पंचविहा पुढविकाइयादीया ।
मणपरिणामविरहिदा जीवा एगेंदिया भणिया ॥...
संबुक्कमादुवाहा संखा सिप्पी अपादगा य किमी ।
जाणंति रसं फासं जे ते बे-इंदिया जीवा ॥
जूगागुंभीमक्कणपिपीलिया विच्छियादिया कीडा ।
जाणंति रसं फासं गंधं ते-इंदिया जीवा ॥
उद्दंसमसयमक्खियमधुकरभमरा पतंगमादीया ।
रूपं रसं च गन्धं फासं पुण ते वि जाणंति ॥
सुरणरणारयतिरिया वण्णरसप्फासगंधसद्दण्हू ।
जलचरथलचरखचरा बलिया पंचेंदिया जीवा ॥"

[Verses 110, 112, 114—117.]

समणा अमणा णेया पंचेंदिय णिम्मणा परे सव्वे ।
बादरसुहमेइंदी सव्वे पज्जत्त इदरा य ॥१२॥*

Samaṇâ amaṇâ ṇeyâ pañchendiya ṇimmaṇâ pare savve.

Bâdarasuhame-indî savve pajjatta idarâ ya (12).

Padapîṭha.—पंचेंदिय Pañchendiya, [Jîvas] possessing five senses. समणा Samaṇâ, having mind. अमणा Amaṇâ, without mind. णेया Ṇeyâ, are known. परे Pare, the rest. सव्वे Savve, all. णिम्मणा Ṇimmaṇâ, without mind. एइंदी Eindî, [Jîvas] possessing one sense. बादर-सुहमा Bâdara-suhamâ, Bâdara and Sûkṣma. सव्वे Savve, all. पज्जत्त Pajjatta, Paryâpta (complete). य Ya, and. इदरा Idarâ, opposite (of Paryâpta).

12. [Jîvas] possessing five senses are known [to be divided into] those having mind and those without mind. All the rest are without mind. [Jîvas] having one sense [are divided into two classes] Bâdara and Sûkṣma. All [of these have again two varieties each] Paryâpta and its opposite.

COMMENTARY.

In this verse the fourteen varieties of Jîva commonly known as Jîva-samâsa in Jain philosophy are briefly described. In Gommatasâra (Jîva-kânda) another work of the author of Dravya-samgraha each of these varieties has been described in detail. The verse in Gommatasâra which is parallel to this verse is as follows:—

"बादर-सुहुमे-इंदिय बितिचउरिंदिय असण्णिसण्णी य ।
पज्जत्ताऽपज्जत्ता एवं ते चोद्दसा होंति ॥"

[गोम्मटसार । जीवकाण्ड । ७२ ।]

i.e., "Jîvas of one sense divided into two classes, Bâdara and Sûkṣma, Jîvas of two, three and four senses, Jîvas having and not having Sañjâ, Paryâpta and Aparyâpta, thus they (the Jîvas) are of fourteen kinds."

* *Sanskrit rendering* :—

समनस्काः अमनस्काः ज्ञेयाः पञ्चेन्द्रियाः निर्मनस्काः परे सर्व्वे ।
बादरसूक्ष्मैकेन्द्रियाः सर्व्वे पर्याप्ताः इतरे च ॥ १२ ॥

Samanaskâḥ amanaskâḥ jñeyâḥ pañchendriyâḥ nirmanaskâḥ pare sarvve.
Bâdara-sûkṣmaikendriyâḥ sarvve Paryâptâḥ itare cha. (12).

5

The accompanying table (Chart No. II.) illustrates these fourteen varieties of Jîvas. It will be remembered that in Verse 11 it was told that Jîvas are first of all divided into two varieties Saṃsâri and Mukta. The Saṃsâri Jîvas are subdivided into Trasa and Sthâvara. The Sthâvara Jîvas possessed of one sense are again divided into Bâdara (gross) and Sukṣma (subtle). A Bâdara form is that which is fettered by matter. A Sukṣma form is not so fettered. That is to say, a Sukṣma is a subtle form unfettered by material things, earth, etc., while Bâdara is exactly its opposite. In Jaina philosophy it is said that all the universe is the place of existence of Sukṣma Jîvas possessing one sense. It is also said that Bâdara Jîvas possessing one sense must have some Âdhâra (substratum) in order to exist.

Jîvas of five senses may be either with mind or without mind. Those with mind are also known as Sañjî, or having Sañjâ.*

Sañjâ consists of attempt to gain what is beneficial and leave what is harmful and a judgment of good and bad.†

Paryâpti has been thus illustrated in Gommata-sâra :—

"जह पुण्णापुण्णाइं गिहघडवत्थादियाइं दव्वाइं ।
तह पुण्णिदरा जीवा पज्जत्तिदरा मुणेयव्वा ॥"

[Jîva-kânda. Verse 118.]

i.e. "As things like rooms, jars, cloths, etc., are full or empty, so Jîvas should be understood to be complete or incomplete (Paryâpta and Aparyâpta)."

Âhâra (taking food and drink), Śarîra (Body), Indriya (the five senses) Âṇaprâṇa (Respiration), Bhâṣâ (Speech) and Manas (Mind), these six exist in Jîvas and make them complete (Paryâpta). Of these the first four make Jîvas having one sense complete, and the first five make Jîvas having two, three and four senses complete. As for Jîvas having five senses, all the six are necessary to make them complete.‡ In absence of these the Jîvas are incomplete (Aparyâpta).

---

* "संज्ञिनः समनस्काः ।" [Tattvârthâdhigama Sûtra II. 5. 24.]

† "हिताहितप्राप्तिपरिहारयोर्गुणदोषविचारणात्मिका संज्ञा" । [Tattvârtha-râja-vârttika on Sûtra II. 5, 24].

‡ "आहारसरीरिंदियपज्जत्ती आणपाणभासमणो ।
चत्तारि पंच छप्पि य एइंदियवियलसण्णीणं ॥"

[गोम्मटसार:, जीवकाण्ड: ११८]

CHART II.—[JIVA-SAMASA.]

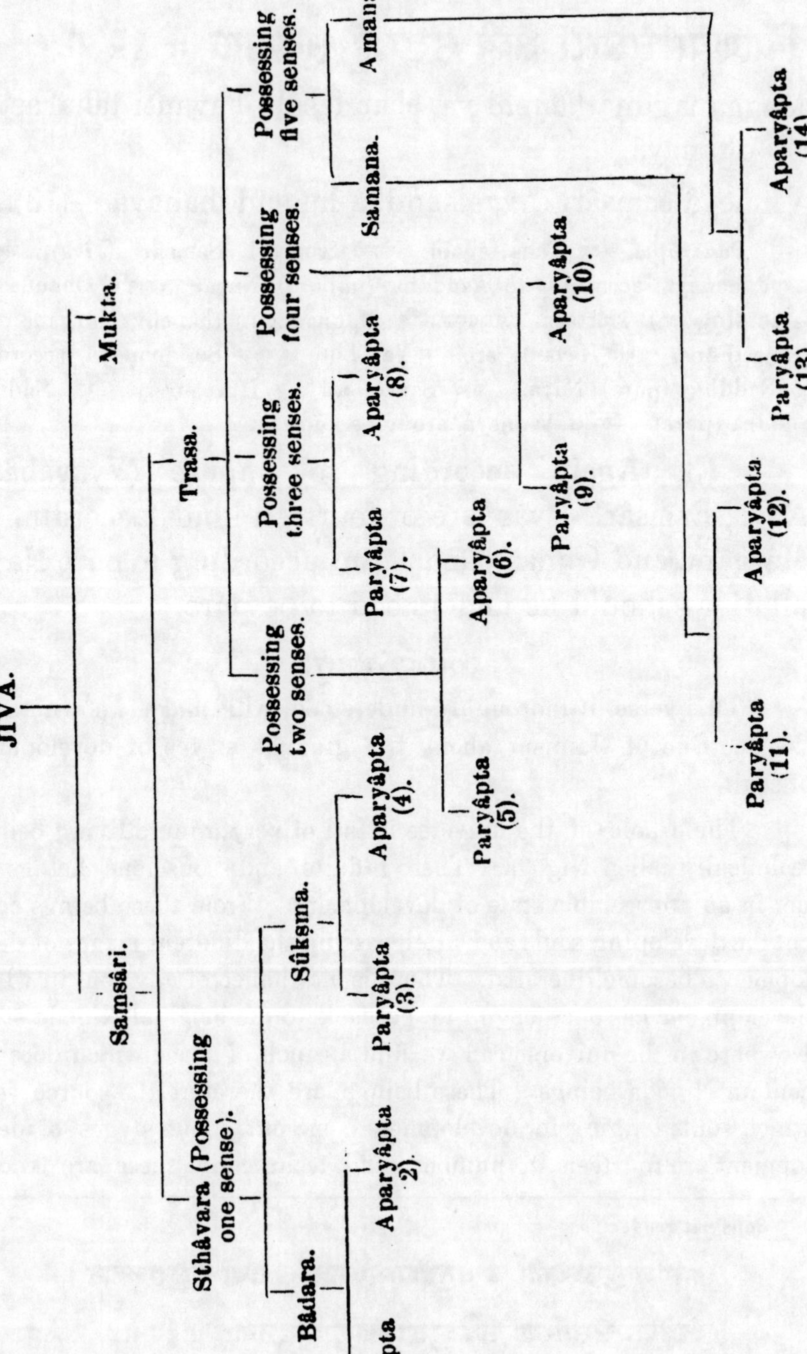

मग्गणगुणठाणेहि य चउदसहि हवंति तह असुद्धणया ।
विण्णेया संसारी सव्वे सुद्धा हु सुद्धणया ॥ १३ ॥ *

Magganagunathânehi ya chaudasahi havanti taha asuddhanayâ.

Vinneyâ samsârî savve suddhâ hu suddhanayâ.—(13).

Padapâtha.—तह Taha, again. संसारी Samsârî, Samsârî (Jîva). असुद्धणया Asuddhanayâ, according to Aśuddha (impure) Naya. चउदसहि Chaudasahi, (according to) fourteen. मग्गणगुणठाणेहि Magganagunathânehi, Mârganâ and Gunasthâna. हवंति Havanti, are. य Ya, but. सुद्धणया Suddhanayâ, according to Śuddha (pure) Naya. सव्वे Savve, all. हु Hu, surely. सुद्धा Suddhâ, Śuddha (pure). विण्णेया Vinneyâ, are to be known.

13. Again, according to impure (Vyavahâra) Naya, Samsârî Jîvas are of fourteen kinds according to Mârganâ and Gunasthâna. But according to pure Naya, all Jîvas should be understood to be pure.

COMMENTARY.

This verse, if thoroughly understood, will make known to us the doctrine of Jainism about the gradual stages of development of soul.

The whole of the universe is full of very minute living beings, technically called Nigoda. These infinite and conscious beings are not in an appreciable state of development. From these beings come out the developing souls and, after passing the different stages of development, become liberated. There is no chance of any soul in which development has once begun to go back to the original Nigoda state. Nowhere in the universe can we find an inch of space which does not contain Nigoda beings. These beings are therefore the source from which souls longing for development come out. The stages of development are fourteen in number, and technically these are known

* *Sanskrit rendering :*

मार्गणागुणस्थानैः च चतुर्दशभिः भवन्ति तथा अशुद्धनयात् ।
विज्ञेयाः संसारिणः सर्वे शुद्धाः खलु शुद्धनयात् ॥ १३ ॥

Mârganâgunasthânaiḥ cha chaturddaśabhiḥ bhavanti tathâ aśuddhanayât.
Vijñeyâḥ samsâriṇaḥ sarvve śuddhâḥ khalu śuddhanayât. (13).

as Guṇasthânas. In Gommatasâra, we have the following list of the fourteen Guṇasthânas :—

"मिच्छो सासण मिस्सो अविरदसम्मो य देसविरदो य ।
विरदा पमत्त इदरो अपुव्व अणियट्ट सुहुमो य ॥
उवसंतखीणमोहो सजोगकेवलिजिणो अजोगी य ।
चउदस जीवसमासा कमेण सिद्धा य णादव्वा ॥ "

[Jîva-kânda, 9, 10.]

i.e., "the fourteen Guṇasthânas should be known to be Mithyâtva, Sâsâdana, Miśra, Avirata-samyaktva, Deśavirata, Virata, Pramatta, Itara (*i. e.* Apramatta), Apûrva, Anivritta, Sûkṣma, Upaśânta-kṣîṇa-moha, Sayogi-kevali-jina and Ayogi."

In the first stage, a person has no belief in the truth of Jaina doctrines. Even when these are taught to him, he does not believe in them, but on the contrary holds false beliefs, whether taught or not. The true doctrines appear to him as distasteful as sweet syrup to a man suffering from fever.* This stage is known as the Mithyâtva Guṇasthâna.

The second is a transitory stage. When one loses true belief and comes to believe false doctrines as in the first stage, he passes through the second stage which is known as Sâsâdana. This is an intermediate stage in the fall from the heights of Samyaktva (right belief) to the level of Mithyâtva (false belief).†

In the third or Miśra stage, a person has true and false beliefs in a mixed way. That is to say, neither a desire to have true beliefs

---

* "मिच्छोदयेण मिच्छत्तमसद्दहणं तु तच्चअत्थाणं ।
... ...
मिच्छत्तं वेदंतो जीवो विवरीयदंसणो होदि ।
ण य धम्मं रोचेदि हु महुरं खु रसं जहा जरिदो ॥
मिच्छाइट्ठी जीवो उवइट्ठं पवयणं ण सद्दहदि ।
सद्दहदि असब्भावं उवइट्ठं वा अणुवइट्ठं ॥"

[Gommatasâra, Jîva-kânda, 15, 17, 18.]

† "सम्मत्तरयणपव्वयसिहरादो मिच्छभूमिसमभिमुहो ।
णासियसम्मत्तो सो सासणणामो मुणेयव्वो ॥"

[Gommatasâra, Jîva-kânda, Verse 20.]

nor a wish to give up false ones, appear in his mind. Samyaktva and Mithyâtva are mixed up, like curd and treacle. *

A person in the fourth stage controls excessive anger, pride, deceit and greed, † and does not doubt the truth of right doctrines. But, while in this stage, he is unable to control the moderate or slight degrees of anger, etc. However, an effort for self-control is made as the person appreciates the value of it, though the effort is successful only to a very limited extent.

In the fifth stage, a person becomes able to control moderate degrees of passions like anger, etc., and succeeds in establishing self-control to a greater extent than in the fourth stage.

In the sixth stage, a person begins to refrain from injury, falsehood, taking any substance which is not given to him, lust and a desire to have worldly possessions. But his attempts are not always successful.

In the seventh stage, a person succeeds in practising, without any transgression, non-injury, truth, chastity, non-acceptance of things not presented and of possessions in general.

In the eighth stage, mild states of passions still arise, but the person enjoys an inexpressible delight by either checking or destroying their consequences.

A person in the ninth stage becomes void of the desire to have enjoyments which he saw, heard or partook of previously, and practises meditation about the true nature of his soul.

In the tenth stage, a person by meditation becomes capable of subduing or destroying the subtle forms of greed.

---

* " दहि-गुडमिव वामिस्सं पुहभावं णेव कारिदुं सक्कं ।
एवं मिस्सयभावो सम्मामिच्छोत्ति णादव्वो ॥ "

[Gommatasâra, Jîva-kânda, Verse 22.]

It should be mentioned here that in Jainism the passions Krodha (anger) Mâna (pride), Mâyâ (deceit) and Lobha (greed) are known as Kaṣâyas. These passions are of four degrees. The first and the most excessive form of these is termed Anantânubandhi. The passions in this state are said to be as permanent as lines cut out on a stone. The next stage is Pratyâkhyâna and the passions last like lines on earth. The third stage is called Apratyâkhyâna in which passions have their existence like lines on dust. In the fourth or Saṃjvalana state, the passions easily disappear like lines on water. The examples given show the gradual stages of duration and permanency of the passions. As a man passes through the successive stages of development, these various classes of passions disappear one by one.

In the eleventh stage, a person gains the power to control all Mohanîya (intoxicating) Karmas,* but these do not disappear altogether.

In the twelfth stage, all the passions and Mohanîya Karmas disappear altogether.

A person in the thirteenth stage destroys the Karmas called Jñânâvaraṇîya, Darśanâ-varaṇîya and Antarâya† and appears like the sun freed from clouds. He attains knowledge of everything existing in the universe. But in this stage, Yoga‡ still remains which disappears in the next or fourteenth stage, and the person attains liberation.

Now we shall see what is meant by Mârgaṇâs. Those states by, or conditions in which, the Jîvas are found are known as Mârgaṇâs; and these are of fourteen kinds, *viz.*, (1) Gati, (2) Indriya, (3) Kâya, (4) Yoga, (5) Veda, (6) Kaṣâya, (7) Jñâna, (8) Saṃyama, (9) Darśana, (10) Leśyâ, (11) Bhavya, (12) Samyaktva, (13) Saṃjñi and (14) Âhâra§.

Gati or condition of existence is of four kinds, *viz.*, existence (1) as inmates of hell (2) as inmates of heaven (3) as human beings and (4) as lower animals.||

Indriya or senses are five, *e.g.*, the senses of sight, hearing, touch, taste and smell.¶

Kâya or body is of six kinds, *viz.*, five kinds of Sthâvara, earth, water, fire, air and vegetable and Trasa.$

* For an explanation of Mohanîya Karmas, see the commentary on Verse 14. (Page 42).

† The first two Karmas have been described in commentaries on Verses 4 and 5. For an account of the third, see the commentary on Verse 14. (Page 42).

‡ Yoga is the fourth Mârgaṇâ described below.

§ "जाहि व जासु व जीवा मग्गिज्जंते जहा तहा दिट्ठा ।
ताओ चोद्दस जाणे सुयणाणे मग्गणा होंति ॥
गइ-इंदियेसु काये जोगे वेदे कसायणाणे य ।
संजमदंसणलेस्सा भवियासम्मत्तसण्णि आहारे ॥"

[गोम्मटसारः । जीवकाण्डः । १४१ । १४२]

|| "गइ-उदयजपज्जाया चउगइगमणस्स हेउ वा हु गई ।
णारयतिरिक्खमाणुसदेवगइत्ति य हवे चदुधा ॥"

[Gommatasâra, Jîva-kânda, 146.]

¶ "फासरसगंधरूवे सद्दे णाणं च चिण्हयं जेसिं ।"

[Gommatasâra, Jîva-kânda, 166.]

$ See a detailed description of Trasa and Sthâvara Jîvas in Verse 11. (Pages 31-32).

Yoga is the power of a Jîva possessing activities of mind, speech and body by which particles of matter are attracted towards it.* Yoga or union is mainly of three kinds, *viz.*, (1) with respect to mind (2) with respect to speech and (3) with respect to body. The first two of these, again, are each of four kinds. Mind may be turned to things which are true, to things which are false, to things which are both true and false, and to things which are neither true nor false. Speech also might be directed to truth, falsehood, mixed truth and falsehood, and neither truth nor falsehood. Unity in body, again, is of seven kinds: (1) as in the bodies of human beings and lower animals which are fixed in limits (2) a mixed state of the first (3) as in the bodies of the inmates of heaven and hell which can increase or diminish (4) a mixed state of the third (5) as in the body which comes out of the head of a sage in the sixth stage of development to go to a Kevali † (6) a mixed state of the fifth and (7) as in the forms which result from the eight kinds of Karma.‡

Veda or sex is of three kinds, male, female and eunuch.

Kaṣâya or passions are four: anger, pride, deceit and greed. Each of these is, again, of four kinds, according to different degrees of intensity.§

Jñâna is of eight kinds, Mati, Śruta, Avadhi, Manaḥ-paryaya, Kevala, Kumati, Kuśruta and Vibhaṅgâvadhi.‖

Saṃyama or restraint consists of keeping the Vratas (vows), observing the Samitis, checking the Kaṣâyas or passions, giving up the Dandas and controlling the Indriyas (senses).¶

Darśana is of four kinds, Chakṣu, Achakṣu, Avadhi and Kevala.$

---

* "पुग्गलविवाइ-देहोदयेण मणवयणकायजुत्तस्स ।
जीवस्स जा हु सत्ती कम्मागमकारणं जोगो ॥"

[Gommatasâra, Jîva-kânda, Verse 216.]

† See the commentary on Verse 10. (Page 20).

‡ For a description of eight kinds of Karma, see the commentary on Verse 14. (Page 42).

§ All these sixteen kinds of Kaṣâyas have been described in a footnote on page 38.

‖ See Verse 5. (Page 11).

¶ "वदसमिदिकसायाणं दंडाण तहिंदियाण पंचण्हं ।
धारणपालणणिग्गहचागजओ संजमो भणियो ॥"

[Gommatasâra, Jîva-kânda, Verse 464.]

See Verse 35. (Page 86) for a detailed description of Vrata and Samiti.

$ See Verse 4. (Page 10).

Leśyâ is that by which a Jîva assimilates virtue and vice with itself.* Feelings arising from Yoga, coloured by passions, lead to Bhâva-Leśyâ and the actual colours of bodies produced by such feelings are called Dravya-Leśyâ. The colours are black, blue, pigeon, golden, lotus-like and white.† The first three are resultants of evil, and the last three of good emotions.

That quality by which a soul attains perfect faith, knowledge and conduct is known as Bhavyatva Guṇa, and that by which these are obstructed is called Abhavyatva Guṇa. Bhavya Mârgaṇâ defines Jîvas which possess each of these sets of qualities.

Samyaktva is perfect faith in the Tattvas or principal tenets of Jainism.

Saṃjñî Jîvas are those who with the help of mind are capable of teaching, of action, of giving advice, and of conversation. Asaṃjñî Jîvas are those who are incapable of these.‡ In Saṃjñî Mârgaṇâ, each of these classes of Jîvas are described.

Âhâra is the assimilation of material particles by Jîvas to preserve bodies.

These are the fourteen kinds of Mârgaṇâ.

Jîvas may be viewed with reference to each of these Mârgaṇâs or with reference to different Guṇasthânas or stages of development. But it must be remembered that all these characteristics are attributed to Jîvas from the ordinary point of view, for none of them really exist in Jîvas.

---

* "लिंपइ अप्पीकीरइ एदीए णियअपुण्णपुण्णं च ।
जीवोत्ति होदि लेस्सा लेस्सागुणजाणयक्खादा ॥"

[Gommatasâra, Jîva-kânda, 488.]

† "किण्हा णीला काऊ तेऊ पम्मा य सुक्कलेस्सा य ।
लेस्साणं णिद्देसा छच्चेव हवंति णियमेण ॥
वण्णोदयेण जणिदो सरीरवण्णो दु दव्वदो लेस्सा ।"

[Gommatasâra, Jîva-kânda, 492, 493]

‡ "सिक्खाकिरियुवदेसालावग्गाही मणोवलंबेण ।
जो जीवो सो सण्णी तव्विवरीयो असण्णी दु ॥"

[Gommatasâra, Jîva-kânda, 660.]

णिक्कम्मा अट्टगुणा किंचूणा चरमदेहदो सिद्धा ।
लोयग्गठिदा णिच्चा उप्पादवयेहि संजुत्ता ॥ १४ ॥*

Ṇikkammâ aṭṭaguṇâ kiṃchûṇâ charamadehado siddhâ.

Loyaggaṭhidâ ṇichchâ uppâdavayehi sañjuttâ.—(14).

Padapâṭha.—णिक्कम्मा Ṇikkammâ, void of Karmas. अट्टगुणा Aṭṭaguṇâ, possessed of eight qualities. चरमदेहदो Charamadehado, than the final body. किंचूणा Kiṃchûṇâ, slightly less. णिच्चा Ṇichchâ, eternal. उप्पादवयेहि Uppâdavayehi, Utpâda and Vyaya. संजुत्ता Saṃjuttâ, consisting of. सिद्धा Siddhâ, liberated. लोयग्गठिदा Loyaggaṭhidâ, existing at the summit of Loka.

14. The Siddhas (or liberated Jîvas) are void of Karmas, possessed of eight qualities, slightly less than the final body, eternal, possessed of Utpâda (rise) and Vyaya (fall), and existent at the summit of Loka.

COMMENTARY.

According to Jainism, Jîvas, as long as they are not liberated, are connected with Karma. But a liberated Jîva is free from all Karmas. Karmas are recognised to be of eight kinds, *viz.*, Jñânâvaraṇîya, Darśanâvaraṇîya, Vedanîya, Mohanîya, Âyu, Nâma, Gotra and Antarâya. It has already been described in the commentaries on Verses 4 and 5 (Pages 10 and 16) that Jñânâvaraṇîya and Darśanâvaraṇîya Karmas are those which obscure infinite Jñâna and Darśana of a Jîva. Vedanîya Karmas tend to produce pain and pleasure in a Jîva. Mohanîya Karmas infatuate Jîvas, making these unable to distinguish right from wrong. Âyu Karmas sustain Jîvas for a certain period and determine their tenure of existence. Nâma Karmas give them their personalities, and Gotra Karmas conduce to their being produced in a particular social surrounding. Antarâya Karmas throw obstacles to the performance of right action

---

* *Sanskrit rendering:*

निष्कर्माणः अष्टगुणाः किञ्चिदूनाः चरमदेहतः सिद्धाः ।
लोकाग्रस्थिताः नित्याः उत्पादव्ययाभ्यां संयुक्ताः ॥ १४ ॥

Niṣkarmâṇaḥ aṣṭaguṇâḥ kiñchidûnâḥ charamadehataḥ siddhâḥ,

Lokâgrasthitâḥ nityâḥ utpâdavyayâvyâṃ saṃjuktâḥ.—(14).

by the Jîvas. Thus all these varieties of Karmas* operate to make a Jîva have different qualities and characteristics in its Saṃsâri or worldly state of existence. But as a Jîva begins to pursue the path of gradual development, these Karmas disappear one by one until at last the said Jîva becomes liberated.

Being void of Karmas, a Jîva resides at the top of the Loka,† and the following eight qualities can then be found in it: Samyaktva, Jñâna, Darśana, Vîrya, Sûkṣma, Avagâhana, Agurulaghu and Avyâvâdha. Samyaktva is perfect faith or belief in the Tattvas or essential principles of Jainism. Jñâna and Darśana have been explained in Verses 4 and 5. Vîrya (literally, power) is the absence of fatigue in having a knowledge of infinite substances. Suksma literally means fineness, and the possession of this quality makes a liberated Jîva incapable of being perceived by the senses, which can perceive the gross bodies only. Avagâha is interpenetrability, that is to say, one liberated Jîva can allow others to exist without obstruction, just as the light of a lamp does not prevent the interpenetration of the light of other lamps. Agurulaghu means "neither heavy nor light." By possessing this quality, a liberated Jîva does neither go up like a light thing nor go down like a heavy object, but remains stationary. Avyâvâdha is undisturbable bliss in which the disturbance of equilibrium caused by happiness or misery is entirely absent. In a word, a liberated Jîva being freed from Karmas goes up to the summit of the Loka and remains there stationary, possessed of perfect faith, power and infinite Jñâna and Darśana and enjoying eternal bliss without obstructing other Jîvas of the same kind. Such a Jîva has a body slightly less than the final body as recognised in the Jaina canons.

A liberated Jîva, again, is eternal in its essential character, though perpetual modifications of it may go on in its condition. To give an example of such modifications, we may say that a ball of gold has certain essential characteristics and may always be said to possess these characteristics throughout its various modifications. Now, if we prepare a ring from this gold, we have an instance of a modification which arises (Utpâda) from the original state of the ball of gold. Again, if the ring be destroyed, we shall have another modification consisting of the destruction (Vyaya) of the stage of existence of

* There are many sub-divisions of each of the eight kinds of Karmas mentioned above. A detailed description of these may be found in works like Tattvârthâdhigama Sûtra, Chapter VIII, Gommatasâra, (Karmakânda,) etc.

† See commentary on Pages 56 and 58.

the ball of gold as a ring. Every substance in the universe is, according to Jainism, possessed of the quality of permanency (Nityatva), with generation (Utpâda) and decay (Vyaya) of the modifications of itself. Being possessed of these qualities, is technically called 'Sat:' and this 'Sat' defines a substance (Dravya) in Jainism.*

अज्जीवो पुण णेश्रो पुग्गल धम्मो श्रधम्म श्रायासं ।
कालो पुग्गल मुत्तो रुवादिगुणो श्रमुत्ति सेसा दु ॥१५॥†

Ajjîvo puṇa ṇeyo puggala dhammo adhmma âyâsaṃ
Kâlo puggala mutto rûvâdiguṇo amutti sesâ du—(15).

Padapâṭha.—पुण Puṇa, again. पुग्गल Puggala, Pudgala. धम्मो Dhammo, Dharma. अधम्म Adhamma, Adharma. आयासं Âyâsaṃ, Âkâśa. कालो Kâlo, Kâla, (Time). अज्जीवो Ajjîvo, Ajîva. णेओ Ṇeyo, to be known. पुग्गल Puggala, Pudgala. रुवादिगुणो Rûvâdiguṇo, possessing the qualities, Rûpa, etc. मुत्तो Mutto, having form. दु Du, but. सेसा Sesâ, the rest. अमुत्ति Amutti, without form.

15. Again, Ajîva should be known to be Pudgala, Dharma, Adharma, Âkâśa and Kâla. Pudgala has form and the qualities, Rûpa, etc. But the rest are without form.

---

*"उत्पादव्ययध्रौव्ययुक्तं सत् ।"
"सद्द्रव्यलक्षणम् ।"

[Tattvârthâdhigama Sûtra V. 30. 29.]

Again—

"स्वजात्यपरित्यागेन भावान्तरावाप्तिरुत्पादः । तथा पूर्वभावविगमो व्ययः । ध्रुवे स्थैर्यकर्मणो ध्रुवतीति ध्रुवः ।"

[Tattvârtharâjavârttika V. 29 (1, 2 and 3.];

i.e., "Utpâda is having a modification by a substance without leaving its own kind, (*e.g.*, the transformation of a lump of clay into a pot.) Vyaya is the change or disappearance of a form, (*e.g.*, the change of a pot into pieces). Dhrauvya consists of the existence of the essential characteristics throughout different modifications (*e.g.*, the existence of clay as such.)"

† *Sanskrit rendering*:

अजीवः पुनः ज्ञेयः पुद्गलः धर्मः अधर्मः आकाशम् ।
कालः पुद्गलः मूर्त्तः रूपादिगुणः अमूर्त्तयः शेषाः तु ॥ १५ ॥

Ajîvaḥ punaḥ jñeyaḥ pudgalaḥ dharmaḥ adharmaḥ âkâśam
Kâlaḥ, pudgalaḥ mûrttaḥ rûpâdiguṇaḥ amûrttayaḥ śeṣâḥ tu—(15).

COMMENTARY.

We have now arrived at the end of the subdivisions of Dravya. The following table will illustrate the varieties of Dravya with sub-classes.

DRAVYA.

Jîva. **Ajîva.**

Dharma. **Adharma.** **Âkâśa.** **Pudgala.** **Kâla.**

Innumerable passages might be quoted from all sorts of Jain works which contain a mention and description of these varieties of Dravya. In Tattvârthâdhigama Sûtra we have :—

"**द्रव्याणि ।**" [V. I].

"**अजीवकाया धर्माधर्माकाशपुद्गलाः ।**" [V. I].

"**जीवाश्च** " [V. 3].

"**कालश्च ।**" [V. 39].

i.e., "The Dravyas are Dharma, Adharma, Âkâśa and Pudgala which are Ajîvas having Kâya (body). The Jîvas also (are Dravyas). Kâla too is Dravya."

Jîva and the four Ajîvas Pudgala, Dharma, Adharma, and Âkâśa have Kâya (body) and are known as Pañchâstikâyas (the Five Astikâyas). Kâla, though an Ajîva, has no body. It is Akâya (or without body). This is why Kâla is mentioned separately and last of all in the Sûtras quted above.

In all the Jaina Purâṇas there is a description of Dravyas. We quote one verse only from a manuscript of Vardhamâna Purâṇa by Bhattâraka Sakalakîrti.

"**अथ पुद्गल एवात्र धर्मोऽधर्मो द्विधा नभः ।**
कालश्च पञ्चधैवेत्यजीवतत्त्वं जगौ जिनः ॥"

[Canto XVI. Śloka 15.]

i.e., "Then Jina (Mahâvîra) spoke about the five sorts of Ajîva, *viz.*, Pudgala, Dharma, Adharma, Âkâśa and Kâla.

As in all the Purâṇas so in all Jain Kâvyas also we find enumeration and description of Dravyas. A peculiarity of Jain Kâvyas is that in the last Canto of nearly all of these works we find a brief summary of the principles of Jainism. It is no wonder therefore that we shall find a description of Dravyas there. Two such passages are quoted here.

"धर्माधर्मौ नभः कालः पुद्गलश्चेति पञ्चधा ।
अजीवः कथ्यते सम्यग्जिनैस्तत्त्वार्थदर्शिभिः ॥
षड्-द्रव्याणीति वर्ण्यन्ते समं जीवेन तान्यपि ।
विना कालेन तान्येव यान्ति पञ्चास्तिकायताम् ॥"

[Dharmaśarmâbhyudaya Kâvya, Canto XXI. 81. 82].

"धर्माधर्मावथाकाशं कालः पुद्गल इत्यपि ।
अजीवः पञ्चधा ज्ञेयो जिनागमविशारदैः ॥
एतान्येव सजीवानि षड्द्रव्याणि प्रचक्षते ।
कालहीनानि पञ्चास्तिकायास्तान्येव कीर्त्तिताः ॥"

[Chandraprabha-Charita Kâvya, Canto XVIII. 67. 68].

i.e., "Dharma, Adharma, Âkâśa, Kâla and Pudgala—these five are called Ajîvas. These with Jîva make up the six Dravyas. Excluding Kâla, the remaining five make up the five Astikâyas."

It is needless to quote any more parallel passages from works like Pañchâstikâyasamayasâra, Dravyânuyogatarkaṇâ, etc.

In the text we have "Pudgala has form." In Tattvârthâdhigama Sûtra, we find "The Pudgalas have Rûpa" ["रूपिणः पुद्गलाः V. 5]. The following explanation of Rûpa in this aphorism is found in the Tattvârtharâja-vâ-rttika: "Though the word Rûpa has various meanings, it is here synonymous with 'shape' according to the authority of the Śâstras. Or it may be taken to mean a certain quality (*viz.*, that quality which is capable of being perceived by the eyes "चक्षुर्ग्रहणयोग्यः")" * The word "Mûrttaḥ" in our text signifies 'that which has Mûrtti (shape).' This Mûrtti should be understood to be the same as "Rûpa" mentioned in Tattvârthâdhigama Sûtra. That is to say the word "Rûpa" in our text is not used in the same sense as it is used in the Tattvârthâdhigama Sûtra. In the latter "Rûpa" is used to denote "Shape or form" but in our text it is used to denote "Colour." In our text "Shape or form" is indicated by the word "Mûrtti" and not "Rûpa." This should be remembered to avoid confusion.

In our text we have "Pudgalas have the qualities, Rûpa, etc." The qualities are touch, taste, smell and colour. All these qualities

* "रूपशब्दस्यानेकार्थत्वे मूर्त्तिपर्यायग्रहणं शास्त्रसामर्थ्यात् ।"
"गुणविशेषवचनग्रहणो वा ।"

[Vârttikas 2, 3 on Aphorism V. 5].

are enumerated in Tattvârthâdhigama Sûtra "स्पर्शरसगन्धवर्णवन्तः पुद्गलाः ।" [V. 23] *i.e.*, "Pudgalas have touch, taste, smell and colour." In Vardhamâna-Purâṇa by Sakalakîrti also we have

"वर्णगन्धरसस्पर्शमयाश्चानन्तपुद्गलाः ।"

[Canto XVI. Verse 16.]

i.e., "Pudgalas are endless and characterised by colour, smell, taste and touch." The varieties of colour, etc., have already been mentioned in the commentary to Verse 7. (Page 23).

Thus we find that among the five varieties of Ajîva, Pudgala has shape and possesses colour, smell, taste and touch. The other four Ajîvas, Dharma, Adharma, Kâla and Akâśa have no form.

सद्दो बंधो सुहमो थूलो संठाणभेदतमछाया ।
उज्जोदादवसहिया पुग्गलदव्वस्स पज्जाया ॥१६॥*

Saddo bandho suhamo thûlo saṃṭhâṇa-bheda-tama-chhâyâ.
Ujjodâdava-sahiyâ puggala-davvassa pajjâyâ.—(16).

Padapâṭha.—सद्दो Saddo, sound. बंधो Bandho, union. सुहमो Suhamo, fineness. थूलो Thûlo, grossness. संठाणभेदतमछाया Saṃṭhâṇa-bheda-tama-chhâyâ, shape, division, darkness, and image. उज्जोदादवसहिया Ujjodâdava-sahiyâ, with lustre and heat. पुग्गलदव्वस्स Puggala-davvassa, of Pudgala substances. पज्जाया Pajjâyâ, modifications.

16. Sound, union, fineness, grossness, shape, division, darkness and image, with lustre and heat (are) modifications of the substance (known as) Pudgala.

COMMENTARY.

Śabda or sound is said to be of two kinds—Bhâṣâ-lakṣaṇa (as incorporated in languages) and Abhâṣâ-lakṣaṇa (which does not find place in any language). The first, again, is of two kinds, *viz.* (1) sounds which are expressed by letters and (2) sounds which are not expressed by letters. It is said that the last-mentioned kind of sounds is made by creatures who possess two, three or four senses, or by the Kevalis.

---

* *Sanskrit rendering*:

शब्दः बन्धः सूक्ष्मः स्थूलः संस्थानभेदतमश्छायाः ।
उद्योतातपसहिताः पुद्गलद्रव्यस्य पर्यायाः ॥१६॥

Śabdaḥ bandhaḥ sûkṣmaḥ sthûlaḥ saṃsthâna-bheda-tama-śchhâyâḥ.
Udyotâtapasahitâḥ pudgaladravyasya paryâyâḥ—(16).

Sounds not finding place in languages are again of two kinds: (1) produced by human beings and (2) resulting from other sources, as the noise of thunder, etc. The first of these, again, are of four kinds: (*a*) Tata or that produced from musical instruments covered by leather, (*b*) Vitata or that produced from string-instruments, (*c*) Ghana or that produced from metallic instruments and (*d*) Sauṣira or that produced from wind-instruments.* It should be mentioned in this connection that there is a difference in the nomenclature of musical instruments between the Jainas and the Hindus, for the latter call Tata by the name of Ânaddha and Vitata by the name of Tata.‡

The following theory of sounds is found in Verse 79 of the Pañchâstikâyasamayasâra:

"सद्दो खंधप्पभवो खंधो परमाणुसंगसंघादो ।
पुट्ठेसु तेसु आयदि सद्दो उप्पादगो णियदो ॥"

i.e., "The combination of atoms is known as Skandha. Sound results when Skandhas strike against one another." Thus it has been laid down that all sounds result from the Skandhas of Pudgala (matter).

Bandha or union is mainly divided into two heads, (1) Prâyogika (produced by the efforts of body, speech, or mind of a person) and (2) Vaisrasika (produced without any kind of effort of any person).

Práyogika may again be (1) Jîva-viṣaya, *i.e.*, union of non-living substances only or (2) Jîvâjîva-viṣaya, *i.e.*, union of living with non-living substances. Jîvâjîva-viṣaya Bandha, again, may result (1)

* "शब्दो द्वेधा भाषालक्षणविपरीतत्वात् ।
भाषात्मक उभयथा अक्षरीकृतेतरविकल्पात् ।
अभाषात्मक द्वेधा प्रयोगविस्रसानिमित्तत्वात् ।
तत्र वैस्रसिको बलाहकादि–प्रभवः ।
प्रयोगश्चतुर्धा ततविततघनसौषिरभेदात् ।"

Tattvârtha-râja-vârttika, V. 24 (2, 3, 4, 5 and 6).

‡ Compare the Hindu nomenclature, *e.g.*

"ततं वीणादिकं वाद्यमानद्धं मुरजादिकम् ।
वंशादिकन्तु सुषिरं कांस्यतालादिकं घनम् ॥" [Amarakoṣa]

with

"चर्म्मततनात्ततः पुष्करभेरीदर्दुरादिप्रभवः ।
विततः तंत्रीकृतो वीणासुघोषादिसमुद्भवः ।"

Tattvârtha-râja-vârttika, V. 24 (6).

from Karma (producing eight kinds of bondage corresponding to eight kinds of Karma, *viz.*, Jñânâvaraṇîya, Darśanâvaraṇîya, Bedanîya, Mohanîya, Nâma, Gotra, Âyu and Antarâya)* or (2) from No-Karma. This last, again, is of five kinds: (1) Âlapana, (*e.g.*, the fastening of a rope or chain to a chariot, etc.) (2) Âlepana (*e.g.*, painting the walls, etc.) (3) Saṃśleṣa (*e.g.*, joining of pieces of wood together by a carpenter, etc.,) (4) Śarîra (*e.g.*, the union of limbs in a body) and (5) Sarîri (*e.g.*, the union of different bodies).

Vaisrasika Bandha, again, is either (1) Anâdi or eternal, as the union of the whole mass or parts of Dharma, Adharma and Âkâśa† or (2) Âdimat or that which has a beginning having resulted from a definite cause, *e.g.*, the union of different colours in a rainbow.

The whole or half or a quarter of each of Dharma, Adharma and Âkâśâ may be said to contain different parts which are attached to one another.‡ Thus there arise nine kinds of union which are eternal.§

Saukṣmya or fineness is of two kinds: (1) that which is found in the atoms, beyond which there is nothing more fine, and (2) that which is found in other substances and which is of different degrees as the same is relative to that of different substances.||

Sthaulya or grossness is, similarly, of two kinds: (1) grossness of the maximum limit, *e.g.*, that of the whole universe and (2) grossness less than the maximum limit which may be of various degrees.¶

Saṃsthâna or shape is of two kinds: (1) that which can be

* See Commentary on Verse 14 for an explanation of these eight kinds of Karma.

† See Verses 17, 18 and 19 for definitions of Dharma, Adharma and Âkâśâ.

‡ "कृत्स्नो धर्मास्तिकायः, तदर्धं देशः, अर्धार्धं प्रदेशः । एवं अधर्माकाशयोरपि ।"—"धर्माधर्माकाशानामेकशः त्रैविध्यान्नवविधः ।"

Tattvârtha-râja-vârttika, V. 24 (11).

§ "बंधोऽपि द्वेधा विस्रसाप्रयोगभेदात् । आद्यो द्वेधा आदिमदनादिविकल्पात् । विस्रसा विधिविपर्यये निपातः। प्रयोगः पुरुषकायवाङ्मनःसंयोगलक्षणः।"

"प्रायोगिकः द्वेधा अजीवविषयो जीवाजीवविषयश्चेति ।......जीवाजीवविषयः कर्मनोकर्मबन्धः । कर्मबन्धो ज्ञानावरणादिरष्टधा । नो-कर्मबन्धः ...पंचविधः आलपनालेपनसंश्लेषशरीरशरीरिभेदात् ।" [तत्वार्थराजवार्त्तिकम् ।५।२४। (१०।११। १२।१३।)]

|| "सौक्ष्म्यं द्विविधं अन्त्यमापेक्षिकं च ।" [तत्वार्थराजवार्त्तिकम् ।५।२४।१४।]

¶ "तथा स्थौल्यम् ।" [तत्वार्थराजवार्त्तिकम् ।५।२४।१५।]

permanently defined (e.g., as round, square, triangular, etc.) and (2) that which cannot be permanently defined (*e.g.*, the shape of clouds).*

Bheda (division or separation) is of six kinds: (1) Utkara (*e.g.*, sawing a piece of wood), (2) Chûrṇa (*e.g.*, grinding wheat into powder,) (3) Khanda (*e.g.*, breaking up a pitcher into its different parts), (4) Chûrṇika (*e.g.*, separating the chaff from rice, pulses, etc.), (5) Pratara (*e.g.*, dividing mica into many slices) and (6) Aṇuchatana (*e.g.*, causing sparks to fly out from a glowing ball of iron)†.

Tamaḥ is darkness.‡ Chhâya is of two kinds: (1) Inverted images, as seen in mirror, etc. and (2) un-inverted images. In the first of these, the left side becomes right and *vice versa.* Herein lies the difference between the two§ Âtapa is heat caused by the sun, and Udyota is the light resulting from the moon, fire-fly, jewels, etc.||

All these things are mere modifications of Pudgala.

---

* "संस्थानं द्वेधेत्थंलक्षणं अनित्थं-लक्षणं च। वृत्तत्र्यस्रचतुरस्रायतनपरिमंडलादित्थमतोन्यदनित्थम्।" [तत्वार्थराजवार्त्तिकम् ५।२४।१६।१७]

† "भेदः षोढोत्कर-चूर्ण-खण्ड-चूर्णिका-प्रतराणुचटनविकल्पात् ।" [तत्वार्थराजवार्त्तिकम् ।५।२४।१८।]

‡ "तमो दृष्टिप्रतिबंधकारणं। [तत्वार्थराजवार्त्तिकम् ५।२४।१९।]

§ "छाया प्रकाशावरणनिमित्ता। सा द्वेधा तद्वर्णादिविकार-प्रतिबिम्बमात्र-ग्रहणविकल्पात्।" [तत्वार्थराजवार्त्तिकम् ५।२४। (२०।२१।)]

|| आतप उष्णप्रकाशलक्षणः। उद्योतश्चन्द्रमणिखद्योतादिविषयः।" [तत्वार्थराजवार्त्तिकम् ५।२४। (२२।२३)]

CHART III.

TABLE I.

ŚABDA

- **Bhâṣâtmaka.**
  - **Akṣarî-krita.**
  - **Anakṣarî-krita.**
- **Abhâṣâtmaka.**
  - **Prâyogika.**
    - **Tata.**
    - **Vitata.**
    - **Ghana.**
    - **Sauṣira.**
  - **Vaisrasika.**

TABLE II.

BANDHA.

- **Vaisrasika.**
  - **Adimat.**
  - **Anâdimat (9 kinds).**
- **Prâyogika.**
  - **Ajîva-viṣaya.**
  - **Jîvâ jîva-viṣaya.**
    - **Karma-bandha (8 kinds).**
    - **No-karma-bandha.**
      - **Âlapana.**
      - **Âlepana.**
      - **Saṃśleṣa.**
      - **Śarîra.**
      - **Sarîri..**

गइ-परिणयाण धम्मो पुग्गलजीवाण गमणसहयारी ।
तोयं जह मच्छाणं अच्छंता णेव सो णेई ॥१७॥*

Gayi-pariṇayâṇa dhammo puggalajîvâṇa gamaṇasahayârî
Toyaṃ jaha machchhâṇaṃ achchhantâ ṇeva so ṇeî.

Padapâṭha.—जह Jaha, as. गइ-परिणयाण Gai-pariṇayâṇa, engaged in moving. मच्छाणं Machchhâṇaṃ, fish. गमणसहयारी Gamaṇa-sahayârî, assisting the movement. तोयं Toyaṃ, water पुग्गलजीवाण Puggala-jîvâṇa, of the Pudgala and Jîvas. धम्मो Dhammo, Dharma. सो So, that. अच्छंता Achchhantâ, those not moving. णेव Ṇeva, does not. णेई Ṇeî, moves.

17. As water assists the movement of moving fish, so Dharma (assists the movement of moving) Pudgala and Jîva. (But) it does not move (Pudgala and Jîva which are) not moving.

COMMENTARY.

In this verse, we have a description of a peculiar substance known as Dharma in Jain philosophy. It should be remembered that the meaning of the word Dharma, as used by the Jainas, has not the slightest resemblance to thatof the same word in Hindu philosophy.†

The Jaina philosophers mean by Dharma a kind of ether, which is the fulcrum of motion. With the help of Dharma, Pudgala and Jîva move. Dharma does not make these move, but only assists them in their movement when they begin to move. In all works in Jaina literature, we have nearly the same illustration given of Dharma. The illustration is as follows. As fish move in water, without being impelled in their movement by water, but only receiving assistance of the water in their movement, so Pudgala and Jîva move, assisted by

---

* *Sanskrit rendering*:

गतिपरिणतानां धर्म्मः पुद्गलजीवानां गमनसहकारी ।
तोयं यथा मत्स्यानां अगच्छतां नैव स नयति ॥१७॥

Gati-pariṇatânâṃ dharmaḥ pudgalajîvânâṃ gamanasahakârî,
Toyaṃ yathâ matsyânâṃ agachchatâṃ naiva sa nayati—(17).

† **"धर्माद्यः संज्ञा सामायिक्यः ।**
आर्हते हि प्रवचनेऽनादिनिधनेऽर्हदादिभिः यथाकालं, अभिव्यक्तज्ञानदर्शनातिशयप्रकाशैरवद्योतितार्थसारे रूढा एताः संज्ञा ज्ञेयाः। क्रियानिमित्ता वा ।"

[तत्वार्थराजवार्त्तिकम् ।५।१।१७।१८।]

Dharma, but not impelled by it. Dharma has no form, is eternal and void of activity. These characteristics of Dharma has been thus enumerated in Varadhamâna Purâṇa by Sakala-Kîrti :

"जीवपुद्गलयोर्धर्म्मः सहकारी गतेर्म्मतः ।
अमूर्त्तो निष्क्रियो नित्यो मत्स्यानां जलवद् भुवि ॥"

(Canto XVI, verse 29.)

i.e., "Dharma is known to be the helper of motion of Jîva and Pudgala, is formless, inactive and eternal. (It acts like) water to fish in the world."

In Pañchâstikâya Samaysâra we have :

"उदयं जह मच्छाणं गमणाणुग्गहयरं हवदि लोए ।
तह जीवपुग्गलाणं धम्मं दव्वं वियाणेहि ॥"

(Verse 85.)

i.e., "Know that, as water helps the movement of fish, so Dharma (helps the movement of) Jîva and Pudgala."

Amrita Chandra Sûri has written in his Tattvârthasâra, "That is called Dharma which help the motion of things which have begun to move by themselves. Jîvas and Pudgalas resort to Dharma when they are going to move, as fish take the help of water in their movement."

"क्रियापरिणतानां यः स्वयमेव क्रियावताम् ।
आदधाति सहायत्वं स धर्म्मः परिगीयते ॥
जीवानां पुद्गलानां च कर्त्तव्ये गत्युपग्रहे ।
जलवन्मत्स्यगमने धर्म्मः साधारणाश्रयः ॥"

[तत्त्वार्थसारः ३ । ३३ । ३४ ।]

In Jain Kâvyas also we have the same illustration of Dharma, and we shall only quote two such passages here :—

"धर्म्मः स तात्त्विकैरुक्तो यो भवेद् गतिकारणम् ।
जीवादीनां पदार्थानां मत्स्यानामुदकं यथा ॥"

[धर्मशर्माभ्युदयम् । २१ । ८३ ।]

i.e., "That which becomes the fulcrum of motion of substances, like Jîvas, etc., as water is to fish is called Dharma by those versed in the Tattvas."

"जलवन्मत्स्ययानस्य तत्र यो गतिकारणम् ।
जीवादीनां पदार्थानां स धर्म्मः परिवर्णितः ॥
लोकाकाशमभिव्याप्य संस्थितो मूर्त्तिवर्जितः ।
नित्यावस्थितिसंयुक्तः सर्वज्ञज्ञानगोचरः ॥"

[चन्द्रप्रभचरितम् । १८ । ६९–७०]

i.e., "That is called Dharma which is the cause of movement of substances, like Jîvas, etc., as water (is the helper) of the movement of fish. It exists pervading Lokâkâśa, is formless and eternal, and is the object of knowledge of only the omniscient."

Dharma is, therefore, that which, not moving in itself and not imparting motion to anything, helps the movement of Jîva and Pudgala. Without Dharma, the motion of Jîva and Pudgala would be impossible.

ठाणजुदाण अधम्मो पुग्गलजीवाण ठाणसहयारी ।
छाया जह पहियाणं गच्छंता णेव सो धरई ॥ १८ ॥ *

Ṭhâṇajudâṇa adhammo puggalajîvaṇa ṭhâṇasahayârî.
Chhâyâ jaha pahiyâṇaṃ gachchhantâ ṇeva so dharayî—(18.)

Padapâṭha.—जह Jaha, as. छाया Chhâyâ, shadow. पहियाणं Pahiyâṇaṃ, of the travellers. ठाणजुदाण Ṭhâṇajudâṇa, stationary. पुग्गलजीवाण Puggalajîvâṇa, of the Pudgalas and Jîvas. ठाणसहयारी Ṭhâṇa-sahayârî, is assistant in making stationary. अधम्मो Adhammo, Adharma. सो So, that. गच्छंता Gachchhantâ, those moving. णेव Ṇeva, does not. धरई Dharaî, holds.

18. As shadow (assists the staying of) the travellers, (so) Adharma assists the staying of the Pudgalas and Jîvas which are stationary. But that (*i.e.*, Adharma) does not hold back moving (Pudgalas and Jîvas).

COMMENTARY.

Adharma is exactly the opposite of Dharma which has been described in Verse 17. Dharma is the fulcrum of motion, and Adharma is the fulcrum of rest. *Vide*—

"जह हवदि धम्मदव्वं तह तं जाणेह दव्वमधम्मक्खं ।
ठिदि-किरियाजुत्ताणं कारणभूदं तु पुढवीव ॥"

[पञ्चास्तिकायसमयसारः । ८६ ।]

Adharma, like Dharma, is eternal, without form and without

* *Sanskrit rendering*:

स्थानयुतानां अधर्मः पुद्गलजीवानां स्थानसहकारी ।
छाया यथा पथिकानां गच्छतां नैव स धरति ॥ १८ ॥

Sthânayutânâṃ adharmaḥ pudgalajîvânâṃ sthâna-sahakârî.
Chhâyâ yathâ pathikânâṃ gachchhatâṃ naiva sa dharati—(18).

activity. It does not stop the motion of Jîva or Pudgala, but it assists them in staying still, while they are in a state of rest. *Vide*—

"स ह्यकर्त्ताप्यधर्मस्याजीवपुद्गलयोः स्थितेः ।
नित्योऽमूर्त्तः क्रियाहीनः छायेव पथिकाङ्गिनाम् ॥"

[Vardhamâna Purâṇa, XVI. 30.]

The following examples are invariably found in all Jaina works, as illustrating Adharma. First, Adharma is likened to earth which does not stop creatures from moving but becomes a support of them when they are at rest. Secondly, Adharma is said to be like shadow which does not forcibly stop the travellers scorched by the rays of the sun from moving, but assists in their rest, while they of their own accord come to sit in the shade.

Both these examples are given in the Verse 84, Canto XXI of Dharmaśarmâbhyudaya Kâvya :

"छायेव घर्मतप्तानामश्वादीनामिव क्षितिः ।
द्रव्याणां पुद्गलादीनामधर्मः स्थितिकारणम् ॥"

i. e., "Adharma is the cause of rest of Dravyas, Pudgala, etc., as shadow is that of (persons) heated by the rays of the sun, or as the earth is that of (creatures like) horses, etc."

In Tattvârthasâra, Chapter III, Verses 35 and 36, we have :

"स्थित्या परिणतानां तु सचिवत्वं दधाति यः ।
तमधर्मं जिनाः प्राहुर्निरावरणदर्शनाः ॥
जीवानां पुद्गलानाञ्च कर्त्तव्ये स्थित्युपग्रहे ।
साधारणाश्रयोऽधर्मः पृथिवीव गवां स्थितौ ॥"

i.e., "Jivas, whose faith is unclouded, call that to be Adharma which ministers to the staying of Jîvas and Pudgalas when these are prone to rest. Adharma supports all (to rest), like the earth allowing rest to the cows."

In Chandraprabhacharita, Canto XVIII, Verse 71, we have :

"द्रव्याणां पुद्गलादीनामधर्मः स्थितिकारणम् ।
लोकेऽभिव्यापकत्वादिधर्मोऽधर्मोऽपि धर्मवत् ॥"

i.e., "Adharma is the cause of rest of Dravyas, Pudgala, etc. Adharma, like Dharma, has the same characteristics, *viz.*, it pervades Lokâkâśa, etc. (the other qualities are that of being eternal, being without form, and being perceptible only by the omniscient.)

We should therefore remember that, without Dharma, it will be impossible for any substance (Dravya) to move. The universe is divided into two parts : (1) Lokâkâśa, which is pervaded throughout by Dharma and Adharma, and in which movement or rest may therefore happen and (2 Alokâkâśa, which is beyond Lokâkâśa, and in which Dharma and Adharma are absent. We have learnt previously that one of the characteristics of a Jîva is to move upwards. When a Jîva makes an attempt to move upwards, in its gradual stages of development, it is able to do so through the assistance of Dharma. By gradually moving higher and higher, it reaches the limits of Lokâkâśa, beyond which there is no Dharma. Hence, it is bound to stay there. This will explain why in Verse 14 we have said that liberated Jîvas stay at the top of Lokâkâśa and, though possessing the characteristic of having an upward motion, they do not proceed any further.

अवगासदाणजोग्गं जीवादीणं वियाण आयासं ।
जेणं लोगागासं अल्लोगागासमिदि दुविहं ॥ १९ ॥*

Avagâsadâṇajoggaṃ jîvâdîṇaṃ viyâṇa âyâsaṃ
Jeṇaṃ logâgâsaṃ allogâgâsamidi dubihaṃ—(19).

Padapâṭha.—जीवादीणं Jîvâdîṇaṃ, of the Jîvas. अवगासदाणजोग्गं Avagâsadâṇajoggaṃ, capable of allowing space. जेणं Jeṇaṃ, Jaina. आयासं Âyâsaṃ, Âkâśa. वियाण Viyâṇa, know. लोगागासं Logâgâsaṃ, Lokâkâśa. अल्लोगागासं Allogâgâsam, Alokâkâśa. इदि Idi, thus. दुविहं Duvihaṃ, of two kinds.

19. Know that which is capable of allowing space to Jîva, etc., to be Akâśa, according to Jainism. Lokâkâśa and Alokâkâśa, thus (Akâśa is) of two kinds.

COMMENTARY.

The word Âkâśa is thus derived: "That in which the substances, Jîva, etc., are revealed or that which reveals itself is known as Âkâśa," or it may be thus derived: "Âkâśa is that which allows space to other substances."†

In our text, the last of the derivations is adopted, as this clearly

* *Sanskrit rendering:*
अवकाशदानयोग्यं जीवादीनां विजानीहि आकाशम् ।
जैनं लोकाकाशं अलोकाकाशमिति द्विविधम् ॥ १९ ॥
Avakâśadânayogyaṃ jîvâdînâṃ vijânîhi âkâśaṃ,
Jainaṃ Lokâkâśaṃ Alokâkâśamiti dvividhaṃ—(19).

† Vide: आकाशंतेऽस्मिन् द्रव्याणि स्वयं वा काशत इत्याकाशम् । (जीवादीनि द्रव्याणि स्वैः स्वैः पर्यायैः अव्यतिरेकेण यस्मिन्नाकाशंते प्रकाशंते तदाकाशं, स्वयं चात्मीयपर्यायमर्यादया आकाशत इत्याकाशम्) अवकाशदानाद् वा । (अथवा इतरेषां द्रव्याणां अवकाशदानादाकाशमिति पृषोदरादिषु निपातितः शब्दः ।)

[Tattvârtha-râja-vârttika, V. I. 21. 22.]

explains the characteristics of Âkâśa. The chief characteristic of Âkâśa is to allow other substances to enter into or penetrate itself. This entering or penetration is expressed by the word Avagâha, which Akalanka Deva explains as Aṇuprabeśa or interpenetration. Umâ Svâmî has also mentioned this characteristic of Âkâśa, *e.g.*

"आकाशस्यावगाहः ।"

[Tattvârthâdhigama Sûtra v. 18].

i.e., "interpenetrability is the characteristic of Âkâśa."

In Pañchâstikâyasamayasâra, verse 90, we have: "That which gives all the room to all Jîvas, Pudgalas and the rest (*i. e.*, Dharma Adharma and Kâla) is Âkâśa"* In Tattvâthasâra, Chapter iii. Verse 38, we have a similar idea:† "Âkâśa is eternal, pervasive and all objects of the universe exist in it,"‡ and "it has no form."§

Akalanka Deva gives the following example to illustrate the interpenetrability of Âkâśa. He says that as water allows a swan to enter in itself, so Âkâśa allows the other substances to penetrate itself.|| But this example, being taken from the material world, should not be accepted in a strict sense. For, really, a swan displaces some water; but Âkâśa being a subtle substance does not obstruct other substances. To have a better example, let us suppose the empty space between a room to be Âkâśa and the substances Dharma, Adharma etc., to be lights of different lamps. Now, the space in a room can be filled up by the lights of different lamps which intermingle and penetrate the space. In the same manner, Âkâśa can allow the substances, Dharma, etc., to penetrate itself.

Âkâśa is of two kinds: Lokâkâśa and Alokâkâśa. These will be explained in the next verse.

---

* "सव्वेसिं जीवाणं सेसाणं तहय पुग्गलाणं च ।
जं देदि विवरमखिलं तं लोए हवदि आयासं ॥"

† "जीवानां पुद्गलानां च कालस्याधर्मधर्मयोः ।
अवगाहनहेतुत्वं तदिदं प्रतिपद्यते ॥"

‡ "नित्यं व्यापकमाकाशमवगाहैकलक्षणम् ।
चराचराणि भूतानि यत्रासंबाधमासते ॥"

§ "लोकालोकनभोभेदादाकाशोऽत्र द्विधा भवेत् ।
अवकाशप्रदः सर्वद्रव्यानां मूर्त्तिवर्ज्जितः ॥"

[Vardhamána-Purâṇa, XVI. 31.]

|| " यथा जलमवगाहते हंसः ।"

[Tattvârtharâjavârttika. V. 18 (2)]

धम्माधम्मा कालो पुग्गलजीवा य संति जावदिये ।
आयासे सो लोगो तत्तो परदो अलोगुत्तो ॥२०॥ *

Dhammâdhammâ kâlo puggala-jîvâ ya santi jâva-diye.

Âyâse so logo tatto parado alogutto.—(20).

Padapâṭha.—जावदिये Jâvadiye, in which. आयासे Âyâse, in Âkâśa. धम्माधम्मा Dhammâdhammâ, Dharma and Adharma. कालो Kâlo, Kâla. य Ya, and. पुग्गलजीवा Puggalajîvâ, Pudgala and Jîva. संति Santi, exist. सो So, that. लोगो Logo, Lokâkâśa. तत्तो Tatto, that. परदो Parado, beyond. अलोगुत्तो Alogutto, is called Alokâkâśa.

20. Lokâkâśa is that in which Dharma, Adharma, Kâla, Pudgala and Jîva exist. That which is beyond (this Lokâkâśa) is called Alokâkâśa.

COMMENTARY.

"Loka is that place in which happiness and misery are seen as results of virtue or vice, or Loka might be said to be that place in which things are got, or Loka is that place which is perceived by the omniscient."† This is how Akalanka Deva derives the word Loka. Âkâśa with reference to Loka, or Âkâśa similar in extent to Loka is Lokákâśa, and Âkâśa beyond Loka is Alokâkâśa‡.

In the accompanying Plate, we have a representation of Lokâkâśa and Alokâkâśa. Loka or the universe, according to the Jain idea, consists of three divisions—Ûrdha Loka or the upper world,

---

* *Sanskrit rendering:*

धर्माधर्मौ कालः पुद्गलजीवाः च सन्ति यावतिके ।
आकाशे स लोकः ततः परतः अलोकः उक्तः ॥ २० ॥

Dharmâdharmau kâlaḥ pudgalajîvâḥ cha santi jâvatike.
Âkâśe sa lokaḥ tataḥ parataḥ alokaḥ'uktaḥ– (20).

† "यत्र पुण्यपापफललोकनं स लोकः । (पुण्यपापयोः कर्मणोः फलं सुखदुःखलक्षणं यत्रालोक्यते स लोकः) लोकतीति वा लोकः । (लोकति पश्यत्युपलभते अर्थानिति लोकः) लोक्यत इति वा लोकः (सर्वज्ञेनानंताप्रतिहतकेवलदर्शनेन लोक्यते यः स लोकः ।)"
[तत्वार्थराजवार्त्तिकम् ५ । १२ । (१० । १२ । १३ ।)]

‡ "तस्याकाशं लोकाकाशं जलाशयवत् । (लोकस्याकाशं लोकाकाशमिति । ......लोक एवाकाशं लोकाकाशमिति समानाधिकरणलक्षणा वृत्तिः ।)"
[Tattvârtharâjavârttika. V. 12. (17)].

To face Gâthâ No. 20 of DRAVYA - SAMGRAHA Vol. 1 of S.B.J.

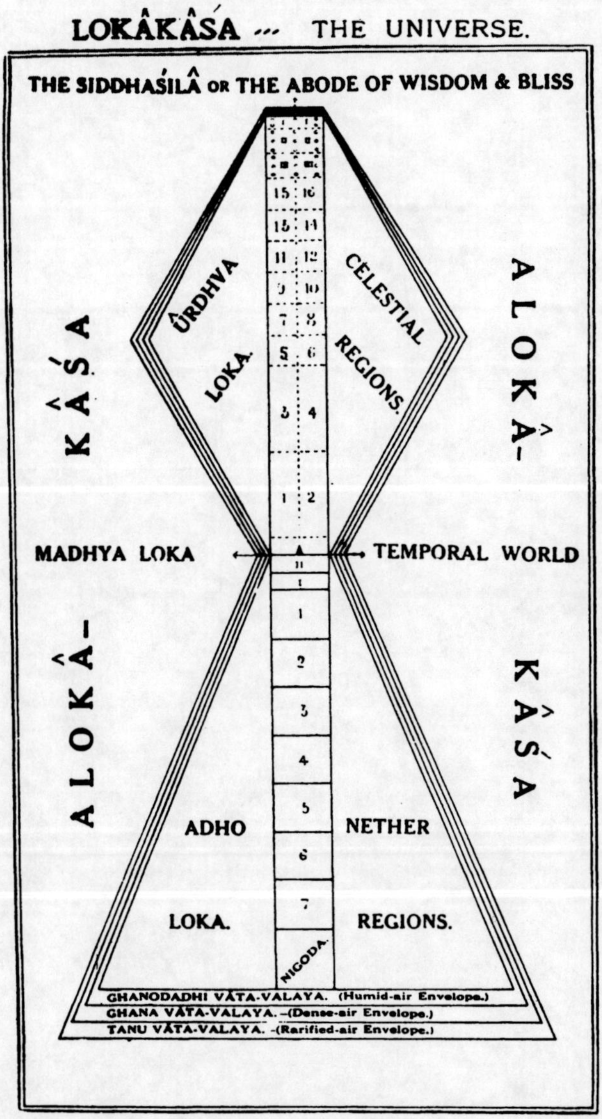

PLATE IX Lokâkâśa containing the Dravyas and Alokâkâśa beyond it

Madhya Loka or the middle world and Adho Loka or the lower world. The first is the abode of celestial beings, the second of men and of other creatures, and the third of the inmates of hell. Surrounding these Lokas, which are situated one above the other, are three layers of air, the inner being humid, the middle dense and the outer rarified. Within the envelope of these layers, there is Lokâkâśa—an invisible substance which allows space to other substances and is equal in extent to the Lokas. In this Lokâkâśa, Jîva, Pudgala, Dharma, Adharma and Kâla exist.*

Beyond this Lokâkâśa, there is Alokâkâśa which is eternal, infinite, formless, without activity and perceptible only by the omniscient.† In Alokâkâśa. there is only the substance Âkâśa and not Dharma, Adharma, Kâla, Pudgala or Jîva.

दव्वपरिवट्टरूवो जो सो कालो हवेइ ववहारो।
परिणामादीलक्खो वट्टणलक्खो य परमट्ठो ॥२१॥‡

Davvaparibaṭṭarûvo jo so kâlo havei vavahâro.
Pariṇâmâdîlakkho vaṭṭaṇalakkho ya paramaṭṭho—(21).

Padapâṭha.—जो Jo, which. दव्वपरिवट्टरूवो Davvaparivaṭṭarûvo, helping changes in substances. परिणामादिलक्खो Pariṇâmâdilakkho, understood from modifications, etc. सो So, that. ववहारो Vavahâro, Vyavahâra. कालो Kâlo, time. हवेइ Havei, is. य Ya, which. वट्टणलक्खो Vaṭṭaṇalakkho, understood from continuity. परमट्ठो Paramaṭṭho, real.

---

* "धर्माधर्मयुताः कालपुद्गलाः जीवपूर्वकाः ।
खे यावत्यत्र तिष्ठन्ति लोकाकाशः स उच्यते ॥"
[Vardhamâna Purâṇa XVI. 32].

"जीवा पुग्गलकाया धम्माधम्मा य लोगदोणण्णा ।
तत्तो अणण्णमण्णं आयासं अंतवदिरित्तं ॥"
[Pañchâstikâyasamayasâra. Verse 91].

"पुद्गलादि-पदार्थानामवगाहैकलक्षणः ।
लोकाकाशः स्मृतो व्यापी शुद्धाकाशो बहिस्ततः ॥"
[Dharmaśarmâbhyudaya XXI. 86].

† "तस्माद् बहिरनन्तो स्यादाकाशो द्रव्यवर्जितः ।
नित्योऽमूर्त्तो क्रियाहीनः सर्वज्ञदृष्टिगोचरः ॥"
[Vardhamâṇa-Purâṇa XVI. 33].

‡ *Sanskrit rendering:*

द्रव्यपरिवर्त्तनरूपः यः स कालः भवेत् व्यवहारः ।
परिणामादिलक्ष्यः वर्त्तनालक्षणा च परमार्थः ॥ २१ ॥

Dravyaparivarttanarûpaḥ yaḥ sa kâlaḥ bhavet vyavahâraḥ.
Pariṇâmâdilakṣyaḥ varttanâlakṣaṇâ cha paramârthaḥ—(21).

21. Vyavahâra Kâla (Time from the ordinary point of view) is that which helps to produce changes in substances and which is known from modifications (produced in substances), while Paramârthika (*i.e.*, real) Kâla is understood from continuity.

COMMENTARY.

Real time is, according to the Jainâ view, that which assists the changes in substances. To give a concrete example, we might say that the stone under a potter's wheel assists in the movement of the wheel. The stone here does not impart motion to the wheel, but without this stone such a kind of motion would not have been possible. Similarly, time, according to Jainism, assists in the changes produced in substances, though it does not cause the same. The Jaina view is, that time does not cause the changes which are produced in the substances, but indirectly aids the production of such changes. This is real time. But time, from the ordinary point of view, consists in hours, minutes, seconds, etc., by which we call a thing to be new or old according to changes produced in the same.* These two kinds of time are technically called Kâla and Samaya respectively. In all the

* "नवजीर्णादिपर्यायैर्द्रव्याणां यः प्रवर्त्तकः ।
समयादिमयः कालो व्यवहाराभिदोऽस्ति सः ॥"

[वर्द्धमानपुराणम् । १६ । ३४ ।]

It is said that Vyâvahârika Kâla is known from Pariṇâma (modification) Kriyâ (action) Paratva (distance) and Aparatva (nearness) of substances. *Vide*-

"व्यावहारिककालस्य परिणामस्तथा क्रिया ।
परत्वं चापरत्वं च लिङ्गान्याहुर्महर्षयः ॥
स्वजातेरविरोधेन विकारो यो हि वस्तुनः ।
परिणामः स निर्दिष्टोऽ परिष्पन्दात्मिकोऽजिनैः ॥
प्रयोगविस्रसाभ्यां या निमित्ताभ्यां प्रजायते ।
द्रव्यस्य सा परिज्ञेया परिष्पन्दात्मिका क्रिया ॥
परत्वं विप्रकृष्टत्वमितरत् सन्निकृष्टता ।
ते च कालकृते ग्राह्ये कालप्रकरणादिह ॥"

[तत्वार्थसारः । ३ । ४५—४८ ॥]

Angas of the Jainas we find the phrase, "In that Kâla and in that Samaya" (**"तेणं कालेणं तेणं समएणं"**). Kâla is eternal, void of form and without beginning or end. Kâla has no varieties. Samaya has a beginning and an end, and consists of varieties, *viz.*, hour, minute, second, etc. Kâla may be said to be the substantial cause (Upâdâna Kâraṇa) of Samaya.

"Some say that there is no other Kâla, except that which consists of acts comprised by the rising and setting of the sun, etc."* That is to say, some deny that there is a real time (Nîśchaya Kâla) behind the apparent time (Vyavahâra Kâla). But this view is untenable, for there must be a time having the characteristics of a substance different from the acts mentioned above. There must be something behind to help these acts. Though in ordinary parlance we apply the word time to such acts, real time is not identical with the same.†

Vartanâ or continuity is the perception of the existence of a substance understood from changes produced in the same in separate moments of time.‡ For example, we put rice in a pot containing water and place the same on a fire. After some time, we find that

---

* **"क्रियां दिनकरादीनामुदयास्तमयादिकाम् ।**
प्रविहायापरः कालो नास्तीत्येके प्रचक्षते ॥"
[चन्द्रप्रभचरितम् । १८ । ७५ ।]

† **"तन्न युक्तं क्रियायां हि लोके काल इति ध्वनिः ।**
प्रवृत्तो गौणवृत्त्यैव वाहीक इव गोध्वनिः ॥
न च मुख्याहृते गौणकल्पना नरसिंहवत् ।
तस्माद्द्रव्यस्वभावोऽन्यो मुख्यः कालोऽस्ति कश्चन ॥"
[चन्द्रप्रभचरितम् । १८ । ७६ । ७७ ।]

"कालो दिनकरादीनामुदयास्त-क्रियात्मकः ।
औपचारिक एवासौ मुख्यकालस्य सूचकः ॥ "
[धर्मशर्माभ्युदयम् । २१ । ८९ ।]

‡ **"प्रतिद्रव्यपर्यायमन्तर्नीतैकसमया स्वसत्तानुभूतिर्वर्त्तना ।"**
[तत्वार्थराजवार्त्तिकम् ।५।२२।४]

"अन्तर्नीतैकसमया प्रतिद्रव्यविपर्ययम् ।
अनुभूतिः स्वसत्तायाः स्मृता सा खलु वर्त्तना ॥"
[तत्वार्थसारः ।३।४१]

the rice has been boiled. From this we infer that slow changes must have been going on in the rice from the moment we put it in the raw state in the vessel, till we saw it in the boiled condition. Throughout this period an existence is to be inferred. This perception of existence is called Vartanâ. Of course, this inference of existence of real time can only be made from the effects of apparent Time (Vyavahârika Kâla), *viz.*, the changes in the rice.*

लोयायपदेसे इक्केक्के जे ट्ठिया हु इक्केक्का ।
रयणाणं रासीमिव ते कालाणू असंखदव्वाणि ॥२२॥†

Loyâyapadese ikkekke je ṭṭhiâ hu ikkekkâ,
Rayaṇâṇaṃ râsîmiva te kâlâṇû asaṃkhadav-vâṇi—(22).

Padapâṭhâ.—इक्केक्के Ikkekke, in each. लोयायपदेसे Loyâyapadese, Pradeśa of Lokâkâśa. जे Je, which. इक्केक्का Ikkekkâ, one by one. कालाणू Kâlâṇû, points of Time. रयणाणं Rayaṇâṇaṃ, jewels. रासीमिव Râsîmiva, heaps. हु Hu, certainly. ट्ठिया Ṭṭhiâ, are. ते Te, that. असंखदव्वाणि Asaṃkhadavvâṇi, innumerable substances.

22. Those innumerable substances which exist one by one in each Pradeśa of Lokâkâśa, like heaps of jewels, are points of time.

COMMENTARY.

Kâla or time consists of minute points or particles which never mix with one another, but are always separate. The universe (Lokâkâśa) is full of these particles of time, no space within it being void of the same. It need not be mentioned that these particles of time are invisible, innumerable, inactive and without form.

In all the Jaina works, these particles have been compared to innumerable jewels. This example illustrates the fact that the

---

* "सानुमानिकी व्यावहारिकदर्शनात् पाकवत् ।"
[तत्वार्थराजवार्त्तिकम् ।५।२१।५।]

† *Sanskrit rendering:*

लोकाकाशप्रदेशे एकैकस्मिन् ये स्थिताः हि एकैकाः ।
रत्नानां राशिः इव ते कालाणवः असंख्यद्रव्याणि ॥२२॥

Lokâkâśa—pradeśe ekaikasmin ye sthitâḥ hi ekaikâḥ,
Ratnânâṃ raśiḥ iva te kâlâṇavaḥ asaṃkhya-dravyâṇi—(22).

particles of time never mix up with one another. In Tattvârthasâra, we have—

"एकैकवृत्त्या प्रत्येकमणवस्तस्य निष्क्रियाः ।
लोकाकाश-प्रदेशेषु रत्नराशिरिव स्थिताः ॥" [३।४४]

i.e., "The particles of that (Time) exist each in its own capacity, like heaps of jewels in the Pradeśas of the Lokâkâśa (universe), and are without activity."

In Vardhamâna Purâṇa, we have—

"लोकाकाशप्रदेशे ये ह्येकैका अणवः स्थिताः ।
भिन्नभिन्नप्रदेशस्था रत्नानामिव राशयः ।"

[Canto XVI., Verse 35.]

i.e., "The particles exist separately in different Pradeśas of Lokâkâśa, like heaps of jewels in different places."

This characteristic of Time differentiates it from the other five kinds of substances; for, while the former consists of separable particles, the latter are collections of indivisible and inseparable parts.

**एवं छव्भेयमिदं जीवाजीवप्पभेददो दव्वं ।
उत्तं कालविजुत्तं णायव्वा पंच अत्थिकाया दु ॥२३॥***

Evaṃ chhavbheyamidaṃ jîvâjîvappabhedado davvaṃ,
Uttaṃ kâlavijuttaṃ ṇâyavvâ pañcha atthikâyâ du. (23).

Padapâṭha.—एवं Evaṃ, in this manner. जीवाजीवप्पभेददो Jîvâjîvappabhedado, according to the subdivisions of Jîva and Ajîva. इदं Idaṃ, this. दव्वं Davvam, Dravya. छव्भेयं Chhavbheyaṃ, of six kinds. उत्तं Uttaṃ, is called. दु Du, and. कालविजुत्तं Kâla-vijuttaṃ, without Kâla. पंच Pañcha, five. अत्थिकाया Atthikâyâ, Astikâyas. णायव्वा Ṇâyavvâ, to be known.

23. In this manner, this Dravya is said to be of six kinds, according to the subdivisions of Jîva and Ajîva. The five, without Kâla, should be understood to be Astikâyas.

---

* *Sanskrit rendering*:

एवं षड्भेदं इदं जीवाजीवप्रभेदतः द्रव्यम् ।
उक्तं कालवियुक्तं ज्ञातव्याः पञ्च अस्तिकायाः तु ॥२३॥

Evaṃ ṣaḍbhedaṃ idaṃ jîvâjîvaprabhedataḥ dravyaṃ,
Uktaṃ kâlaviyuktaṃ jñâtavyâḥ pañcha astikâyâḥ tu.—(23).

COMMENTARY.

Dravya is divided into Jîva and Ajîva. Ajîva, again, is subdivided into Pudgala, Dharma, Adharma, Âkâśa and Kâla. These five Ajîvas, with Jîva, make up the six varieties of Dravya.

DRAVYA.

Jîva. Ajîva.

Pudgala. Dharma. Adharma. Âkâśa. Kâla.

Of these six varieties, Jîva, Pudgala, Dharma, Adharma and Âkâśa are technically known as the five Astikâyas.* The meaning of the word Astikâya will be understood from Verse 24, Page 65 and the reason why Kâla, the sixth variety of Dravya, is not called Astikâya, will be explained in Verse 25. Page 66.

संति जदो तेणेदे अत्थीति भणंति जिणवरा जम्हा ।
काया इव वहुदेसा तम्हा काया य अत्थिकाया य ॥२४॥†

Santi jado teṇede atthîti bhaṇanti jiṇavarâ jamhâ,
Kâyâ iva vahudesâ tamhâ kâyâ ya atthikâyâ ya.—(24).

* Compare:

"धर्माधर्मौ नभः कालः पुद्गलश्चेति पञ्चधा ।
अजीवः कथ्यते सम्यग् जिनैस्तत्वार्थदर्शिभिः ॥
षड्द्रव्याणीति वर्ण्यन्ते समं जीवेन तान्यपि ।
विना कालेन तान्येव यान्ति पञ्चास्तिकायताम् ॥"
[धर्मशर्माभ्युदयम् ।२१।८१। ८२]

Also—

"धर्माधर्मावथाकाशं कालः पुद्गल इत्यपि ।
अजीवः पञ्चधा ज्ञेयो जिनागमविशारदैः ॥
एतान्येव सजीवानि षड् द्रव्याणि प्रचक्षते ।
कालहीनानि पञ्चास्तिकाया स्तान्येव कीर्त्तिताः ॥"
[चन्द्रप्रभचरितम् ।१८।६७।६८।]

† *Sanskrit rendering:*

सन्ति यतः तेन अस्ति इति भणन्ति जिनवराः यस्मात् ।
काया इव बहुदेशाः तस्मात् कायाः च अस्तिकायाः च ॥२४॥

Santi yataḥ tena asti iti bhaṇanti jinavarâḥ Gasmât,
Kâyâ iva vahudeśâḥ tasmât kâyâḥ cha astikâyâḥ, cha.—(24).

Padapâṭha.—जदो Jado, because, एदे Ede, these. संति Santi, exist. तेण Teṇa, on that account. जिणवरा Jiṇavarâ, the great Jiṇas. अत्थीति Atthîti, as "Asti." भणंति Bhaṇanti, say. य Ya, and. जम्हा Jamhâ, because. काया Kâyâ, bodies. इव Iva, like. बहुदेसा Vahudesâ, having many Pradeśas. तम्हा Tamhâ, therefore काया Kâyâ, Kâyas. य Ya, and. अत्थिकाया Atthikâyâ, Astikâyas.

24. As these exist, they are called "Asti" by the great Jinas, and because (they have) many Pradeśas, like bodies, therefore [they are called] Kâyas. [Hence these are called] Astikâyas.

COMMENTARY.

"Asti-kâya"† consists of two words, "Asti" and "Kâya." "Asti" literally means "exists." Now, the five kinds of substances, *viz.*, Jîva, Pudgala, Dharma, Adharma, and Âkâśa always exist; hence, while mentioning any of these, one might say "it exists." Again, each of these substances has many Pradeśas, like bodies. Hence, each of these might also be said to be "Kâya" (literally, body). These two characteristics being combined, each of the aforesaid five substances are named 'Astikâya' or 'that which exists and has different Pradeśas like a body' It should be remembered that to be an Astikâya, a substance must have both these characteristics. The substance Kâla, (Time) though having the first characteristic (*viz.* existence), is not called Astikâya, because it does not have many Pradeśas.

To be more clear, first let us understand what is meant by a Pradeśa. Pradeśa has been defined in Verse 27 to be that part of space which is obstructed by one indivisible atom of matter. A Pradeśa can contain not only atoms of matter, but of particles of other substances also. Thus each of the substances have Pradeśas. Now, Jîva, Pudgala, Dharma, Adharma and Âkâśa have many Pradeśas, as these consist of many indivisible and inseparable parts, or, in other words, the particles of these are not separate, but are mixed up or capable of being mixed up. Hence, as we are unable to locate these particles, in definite Pradeśas, these substances can be said to

† The word Astikâya is thus derived:

"अस्ति इति तिङन्तप्रतिरूपकमव्ययम् ।"

"Asti" is an indeclinable (Avyaya) resembling a verb in form.

That which acts like Kâya is "Kâya."

(काय इव आचरति इति कायः । आचारार्थे क्विप् ।)

That in which there is existence (Asti) and Kâya is called Astikâya.

occupy many Pradeśas. But Kâla consists of particles which never mix up, and consequently each of these particles occupies a particular Pradeśa. Hence Kâla is said to have one Pradeśa only. But the other substances Jîva, Pudgala, Dharma, Adharma and Âkâśa having no separable and distinct particles occupying distinct Pradeśas, are said to be of many Pradeśas.

Kâya is that which has many Pradeśas. The five substances, Jîva, Pudgala, Dharma, Adharma and Akâśa have many Pradeśas, and hence these are called Kâyas ; but Kâla, having but a single Pradeśa, is not called so. This is the reason why Kâla is not called an "Astikâya."

होंति असंखा जीवे धम्माधम्मे अणंत आयासे ।
मुत्तेतिविहपदेसा कालस्सेगो ण तेण सो काओ ॥२५॥*

Honti asaṃkhâ jîve dhammâdhamme aṇanta âyâse.
Mutte tivaha padesâ kâlassego ṇa teṇa so kâyo—(25).

Padapâṭha.—जीवे Jîve, in Jîva. धम्माधम्मे Dhammâdhamme, in Dharma and Adharma. असंखा Asaṃkhâ, innumerable. पदेसा Padesâ, Pradeśas. होंति Honti, are. आयासे Âyâse, in Âkâśa. अणंत Aṇanta, infinite. मुत्ते Mutte, in that which has form. तिविह Tiviha, of three sorts. कालस्स Kâlassa, of Kâla. एगो Ego, one. तेण Teṇa, for that. सो So, that. काओ Kâyo, having body. ण Ṇa, not.

25. In Jîva and in Dharma and Adharma, the Pradeśas are innumerable, in Âkâśa (the Pradeśas are) infinite and in that which has form (*viz.*, Pudgala) (these are) of three kinds, (*viz.*, numerable, innumerable and infinite). Kâla (Time) has one (Pradesa). Therefore, it is not (called) Kâya.

COMMENTARY.

Every kind of substance is made up of ultimate indivisible particles. The space occupied by one such particle is known as Pradeśa. Now, the substances, Jîva, Dharma and Adharma have

---

* *Sanskrit rendering* :

भवन्ति असंख्याः जीवे धर्माधर्मयोः अनन्ताः आकाशे ।
मूर्त्ते त्रिविधाः प्रदेशाः कालस्य एकः न तेन स कायः ॥ २५ ॥

Bhavanti asaṃkhyâḥ jîve dharmâdharmayoḥ anantâḥ âkâśe,
Mûrtte trividhâḥ pradeśâḥ kâlasya ekaḥ na tena sa kâyaḥ (25).

innumerable Pradeśas.* That is to say, the Pradeśas of Jîva, Dharma and Adharma are beyond calculation. Lokâkâśa or the universe contains innumerable Pradeśas and, as Jîva can fill up the whole of the universe by expansion, it is said to contain innumerable Pradeśas. Dharma and Adharma also pervade all parts of the universe, as oil pervades the whole portion of a mustard seed.† Hence these two substances also have innumerable Pradeśas. Âkâśa is infinite, for it not only pervades the universe, but is even existent beyond it; hence its Pradeśas are infinite. The distinction between innumerable and infinite Pradeśas consists in this that, while the former have a limit, though it is beyond the power of even an omniscient being to count them, the latter is without limits.

It may be urged that, without knowing the number of the Pradeśas belonging to Âkâśa, how can one become omniscient? Akalanka Bhatta has replied to this that, to be ominiscient, it is sufficient to know that these are innumerable.

When we say that Pradeśas of such and such a substance are innumerable, we mean that in reality these are incapable of being counted by anyone. We are not speaking this with reference to the ordinary human beings who have limited powers of perception, but with reference to all beings.‡ Hence, it must be supposed that an omniscient being only knows that Pradeśas of such substances are innumerable. This is also the case when we speak of the infinite Pradeśas.

---

* "असंख्येयाः प्रदेशा धर्माधर्मैकजीवानाम् ।"
[तत्वार्थाधिगमसूत्रम् ५ । ८ ।]
"एकस्य जीवद्रव्यस्य धर्माधर्मास्तिकाययोः ।
असंख्येयप्रदेशत्वमेतेषां कथितं पृथक् ॥"
[तत्वार्थसारः । ३ । १९ ।]

† "संहाराच्च विसर्पाच्च प्रदेशानां प्रदीपवत् ।
जीवस्तु तदसंख्येयभागादीनवगाहते ॥
लोकाकाशे समस्तेऽपि धर्माधर्मास्तिकाययोः ।
तिलेषु तैलवत् प्राहुरवगाहं महर्षयः ।"
[तत्वार्थसारः । ३ । १४ । २३ ।]

‡ "संख्याविशेषातीतत्वादसंख्येयाः ।"
"तदनुपलब्धेरसर्वज्ञत्वप्रसंग इति चेन्न तेनात्मनावसिततत्वात् ।"
[तत्वार्थराजवार्त्तिकम् । ५ । ८ । १ । ३ ।]

Pudgala has Pradeśas which are numerable, innumerable and infinite. To be more explicit, Pudgala or matter consists of ultimate indivisible particles which we might call atoms, remembering, however, that these atoms are more fine than the atoms as understood in the modern science. Now, two or more atoms of matter may combine and produce what is technically known as a Skandha.† A Skandha may contain two, four, six, a hundred, a million or more atoms. The Pradeśas or spaces obstructed by atoms in the state of Skandha can, therefore be counted, and hence we might say in this respect that matter (Pudgala) has numerable Pradeśas. From another point of view, if we do away with the combination which produce Skandhas and suppose the atoms to exist separately, contemplating a division, Pudgala should be understood to have innumerable atoms ; for Pudgala, as mentioned before, exists throughout Lokâkâśa or the universe. Again, Pudgala may be said to have infinite Pradeśas also from another point of view, *viz.*, the atoms of matter in a subtle state may be considered to be infinite.

If a doubt be started that how can infinite atoms exist in finite Lokâkâśa, we reply that atoms in a subtle state, though infinite, can exist in one Pradeśa of Âkâśa, though in the gross state this is not possible.‡ Thus matter in subtle state may be said to possess infinite Pradeśas.

It has already been mentioned in the Commentary on Verse 24 that Kâla has only one Pradeśa, and this is the reason why we do not call it Kâya, for a Kâya is that which has more than one Pradeśa.

एयपदेसो वि अणू णाणाखंधप्पदेसदो होदि ।
बहुदेसो उवयारा तेण य काओ भणंति सव्वण्हु ॥२६।*

Eyapadeso vi aṇû ṇâṇâkhandhappadesado hodi.

---

† "अणवः स्कन्धाश्च ।" "भेदसंघातेभ्य उत्पद्यन्ते ।"
"भेदादणुः ।" "भेदसंघाताभ्यां चाक्षुषः ।"
[तत्वार्थाधिगमसूत्रम् । ५ । २५—२८ ।]

‡ "अधिकरणविरोधादानन्त्याभाव इति चेन्न सूक्ष्मपरिणामावगाहनसामर्थ्यात् ।
[तत्वार्थराजवार्त्तिकम् । ५ । १ । ३]

* *Sanskrit rendering :*

एकप्रदेशः अपि अणुः नानास्कन्धप्रदेशतः भवति ।
बहुदेशः उपचारात् तेन च कायः भणन्ति सर्वज्ञाः ॥ २६ ॥
Ekapradeśaḥ api aṇuḥ nânâskandhapradeśataḥ bhavati.
Vahudeśaḥ upachârât tena cha kâyaḥ bhaṇanti sarvajñâḥ—(26).

Bahudeso uvayârâ teṇa ya kâyo bhaṇanti savvaṇhu—(26.)

Padapâṭha.—एयपदेसोवि Eyapadesovi, though of one Pradeśa. अणू Aṇû, atom. णाणाखंधप्पदेसदो Ṇâṇâkhandhappadesado, on account of being Pradeśa of many Skandhas. बहुदेसो Bahudeso, of many Pradeśas. होदि Hodi, becomes. तेण Teṇa, therefore. य Ya, and. सव्वण्हु Savvaṇhu, the omniscient. उवयारा Uvayârâ, ordinarily. काओ Kâyo, Kâya. भणंति Bhaṇanti, say.

26. An atom (of Pudgala), though having one Pradeśa, becomes of many Pradeśas, through being Pradeśa in many Skandhas. For this reason, from the ordinary point of view, the omniscient ones call (it to be) Kâya.

COMMENTARY.

It may be urged that, as each particle of Kâla occupies a separate Pradeśa, so we have said that Kâla has one Pradeśa only; in the same manner, each atom of matter occupies one Pradeśa, and consequently matter might also be said to have only one Pradeśa. To this, we reply that it is true that a single atom of matter occupies a single Pradeśa, but this atom may combine with other atoms and form different Skandhas which have many Pradeśas. With reference to this stage, an atom may be said to have many Pradeśas. For this reason, from the ordinary point of view, we recognise even one atom to have many Pradeśas. And, as that which has many Pradeśas is called Kâya, so this atom also is known as Kâya.

The atoms in matter are capable of combining with one another and form Skandhas, but particles of Time cannot combine in this manner. It has been mentioned before that each particle of Time exists separately. Hence, though from the ordinary point view we may say an atom of matter to have many Pradeśas with reference to its existence in a Skandha stage, we cannot say that a particle of Time in the same manner contains many Pradeśas.

जावदियं आयासं अविभागीपुग्गलाणुवट्ठद्धं ।
तं खु पदेसं जाणे सव्वाणुट्ठाणदाणरिहं ॥ २७ ॥*

Jâvadiyaṃ âyâsaṃ avibhâgîpuggalâṇuvaṭṭhaddhaṃ,

* *Sanskrit rendering*:
यावन्मात्रं आकाशं अविभागिपुद्गलाण्ववष्टब्धम् ।
तं खलु प्रदेशं जानीहि सर्वाणुस्थानदानार्हम् ॥ २७ ॥
Yâvanmâtraṃ âkâśaṃ avibhâgipudgalâṇvavaṣṭavdhaṃ,
Taṃ khalu pradeśaṃ jânîhi sarvâṇusthânadânârhaṃ—(27).

Taṃ khu padesaṃ jâṇe savvâṇuṭṭhâṇadâṇarihaṃ.—(27)

Padapâṭha.—जावदियं Jâvadiyaṃ, which portion. आयासं Âyâsaṃ, Âkâśa. अविभागीपुग्गलाणुवट्ठद्धं Avibhâgîpuggalâṇuvaṭṭhaddhaṃ, is obstructed by one indivisible atom of Pudgala. तं Taṃ, that. खु Khu, surely. सव्वाणुट्ठाणदाणरिहं Savvâṇuṭṭhâṇadâṇarihaṃ, capable of giving space to particles of all. पदेसं Padesaṃ, Pradeśa. जाणे Jaṇe, know.

27. Know that (to be) surely Pradeśa which is obstructed by one indivisible atom of Pudgala and which can give space to all particles.

COMMENTARY.

We have already mentioned more than once what is meant by a Pradeśa. In this verse, we have a definition of Pradeśa. That portion of Âkâśa which is obstructed by one indivisible ultimate atom of matter is known as a Pradeśa. In such a Pradeśa of Lokâkâśa, one Pradeśa of Dharma, one Pradeśa of Adharma, one particle of Kâla and innumerable atoms of matter, or even Skandhas in a subtle state may exist.* The characteristic of Âkâśa is to give space to all these.

आसवबंधणसंवरणिज्जरमोक्खा सपुण्णपावा जे ।
जीवाजीवविसेसा ते वि समासेण पभणामो ॥ २८ ॥†

Âsavabandhaṇasaṃvaraṇijjaramokkhâ sapuṇṇapâvâ je,
Jîvâjîvavisesâ te vi samâseṇa pabhaṇâmo—(28).

Padapâṭha.—जे Je, those. सपुण्णपावा Sapuṇṇapâvâ, with Puṇya and Pâpa. आसवबंधणसंवरणिज्जरमोक्खा Âsava-bandhaṇa-saṃvara-ṇjjara-mokkhâ, Âsrava, Bandha,

* "लोकाकाशस्य तस्यैकप्रदेशादींस्तथा पुनः ।
पुद्गला अवगाहन्ते इति सर्वज्ञशासनम् ॥
अवगाहनसामर्थ्यात् सूक्ष्मत्वपरिणामिनः ।
तिष्ठन्त्येकप्रदेशेऽपि बहवोऽपि हि पुद्गलाः ॥"
[तत्वार्थसारः । ३ । २५ । २६ ।]

† *Sanskrit rendering:*

आस्रवबन्धनसंवरनिर्जरामोक्षाः सपुण्यपापाः ये ।
जीवाजीवविशेषाः तान् अपि समासेन प्रभणामः ॥ २८ ॥

Âsrava-bandhana-saṃvara nirjarâ-mokṣâḥ sapuṇyapâpâḥ ye.
Jîvâjîvaviśeṣâḥ tân api samâsena prabhaṇâmaḥ—(28).

Saṃvara, Nirjarâ and Mokṣa. जीवाजीवविसेसा Jîvâjîva-visesâ, varieties of Jîva and Ajîva. तेवि Tevi, those also. समासेन Samâsena, briefly. पभणामो Pabhaṇâmo, say.

28. We shall describe briefly those varieties of Jîva and Ajîva also which are (known as) Âsrava, Bandha, Saṃvara, Nirjarâ and Mokṣa, with Puṇya and Pâpa.

COMMENTARY.

The author now takes up the subject of Âsrava, Bandha, Saṃvara, Nirjarâ, Mokṣa, Puṇya and Pâpa. The first five together with Jîva & Ajîva are commonly known as the seven Tattvas of Jainism. Adding Puṇya and Pâpa to these, we get the nine Padârthas of Jainism. Each of these seven will be taken up and discussed one by onc in Verses 29-38.

आसवदि जेण कम्मं परिणामेणप्पणो स विगणेओ ।
भावासवो जिणुत्तो कम्मासवणं परो होदि ॥ २९ ॥*

Âsavadi jeṇa kammaṃ pariṇâmeṇappaṇo sa viṇṇeo,
Bhâvâsavo jiṇutto kammâsavaṇaṃ paro hodi—(29).

Padapâṭha.—अप्पणो Appaṇo, of the soul. जेण Jeṇa, that. परिणामेण Pariṇâmeṇa, modification. कम्मं Kammaṃ, Karma. आसवदि Âsavadi, gets in. स Sa, that. जिणुत्तो Jiṇutto, called by the Jiṇa. भावासवो Bhâvâsavo, Bhâvâsrava. विण्णेओ Viṇṇeo, to be known. कम्मासवणं Kammâsavaṇaṃ, influx of Karmas. परो Paro, the next. होदि Hodi, is.

29. That modification of the soul by which Karma gets into (it), is to be known as Bhâvâsrava, as told by the Jîṇa, and the other (kind of Âsrava) is the influx of Karma.

COMMENTARY.

Âsrava has been defined to be the cause of the bondage of Karma, *i.e.*, that by which the Karmas enter the soul.† Elsewhere,

* *Sanskrit rendering :*

आस्रवति येन कर्म परिणामेन आत्मनः स विज्ञेयः ।
भावास्रवः जिनोक्तः कर्मास्रवणं परः भवति ॥ २९ ॥

Âsravati yena Karma pariṇâmena âtmanaḥ sa vijñeyaḥ.
Bhâvâsravaḥ jinoktaḥ karmâsravaṇaṃ paraḥ bhavati—(29).

† "आश्रवन्ति प्रविशन्ति येन कर्माणि आत्मनि इति आश्रवः कर्मबन्धहेतुरिति भावः ।"

[Abhayadeva's Commentary on Sthânânga.]

we have "those from which Karmas flow are called Âsravas."* These definitions are in keeping with the derivative meaning of the word Âsrava, and throughout Jaina literature the word Âsrava is used in this sense. We should mention in this connection that this use of the word Âsrava, in its original and derivative sense, has been supposed to support the view that Jainism was prevalent before Buddhism. "We meet with many terms which are used alike by the Jainas and the Buddhists. Among them there is one which the Buddhists must have borrowed from the Jainas. The term Âsrava, in Pali Âsava, is, according to the Buddhists, synonymous with Kleśa, and it means human passion, sin, corruption, depravity. Âsrava, etymologically, meant 'flowing in' or 'influx,' and it was difficult to imagine why the Buddhists should have chosen just that word to denote sin, corruption, depravity. Even if taken in a metaphorical sense, it is not easy to see how, from the Buddhist point of view, it could come to express the idea of depravity and sin, for it might be asked what is to flow in and where is it to flow in? But with the Jainas, Âsrava retained its etymological meaning and it adequately exprsssed the idea denoted by the term Âsrava, for, according to Jaina philosophy, Âsrava meant the influx of matter into the soul. Hence the term Âsrava had its literal meaning, for there really was something flowing in, and the result of it was defilement or depravity. It is therefore easily imaginable that, in common parlance, Âsrava should have got the meaning defilement or depravity, irrespective of the etymology; and this was just what happened to the word Âsrava before it was received into Buddhist terminology. But the word could never have been used in its derivative meaning (sin), if it had not before been used in its literal meaning. And since the Jainas used the word in its original, *i.e.*, literal or etymological meaning, those who used it in the derived meaning must have adopted it from the Jainas. Thus the use of the word Âsrava by the Buddhists is a proof of their posteriority with regard to the Jainas."†

Umâsvâmi says that Âsrava results from the actions of the

* "अभिविधिना श्रौति श्रवति कर्म येभ्यस्ते आश्रवाः।"

[Abhayadeva's Commentary on Praśna Vyâkaraṇa].

† Presidential address by H. Jacobi, delivered at Benares, on the 29th December, 1913.

body and the mind and also from speech.* Svâmi Kârtikeya says that Âsravas are certain movements of Jîva resulting from actions of speech and those of the mind and the body, either accompanied by or bereft of Moha Karma.† As water enters a pond through various channels, so Karmas enter a soul through the Âsravas.‡ As water enters a boat through holes, so Karma enters a soul through Âsravas.

Âsravas are broadly divided into (*a*) Bhâvâsrava and (*b*) Karmâsrava or Dravyâsrava. The former consists of the thought-activities which cause the influx of karmic matter into a soul while the latter is the karmic matter itself, which enters a soul in this manner. In other words, in Bhâvâsrava we are concerned with thought activities, while in Dravyâsrava or Karmâsrava we have connection with matter. Abhayadeva says that Dravyâsrava is the entrance of water through holes in a boat, etc., when the boat is on the water, and Bhâvâsrava is the influx of Karma, through the five senses of Jivas.§ In Vardhamâna, Purâṇa, we have "that Bhâva made impure by attachment (Râga), etc., by which Karmas adhere to men possessing attachment, is

* "कायवाङ्मनःकर्म योगः ।"
"स आस्रवः ।"
[तत्वार्थाधिगमसूत्रम् । ६ । १ । २ ।]

Amritachandra Sûri, in his Tattvârthasâra (IV-2) has combined the above two Sûtras in a single line of a verse as follows :—

"कायवाङ्मनसां कर्म स्मृतो योगः स आस्रवः ।"

Vide also.—

"कर्मणामागमद्वारमास्रवं संप्रचक्षते ।
स कायवाङ्मनःकर्मयोगत्वेन व्यवस्थितः ॥"
[चन्द्रप्रभचरितम् । १८ ॥ ८२ ।]

† "मणवयणकायजोया जीवपवेसाण–फंदणविसेसा ।
मोहोदएण जुत्ता विजुत्ता वि य आसवा होंति ॥"
[स्वामिकार्त्तिकेयानुप्रेक्षा । ८८ ।]

‡ "सरसः सलिलावाहि द्वारमत्र जनैर्यथा ।
तदास्रवणहेतुत्वादास्रवो व्यपदिश्यते ॥"
[तत्वार्थसारः । ३ । २ ।]

§ "तत्र द्रव्यास्रवा यज्जलान्तर्गतनावादौ तथाविधपरिणामेन छिद्रैः जलप्रवेशनं, भावास्रवस्तु यज्जीवानां पञ्चेन्द्रियादिछिद्रतः कर्मजलसञ्चय इति ।"
[स्थानाङ्ग–टीका]

called Bhâvâsrava. The influx of matter, in the shape of Karma, in a Jîva grasped by impure Bhâvas, is known as Dravyâsrava." *

Varieties of each of these classes of Âsrava will be mentioned in Verses 30 and 31 respectively.

मिच्छत्ताविरदिपमादजोगकोहादश्रो थ विरणेया ।
पण पण पणदह तिय चदु कमसो भेदा दु पुव्वस्स ॥ ३० ॥†

Michchhattâviradipamâdajogakohâdayo tha viṇ-
neyâ,
Paṇa paṇa paṇadaha tiya chadu kamaso bhedâ du
puvvassa—(30).

Padapâṭha—अथ Atha, then. पुव्वस्स Puvvassa, of the former. मिच्छत्ताविरदिपमादजोगकोहादश्रो Michchhattâ-viradi-pamâda-joga-kohâdayo, Mithyâtva, Avirati, Pramâda, Yoga, and Krodha, etc. कमसो Kamaso, respectively. पण-पण-पणदह-तिय-चदु. Paṇa-paṇa-paṇadaha-tiya-chadu, Five, five, fifteen, three and four. भेदा Bhedâḥ, classes विण्णेया Viṇṇeyâ, are to be known.

30. Then, it should be known that of the former (*i.e.*, Bhâvâsrava) (the subdivisions are) Mithyâtva, Avirati, Pramâda, Yoga, Anger, etc., (which are again of) five, five, fifteen, three and four classes, respectively.

COMMENTARY.

In this verse, the varieties of Bhâvâsrava are described to be of five kinds, *viz.* :Mithyâtva (Delusion), Avirati (Lack of Control), Pramâda (Inadvertence), Yoga (Activities) and Kaṣâya (Passions).

I. Mithyâtva or Delusion is of five kinds, Ekânta, Viparîta, Vinaya, Saṃśaya and Ajñâna:

---

* "रागादि-दूषितैनैव येन भावेन रागिणाम् ।
आस्रवन्त्यत्र कर्माणि स भावास्रव एव हि ॥
दुर्भावकलिते जीवे पुद्गलानां य आगमः ।
प्रत्ययैः कर्मरूपेण द्रव्यास्रवो मतोऽत्र सः ॥"
[वर्द्धमानपुराणम् । १६ ॥ ४० । ४१ ।]

† *Sanskrit rendering :*

मिथ्यात्वाविरतिप्रमादयोगक्रोधादयोऽथ विज्ञेयाः ।
पञ्च पञ्च पञ्चदश त्रय चत्वारः क्रमशः भेदा तु पूर्वस्य ॥ ३० ॥

Mithyâtvâviratipramâdayogakrodhâdayo' tha vijñeyâḥ,
Pañcha pañcha pañchadaśa traya chatvâraḥ kramaśaḥ bhedâḥ tu pûrvasya
—(30).

(*a*) Ekânta Mithyâtva is that state of delusion when we have a false belief, without knowing the same to be false or without even attempting to examine the same. A person who is born and brought up in a family where the tenets of Jainism are unknown and who consequently takes up the doctrines of that family to be true may be said to have Ekânta Mithyâtva with respect to Jainism.

(*b*) Viparîta Mithyâtva is that state of delusion in which we think that this or that may both be true. A belief that one religion is as good as another, for both of these are true, may be said to be such a delusion according to Jainaism.

(*c*) Vinaya Mithyâtva is retaining a belief, even when we know it to be false. This state exists in those who, even when convinced of the falsity of their doctrines, stick to the same.

(*d*) Saṃśaya Mithyâtva consists of a state of doubt as to whether a course is right or wrong. This state arises when a person begins to lose faith in the doctrines which he holds and is going to have a belief in others.

(*e*) Ajñâna Mithyâtva is the state when a person has no belief at all. A man who does not employ his reasoning faculties, and is unable to form any definite idea about doctrines might be said to have this kind of delusion, which obstructs knowledge.

II. Avirati or lack of control is also of five kinds, *viz.* : (*a*) Hiṃsâ (Injury), (*b*) Anrita (Falsehood), (*c*) Chaurya (Stealing), (*d*) Abrahma (Incontinence) and (*e*) Parigrâhâkâṅkhâ (Desire to possess a thing which is not given). In some works, these five only are mentioned as subdivisions of Âsrava. For example, in the tenth Aṅga of the Jainas, called Praśna Vyâkaraṇa, we have a description of Asravas and Saṃvaras, with their subdivisions; and in that work we have only the mention of the above five kinds of Avirati as subdivisions of Âsrava.* Abhayadeva, in his Commentary on Praśna Vyâkaraṇa, says that, though in that work Âsrava is said to be of five kinds, from another point of view, forty-two varieties of Âsrava are also recognised.† Abhayadeva quotes this passage to support

* "पंचविहो पण्णत्तो जिणेहिं इह अराहओ अणादीवो हिंसा-मोस-मदत्त-मबंभ-परिग्गहं चेव ।" [पण्हा वागरणम् । १]

† "हिंसादि-भेदतः एवं पञ्चविधः । प्रकारान्तरेण तु द्वि-चत्वारिंश-द्विधः।" [प्रश्नव्याकरणटीका ।]

his view: "There are forty-two Âsravas, *viz.*, those arising from five Indriyas, four Kaṣâyas, five Avratas, twenty-five Kriyâs and three Yogas.* In Dravyasaṃgraha, we have a mention of thirty-two varieties only of Âsrava.

The five Aviratis are called Avratas by Umâsvâmi. † He, however, mentions many subdivisions of Âsrava.‡ Svâmi Kârtikeya seems to support the author of Dravyasaṃgraha, by saying, "Know these Asravas to be of various kinds, *viz.*, Mithyâtva, etc." §.

III. Pramâda or Inadvertance is said to consist of (*a*) Vikathâ (Reprehensible talk), (*b*) Kaṣâya (Passions), (*c*) Indriya (Senses), (*d*) Nidrâ (Sleep) and (*e*) Râga (Attachment):

(*a*) Vikathâ or reprehensible talk may be about the king (Râja-kathâ), the state (Râṣṭra-kathâ), women (Strîkathâ) or food (Bhojana—kathâ). Thus it is of four varieties;

(*b*) Kaṣâya or passions are Krodha (Anger), Mâna (Pride), Mâyâ (Deceipt) and Lobha (Greed);

---

* "इंदिय-कसाय-अव्वय-किरिया पण-चउअ-पंच-पणवीसा जोगा तिणे वभवे आसवेयाउ वायालत्ति ।"

Vide also—"स च इंद्रियकषायाव्रतक्रियायोगरूपक्रमेण पञ्च-चतुः-पञ्च-पञ्चविंशति-त्रि-भेदाः" [स्थानाङ्ग-टीका]

† "प्रमत्तयोगात् प्राणव्यपरोपणं हिंसा ।"
"असदभिधानमनृतम् ।"
"अदत्तादानं स्तेयम् "
"मैथुनमब्रह्म ।"
"मूर्च्छा परिग्रहः ।"

[तत्वार्थाधिगमसूत्रम् । ७ ॥ १३–१७ ।]

‡ Umâsvâmi mentions Sâmparâyika and Îryâpatha as varieties of Âsrava, the former existing in Jîvas with passions, and the latter in Jîvas without passions. Sâmparâyika Âsrava is, again, subdivided into five Indriyas, four Kaṣâyas, five Avratas and twenty-five Kriyâs.

Vide—

"सकषायाकषाययोः साम्परायिकेर्यापथयोः ।"
"इंद्रियकषायाव्रतक्रियाः पञ्च-चतुः-पञ्च-पञ्चविंशतिसंख्याः पूर्वस्य भेदाः।"

[तत्वार्थाधिगमसूत्रम् । ६ ॥ ४ । ५]

§ "ते आसवा मुणिज्जसु मिच्छत्ताई अणेयविहा ।"

[स्वामिकार्त्तिकेयानुप्रेक्षा । ७ । ८९ ।]

The Commentator says that by "Mithyâtva, etc." Mithyâtva, Avirati, Pramâda, Yoga and Kaṣâya are meant.

(c) Indriya or the senses are five, *viz.*, the senses of touch, taste, smell, sight and hearing;

(d) Nidrâ (Sleep) and (e) Râga (Attachment) to worldly objects, are the last two varieties of Pramâda.

In some works, Pramâda or Inadvertance has not been mentioned as a sub-class of Bhâvâsrava. The author of Dravya-Saṃgraha himself, in his another work called Gommata Sâra, only mentions Mithyâtva, Avirati, Kaṣâya and Yoga to be subdivisions of Âsrava.*

IV. Yoga consists of the activities of the Manas (Mind), Vachana (speech) and Kâya Body). Though the author of Dravya-Saṃgraha stops here, in other works we meet with further subdivisions, *e.g.*, the activities of mind and speech are each divided into four classes, according as the same are true, untrue or mixed, and the activities of the body also are said to be of seven kinds.

V. Kaṣâyas or passions are four in number, *viz.*, Anger, Pride, Deceit and Greed. Each of these, again, are of four varieties, according as the same are of intense, great, moderate or mild degrees. Thus we get sixteen varieties of Kaṣâya.† In some works, we get a mention of nine No-Kaṣâyas which, together with the sixteen, make up twenty-five varieties of Kaṣâyas. The No-Kaṣâyas are Hâsya (Laughter), Rati (Pleasure), Arati (Pain) Śoka (Grief), Bhaya (Fear), Jugupsâ (Hatred), Strîveda (knowledge of the feminine gender), Puruṣa-veda (knowledge of the masculine gender) and Napuṃsaka-veda (knowledge of the gender of a eunuch.)

---

* "मिच्छत्तमविरमणं कसायजोगा य आसवा होंति ।
पण बारस पणुवीसं पण्णरसा होंति तब्भेया ॥"

i.e., "five kinds of Mithyâtva, twelve kinds of Avirati, twenty-five kinds of Kaṣâya and fifteen kinds of Yoga, are subdivisions of Âsrava."

[Gommatasâra Karmakânda, Verse 786.]

† See footnote or Page 38.

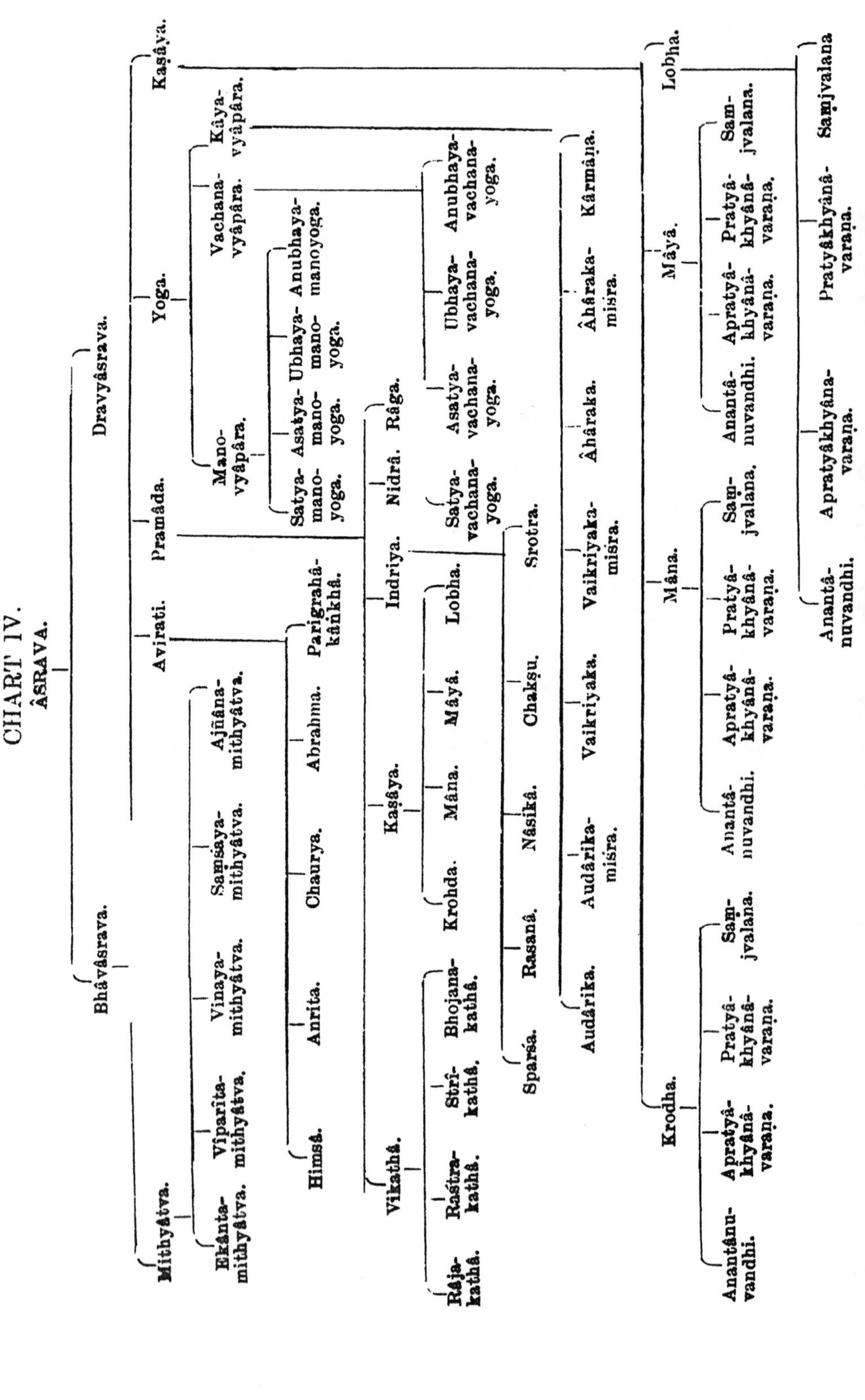
CHART IV.
ÂSRAVA.
Bhâvâsrava.
Dravyâsrava.
Mithyâtva.
Avirati.
Pramâda.
Yoga.
Kaṣâya.
Ekânta-mithyâtva.
Viparîta-mithyâtva.
Vinaya-mithyâtva.
Samśaya-mithyâtva.
Ajñâna-mithyâtva.
Himsâ.
Anrita.
Chaurya.
Abrahma.
Parigrahâ-kâṅkhâ.
Vikathâ.
Kaṣâya.
Indriya.
Nidrâ.
Râga.
Râja-kathâ.
Rastra-kathâ.
Strî-kathâ.
Bhojana-kathâ.
Krohda.
Mâna.
Mâyâ.
Lobha.
Sparśa.
Rasanâ.
Nâsikâ.
Chakṣu.
Srotra.
Mano-vyâpâra.
Vachana-vyâpâra.
Kâya-vyâpâra.
Satya-mano-yoga.
Asatya-mano-yoga.
Ubhaya-mano-yoga.
Anubhaya-manoyoga.
Satya-vachana-yoga.
Asatya-vachana-yoga.
Ubhaya-vachana-yoga.
Anubhaya-vachana-yoga.
Audârika.
Audârika-misra.
Vaikriyaka.
Vaikriyaka-misra.
Âhâraka.
Âhâraka-misra.
Kârmâṇa.
Krodha.
Mâna.
Mâyâ.
Lobha.
Anantânu-vandhi.
Apratyâ-khyânâ-varaṇa.
Pratyâ-khyânâ-varaṇa.
Sam-jvalana.
Anantâ-nuvandhi.
Apratyâ-khyânâ-varaṇa.
Pratyâ-khyânâ-varaṇa.
Sam-jvalana.
Anantâ-nuvandhi.
Apratyâ-khyânâ-varaṇa.
Pratyâ-khyânâ-varaṇa.
Sam-jvalana.
Anantâ-nuvandhi.
Apratyâkhyâna-varaṇa.
Pratyâkhyânâ-varaṇa.
Saṃjvalana

णाणावरणादीणं जोग्गं जं पुग्गलं समासवदि ।
दव्वासवो स णेओ अणेयभेओ जिणक्खादो ॥३१॥ *

Ṇâṇâvaraṇâdîṇaṃ joggaṃ jaṃ puggalaṃ samâsavadi,

Davvâsavo sa ṇeo aṇeyabheo jiṇakkhâdo.—(31.)

Padapâṭha—णाणावरणादीणं Ṇâṇâvaraṇâdîṇaṃ, of Jñânâvaraṇîya, etc. जोग्गं Joggaṃ, fit. जं Jam, which. पुग्गलं Puggalaṃ, Pudgala. समासवदि Samâsavadi, inflows. स Sa, that. जिणक्खादो Jiṇakkhâdo, told by the Jiṇa. अणेयभेदो Aṇeyabhedo, of many kinds. दव्वासवो Davvâsavo, Dravyâsrava. णेओ Ṇeyo, to be known.

31. That influx of matter which causes Jñânâvaraṇîya, etc., is to be known as Dravyâsrava as called by the Jina and possessing many varieties.

COMMENTARY.

We have observed that Bhâvâsravas are thought-activities which prepare the way for the influx of matter into Jîva. Dravyâsrava is the actual flowing in of matter into the soul by which the eight kinds of Karma mentioned in Verse 14, are produced. As it is easy for particles of dust to stick to the body of a person if the same be smeared with oil, so it becomes easier for particles of matter to enter a soul when it is vitiated by certain thought-activities (Bhâvâsravas). First of all, therefore, there are the reprehensible thought-activities (Bhâvâsrava). These are followed by the influx of matter (Dravyâsrava). When matter enters the soul in this manner, the eight kinds of Karma are produced.

Thus, Dravyâsrava may be said to be primarily of eight kinds, according to the eight varieties of Karma, *viz.*, Jñânâvaraṇiya, Darśanâvarṇiya, Vedanîya, Mohanîya, Âyu, Nâma, Gotra and Antarâya. Further subdivisions are also made of each of these kinds of Karmas. Jñânâvaraṇiya is said to be of five kinds—Darśanâvaraṇîya of nine, Vedanîya of two, Mohanîya of twenty-eight, Ayu of four, Nâma of ninety-three, Gotra of two and Antarâya of five kinds. The total number of the varieties of Dravyâsrava is, therefore, one hundred and

* *Sanskrit rendering*:

ज्ञानावरणादीनां योग्यं यत् पुद्गलं समास्रवति ।
द्रव्यास्रवः स ज्ञेयः अनेकभेदः जिनाख्यातः ।३१।।

Jñânâvaraṇâdînâṃ yogyam yat pudgalaṃ samâsravati.
Dravyâsravaḥ sa jñeyaḥ anekabhedaḥ jinâkhyâtaḥ—(31).

forty-eight. The author of Dravya-Saṃgraha has treated these varieties in detail, in his work named Gommata Sâra (Karma-kâṇḍa). Here verse, he simply says that Dravyâsrava is of many varieties. Consequently, we need not go into these detailed subdivisions.

वज्झदि कम्मं जेण दु चेदणभावेण भावबंधो सो ।
कम्मादपदेसाणं अण्णोण्णपवेसणं इदरो ॥३२॥*

Bajjhadi kammaṃ jeṇa du chedaṇabhâveṇa bhâvabandho so,
Kammâdapadesâṇaṃ aṇṇoṇṇapavesaṇaṃ idaro.—(32).

Padapâṭha.—जेण Jeṇa, which. चेदणभावेण Chedaṇabhâveṇa, conscious state. कम्मं Kammaṃ, Karma. वज्झदि Bajjhadi, is bound. स Sa, that. भावबंधो Bhâvabandho, Bhâva-bandha. दु Du, but कम्मादपदेसाणं Kammâdapadesâṇaṃ, of the Pradeśas of Karma and Âtmâ (soul). अण्णोण्णपवेसणं Aṇṇoṇṇapavesaṇaṃ, inter-penetration. इदरो Idaro, the other.

32. That conscious state by which Karma is bound (with the soul) is called Bhâva-bandha, while the interpenetration of the Pradeśas of Karma and the soul is the other (*i.e.*, Dravyabandha).

COMMENTARY.

We have learnt in Verses 29-31 the causes, on account of which Karmas enter a soul. Now, when there is such an influx of Karmas, there is a bondage of the soul with these Karmas. This bondage is called Bandha.

Bondage of the soul with Karmas is made by the conscious states of mind, when a soul is excited with attachment or aversion. These states of consciousness are known as Bhâva-bandha. In Vardhamâna-Purâṇa (Canto XVI, Verse 43) we have:—

"चेतनापरिणामेन रागद्वेषमयेन च ।
येन कर्माणि बध्यन्ते भावबन्धः स एव हि ॥"

i.e., "That modification of consciousness consisting of attachment or aversion by which Karmas are tied (to the soul), is known as

* *Sanskrit rendering:*

बध्यते कर्म येन तु चेतनभावेन भावबंधः सः ।
कर्मात्मप्रदेशानाम् अन्योन्यप्रवेशनम् इतरः ॥३२॥

Badhyate karma yena tu chetanabhâvena bhâvabandhaḥ saḥ,
Karmâtmapradeśânâṃ anyonyapraveśanaṃ itaraḥ.—(32).

Bhâva-bandha." Bhâva-bandha is, therefore, the alliance of the soul with mental activities which are produced when we are excited with attachment or aversion to worldly objects.

First of all, therefore, there is an influx of Karmas, through Âsravas. Then, there are some activities of consciousness which attach themselves to the soul, producing a peculiar kind of bondage. This is what we call Bhâva-bandha. After this Bhâva-bandha, there is a union of Jîva with actual Karmas. This union consists of the interpenetration of the soul and Karmas, and the bondage resulting from this, is known as Dravya-bandha. In Vardhamâna-Purâṇa (Canto XVI, Verse 44), we have :—

"भावबन्धनिमित्तेन संश्लेषो जीवकर्मणोः ।
योऽसौ चतुःप्रकारोऽत्र द्रव्यबन्धो बुधैः स्मृतः ॥"

i.e., "That union of Jîva and Karma which is caused by Bhâvabandha and is of four kinds, is called Dravya-bandha by the learned."

Bandha is, therefore, the assimilation of matter existing in many Pradeśas by Jîva, when it is excited by Kasâya (*i.e.*, attachment and aversion)* We have already described the results of this bondage in the commentary on Verse 7.†

**पयडिट्ठिदिअणुभागप्पदेसभेदा दु चदुविधो बंधो ।
जोगा पयडिपदेसा ठिदिअणुभागा कसायदो होंति ॥३३॥ ‡**

Payaditthidianubhâgappadesabhedâ du chaduvidho bandho,

---

* "सकषायतयादत्ते जीवोऽसंख्यप्रदेशगान् ।
पुद्गलान् कर्मणो योग्यान् बन्धः स इह कथ्यते ॥"
[धर्मशर्माभ्युदयम् ।२१।१०६।]

"सकषायतया जन्तोः कर्मयोग्यैर्निरन्तरम् ।
पुद्गलैः सह संबन्धी बन्ध इत्यभिधीयते ॥"
[चन्द्रप्रभचरितम् ।१८।९६।]

"सकषायत्वाज्जीवः कर्मणो योग्यान् पुद्गलानादत्ते स बन्धः ।"
[तत्वार्थाधिगमसूत्रम् ।८।२।]

† See pages 22-23.

‡ *Sanskrit rendering* :
प्रकृतिस्थित्यनुभागप्रदेशभेदात् तु चतुर्विधः बन्धः ।
योगात् प्रकृतिप्रदेशौ स्थित्यनुभागौ कषायतः भवन्ति ॥३३॥
Prakritisthityanubhâgapradeśabhedât tu chaturvidhaḥ bandhaḥ,
Yogât prakritipradeśau sthityanubhâgau kaṣâyataḥ bhavanti.—(33).

Jogâ payaḍipadesâ ṭhidiaṇubhâgâ kasâyado honti.
—(33).

Padapâṭha.—बंधो Bandho, Bandha. पयडिट्ठिदि अणुभागप्पदेसभेदा Payaḍiṭṭhidi-aṇubhâgappadesabhedâ, according to the subdivisions, Prakriti, Sthiti, Anubhâga and Pradeśa. चदुविधो Chaduvidho, is of four kinds. पयडिपदेसा Payaḍi-padesâ, Prakriti and Pradeśa. जोगा Jogâ, from Yoga. होंति. Honti, are. दु Du, but. ठिदि-अणुभागा Ṭhidianubhâgâ, Sthiti and Anubhâga. कसायदो Kasâyado, from Kaṣâya.

33. Bandha is of four kinds, according to the (subdivisions, *viz.*) Prakriti, Sthiti, Anubhâga and Pradeśa. Prakriti and Pradeśa are (produced) from Yoga. but Sthiti and Anubhâga are from Kaṣâya.

COMMENTARY.

When there is an influx of matter into the soul, certain energies (Karma) are produced which consist of bondage of the soul with matter. It has been stated before (see page 42) that Karma is of eight kinds Jnânâvaraṇîya, Darśanâvaraṇîya, Vedanîya, Mohanîya, Âyu, Nâma, Gotra and Antarâya. What is the nature of each of these eight kinds of Karma? The nature of the first two kinds of Karma is to obscure Jñâna and Darśana respectively; that of the third to produce happiness or misery; that of the fourth to produce illusion; that of the fifth to attach a soul to a body for a certain period; that of the sixth to produce shape; that of the seventh to cause birth in high and low families; and that of the eighth to put obstacles to several characteristics of the soul. Now, all these are the different natures (Prakritis) of Karma. Bandha or bondage can also be regarded to be of various natures, corresponding to the different natures of Karmas. The first variety of Bandha or bondage is, therefore, with respect to its Prakriti or nature.

Now, the time during which the various kinds of Karma will stay in a soul, is called its Sthiti or duration. Bandha or bondage also has a duration equal in extent with the duration of Karmas. The second variety of Bandha is, therefore, recognised with respect to this duration (Sthiti).

Karmas may be of intense, mediocre or mild degrees, as regards the results which these may produce. Bandha or bondage also may be of these three degrees of intensity. We therefore recognise the third variety of Bandha, with regard to its Anubhâga (Intensity).

The fourth variety of Bandha is with regard to its Pradeśa (or mass). The Karmas interpenetrate Pradeśas of the soul and attach themselves to the same. Considering this existence of Karma and soul in one place, we speak of the fourth variety of Bandha with respect to its mass (Pradeśa).

Umâsvâmi has also mentioned these four varities of Bandha* In Vardhamâna Purâṇa we have: "Bandha which is of an evil nature and productive of all evils is of four kinds, *viz.*, Prakriti, Sthiti, Anubhâga and Pradeśa."† Harichandra and Vîranandi also mention the same.‡

In a word, we consider bondage with respect to its nature (Prakriti), duration (Sthiti), intensity (Anubhâga) and mass (Pradeśa).

The nature (Prakriti) and mass (Pradeśa) of bondage result from the activities of thought, speech and body, while the duration of bondage (Sthiti) and intensity (Anubhâga) result from the attachment and aversion of the soul towards worldly objects. In other words, Kaṣâya or attachment and aversion of the soul towards worldly objects is the Antaraṅga (internal) cause of bondage, and determines the duration and intensity of it; while the activities of mind, speech and body are the Vahiraṅga (external) cause of the bondage and determines its nature and mass. In Pañchâstikâya-samaya-sâra also we have a similar idea.§

---

* "प्रकृतिस्थित्यनुभागप्रदेशास्तद्विधयः ।"
[तत्वार्थाधिगमसूत्रम् । ८ । ३ ।]

† "प्रकृतिस्थितिबंधोऽ नुभागः प्रदेश-संज्ञकः ।
इति चतुर्विधो बंधः सर्वानर्थकरोऽ शुभः ॥"
[वर्द्धमानपुराणम् । १६ । ४५ ।]

‡ "प्रकृतिस्थित्यनुभागप्रदेशानां विभेदतः ।
चतुर्विधः प्रणीतोऽ सौ जैनागमविचक्षणैः ॥"
[धर्मशर्माभ्युदयम् । २१ । १०८ ।]

"विभेदात् प्रकृतिस्थित्योरनुभागप्रदेशयोः ।
जिनागमनदीष्णानैर्विज्ञेयः स चतुर्विधः ॥"
[चन्द्रप्रभचरितम् । १८ । ९७ ।]

§ "जोगणिमित्तं गहणं जोगो मणवयणकायसंभूदो ।
भावणिमित्तो बंधो भावो रदिरागदोसमोहजुदो ॥
[Verse 148.]

चेदणपरिणामो जो कम्मस्सासवणिरोहणे हेऊ ।
सो भावसंवरो खलु दव्वासवरोहणे अण्णो ॥३४॥*

Chedaṇapariṇâmo jo kammassâsavaṇirohaṇe heû.
So bhâvasaṃvaro khalu davvâsavarohaṇe aṇṇo.—(34).

Padapâṭha.—जो Jo, which. चेदणपरिणामो Chedaṇapariṇâmo, the modification of consciousness. कम्मस्स Kammassa, of Karma. आसवणिरोहणे Âsavaṇirohaṇe, in checking Âsrava. हेऊ Heû, the cause. सो So, that. खलु Khalu, surely. भावसंवरो Bhâva-saṃvaro, Bhâva-saṃvara. दव्वासवरोहणे Davvâsava-rohaṇe, in checking Dravyâsrava. अण्णो Aṇṇo, the other.

34. That modification of consciousness which is the cause of checking Asrava (influx) of Karma, is surely Bhâvasaṃvara, and the other (known as Dravyasaṃvara is known from) checking Dravyâsrava.

COMMENTARY.

Saṃvara is the antagonistic principle of Âsrava.† The word is thus derived: that which checks the causes of Karma, such as killing, etc. (*i.e.*, that which stops Âsrava, is known to be Saṃvara.‡ Those by which the water of Karma is prevented from entering the pond of self, are known as Saṃvaras. Saṃvaras are refraining from killing, etc.§

To be more explicit, Âsrava being the influx of Karma, through some openings (as we have seen before), Saṃvara is the stoppage of

* *Sanskrit rendering :*

चेतनपरिणामः यः कर्मणः आस्रवनिरोधने हेतुः ।
स भावसंवरः खलु द्रव्यास्रवरोधने अन्यः ॥ ३४ ॥

Chetana-pariṇâmaḥ yaḥ karmaṇaḥ âsravanirodhane hetuḥ,
Sa bhâvasaṃvaraḥ khalu dravyâsrava-rodhane anyaḥ—(34).

† "आस्रवप्रतिपक्षभूतः संवरः ।"

[Commentary on Sthânânga, Adhayana I.]

‡ "संव्रियते कर्मकारणं प्राणातिपातादि निरुध्यते येन परिणामेन स संवरः, आस्रव-निरोध इत्यर्थः ।

[Commentary on Sthânânga. I.]

§ "संव्रियते निरुध्यते आत्मतडागे कर्मजलं प्रविशत् एभिः इति संवराः प्राणातिपातविरमणादयः ।"

[Commentary on Prasnavyâkaraṇa. I.]

these opinings leading to the stoppage of Âsrava. To use our old illustration, the holes will allow influx (Âsrava) of water (Karma) in a boat (Jîva); but if these holes be stopped (Saṃvara), there will be no advent of water (Karma) in the boat (Jîva).

As there are two kinds of Âsravas, so two kinds of Saṃvaras are also recognised as opposite principles to each of these kinds of Âsrava. These are called Bhâva-saṃvara and Dravya-saṃvara, as opposed to Bhâvâsrava and Dravyâsrava, respectively. Abhayadeva Âcharya has said that Bhâvasaṃvara is the stoppage of the inlets of senses through which Karma enters the soul, and Dravyasaṃvara is the stoppage, for example, of holes through which water enters a boat*. In Vardhamâna Purâṇa we have: "That modification of consciousness which is void of attachment and aversion, and by which the influx of Karmas is stopped, is called Bhâva-saṃvara." And "that by which the Yogis stop all kinds of influx through the great vows and meditation is called Dravya-saṃvara." †

These are the two principal varieties of Saṃvara, but the first variety, *viz.*, Bhâvasaṃvara is, again, subdivided into many classes which will be described in the following verse.

वदसमिदीगुत्तीश्रो धम्माणुपिहा परीसहजश्रो य ।
चारित्त वहुभेयं णायव्वा भावसंवरविसेसा ॥३५॥ ‡

---

* "अथवा यद् द्विधा द्रव्यतो भावतश्च । तत्र द्रव्यतो जलमध्यगतनावादेरनवरतप्रविशज्जलानां छिद्राणां तथाविधद्रव्ये स्थगनं संवरः । भावतस्तु जीवद्रोण्यामास्रवत्-कर्मजलानामिन्द्रियादि-छिद्राणां समित्यादिना निरोधनं संवर इति ।"

[Commentary on Sthânâṅga.]

† "चैतन्यपरिणामो यो रागद्वेषातिगो महान् ।
कर्मास्रवनिरोधस्य हेतुः स भावसंवरः ॥"
"सर्वास्रव-निरोधो यः क्रियते तेन योगिभिः ।
महाव्रतादि-सद्ध्यानैर्द्रव्याख्यः स सुखाकरः ॥"

[Vardhamâna Purâṇa XVI. 67-68.]

‡ *Sanskrit rendering*:
व्रत-समिति-गुप्तयः धर्मानुप्रेक्षाः परीषहजयश्च ।
चारित्रं बहुभेदं ज्ञातव्याः भावसंवरविशेषाः ॥ ३५ ॥
Vrata-samiti-guptayaḥ dharmânuprekṣâḥ parîṣahajayaścha.
Châritraṃ vahubhedaṃ jñâtavyâḥ bhâvasaṃvaraviśeṣâḥ—(35).

Vadasamidîguttîo dhammâṇupihâ parîsahajao ya.
Chârittaṃ vabubheyaṃ ṇâyavvâ bhâvasaṃvara-visesâ.—(35).

Padapâṭha.—वद-समिदीगुत्तीओ Vada-samidîguttîo, Vratas, Samitis and Guptis. य Ya, and. धम्माणुपिहा Dhammâṇupihâ, Dharmas and Anuprekṣâs. परीसहजओ Parîsahajao, Parîṣahajaya. बहुभेयं Vahubheyaṃ, of many kinds. चारित्तं Chârittaṃ. Châritra. भावसंवरविसेसा Bhâvasaṃvaravisesâ, the varieties of Bhâva-saṃvara. णायव्वा Ṇâyavvâ, to be known.

35. The Vratas (Vows), Samitis (Attitudes of carefulness), Guptis (Restraints), Dharmas (Observances), Anuprekṣâs (Meditations), Parîṣaha-jayas (the victories over troubles) and various kinds of Châritra (Conduct) are to be known as varieties of Bhâva-saṃvara.

COMMENTARY.

From this verse, we learn that Bhâvasaṃvara is of seven varieties: Vrata, Samiti, Gupti, Dharma, Anuprekṣâ, Parîṣaha-jaya and Châritra. Each of these, again, are divided into various sub-classes.

A. Vrata or vows is of five kinds, *viz.* Ahiṃsâ (Abstinence from injury), Satya (Truthfulness), Achaurya or Asteya (Abstinence from stealing), Brahmacharya (Abstinence from sexual pleasures) and Aparigraha Abstinence from acceptance of worldly objects). Umâsvâmi has mentioned these five varieties of Vrata, and has defined each of them* In Prasna Vyâkaraṇa, Saṃvara is said to consist of these five varities only.† The five rules of conduct (Pañcha Sîlas) of the Buddhists correspond to the five Vratas of Jainism; and a parallel may also be found in the commandments, such as, "Thou shalt not kill," "Thou shalt not steal," "Thou shalt not commit adultery," etc., which are promulgated by Christianity.

* "हिंसाऽनृतास्तेयाब्रह्मपरिग्रहेभ्यो विरति-र्व्रतम् ।"

[तत्वार्थाधिगमसूत्रम् । ६ । १ ।]

† "एत्तो संवर-दाराइं पंच वोच्छामि आणुपुव्वीए जह भणियाणि भगवया सव्वदुक्खविमोक्खणट्ठाए । पढमं हुंति अहिंसा, वितियं सच्चवयणंति पण्णत्तं दत्तमणुण्णाय संवरो बंभचेरमपरिग्गहत्तं च ।"

[प्रश्नव्याकरणम् । ६ अध्ययनम]

B Samiti or carefulness is of five kinds. (*a*) Îryâ, *i.e.*, using paths trodden by men and beasts in such a manner as not to cause injury to any creature, (*b*) Bhâṣâ, *i.e.*, gentle and beneficial talk, (*c*) Eṣaṇâ, *i.e.*, receiving alms, avoiding the faults reprehended in Jaina canons, (*d*) Adâna-nikṣepa, *i.e.*, receiving and keeping things which are necessary for religious purposes only, after examination and (*e*) Utsarga, *i.e.*, attending to calls of nature in unfrequented places.*

C. Gupti † or restraint is of three kinds: (*a*) Kâya-gupti or restraint of movements of the body, (*b*) Vâg-gupti or restraint of the tongue, so that it might not utter bad language and (*c*) Mano-gupti or restraint of mind from thinking about forbidden matter.

D. Dharma or observance is of ten kinds, *viz.*, the observance of (*a*) Uttama Kṣamâ or excellent forgiveness, (*b*) Uttama Mârdava or excellent humility (*c*) Uttama Ârjava or excellent straightforwardness, (*d*) Uttama Satya or excellent truth, (*e*) Uttama Śaucha or excellent cleanliness, (*f*) Uttama Saṃyama or excellent restraint, (*g*) Uttama Tapa or excellent penance, (*h*) Uttama Tyâga or excellent abandonment, (*i*) Uttama Âkiñchanya or excellent indifference and (*j*) Uttama Brahmacharya or excellent celibacy. ‡

The seventh variety of Dharma, *viz.*, Uttama Tapa is, again, of two kinds: Vâhya (external) and Âvyantara (internal). Vâhya Tapa (external penance) consists of Anaśana (fasting), Avamodârya (regulation of diet), Vritti-parisankhyâna (regulation of meals by observing the rules enjoined in the Jaina scriptures for begging alms), Rasaparityâga (abstinence from appetising food), Vivikta-śayyâsana (sitting and lying at quiet and solitary places) and Kâya-Kleśa (practice of bodily austerities). Âvyantara Tapa (internal penance) consists of Prâyaśchitta (expiation), Vinaya (reverence), Vaiâvritya (service), Svâdhyâya (study of scriptures), Vyutsarga (giving up

---

*"ईर्याभाषैणादाननिक्षेपोत्सर्गाः समितयः।"

[तत्वार्थाधिगमसूत्रम् । ९ । ५ ।]

†"सम्यग् योगनिग्रहो गुप्तिः ।"

[तत्वार्थाधिगमसूत्रम् । ९ । ४ ।]

‡"उत्तमक्षमा-मार्दवार्जवसत्यशौचसंयमतपस्त्यागाकिञ्चन्यब्रह्मचर्याणि धर्मः ।"

[तत्वार्थाधिगमसूत्रम् । ९ । ६. ।]

mundane objects and thoughts about the same) and Dhyâna (meditation). *

E. Anupreksâ or reflection is of twelve kinds: (a) Anityânupreksâ or reflection that everything in this world is transient, (b) Asaranânupreksâ or reflection that there is no other refuge of us in this world, except our own truth, (c) Saṃsârânupreksâ or reflection about the cycles of worldly existence, (d) Ekatvânupreksâ or reflection that a person is solely and individually responsible for his own acts, whether good or bad, (e) Anyatvânupreksâ or reflection that non-ego is separate from the ego, (f) Asuchitvânupreksâ or reflection that the body and all that appertains to it is unclean, (g) Âsravânupreksâ or reflection about the influx of Karma, (h) Saṃvarânupreksâ or reflection about stoppage of the influx of Karma, (i) Nirjarânupreksâ or reflection about the removal of foreign energies which have already entered the soul, (j) Lokânupreksâ or reflection about soul and matter and the real substances of this universe, (k) Bodhidurlabhânupreksâ or reflection about the difficulty of attaining perfect faith, perfect knowledge and perfect conduct, and (l) Dharmânupreksâ or constant reflection about the essential principles of the universe. †

F. Parîsaha-jaya or conquering the troubles is the sixth kind of Saṃvara. The troubles which may afflict a hermit are of various kinds. Gaining victory over all these troubles is what is known as

---

* "अनशनावमौदर्य्यवृत्तिपरिसंख्यानरसपरित्यागविविक्तशय्यासनकायक्लेशा वाह्यं तपः।"

"प्रायश्चित्त-बिनय-वैयावृत्य-स्वाध्याय-व्युत्सर्ग-ध्यानान्युत्तरम्।"

[तत्वार्थाधिगमसूत्रम्। ९। १९। २०]

"बाह्यमाभ्यन्तरञ्चेति मूलभेदद्वयान्वितम्॥
उपवासावमोदर्य वृत्तिसंख्य रसोप्सनम् (?)।
विविक्तवासना कायक्लेशश्चेति बहिर्भवम्॥
स्वा-ध्यायेा व्यावृत्तिर्ध्यानं व्युत्सर्गो विलयस्तथा।
प्रायश्चित्तमिति ज्ञेयमान्तरं षड्विधं तपः॥"

[चन्द्रप्रभचरितम्। १८। १११ –११३।]

† "अनित्याशरणसंसारैकत्वान्यत्वाशुच्यास्रवसंवरनिर्जरालोकबोधिदुर्लभधर्मस्वाख्यातत्त्वानुचिन्तनमनुप्रेक्षाः।"

[तत्वार्थाधिगमसूत्रम्। ९। ७]

Parîṣahajaya. The varieties of these are (*a*) Kṣudhâparîṣahajaya or the victory over the troubles of hunger, (*b*) Pipâsâ-parîṣaha-jaya or the victory over the troubles of thirst, (*c*) Śîta-parîṣahajaya or victory over the troubles of cold, (*d*) Uṣṇaparîṣahajaya or the victory over the troubles of heat, (*e*) Daṃśa-maśaka-parîṣahajaya or the victory over the troubles from mosquitoes and gnats, (*f*) Nâgnyaparîṣahajaya or the victory over the feelings of shame arising from nudity, (*g*) Aratiparîṣahajaya or the victory over the feelings of dissatisfaction with hunger, thirst, etc., (*h*) Strîparîṣahajaya or the victory over the disturbance of tranquility at the sight of fair women or the movements of them, (*i*) Charyâparîṣahajaya or the victory over the feelings of fatigue arising from travelling on the roads, (*j*) Niṣadyâparîṣahajaya or victory over the desire of moving from a fixed posture in meditation, (*k*) Śayyâ-parîṣahajaya or the victory over the desire of having a bed prohibited in the Jaina scriptures, (*l*) Âkrośa-parîṣahajaya is conquering the feelings of anger when one is insulted by another, (*m*) Badha-parîṣahajaya or the conquering of ill-feeling against an enemy who comes to kill (*n*) Yâchana-parîṣaha-jaya or conquering the desire to ask anything from anyone, even at the time of greatest need, (*o*) Alâbha-parîṣaha-jaya is the victory over the feelings of disappointment arising from not getting worldly objects, (*p*) Roga-parîṣahajaya or the victory over the pains of disease, (*q*) Triṇa-sparśa-parîsaha-jaya or the victory over the feeling of pain arising from wounds in the feet by treading over thorns, etc., (*r*) Mala-parîṣahajaya is conquering the feeling of disgust which arises from seeing one's body to be unclean, (*s*) Satkârapuraskâraparîṣahajaya or the victory over the desire to gain respect, praise or reward, (*t*) Prajñâ-parîṣaha-jaya or the victory over the feeling of pride at one's learning (*u*) Ajñâna-parîṣahajaya or the victory over the feeling of despair arising out of failure to gain knowledge by certain hindrances and (*v*) Adarśana-parîṣaha-jaya or conquering the feeling of sadness or despair when one fails to obtain desired fruits, even after practise of penances, etc. These are the twenty-two kinds of victory over troubles. *

* "क्षुत्पिपासा—शीतोष्ण—दंशमशकनाग्न्यारतिस्त्रीचर्यानिषद्याशय्याक्रोशवधयाचनाऽलाभरोगतृणस्पर्शमलसत्कारपुरस्कारप्रज्ञाज्ञानादर्शनानि ।"

[तत्त्वार्थाधिगमसूत्रम् ।९।९।]

G. Châritra or Right Conduct is of five kinds* :—(*a*) Sâmâyika-châritra (Equanimity) consisting of self-absorption in which a person refrains during his whole life or for a certain fixed period from injury, false-hood, lust, stealing and acceptance of things which are not given† (*b*, Chhedopasthâpanâ (Resettling after a break) consisting of penalties for faults arising from inadvertence or negligence, on account of which one loses equanimity. (This therefore may be said to consist of an attempt to recover equanimity ; after a fall from the same)‡ (*c*) Parihâra-viśuddhi (Purity obtained by refraining from injury to living beings) which is only found in a saint who being thirty years old, serves a Tîrthankar from three to nine years, who is devoid of inadvertence and absorbed in self-contemplation and who practises other observances § (*d*) Sûkṣmasâmparâya consisting of conduct in which only the passion greed is present in a very subtle state while all other passions have subsided or have been destroyed. (This kind of conduct is only found in one who has reached the tenth stage of development)|| (*e*) Yathâkhyâta (Perfect Right Conduct) characterised by subsidence or destruction of all the passions. It is present in beings who are in the eleventh, twelfth, thirteenth and fourteenth stages of development.¶

* "वृत्तं सामायिकं ज्ञेयं छेदोपस्थापनं तथा ।
परिहारं च सूक्ष्मं च यथाख्यातं च पञ्चमम् ॥"
[तत्वार्थसारः ॥ ६ । ४४ ॥]

† "प्रत्याख्यानमभेदेन सर्वसावद्यकर्मणः ।
नित्यं नियतकालं वा वृत्तं सामायिकं स्मृतम् ॥"
[तत्वार्थसारः ॥ ६ । ४५ ॥]

‡ "यत्र हिंसादिभेदेन त्यागः सावद्यकर्मणः ।
व्रतलोपे विशुद्धिर्वा छेदोपस्थापनं हि तत् ॥"
[तत्वार्थसारः ॥ ६ । ४६ ॥]

§ "विशिष्टपरिहारेण प्राणिघातस्य यत्र हि ।
शुद्धिर्भवति चारित्रं परिहारविशुद्धि तत् ॥"
[तत्वार्थसारः ॥ ६ । ४७ ॥]

|| "कषायेषु प्रशान्तेषु प्रक्षीणेष्वखिलेषु वा ।
स्यात् सूक्ष्मसांपरायाख्यं सूक्ष्मलोभवतो यतेः ॥
[तत्वार्थसारः ॥ ६ । ४८ ॥]

¶ "क्षयाच्चारित्रमोहस्य कात्स्न्येनोपशमात्तथा ।
यथाख्यातमथाख्यातं चारित्रं पञ्चमं जिनैः ॥"
[तत्वार्थसारः ॥ ६ । ४९ ॥]

We have thus seen that Saṃvara is first divided into two classes, Bhâva-saṃvara and Dravya-saṃvara, the first of which, again, has many subdivisions. The first variety of Bhâva-saṃvara *viz.*, Vrata is not counted as such by Umâswâmi,* Amrita-chandra Sûri,† and Svâmi-kârtikeya.‡ Abhayadeva Âchârya, again, in his commentary on Sthânâṅga says that Saṃvara is of forty-two kinds.§

In the Jaina epics also we do not find Vrata included in the sub-divisions of Saṃvara, but only Gupti, Samiti, Dharma Anuprekṣâ, Parîṣahajaya and Charîtra are mentioned as varieties of Saṃvara|| Vrata, with all its five varieties, is, however, mentioned in all the above-mentioned works—though not as a sub-division of Saṃvara, yet as a factor opposed to Avrata.¶

* "स गुप्ति-समितिधर्मानुप्रेक्षा-परीषहजयचारित्रैः ।"

[तत्त्वार्थाधिगमसूत्रम् । ९ । २ ।]

† "गुप्तिः समितयो धर्म्मः परीषहजयस्तपः ।
अनुप्रेक्षाश्च चारित्रं सन्ति संवरहेतवः ॥"

[तत्त्वार्थसारः । ६ । २]

‡ "गुत्ती समिदी धम्मो अणुवेक्खा तह परीसहजओ वि ।
उक्किट्ठं चारित्तं संवरहेदू विसेसेण ॥"

[स्वामिकार्तिकेयानुप्रेक्षा । ९६ ।]

§ "तदेवमयं द्विचत्वारिंशद्विधो ।"

[स्थानाङ्ग-टीका]

|| "आस्रवस्य निरोधो यः संवरः स निगद्यते ।
कर्म संव्रियते येनेत्येवं व्युत्पत्तिसंश्रयात् ॥
चारित्रगुप्त्यनुप्रेक्षापरीषहजयादसौ ।
दशलक्षणधर्म्माच्च समितिभ्यश्च जायते ॥"

[चन्द्रप्रभचरितम् ॥ १८ ॥ १०६—१०७]

"आस्रवाणामशेषाणां निरोधः संवरः स्मृतः ।
कर्म संव्रियते येनेव त्यन्वयस्यावलोकनात् ॥
आस्रवद्वाररोधेन शुभाशुभविशेषतः ।
कर्म संव्रियते येन संवरः स निगद्यते ॥
धर्मात् समिति-गुप्तिभ्यामनुप्रेक्षानुचिन्तनात् ।
असावुदेति चारित्रादरिषट्कजयादपि ॥"

[धर्मशर्माभ्युदयम् ॥ २१ ॥ ११७—११९॥]

¶ "हिंसानृतास्तेयाब्रह्मपरिग्रहेभ्यो विरतिर्व्रतम् ।"

[तत्त्वार्थाधिगमसूत्रम् ॥ ७ । २ ॥]

CHART V.

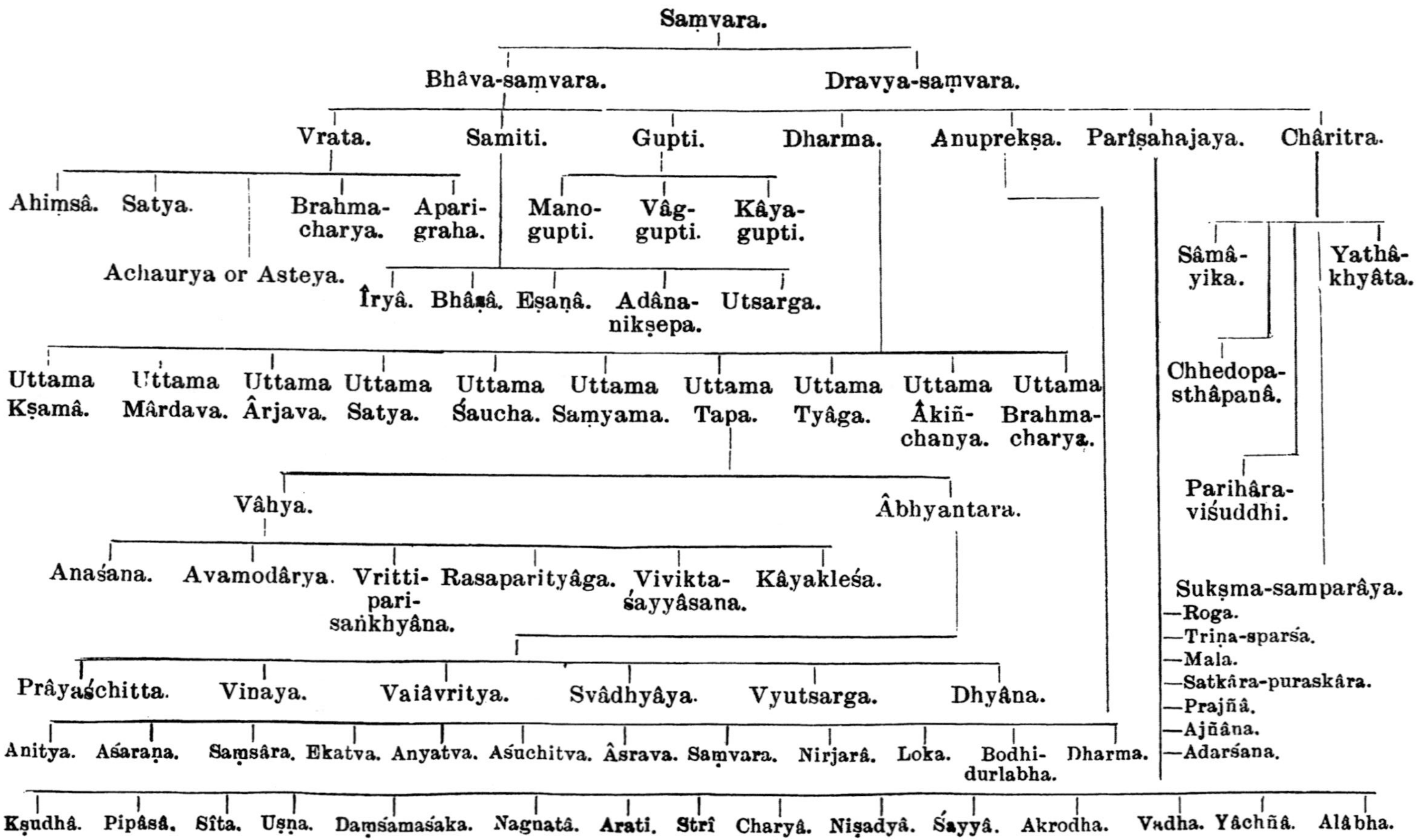
Saṃvara.
Bhâva-saṃvara.
Dravya-saṃvara.
Vrata.
Samiti.
Gupti.
Dharma.
Anuprekṣa.
Parîṣahajaya.
Châritra.
Ahiṃsâ.
Satya.
Brahma-charya.
Apari-graha.
Achaurya or Asteya.
Mano-gupti.
Vâg-gupti.
Kâya-gupti.
Îryâ.
Bhâṣâ.
Eṣaṇâ.
Adâna-nikṣepa.
Utsarga.
Sâmâ-yika.
Yathâ-khyâta.
Chhedopa-sthâpanâ.
Parihâra-viśuddhi.
Sukṣma-samparâya.
Uttama Kṣamâ.
Uttama Mârdava.
Uttama Ârjava.
Uttama Satya.
Uttama Śaucha.
Uttama Saṃyama.
Uttama Tapa.
Uttama Tyâga.
Uttama Âkiñ-chanya.
Uttama Brahma-charya.
Vâhya.
Âbhyantara.
Anaśana.
Avamodârya.
Vritti-pari-saṅkhyâna.
Rasaparityâga.
Vivikta-śayyâsana.
Kâyakleśa.
Prâyaśchitta.
Vinaya.
Vaiâvritya.
Svâdhyâya.
Vyutsarga.
Dhyâna.
—Roga.
—Triṇa-sparśa.
—Mala.
—Satkâra-puraskâra.
—Prajñâ.
—Ajñâna.
—Adarśana.
Anitya.
Aśaraṇa.
Saṃsâra.
Ekatva.
Anyatva.
Aśuchitva.
Âsrava.
Saṃvara.
Nirjarâ.
Loka.
Bodhi-durlabha.
Dharma.
Kṣudhâ.
Pipâsâ.
Sîta.
Uṣṇa.
Daṃśamaśaka.
Nagnatâ.
Arati.
Strî
Charyâ.
Niṣadyâ.
Śayyâ.
Akrodha.
Vadha.
Yâchñâ.
Alâbha.

जहकालेण तवेण य भुत्तरसं कम्मपुग्गलं जेण ।
भावेण सडदि णेया तस्सडणं चेदि णिज्जरा दुविहा ॥३६॥*

Jahakâleṇa taveṇa ya bhuttarasaṃ kammapuggalaṃ jeṇa
Bhâveṇa saḍadi ṇeyâ tassaḍaṇaṃ chedi ṇijjarâ duvihâ—(36.)

Padapâṭha. जहकालेण Jahakâleṇa, in proper time. भुत्तरसं Bhuttarasaṃ, whose fruits are enjoyed. कम्मपुग्गलं Kammapuggalaṃ, the matter of Karma. जेण Jeṇa, that. भावेण Bhâveṇa, Bhâva. सडदि Saḍadi, disappears. य Ya, and. तवेण Taveṇa, by penance. च Cha, and. तस्सडणं Tassaḍaṇaṃ, that disappearance. इदि Idi, thus. णिज्जरा Ṇijjarâ, Nirjarâ. दुविहा Duvihâ, of two kinds. णेया Ṇeyâ, to be known.

36. That Bhâva (modification of the soul) by which the matter of Karma disappears in proper time after the fruits [of such Karma] are enjoyed [is called Bhâva-Nirjarâ], also [the destruction of Karmic matter] through penances [is known as Bhâva-Nirjarâ.] And that destruction [itself] [is known as Dravya-Nirjarâ]. Thus Nirjarâ should be known to be of two kinds.

COMMENTARY.

We have seen how the matter of Karma enters the soul through Âsrava and how this influx might be stopped by Saṃvara. But now the question arises, that we might stop a further influx of Karmic matter by Saṃvara, but how can we be freed from the same which has already taken possession of the soul? The answer to this is given in this verse, where it is laid down that by Nirjarâ we can free ourselves from the Karmic matter which has already entered the soul.

What is Nirjarâ? The destruction of Karmas is called Nirjarâ.†

---

* ***Sanskrit rendering*** :—

यथाकालेन तपसा च भुक्तरसं कर्मपुद्गलं येन ।
भावेन सडति ज्ञेया तत् सडनं चेति निर्जरा द्विविधा ॥ ३६ ॥

Yathâkâlena tapasâ cha bhuktarasaṃ karma-pudgalaṃ yena,
Bhâvena saḍati jñeyâ ṭat saḍanaṃ cheti nirjarâ dvividhâ. (36.)

† "एगा णिज्जरा ।" स्थानाङ्ग । १ । "निर्जरणं निर्जरा विशरणं परिशटनमित्यर्थः कर्मक्षयो निर्जरा ।"

[स्थानाङ्ग-टीका]

This destruction may be of two kinds, Bhâva-Nirjarâ and Dravya-Nirjarâ. Bhâva-Nirjarâ consists of that modification of the soul which precedes and favours the separation of Karmic matter from the soul. Dravya-Nirjarâ is the actual separation of the Karmic matter from the soul. In other words, Bhâva-Nirjará is that state of the soul when the material particles arising from Karma disappear while Dravya-Nirjarâ is the disappearance itself.

Bhâva-Nirjarâ is of two kinds, Savipâka or Akâma and Avipâka or Sakâma. That is to say, Karmas are destroyed in two ways, *viz.*, (1) after their fruits are fully enjoyed and (2) through penances before such enjoyment of fruits. * Every person is affected with good or bad Karmas, the fruits of which are enjoyed by them in an existence in earth heaven or hell, according to the kind of Karma possessed by them. There is a fixed period of such enjoyment of the fruits of Karmas, and after the lapse of that period when the said fruits of Karmas are fully enjoyed, a person is freed from Karmas which disappear of their own accord. This is what is known as Savipâka Nirjarâ (or destruction of Karmas after the enjoyment of fruits.) This kind of Nirjarâ can happen to all beings, for all kinds of Karmas of all beings disappear in this manner after a proper period. As this disappearance takes place without the activity of a person, it is also called Akâma (or un-intentional) Nirjarâ.

The second kind of destruction of Karmas takes place when the sages practise penances, by the force of which the Karmas disappear even before their fruits are enjoyed. This is consequently known as Avipâka Nirjarâ (or destruction of Karmas without the enjoyment of their fruits.) As such a kind of destruction can only be produced by intentional effort on behalf of a person, it is known as Sakâma (intentional) Nirjarâ.

The soul is like a mirror which becomes dim when the dust of Karma accumulates on its surface. By Nirjarâ this dust of Karma

---

* उपात्तकर्मणः पातो निर्जरा द्विविधा च सा ।
आद्या विपाकजा तत्र द्वितीया चाविपाकजा ॥
अनादिबन्धनोपाधिविपाकवशवर्त्तिनः ।
कर्मारब्धफलं यत्र क्षीयते सा विपाकजा ॥
अनुदीर्णं तपःशक्त्या यत्रोदीर्णोदयावलीम् ।
प्रवेश्य वेद्यते कर्म सा भवत्यविपाकजा ॥"

[तत्त्वार्थसारः ॥ ७ ॥ २–४]

is removed and the soul attains clearness.* The good or bad Karmas disappear either of their own accord without any activity on the part of a soul when their fruits are enjoyed in earth heaven or hell, or by the effort on the part of a person consisting of practice of penances.† We have already mentioned that there are twelve kinds of penances, according as they are external or internal. A person must practise first of all Saṃvara so as to stop all further influx of Karmas, and then begin to destroy the Karmas already amalgamated with the soul, by means of penances.‡ This is the

---

* " कर्मणां फलभोगेन संक्षयो निर्जरा मता ।
भूत्यादर्श इवात्मायं तथा स्वच्छत्वमृच्छति ॥"
[नेमिनिर्वाणम् । १५ । ७४ ।]

† " यथाकालकृता काचिदुपक्रमकृतापरा ।
निर्जरा द्विविधा ज्ञेया कर्मक्षपणलक्षणा ॥
या कर्मभुक्तिः श्वभ्रादौ सा यथाकालजा स्मृता ।
तपसा निर्जरा या तु सा चोपकर्मनिर्जरा ॥
स्थितं द्वादशभिर्भेदैर्निर्जराकरणं तपः ।
बाह्यमाभ्यन्तरञ्चेति मूलभेदद्वयान्वितम् ॥ "
[चन्द्रप्रभचरितम् । १८ । १०९ — १२१]

" दुर्जरा निर्जरत्यात्मा यथा कर्म शुभाशुभम् ।
निर्जरा सा द्विधा ज्ञेया सकामाकामभेदतः ॥
सा सकामा स्मृता जैनैर्या व्रतोपक्रमैः कृता ।
अकामा स्वविपाकेन यथा श्वभ्रादिवासिनाम् ॥"
[धर्मशर्माभ्युदयम् । ५१ ॥१२२ — १२३ ।]

"सविपाकाविपाकाभ्यां द्विधा स्यान्निर्जराङ्गिनाम् ।
अविपाका मुनीन्द्राणां सविपाकाखिलात्मनाम् ॥ "
[वर्द्धमानपुराणम् । १६ ॥ ९० ।]

"सव्वेसिं कम्माणं सत्तिविवाओ हवेइ अणुभाओ ।
तदणंतरं तु सडणं कम्माणं णिज्जरा जाण ॥
सा पुण दुविहा णेया सकालपत्ता तवेण कयमाणा ।
चादुगदीणं पढ़मा वयजुत्ताणं हवे विदिया ॥"
[स्वामिकार्त्तिकेयानुप्रेक्षा । १०३ - १०४]

‡ " संवर-जोगेहिं जुदो तवेहिं जो चिट्ठदे बहुविहेहिं ।
कम्माणं णिज्जरणं बहुगाणं कुणदि सो णियदम् ॥"
[पञ्चास्तिकायसमयसारः । १४४]

way in which the destruction of Karmas takes place in the case of sages, while, ordinarily, with respect to all classes of beings, the Karmas disappear only after their fruits are fully enjoyed.

सव्वस्स कम्मणो जो खयहेदू अप्पणो हु परिणामो ।
णेओ स भावमोक्खो दव्वविमोक्खो य कम्मपुधभावो ॥३७॥*

Savvassa Kammaṇo jo khayahedû appaṇo hu pariṇâmo,
Ṇeo sa bhâva-mokkho davva-vimokkho ya kammapudha-bhâvo—(37).

Padapâṭha.—जो Jo, that. अप्पणो Appaṇo, soul's. परिणामो Pariṇâmo, modification. सव्वस्स Savvassa, of all. कम्मणो Kammaṇo, Karma. खयहेदू Khaya-hedû, the cause of destruction. स Sa, that. हु Hu, surely. भावमोक्खो Bhâva-mokkho, Bhâva-mokṣa. णेओ Ṇeyo, to be known. य Ya, and. कम्मपुधभावो Kammapudha-bhâvo, separation of Karma. दव्वविमोक्खो Davva-vimokkho, Dravya-mokṣa.

37. That modification of the soul which is the cause of the destruction of all Karmas, is surely to be known as Bhâva-mokṣa and the (actual) separation of the Karmas [is] Dravya-mokṣa.

COMMENTARY.

When a person is desirous of having liberation, he attempts to have perfect faith, perfect knowledge and perfect conduct. (See Verse 39.) Having perfect faith, knowledge and conduct, he becomes free from the four kinds of Ghâtiya Karmas, Jñânâvaraṇîya, Darśanâ-varaṇîya, Mohanîya and Antarâya (see Commentary on Verse 14). This modification of the soul which leads to the destruction of the Karmas mentioned above is called Bhâvamokṣa. The commentator Brahmadeva, says† that by the words "all Karmas" in the verse, the four

---

* *Sanskrit rendering:*

सर्वस्य कर्मणः यः क्षयहेतुः आत्मनः हि परिणामः ।
ज्ञेयः स भावमोक्षः द्रव्यविमोक्षः च कर्मपृथग्भावः ॥३७॥

Sarvasya karmaṇaḥ yaḥ kṣayahetuḥ âtmanaḥ hi pariṇâmaḥ,
Jñeyaḥ sa bhâvamokṣaḥ dravya-vimokṣaḥ cha karma-prithag-bhâvaḥ—(37).

† "सर्वस्य द्रव्यभावरूपमोहनीयादिघातिचतुष्टयकर्मणो ।"

[ब्रह्मदेवविरचितटीका]

Ghâtiya Dravya and Bhâva Karmas only are meant. In Vardhamâna Purâṇa we have :—

"सर्वेषां कर्मणां योऽत्र क्षयहेतुः शिवार्थिनः ।
परिणामोऽतिशुद्धः स भावमोक्षो जिनैर्मतः ॥"

[Canto XVI. 72.]

i.e., "The extremely pure modification of the soul which is the cause of destruction of all kinds of Karma in a person desirous of good, is regarded as Bhâva-mokṣa by the Jinas."

Now, there is another kind of Mokṣa, called Dravya-mokṣa, which consists of the separation of the soul from the Aghâtiya Karmas, *viz.*, Âyu, Nâma, Gotra and Vedanîya Karmas which disappear last of all. This happens when a being is in the last stage of development which is known as Ayogi. (See Commentary on Verse 13). In Vardhamâna Purâṇa we have :—

"कृत्स्नेभ्यः कर्मजातेभ्यो विश्लेषो यश्चिदात्मनः ।
परमसद्ध्यानयोगेन द्रव्यमोक्षः स कथ्यते ॥"

[Canto XVI. 73.]

i.e., "The separation of the conscious soul from all kinds of Karmas by excellent meditation is known as Dravya-mokṣa."

By Bhâva-mokṣa, therefore, one is freed from the first four, and by Dravya-mokṣa from the last four kinds of Karmas. Both these kinds of Mokṣa together lead to perfect liberation.

Umâsvâmi has written in his Tattvârtha Sûtra X. 1. 2 that a person attains Kevala Jñâna (Omniscience) when first his Mohanîya Karmas and then his Jñânâvaraṇiya, Darśanâvaraṇiya and Antarâya Karmas are destroyed. After attaining Kevala Jñâna, the cause producing bondage being absent and Nirjarâ being present, a person becomes free from the remaining Karmas, *viz.*, Vedanîya, Âyu, Nâma and Gotra Karmas, and thus being void of all kinds of Karma attains liberation *

We have seen that Karmas take possession of a soul through Âsravas. This influx of Karmas can be stopped by Saṃvaras. By

* "मोहक्षयाज्ज्ञानदर्शनावरणान्तरायक्षयाच्च केवलम् ।"
"बन्धहेत्वभावनिर्जराभ्यां कृत्स्नकर्मविप्रमोक्षो मोक्षः ।"

[तत्वार्थाधिगमसूत्रम् । १० । १ । २]

See also :

"अभावाद्बन्धहेतूनां बन्धनिर्जरया तथा ।
कृत्स्नकर्मप्रमोक्षो हि मोक्ष इत्यभिधीयते ॥" [तत्वार्थसारः ।]

this stoppage, fresh Karmas cannot enter the soul. But even after stopping the entrance of fresh Karmas, it is necessary to purge the soul from Karmas which have already taken possession of the former. This can be done by Nirjarâ. Then only the Karmas, Vedanîya, Nâma, Gotra and Âyu which cause worldly existence disappear and a being attains liberation. In Pañchâstikâya-samaya-sâra we have :

"जो संवरेण जुत्तो णिज्जरमाणोध सव्वकम्माणि ।
ववगदवेदाउस्सो मुयदि भवं तेण सो मोक्खो ॥"

[Verse 153.]

i.e., "He who having Saṃvara and destroying all Karmas through Nirjarâ becomes free from Vedanîya, Nâma, Gotra and Âyu Karmas, leaves the world. Therefore this is called Mokṣa (liberation)". *

सुह-असुह-भाव-जुत्ता पुण्णं पावं हवंति खलु जीवा ।
सादं सुहाउ णामं गोदं पुण्णं पराणि पावं च ॥३८॥†

Suha-asuha-bhâva-juttâ puṇṇaṃ pâvaṃ havanti khalu jîvâ,
Sâdaṃ suhâu ṇâmaṃ godaṃ puṇṇaṃ parâṇi pâvaṃ cha—(38).

Padapâtha.—जीवा Jîvâ, Jîvas. सुह-असुह-भाव-जुत्ता Suha-asuha-bhâva-juttâ, having auspicious and inauspicious Bhâvas. खलु Khalu. surely. पुण्णं Puṇṇaṃ, Puṇya. पावं Pâvaṃ, Pâpa. हवंति Havanti, become. सादं Sâtaṃ, Sâtâvedanîya. सुहाउ Suhâu, auspicious life. णामं Ṇâmaṃ, name. गोदं Godaṃ, Gotra. पुण्णं Puṇṇaṃ. Puṇya. च Cha, and. पराणि Paṛâṇi the rest. पावं Pâvaṃ, Pâpa.

---

* Compare also :—

"अनेकजन्मबद्धानां सर्वेषामपि कर्मणाम् ।
विप्रमोक्षः स्मृतो मोक्ष आत्मनः केवलस्थितेः ॥"

[नेमिनिर्वाणम् । १५ ॥ ७६ ।]

"कृत्स्नकर्मक्षयो मोक्षो भव्यस्य परिणामिनः ।"

[चन्द्रप्रभचरितम् । १८ ॥ १२३ ।]

† *Sanskrit rendering* :—

शुभाशुभभावयुक्ताः पुण्यं पापं भवन्ति खलु जीवाः ।
सातं शुभायुः नाम गोत्रं पुण्यं पराणि पापं च ॥ ३८ ॥

Śubhâśubhabhâvayuktâḥ puṇyaṃ pâpaṃ bhavanti khalu jîvâḥ,
Sâtaṃ śubhâyuḥ nâma gotraṃ puṇyaṃ parâṇi pâpaṃ cha—(38).

38. The Jîvas consist of Puṇya and Pâpa surely having auspicious and inauspicious Bhâvas (respectively). Puṇya is Sâtâvedanîya, auspicious life, name, and class, while Pâpa is (exactly) the opposite (of these).

COMMENTARY.

The real characteristic of a Jîva is consciousness, purity and bliss. But through the eternal chain of Karmas, bondage is produced and Jîvas enjoy weal (Puṇya) or woe (Pâpa), according as they are possessed by auspicious and inauspicious Bhâvas. The auspicious Bhâvas are said to consist of freedom from delusion, acquirement of perfect faith and knowledge, practice of reverence and obeisance, observance of the five vows, *viz.*, truth, non-injury, chastity, non-acceptance of worldly objects and refraining from stealing, subduing of the four passions, Anger, Pride, Illusion and Greed, victory over the uncontrollable senses and practice of penances. The inauspicious Bhâvas are opposites of each of these. According as a Jîva is possessed of these auspicious or inauspicious Bhâvas, it has merits or demerits resulting in weal or woe.*

Thus, a Jîva enjoys happiness or misery, according as it is actuated by different kinds of Bhâvas mentioned above.†

In Tattvârthâdhigama Sûtra, we have—"Puṇya consits of Sâtâvedanîya, Śubha Âyu, Śubha Nâma and Śubha Gotra, and Pâpa consists of the opposites of each of these." ‡ We have seen that there

* "उद्वम मिथ्यात्वविषं भावय दृष्टिं च कुरु परां भक्तिम् ।
भावनमस्कारतो ज्ञाने युक्तो भव सदापि ॥
पञ्चमहाव्रतरक्षां कोपचतुष्कस्य निग्रहं परमम् ।
दुर्दान्तेन्द्रियविजयं तपःसिद्धविधौ कुरूद्योगम् ॥
इत्यार्याद्वयकथितलक्षणेन शुभोपयोगभावेन परिणामेन
तद्विलक्षणेनाशुभोपयोगपरिणामेन च युक्ताः परिणताः ।"

[Brahmadeva's Commentary.]

† "सुहपरिणामो पुण्णं असुहो पावंति हवदि जीवस्स ।
दोण्हं पोग्गलमत्तो भावो कम्मत्तणं पत्तो ॥"

[पञ्चास्तिकायसमयसारः । १३२ ।]

‡ "सद्वेद्यशुभायुर्नामगोत्राणि पुण्यम् ।"
"अतोऽन्यत् पापम् ।"

[तत्वार्थाधिगमसूत्रम् । ८ ॥ २५ । २६]

are eight kinds of Karma—Jñânâvaraṇîya, Darśanâvaraṇîya, Mohanîya, Antarâya, Vedanîya, Âyu, Nâma and Gotra and that the first four of these are known as Ghâtiya Karmas while the last four are named Aghâtiya Karmas. Among these, all the Ghâtîya Karmas may be said to be Pâpa, while the Aghâtiya Karmas may be either Puṇya or Pâpa.

Sâtâvedanîya is that Karma by which a soul feels pleasure in external objects and by the assistance of which things which are gratifying to the soul may be procured. Subha Âyu (Auspicious life) consists in having an existence as a God, human being or a beast. Śubha Gotra (Auspicious family) consists in being born in a high status of life. Śubha Nâma (Auspicious name) consists of fame, etc., and is of various kinds. All these make up what is known as Puṇya.

Pâpa, on the other hand, consists of Asâtavedanîya or that Karma which produces pain and procures objects causing pain, Aśubha Âyu (Inauspicious life), *viz.*, an existence in hell, Aśubha Gotra (Inauspicious family) comprising a birth in low stations and Aśubha Nâma (Inauspicious name) consisting of disgrace, etc.

With this ends that section of Dravya-saṃgraha which treats of the seven Tattvas (principles), *viz.*, Âsrava, Bandha, Saṃvara, Nirjarâ, Mokṣa, Puṇya and Pâpa. The next section will deal with the manner by which one can attain liberation.

सम्मद्दंसण णाणं चरणं मोक्खस्स कारणं जाणे ।
ववहारा णिच्चयदो तत्तियमइओ णिओ अप्पा ॥३९॥ *

Sammaddaṃsaṇa ṇâṇaṃ charaṇaṃ Mokkhassa kâraṇaṃ jâṇe,
Vavahârâ Ṇichchayado tattiyamaio ṇio appâ. (39).

Padapâṭha.—ववहारा Vavahârâ, from the ordinary point of view. सम्मद्दंसण णाणं चरणं Samaddaṃsaṇa ṇâṇaṃ charaṇaṃ, perfect faith, knowledge and conduct. मोक्खस्स Mokkhassa, of liberation. कारणं Kâraṇaṃ, cause. जाणे Jâṇe, know. णिच्चयदो Ṇichchayado, really. तत्तियमइओ Tattiyamaio, consisting of of these three. णिओ Ṇiyo, of one's own. अप्पा A'ppâ, soul.

---

* ***Sanskrit rendering*** :

सम्यग्दर्शनं ज्ञानं चरणं मोक्षस्य कारणं जानीहि ।
व्यवहारात् निश्चयतः तत्त्रितयमयः निजः आत्मा ॥ ३९ ॥

Samyagdarśanaṃ jñânaṃ charaṇaṃ mokṣasya kâraṇaṃ jânîhi.
Vyavahârât niśchayataḥ tattritayamayaḥ nijaḥ âtmâ. (39).

39. Know that from the ordinary point of view, perfect faith, knowledge and conduct are the causes of of liberation, while really one's own soul consisting of these three (is the cause of liberation).

Commentary.

Now the author proceeds to lay down the ways and means to liberation. To attain liberation, one must have Perfect Faith, Perfect Knowledge and Perfect Conduct.* These three will be further explained in Verses 41—43. These are technically known as the three jewels in Jaina works. The three jewels are means to liberation from the ordinary point of view. But really these three jewels cannot exist elsewhere than in the soul; so, to be accurate, it is the soul which can produce liberation. This will be emphasised in the next verse.

रयणत्तयं ण वट्टइ अप्पाणं मुयतु अण्णदवियम्हि ।
तम्हा तत्तियमइओ होदि हु मोक्खस्स कारणं आदा ॥४०॥†

Rayaṇattayaṃ ṇa vaṭṭai appâṇaṃ muyatu aṇṇa-daviyamhi,

Tamhâ tattiya-mayio hodi hu mokkhassa kâraṇaṃ âdâ (40.)

Pada pâṭha.—अप्पाणं Appâṇaṃ, the soul. मुयतु, Muyatu, excepting. अण्णदवियम्हि Aṇṇadaviyamhi, in any other substances रयणत्तयं, Rayaṇattayaṃ the

---

* "सम्यग्दर्शनज्ञानचारित्राणि मोक्षमार्गः ।"

[तत्त्वार्थाधिगम-सूत्र १ । १ ।]

"कृत्स्नकर्मक्षयो मोक्षो भव्यस्य परिणामिनः ।
ज्ञानदर्शनचारित्रत्रयोपायः प्रकीर्त्तितः ॥"

[चन्द्रप्रभचरितम् । १८ । १२३ ॥]

"ज्ञानदर्शनचारित्रैरुपायैः परिणामिनः ।
भव्यस्यायमनेकाङ्गविकलैरेव जायते ॥"

[धर्मशर्माभ्युदयम् । २१ ॥ १६१ ।]

† *Sanskrit rendering*:—

रत्नत्रयं न वर्त्तते आत्मानं मुक्त्वा अन्यद्रव्ये ।
तस्मात् तत्त्रितयमयः भवति खलु मोक्षस्य कारणं आत्मा ॥४० ॥

Ratnatrayaṃ na varttate âtmânam muktvâ anya—Dravye.
Tasmât tattritayamayaḥ bhavati khalu mokṣasya kâraṇam âtmâ. (40.)

three jewels. ण Na, not. वट्टइ Vaṭṭai, exist. तम्हा, Tamhâ, therefore. तत्तियमइओ Tattiyamaio, consisting of these three. आदा Âdâ, the soul. हु Hu, surely. मोक्खस्स Mokkhassa, of liberation. कारणं Kâraṇaṃ, cause of. होदि Hodi, becomes.

40. The three jewels (*i. e.*, Perfect Faith, Perfect Knowledge and Perfect Conduct) do not exist in any other substance excepting the soul. Therefore, the soul surely is the cause of liberation.

COMMENTARY.

It has been laid down that, in order to attain Mokṣa or liberation, one must have Perfect Faith, Perfect Knowledge and Perfect Conduct. These three are therefore the means to liberation. But these should not be considered to be apart from the soul, for nowhere but in the soul can each or all of these exsist. It is the soul possessed of all these three jewels that is really fit for liberation. Strictly speaking, therefore, the soul itself attains liberation when it is possessed of certain characteristics (viz., these three jewels). But from the ordinary point of view, we regard the three jewels as apart from the soul as the causes of liberation though from the realistic point of view, the soul possessed of these three jewels is the cause of Mokṣa.

जीवादीसद्दहणं सम्मत्तं रुवमप्पणो तं तु ।
दुरभिणिवेसविमुक्कं णाणं सम्मं खु होदि सदि जम्हि ॥४१॥*

Jîvâdîsaddahaṇaṃ sammattaṃ rûvamappaṇo taṃ tu,

Durabhiṇivesavimukkaṃ ṇâṇaṃ sammaṃ khu hodi sadi jamhi (41).

Padapâṭha.—जीवादि-सद्दहणं Jîvâdi-saddahaṇaṃ, faith in Jîva, etc. सम्मत्तं Sammattaṃ, Samyaktva (Perfect Faith). तं Taṃ, that. अप्पणो Appaṇo, of soul. रुवं Rûvaṃ, quality. तु Tu, and. जम्हि Jamhi, that. सदि Sadi, being. खु Khu, surely. णाणं Nâṇaṃ, Jñâna (knowledge). दुरभिणिवेसविमुक्कं Durabhinivesa-vimukkaṃ, free from errors. सम्मं Saṃmaṃ, perfect होदि Hodi, becomes.

* *Sanskrit rendering :—*

जीवादिश्रद्धानं सम्यक्त्वं रूपं आत्मनः तत् तु ।
दुरभिनिवेशविमुक्तं ज्ञानं सम्यक् खलु भवति सति यस्मिन् ॥ ४१ ॥

Jîvâdi-sraddhânaṃ samyaktvaṃ rûpaṃ âtmanaḥ tat tu.
Durabhinivesa-vimuktaṃ jñânaṃ samyak khalu bhavati sati yasmin (41).

41. Samyaktva (perfect faith) is the belief in Jîva, etc. That is a quality of the soul, and when this arises, Jñâna (knowledge), being free from errors surely becomes perfect.

COMMENTARY.

Jîva, Ajîva, Âsrava, Bandha, Saṃvara, Nirjarâ and Mokṣa are the seven Tattvas (essential principles) of Jainism.* A sincere belief in these Tattvas is called Samyaktva or Perfect Faith.† The first step to liberation, according to Jainism, is to have a belief in these essential principles of Jainism. It is only after a person has this faith that he can attain Perfect Knowledge. He may have knowledge of substances before he attains Perfect Faith; but this knowledge is apt to be fallacious, for errors might creep in the same. For example, a person may have a knowledge of the aforesaid seven principles of Jainism, but that knowledge may be vague or indefinite or it may be full of doubts, or it may be entirely wrong. These defects of knowledge arise, because the person has not at that time perfect faith in the essential principles of Jainism, for Perfect Faith in such principles is incompatible with doubts and indecision or a belief in opposite principles. Consequently, the knowledge of these principles which succeeds Perfect Faith is free from errors or fallacy. This knowledge is known as Samyak Jñâna (or Perfect Knowledge.)

संसयविमोहविब्भमविवज्जियं अप्पपरसरुवस्स ।
गहणं सम्मं-णाणं सायारमणेयभेयं च ॥४२॥‡

Saṃsaya-vimoha-vibbhama-vivajjiyaṃ appaparasa-rûvassa,

---

* "जीवाजीवास्रवबन्धसंवरनिर्जरामोक्षास्तत्त्वम् ।"
[तत्त्वार्थाधिगमसूत्रम् । १ । ४]

† "तत्त्वार्थश्रद्धानं सम्यग्दर्शनम् ॥"
[तत्त्वार्थाधिगमसूत्रम् । १ । २]

‡ Sanskrit rendering:

संशयविमोहविभ्रमविवर्जितं आत्मपरस्वरूपस्य ।
ग्रहणं सम्यग् ज्ञानं साकारं अनेकभेदं च ॥ ४२ ॥

Saṃśayavimohavibhramavivarjitam âtmaparasvarûpasya.
Grahaṇaṃ samyag-Jñanaṃ sâkâraṃ anekabhedaṃ cha. (42).

Gahaṇaṃ sammaṃ—ṇâṇaṃ sâyâramaneyabheyaṃ cha (42.)

Padapâṭha.—संसयविमोहविब्भमविवज्जियं Saṃsaya-vimohavibbhama-vivajjiyaṃ, freed from Saṃśaya (Doubt), Vimoha (Perversity) and Vibbhrama (Indefiniteness). सायारम् Sâyâraṃ, detailed. अप्पपरसरूवस्स Appaparasarûvassa, of the real nature of ego and non-ego. गहणं Gahaṇaṃ, cognition. सम्मं-णाणं Sammaṃ Ṇâṇaṃ, Samyak Jñâna or Perfect Knowledge. च Cha, and. अणेयभेयम् Aṇeyabheyaṃ, of many varieties.

42. Samyak Jñâna (Perfect Knowledge) is the detailed cognition of the real nature of the ego and non-ego, is freed from Saṃśaya (Doubt), Vimoha (Perversity) and Vibhrama (Indefiniteness), and is of many varieties.

COMMENTARY.

Correct knowledge, according to Jaina Nyâya philosophy must be free from the Samâropa (*i.e.*, fallacies).* This Samâropa is said to be of three kinds, Viparyaya or Vimoha (Perversity), Saṃśaya (Doubt) and Anadhyavasâya or Vibhrama (Indefiniteness.)† The cognition of an object as something which is quite the contrary of its real self, is known as Viparyaya or Vimoha. For example, if we think nacre to be silver, we have a knowledge vitiated by Viparyaya or Vimoha (Perversity.)‡ Saṃsaya consists of doubt when our mind sways between this or that, without being able to assert the true nature of anything. For example, when we see a certain object from a distance and are unable to say whether it is a man or a post, we have an instance of Saṃśaya

* "अतस्मिँस्तदध्यवसायः समारोपः ।"

[प्रमाणनयतत्त्वालोकालङ्कारः १ । ७ ।]

† "स विपर्ययसंशयानध्यवसायभेदात् त्रेधा ॥"

[प्रमाणनयतत्त्वालोकालङ्कारः १ । ८]

‡ "विपरीतैककोटिनिष्टङ्कनं विपर्ययः ।" "यथा शुक्तिकायामिदं रजतमिति ।"

[प्रमाणनयतत्त्वालोकालङ्कारः । १ । ९ । १० ।]

"विपरीतैककोटिनिश्चयो विपर्ययः । यथा शुक्तिकायामिदं रजतमिति ज्ञानम् । अत्रापि सादृश्यादिनिमित्तवशात् शुक्तिविपरीते रजते निश्चयः ।"

[न्यायदीपिका]

"अतस्मिंस्तदेवेति विपर्ययः ।" [प्रमाणमीमांसा । १ । १ । ७ ।]

or doubt.* A knowledge that this is something without any clear dea of what it is, is called Anadhyavasâya or Vibhrama. For example, such a knowledge arises in the mind of a person when he touches something while he is moving. He is conscious that he has touched something, but is unable to say what it is.† These being the varieties of fallacy, there is no doubt that in Perfect Knowledge these are entirely absent. In the state of Perfect Knowledge we have a clear idea of the real nature of everything, ego and non-ego. This idea is not of a shadowy kind, but consists of detailed knowledge. We have already described the difference between detailed and detailless knowledge in the commentary on Verse 4, page 9.

जं सामण्णं गहणं भावाणं णेव कट्टुमायारं ।
अविसेसिदूण अट्टे दंसणमिदि भण्णये समये ॥४३॥‡

Jaṃ sâmaṇṇaṃ gahaṇaṃ bhâvâṇaṃ ṇeva kaṭṭumâyâraṃ,
Avisesidûṇa aṭṭe daṃsaṇamidi bhaṇṇaye samaye—(43).

---

* "साधकबाधकप्रमाणाभावादनवस्थिताऽनेककोटिसंस्पर्शि ज्ञानं संशयः ।"
"यथाऽयं स्थाणुर्वा पुरुषो वा ।"
[प्रमाणनयतत्त्वालोकालङ्कारः । १ । ११-१२ ।]

"विरुद्धानेककोटिस्पर्शि ज्ञानं संशयः । यथाऽयं स्थाणुर्वा पुरुषो वेति । स्थाणुपुरुषसाधारणोर्ध्वतादि-दर्शनात्तद्विशेषस्य वक्रकोटरशिरः—पाण्यादेः साधक-प्रमाणस्याभावादनेककोट्यवलम्बितत्वं ज्ञानस्य ।" [न्यायदीपिका ।]

"अनुभयत्रोभयकोटिसंस्पर्शि-प्रत्ययः संशयः ।"
[प्रमाणमीमांसा । १ । १ । ५]

† "किमित्यालोचनमात्रमनध्यवसायः । यथा गच्छत्तृणस्पर्शज्ञानम् ।"
[प्रमाणनयतत्त्वालोकालङ्कारः । १ । १३ । १४]

"किमित्यालोचनमात्रमनध्यवसायः । यथा पथि गच्छतस्तृणस्पर्शादि-ज्ञानम् [न्यायदीपिका ।]

"विशेषानुल्लेख्यमनध्यवसायः ।" [प्रमाणमीमांसा । १ । १ । ७]

‡ *Sanskrit rendering* :

यत् सामान्यं ग्रहणं भावानां नैव कृत्वा आकारम् ।
अविशेषयित्वा अर्थान् दर्शनम् इति भण्यते समये ॥ ४३ ॥

Yat sâmânyaṃ grahaṇaṃ bhâvânâṃ naiva kritvâ âkâraṃ,
Aviśeṣayitvâ arthân darśanaṃ iti bhaṇyate samaye—(43).

Padapâṭha.—अट्टे Aṭṭe, things. अविसेसिदूण Avisesidûṇa, without particulars. आयारम् Âyâraṃ, detail. णेव Ṇeva, not. कट्टुम् Kaṭṭuṃ, grasping. जं Jaṃ, which. भावाणं Bhâvâṇaṃ, things. सामण्णं Sâmaṇṇaṃ, general. गहणं Gahaṇaṃ, perception. दंसणम् Daṃsaṇaṃ, Darśana. इदि Idi, this. समये Samaye, in the scriptures. भण्णये Bhaṇṇaye, is called.

43. That perception of the generalities of things without particularities in which there is no grasping of details, is called Darśana in (Jaina) scriptures.

COMMENTARY.

Darśana is knowledge without details. For example, when a person sees a cloth, as long as he is only conscious of the existence of something called cloth, he is said to have Darśana. But when he begins to have knowledge of the details, *viz.*, the size, colour, etc., of that piece of cloth, he is said to have Jñâna. We have already made this clear in the commentary on Verse 4, page 9.

In Tattvârthâdhigama Sûtra of Umàsvâmi, we have "Samyak Darśana is faith in the principles of Jainism" ["तत्वार्थश्रद्धानं सम्यग्दर्शनम्" १।२] That Darśana is not the same as the Darśana which we have described above. There Samyak Darśana means perfect faith, and details are present there, while here it means knowledge without details.*

दंसणपुव्वं णाणं छदुमत्थाणं ण दुण्णि उवओगा ।
जुगवं जम्हा केवलिणाहे जुगवं तु ते दोवि ॥४४॥†

Daṃsaṇapuvvaṃ ṇâṇaṃ chhadumatthâṇaṃ ṇa duṇṇi uvaogâ.
Jugavaṃ jaṃhâ kevaliṇâhe jugavaṃ tu te dovi—(44).

Padapâṭha.—छदुमत्थाणं Chhadumatthâṇaṃ, of the Saṃsârî Jîvas. दंसणपुव्वं Daṃsaṇapuvvaṃ, preceded by Darśana. णाणं Ṇâṇaṃ, Jñâna. जम्हा Jaṃhâ, for this reason. दुण्णि Duṇṇi, two. उवओगा Uvayogâ, Upayoga. जुगवं Jugavaṃ,

* "नेदमेव तत्वार्थश्रद्धानलक्षणं सम्यग्दर्शनम् वक्तव्यम् । कस्मादिति चेत् ? तत्र श्रद्धानं विकल्परूपम्, इदं तु निर्विकल्पम् ।"

[Brahmadeva's Commentary]

† *Sanskrit rendering:*

दर्शनपूर्वं ज्ञानं छद्मस्थानां न द्वौ उपयोगौ ।
युगपत् यस्मात् केवलिनाथे तु ते द्वौ अपि ॥ ४४ ॥

Darśanapûrvaṃ jñânaṃ chhadmasthânâṃ na dvau upayogau.
Yugapat yasmât kevalinâthe tu te dvau api. -(44).

simultaneously. ण Ṇa, not. तु Tu, but. केवलिणाहे Kevaliṇâhe, in Kevalis. ते Te, those. दो Do, two. वि Vi, together. जुगवं Jugavaṃ, simultaneously.

44. In Saṃsârî Jîvas, Jñâna is preceded by Darśana. For this reason (in him), the two Upayogas (*viz.*, Jñâna and Darśana) do not (arise) simultaneously. But in Kevalis, both of these two (arise) simultaneously.

COMMENTARY.

Saṃsârî Jîvas or beings leading a mundane existence have Darśana or detail-less knowledge. first of all. Then they have Jñâna or knowledge, with details. But this is not the case with Kevalis, who have Darśana and Jñâna at once. The reason for this difference is that in Saṃsârî Jîvas, there are hindrances, known as Darśanâvaraṇîya and Jñânâvaraṇîya Karmas (*i.e.*, Karmas obscuring Darśana and Jñâna), which must be destroyed or mitigated (Kṣaya or Upaśama), before Darśana or Jñâna can arise. But in a Kevali, these obscuring Karmas are entirely absent; so Darśana and Jñâna can both arise at the same time. Brahmadeva has illustrated this as follows. In the case of Saṃsârî Jîvas, the knowledge of the objects through Darśana and Jñâna is gradual, first, without, and then with details like the revelation of objects by the light of the sun when it is obscured by clouds, but the appearance of Darśana and Jñâna in Kevalis is like the sudden illumination of every object when the sun appears in a cloudless sky.* The clouds represent the Karmas which obscure Jñâna and Darśana.

असुहादो विणिवित्ती सुहे पवित्ती य जाण चारित्तं ।
वदसमिदिगुत्तिरुवं ववहारणया दु जिणभणियं ॥४५॥†

Asuhâdo viṇivittî suhe pavittî ya jâṇa chârittaṃ.
Vadasamidiguttirûvaṃ vavahâraṇayâ du jiṇabhaṇiyaṃ—(45.)

---

* "केवलिनां तु भगवतां निर्विकारस्वसंवेदनसमुत्पन्ननिराकरणक्षायिकज्ञानसहितत्वात् निर्मेघादित्ये युगपदातपप्रकाशवद्दर्शनं ज्ञानं च युगपदेव इति विज्ञेयम् ।" [Brahmadeva's Commentary.]

† *Sanskrit rendering*:

अशुभात् विनिवृत्तिः शुभे प्रवृत्तिः च जानीहि चारित्रम् ।
व्रतसमितिगुप्तिरूपं व्यवहारनयात् तु जिनभणितम् ॥ ४५ ॥

Aśubhât vinivrittiḥ śubhe pravrittiḥ cha jânîhi chârittraṃ.
Vrata-samitiguptirûpaṃ vyavahâranayât tu jiṇabhaṇitaṃ—(45.)

Padapâṭha.—असुहादो Asuhâdo, from what is harmful. विणिवित्ती Viṇivittî, refraining. य Ya, and. सुहे Suhe, in what is beneficial. पवित्ती Pavittî, engagement. चारित्तं Chârittaṃ, Châritra (Conduct). जाण Jâṇa, know. दु Du, but. ववहारणया Vavahâraṇayâ, according to Vyavahâra Naya. वदसमिदिगुत्तिरूवं Vadasamidiguttirûvaṃ, consisting of Vrata, Samiti and Gupti. जिणभणियं Jiṇabhaṇiyaṃ, mentioned by the Jina.

45. Know Châritra to be refraining from what is harmful and engagement in what is beneficial. But according to Vyavahâra Naya, Châritra (Conduct) has been mentioned by the Jina to consist of Vrata, Samiti and Gupti.

COMMENTARY.

From the ordinary point of view, Vratas (Vows), Samitis (Attitudes of carefulness) and Guptis (Restraints) may be said to constitute Châritra (Conduct.) We have already described what Vratas, Samitis and Guptis are in Verse 35. One who is immersed in worldly aspirations and attached to worldly objects, one whose soul is possessed of attachment and aversion, one who listens non-Jaina scriptures, one who has a vicious mind, keeps evil company and follows the terrible evil path of life, is said to be active in the pursuit of what is harmful (Aśubha).* Refraining from these and engagement in the opposite of these by practising the five Vratas, five Samitis and three Guptis lead to what is beneficial (Śubha). Châritra (Conduct) consists in the pursuit of what is beneficial and avoidance of what is harmful.

What is really Samyak Châritra (Perfect Conduct) will appear from the next verse.

बहिरब्भंतरकिरियारोहो भवकारणप्पणासट्ठं ।
णाणिस्स जं जिणुत्तं तं परमं सम्मचारित्तम् ॥४६॥†

Bahirabbhaṃtarakiriyâroho bhavakâraṇappaṇâsaṭṭhaṃ,

---

* "विसयकसाओगाढोदुस्सुदिदुच्चित्तदुट्ठगोट्ठिजुदो ।
उग्गो उम्मग्गपरो उवओगो जस्स सो असुहे ॥"
[Verse quoted in Brahmadeva's Commentary.]

† *Sanskrit rendering* ;
बहिरभ्यंतरक्रियारोधः भवकारणप्रणाशार्थम् ।
ज्ञानिनः यत् जिनोक्तं तं परमं सम्यक् चारित्रम् ॥ ४६ ॥
Bahirabhyantarakriyârodhaḥ bhavakâraṇapraṇâśârthaṃ,
Jñâninaḥ yat jinok-taṃ taṃ paramaṃ samyak chârittraṃ—(46)

Ṇâṇissa jaṃ jiṇuttaṃ taṃ paramaṃ samma-chârittaṃ—
(46).

Padapâtha. भवकारणप्पणासट्ठं Bhavakâraṇappaṇâsaṭṭhaṃ, to destroy the causes of Saṃsâra. जं Jaṃ, which. णाणिस्स Ṇâṇissa, of one who has knowledge. बहिरब्भंतरकिरियारोहो Bahirabbhaṃtarakiriyâroho, the checking of external and internal actions. तं Taṃ, that. जिणुत्तं Jiṇuttaṃ, mentioned by the Jinas. परमं Paramaṃ, excellent. सम्मचारित्तं Sammachârittaṃ, perfect conduct.

46. That checking of external and internal actions by one who has knowledge, in order to destroy the causes of Saṁsâra, is the excellent Samyak Châritra (Perfect Conduct) mentioned by the Jina.

COMMENTARY.

In the previous verse, Châritra (Conduct) from the ordinary point of view has been described. In this verse, we are introduced to Châritra from the realistic point of view.

When a person checks all external activities of body and speech, together with all internal activities of the mind, so that all hindrances to the understanding of the true character of the soul are removed, he is said to have Samyak Châritra (Perfect Conduct).* By this means, the person becomes free from all influx of beneficial or harmful Karmas, which cause Samsâra or worldly existence.† Perfect Conduct therefore consists in checking all kinds of activities which are opposed to the characteristics of the soul, which is void of all actions, eternal and consisting of pure Jñâna and Darśana.

दुविहंपि मोक्खहेउं झाणे पाऊणदि जं मुणी णियमा ।
तम्हा पयत्तचित्ता जूयं झाणं समब्भसह ॥४७॥‡

Duvihaṃpi mokkhaheuṃ jhâṇe pâûṇadi jaṃ muṇî ṇiyamâ,

---

* "निष्क्रियनित्यनिरञ्जनविशुद्धज्ञानदर्शनस्वभावस्य निजात्मनः प्रतिपक्षभूतस्य बहिर्विषये शुभाशुभवचनकायव्यापाररूपस्य तथैवाभ्यन्तरे शुभाशुभमनोविकल्परूपस्य च क्रियाव्यापारस्य योऽसौ निरोधस्त्यागः ।"
[Brahmadeva's Commentary.]

† "भवस्य संसारस्य व्यापार कारणभूतो योऽसौ शुभाशुभकर्मास्रवस्तस्य प्रणाशार्थं विनाशार्थमिति ।"

‡ *Sanskrit rendering :*

द्विविधमपि मोक्षहेतुं ध्यानेन प्राप्नोति यत् मुनिः नियमात् ।
तस्मात् प्रयत्नचित्ताः यूयं ध्यानं समभ्यसध्वम् ॥४७॥

Dvividhamapi mokṣahetuṃ Dhyânena prâpnoti yat muniḥ niyamât,
Tasmât prayatnachittâḥ yûyaṃ Dhyânaṃ samabhyasadhvaṃ—(47).

Tamhâ payattachittâ jûyam jhâṇam samavbhasaha— (47).

Padapâṭha.—जं Jaṃ, because. मुणी Muṇî, a sage. णियमा Ṇiyamâ, by the rule. दुविहं Duviham, two kinds. पि Pi, both. मोक्खहेउं Mokkhaheum, the cause of liberation. झाणे Jhâṇe, by meditation. पाउणदि Pâûṇadi, gets. तम्हा Tamhâ, therefore. जूयं Jûyam, you. पयत्तचित्ता Payattachîttâ, with careful mind झाणं Jhâṇam meditation. समब्भसह Samabhasaha, practise.

47. Because by the rule a sage gets both the (Vyavahâra and Niśchaya) causes of liberation by meditation, therefore (all of) you practise meditation with careful mind.

COMMENTARY.

Perfect faith, perfect knowledge and perfect conduct are the causes of liberation from the ordinary point of view, while really the soul itself possessed of these three is the cause of liberation. By meditation, one can have perfect faith, perfect knowledge and perfect conduct, and one can understand the soul also only through meditation. Therefore, Dhyâna or meditation is of supreme importance for a person who seeks liberation. The author therefore in this verse asks everyone who is eager to attain liberation to practise meditation.

मा मुज्झह मा रज्जह मा दुस्सह इट्ठणिट्ठअत्थेसु ।
थिरमिच्छह जइ चित्तं विचित्तझाणप्पसिद्धीए ॥४८॥*

Mâ mujjhaha mâ rajjaha mâ dussaha iṭṭhaṇiṭṭhaatthesu,
Thiramichchhaha jai chittam vichittajhâṇappasiddhîe— (48).

Padapâṭha.—जइ Jai, if. विचित्तझाणप्पसिद्धीए Vichittajhâṇappasiddhîe, to succeed in various kinds of meditation. चित्तं Chittam, mind. थिरं Thiram, fixed. इच्छह Ichchhaha, wish. इट्ठणिट्ठअत्थेसु Iṭṭhaṇiṭṭha-atthesu, in beneficial and harmful objects. मा Mâ, do not. मुज्झह Mujjhaha, be deluded. मा Mâ, do not. रज्जह Rajjaha, be attached to. मा Mâ, do not. दुस्सह Dussaha, be averse to.

48. If you wish to have your mind fixed, in order to succeed in various kinds of meditation, do not be

* *Sanskrit rendering:*

मा मुह्यत मा रज्यत मा द्विष्यत इष्टानिष्टार्थेषु ।
स्थिरं इच्छथ यदि चित्तं विचित्रध्यानप्रसिद्ध्यै ॥४८॥

Mâ muhyata mâ rajyata mâ dviṣyata iṣṭâniṣṭârtheṣu,
Sthiram ichchhatha yadi chittam vichitra-Dhyânaprasiddhyai—(48).

deluded by or attached to beneficial objects and do not be averse to harmful objects.

COMMENTARY.

To succeed in the practice of meditation, one must be free from all disturbing feelings. He should neither be attracted to pleasant objects nor repulsed by unpleasant objects. He should be indifferent to everything, may it be beneficial or harmful. By this means, he would be able to fix his soul upon itself, as the calmness of his mind would remain undisturbed through the disappearance of disturbances arising from attachment and aversion.

पणतीस सोल छप्पण चदु दुगमेगं च जवह झाएह ।
परमेट्ठिवाचयाणं अण्णं च गुरूवएसेण ॥४६॥*

Paṇatîsa sola chhappaṇa chadu dugamegaṃ cha javaha jhâeha,
Parameṭṭhivâchayâṇaṃ aṇṇaṃ cha gurûvaesena—(49.)

Padapâṭha.—परमेट्ठिवाचयाणं Parameṭṭhivâchayâṇaṃ, signifying the Parameṣṭhis. पणतीस Paṇatîsa, thirty-five. सोल Sola, sixteen. छ Chha, six. पण Paṇa, five. चदु Chadu, four. दुगम् Dugaṃ, two. च Cha, and. एगं Egaṃ, one. च Cha, and. गुरुवएसेण Gurûva—eseṇa, by instruction of the Guru (preceptor). अण्णं Aṇṇaṃ, others जवह Javaha. repeat. झाएह Jhâeha, meditate.

49. Repeat and meditate on (the Mantras), signifying the Parameṣṭhis and consisting of thirty-five, sixteen, six, five, four, two and one (letter) and other (mantras) taught by the Guru (preceptor).

COMMENTARY.

In this verse, we are introduced to the daily prayer of the Jainas. In all religions, a formula consisting of the daily prayer has been prescribed; and in Jaina religion, this prayer can be lengthened or shortened, according to the occasion or capacity of the worshipper.

---

* *Sanskrit rendering* :

पञ्चत्रिंशत् षोडश षट् पञ्च चत्वारि द्विकम् एकं च जपत ध्यायेत ।
परमेष्ठिवाचकानाम् अन्यत् च गुरूपदेशेन ॥ ४९ ॥

Pañchatrinśat ṣoḍaśa ṣat pañcha chatvâri dvikaṃ ekaṃ cha japata dhyayeta,
Parameṣṭhivâchakânâṃ anyat cha gurûpadeśena—(49.)

The full prayer is as follows :—

" Ṇamo Arihantâṇaṁ, ṇamo Siddhâṇaṃ, ṇamo Âyariyâṇaṃ, ṇaṃo Uvajjhâyâṇaṃ, ṇamo loe savvasâhûṇaṃ."—

["णमो अरिहंताणं णमो सिद्धाणं, णमो आयरियाणं, णमो उवज्झायाणं, णमो लोए सव्वसाहूणम् ।"]

I.E., " Obeisance to the Arhats, obeisance to the Siddhas, obeisance to the Âchâryas, obeisance to the Upâdhyâyas and obeisance to all Sâdhus in the universe." This prayer in original consists of thirtyfive words.

Who are meant by the words Arhat, Siddhas, Âchâryas, Upâdhyâyas and Sâdhus, will appear from Verses 50, 51, 52, 53 and 54 respectively. These five classes of beings who are to be revered are known as Pañcha Parameṣṭhis (the five supreme beings). [See Illustration.]

Instead of the full Mantra, one may utter " Arihanta Siddha Âyiriâ Uvajjhâyâ Sâhû" **["अरिहंत सिद्ध आइरिया उवज्झाया साहू"]** which consists of sixteen letters. The following Mantras, each consisting of six letters, may also be uttered : " Arihanta Siddhâ " **["अरिहंत सिद्धा"]** " Arihanta si sâ **["अरिहंत सि सा"]** or " Om ṇamo siddhâṇaṃ " **["ओं णमो सिद्धाणं"]** A Mantra still shorter, consisting of five letters, *viz.*, " A si â u sâ " **["अ सि आ उ सा"]** in which only the first letters of the words Arhat, Siddha, Âchârya, Upâdhyâya and Sâdhu are taken, may also be used. Again the following Mantras, each consisting of four letters, may be employed : **"अरहंत"** [Arahanta] or " A si sâhû " **["अ सि साहू"]**. There are three Mantras, each consisting of two letters, *viz.*, " Siddha " **["सिद्ध"]** " A sâ " **["अ सा"]** " and " Oṃ ṇhî " **["ओं ह्रीं"]** Lastly, combining the first letter of the five words, denoting the Pañcha Parameṣṭhis we get a Mantra of one letter, *viz.*, " Oṃ " **["ओम्"]*** Some say that " A " **["अ"]** is also a Mantra of one letter.

---

* The word " Oṃ " is thus derived : 'A,' the first letter of Arhat, the letter "A" representing Aśarîra (*i.e.*, without body) Siddha, " Â," the first letter of Âchârya, " U "—the first letter of Upâdhyâya and " Ma," the first letter of Muni (or Sâdhu) being conjoined by the rules of Sandhi become " Oṃ " [*vide* "[illegible] ।" "[illegible] ।" Śâkatâyana's Grammar, I. I. 77 and I. I. 82.]

C. F. "अरहंता असरीरा आइरिया तह उवज्झया मुणियो ।
पढमक्खरणिप्पण्णो ओंकारो पंचपरमेट्ठी ॥ "

PLATE X The Pancha Paramesṭhis

These, therefore, are the Mantras consisting of thirty-five, sixteen, six, five, four, two and one letter respectively. These Mantras, should be uttered audibly or repeated mentally. Besides these Mantras, one may utter or meditate on other Mantras taught by one's spiritual preceptors. The commentator, Brahmadeva, says that examples of such Mantras may be found in the work entitled "Pañcha-namaskâra," consisting of twelve thousand verses.*

णट्ठचदुघाइकम्मो दंसणसुहणाणवीरियमईओ ।
सुहदेहत्थो अप्पा सुद्धो अरिहो विचिंतिज्जो ॥५०॥†

Ṇaṭṭhachadughâikammo daṃsaṇa-suha-ṇâṇa-vîri-yamaîo,
Suhadehattho appâ suddho ariho vichintijjo—(50).

Padapâṭha.—णट्ठचदुघाइकम्मो Naṭṭhachadughâikammo, one who has destroyed the four Ghâtiya Karmas. दंसणसुहणाणवीरियमईओ Daṃsaṇa-suha-ṇâṇa-vîriya-mayîo, possessed of faith, happiness, knowledge and power. सुहदेहत्थो Suhadehattho, existing in an auspicious body. सुद्धो Suddho, pure. अप्पा Appâ, soul. अरिहो Ariho, Arhan. विचिंतिज्जो Vichintijjo, to be meditated on.

50. That pure soul existing in an auspicious body, possessed of (infinite) faith, happiness, knowledge and power which has destroyed the four Ghâtiya Karmas, is to be meditated on as an Arhat.

COMMENTARY.

The four kinds of Karma, *viz.*, Jñânâvaraṇîya, Darśaṇâvaraṇîya, Mohanîya and Antarâya destroy the natural characteristics of a soul.

---

* "द्वादशसहस्रप्रमितपञ्चनमस्कारग्रन्थकथितक्रमेण लघुसिद्धचक्रं बृहत्सिद्धचक्रमित्यादिदेवार्चनविधानं भेदाभेदरत्नत्रयाराधकगुरुप्रसादेन ज्ञात्वा ध्यातव्यम् ।"

i. e., "One should meditate on the manner of worshipping supreme beings, known as Laghu Siddha Chakra and Brihat Siddha Chakra, as is mentioned in the work called, Pañcha-namaskâra, consisting of twelve thousand verses, after one is aware of the same through the kindness of a spiritual preceptor, who practises the three jewels." [Brahmadeva's Commentary.]

† *Sanskrit rendering* :

नष्टचतुर्घातिकर्मा दर्शनसुखज्ञानवीर्यमयः ।
शुभदेहस्थ आत्मा शुद्धः अर्हन् विचिन्तनीयः ॥५०॥

Naṣṭachaturghâtikarmâ darśanasukhajñânavîryamayaḥ,
Śubhadehasthaḥ âtmâ śuddhaḥ arhan vichintanîyaḥ—(50).

For this reason, these are known as Ghâtiya Karmas (destroying Karmas). (1) An Arhat is freed from these four kinds of Karmas, and consequently he possesses the following four excellent qualities, each of which appears at the disappearance of each of the four Ghâtiyâ Karmas: *viz.*, perfect knowledge (arising from the destruction of Jñânavaraṇîya Karma), perfect faith (arising from the destruction of Darśanâvaraṇîya Karma), infinite happiness (arising from the destruction of Mohanîya Karma) and infinite power (arising from the destruction of Antarâya Karma). An Arhat is, therefore, bereft of Jñânâvaraṇîya, Darśanâvaraṇîya, Mohanîya and Antarâya Karmas and possessed of infinite faith, knowledge, happiness and power. An Arhat is also Śuddha (pure), as he is void of eighteen kinds of faults, *viz.*, hunger, thirst, fear, aversion, attachment, illusion, anxiety, old age, sickness, death, fatigue, perspiration, pride, displeasure, astonishment, birth, sleep and sorrow.* From the realistic point of view, an Arhat is without a body; but from the ordinary point of view, we speak of an Arhat to possess a body known as Audârika, which is brilliant as a thousand suns.†

An Arhat has one thousand and eight synonyms Vîtarága, Sarvajña, etc. According to Jainism, when an Arhat is conceived, is born, is first engaged in penances, is in a state of attaining perfect knowledge and is in the last stage of obtaining Nirvâṇa, the gods Indra, etc., are said to worship him. These worshippings are technically known as Pañcha-mahâkalyâṇa.‡

---

* "क्षुधा तृषा भयं द्वेषो रागो मोहश्च चिन्तनम् ।
जरा रुजा च मृत्युश्च खेदः स्वेदो मदोऽरतिः ।
विस्मयो जननं निद्रा विषादोष्टादश स्मृताः ।
एतैर्दोषैर्विनिर्मुक्तः सोऽयमाप्तो निरञ्जनः ॥"

[Verses quoted in Brahmadeva's Commentary].

† "निश्चयेनाशरीरोऽपि व्यवहारेण सप्तधातुरहितदिवाकरसहस्रभासुरपरमौदारिकशरीरत्वात् शुभदेहस्थः ।"

[Brahmadeva's Commentary].

‡ "इन्द्रादिभिर्विनिर्मितां गर्भावतरण-जन्माभिषेक-निष्क्रमण-केवलज्ञानोत्पत्तिनिर्वाणाभिधानपञ्च-महाकल्याणरूपां पूजामर्हन्ति ।"

[Brahmadeva's Commentary].

णट्ठट्ठकम्मदेहो लोयालोयस्स जाणग्रो दट्ठा ।
पुरिसायारो अप्पा सिद्धो झाएह लोयसिहरत्थो ॥५१॥*

Naṭṭhaṭṭhakammadeho loyâloyassa jâṇao daṭṭhâ,
Purisâyâro appâ siddho jhâeha loyasiharattho—(51).

Padapâṭha.—णट्ठट्ठकम्मदेहो Naṭṭhaṭṭhakammadeho, void of bodies, produced by eight kinds of Karma. लोयालोयस्स Loyâloyassa, of Loka and Aloka. जाणओ Jâṇao, knower. दट्ठा Daṭṭhâ, seer. पुरिसायारो Purisâyâro, having the shape of a Puruṣa. लोयसिहरत्थो Loyasiharattho, staying at the summit of the universe. अप्पा Appâ, soul. सिद्धो Siddho, Siddha. झाएह Jhâeha, meditate.

51 Meditate on the Siddha—the soul which is bereft of the bodies produced by eight kinds of Karma, which is the seer and knower of Loka and Aloka, which has a shape like a human being and which stays at the summit of the universe.

COMMENTARY.

Really speaking, a Siddha is without a body, and hence incapable of being perceived by the senses. But from the ordinary point of view, a Siddha is said to have a shadowy shape, resembling the figure of a human being† That is to say, the shape of a Siddha resembles a human figure, but is not clearly defined. The body is like the shadow of a human being. A Siddha may attain a higher stage which is the final one. A Siddha's body is therefore a little less than the final body.

A Siddha has not therefore a gross body which results from eight kinds of Karmas. He lives at the summit of Lokâkâśa, or the universe in a place called the Siddha-śilâ, beyond which Alokâkâsa begins. A Siddha, however, has knowledge of everything in Lokâkâsa and Alokâkâsa which existed in the past, exists in the present or

* *Sanskrit rendering:*

नष्टाष्टकर्मदेहः लोकालोकस्य ज्ञायकः द्रष्टा ।
पुरुषाकारः आत्मा सिद्धः ध्यायेत लोकशिखरस्थः ॥५१॥

Naṣṭâṣṭakarmadehaḥ lokâlokasya jñâyakaḥ draṣṭâ,
Puruṣâkâraḥ âtmâ siddhaḥ dhyâyeta lokaśikharasthaḥ—(51).

† "निश्चयनयेनातीन्द्रियामूर्त्तपरमचिदुच्छलननिर्भरशुद्धस्वभावेन निराकारोऽपि व्यवहारेण भूतपूर्वनयेन किञ्चिदूनचरमशरीराकारेण गतसिक्थमूषागर्भाकारवच्छायाप्रतिमावद् वा पुरुषाकारः ।"

[Brhmadeva's Commentary].

will exist in the future.* Such is a Siddha according to Jainism, and he should be distinguished from persons ordinarily known as Siddhas, who attain wonderful powers† In the Yoga philosophy, such powers are known as Bibhûtis.

दंसणणाणपहाणो वीरियचारित्तवरतवायारे ।
अप्पं परं च जुंजइ सो आयरिओ मुणी झेओ ॥५२॥‡

Damsananânapahâne vîriyachârittavaratavâyâre,
Appam param cha juñjai so âyario munî jheo—(52).

Padapâtha.—दंसणणाणपहाणे Damsananânapahâne, in which faith and knowledge are eminent. वीरियचारित्तवरतवायारे Vîriyachârittavaratavâyâre, in the practice of Vîrya, Châritra and excellent Tapa. अप्पं Appam, himself. च Cha, and. परं Param, others. जुंजइ Juñjai, fixes. सो So, he. मुणी Munî, sage. आयरिओ Âyario, Âchârya. झेओ Jheo, to be meditated.

52. That sage who attaches himself and others to the practice of Vîrya (Power), Châritra (Conduct) and Tapa (Penance) in which faith and knowledge are eminent is to be meditated, as Âchârya (Preceptor).

COMMENTARY.

An Âchârya is one who practises the five Âchâras (kinds of conduct) and advises his disciples to do the same. The five kinds of Âchâras are Darśanâchâra, Jñânâchâra, Châritrâchâra, Tapâchâra and Vîryâchâra. Darśanâchâra is the turning of oneself to the faith that the soul, consisting of supreme consciousness, is separate from everything else and is the only thing to be meditated on. Jñânâchâra is the turning of oneself to attainment of the knowledge that the

* "लोकालोकगतत्रिकालवर्त्तिसमस्तवस्तुसम्बन्धिविशेषसामान्यस्वभावाना मेकसमयज्ञापकदर्शकत्वात् ।"

[Brahmadeva's Commentary].

† "अञ्जनसिद्ध-पादुकासिद्ध-गुटिकासिद्ध-खड्गसिद्ध-मायासिद्धादिलौकिक सिद्ध-विलक्षणः ।"

[Brahmadeva's Commentary]

‡ *Sanskrit rendering:*

दर्शनज्ञानप्रधाने वीर्यचारित्रवरतपाचारे ।
आत्मानं परं च युनक्ति स आचार्यः मुनिः ध्येयः ॥ ५२ ॥

Darśanajñânapradhâne Vîryachâritravaratapâchâre.
Âtmânam param cha yunakti Sa Âchâryahmunih Dhyeyah (52).

natural characteristics of the soul have no connection with delusion, etc., or attachment and aversion. Chârilrâchâra consists in making the soul tranquil after freeing it from all kinds of disturbances arising from attachment, etc., so that it may enjoy perfect bliss. Tapâchâra consists in the practice of various kinds of penances by which one can conquer reprenensible desires and attain a true conception of the soul. Vîryâchâra is giving full scope to one's inherent power; so the first four Âchâras might not be hindered or destroyed.*

An Âchârya is therefore one who is always engaged in all these five kinds of practices, and by precept as well as by example makes his disciples perform the same. Brahmadeva in his commentary quotes the following verse which gives the characteristics of an Âchârya :—

"छत्तीसगुणसमग्गे पंचविहाचारकरणसण्दरिसे ।
सिस्साणुग्गहकुसले धम्मायरिए सदा वंदे ॥"

i.e., " I always bow to Dharmâchârya (the preceptor of religion) who possesses the thirty-six qualities, advises the practice of the five kinds of Âchâras and is always kind to his disciples."

जो रयणत्तयजुत्तो णिच्चं धम्मोवएसणे णिरदो ।
सो उवझाओ अप्पा जदिवरवसहो णमो तस्स ॥५३॥†

Jo rayaṇattayajutto ṇichchaṃ dhammova-esaṇe ṇirado,
So uvajhâyo appâ jadivaravasaho ṇamo tassa—(53).

---

* "समस्तपरद्रव्येभ्यो भिन्नः परमचैतन्यविलासलक्षणः स्वशुद्धात्मैवोपादेय इति रुचिरूपसम्यग्दर्शनम्, तत्राचरणं परिणमनं निश्चयदर्शनाचारः। तस्यैव शुद्धात्मनो ... मिथ्यात्वरागादिपरभावेभ्यः पृथक्परिच्छेदनं सम्यक्ज्ञानं, तत्राचरणं परिणमनं निश्चयज्ञानाचारः। तत्रैव रागादिविकल्पोपाधिरहितस्वाभाविकसुखास्वादेन निश्चलचित्तं वीतरागचारित्रम्, तत्राचरणं परिणमनं निश्चयचारित्राचारः। समस्तपरद्रव्येच्छा निरोधेन......स्वस्वरूपे प्रतपनं विजयनं निश्चयतपश्चरणं, तत्राचरणं परिणमनं निश्चयतपश्चरणाचारः। तस्यैव निश्चयचतुर्विधाचारस्य रक्षणार्थं स्वशक्त्यनवगूहनं निश्चयवीर्याचारः।"

[Brahmadeva's Commentary].

† *Sanskrit rendering :—*

यः रत्नत्रययुक्तः नित्यं धर्मोपदेशने निरतः ।
स उपाध्यायः आत्मा यतिवरवृषभः नमस्तस्मै ॥५३॥

Yaḥ ratnatrayayuktaḥ nityaṃ dharmopadesane nirataḥ,
Sa upâdhyâyaḥ âtmâ yativaravriṣabhaḥ namastasmai.—(53).

Padapâṭha.—जो Jo, who. रयणत्तयजुत्तो Rayaṇattaya-jutto, possessed of the three jewels. णिच्चं. Ṇichcham̩, always. धम्मोवएसणे Dhammovaesaṇe, in preaching religious truths. णिरदो Ṇirado, engaged. सो So, he. जदिवरवसहो Jadivaravasaho, the greatest of the great sages. अप्पा Appâ, soul. उवज्झाओ Uvajhâyo Upâdhyâya (teacher). तस्स Tassa, to him. णमो Ṇamo, salutation.

53. That being, the greatest of the great sages who being possessed of the three jewels is always engaged in preaching the religious truths, is (known as) Upâdhyâya (Teacher). Salutation to him.

COMMENTARY.

Upâdhyâya or Teacher is one who is always engaged in teaching others the tenets of Jainism. He is a man possessed of perfect faith, perfect knowledge and perfect conduct. From his preachings a person knows his duties and regulates himself by practising what is desirable and avoiding what is undesirable. The place of Upâdhyâya is high among the Jaina sages, as he directly encourages practice of religion by continually preaching the principles of religion.

दंसणणाणसमग्गं मग्गं मोक्खस्स जो हु चारित्तं।
साधयदि णिच्चसुद्धं साहू स मुणी णमो तस्स ॥५४॥*

Dam̩saṇa-ṇâṇa-samaggam̩ maggam̩, mokkhassa jo hu chârittam̩,
Sâdhayadi ṇichchasuddham̩ sâhû sa muṇî ṇamo tassa—(54).

Padapâṭha.—जो Jo, that. मुणी Muṇî, sage. दंसणणाणसमग्गं Dam̩saṇa-ṇâṇa-samaggam̩, with perfect faith and perfect knowledge. मोक्खस्स Mokkhassa, of liberation. मग्गं Maggam̩, path. णिच्चसुद्धं Ṇichchasuddham̩, always pure. चारित्तं Chârittam̩, conduct. हु Hu, well. साधयदि Sâdhayadi, practises. स Sa, he. साहू Sâhû, Sâdhu. तस्स Tassa, him. णमो Ṇamo, obeisance.

54. That sage who practises well conduct—which is always pure and which is the path of liberation, with perfect faith and knowledge—is a Sâdhu. Obeisance to him.

* दर्शनज्ञानसमग्रं मार्गं मोक्षस्य यः हि चारित्रम्।
साधयति नित्यशुद्धं साधुः स मुनिः नमः तस्मै ॥ ५४ ॥

Darśanajñâna samagram̩ mârgam̩ mokṣasya yaḥ hi châritram̩,
Sâdhayati nityaśuddham̩ sâdhuḥ sa muniḥ namaḥ tasmai.—(54).

COMMENTARY.

A Sâdhu is one who is always active in attaining perfect conduct with perfect faith and perfect knowledge, and practises penances. The external effort of a Sâdhu is seen when he tries to have perfect faith, knowledge and conduct, and practises excellent penances.* The internal effort of a Sâdhu is made when he fixes his mind upon the soul itself, which is the only receptacle of perfect faith, knowledge and conduct and excellent penances.† A Sâdhu is, therefore, one who is characterised by activity while moving in the path of liberation. This activity is solely directed to the attainment of means to liberation.

Herewith ends the detailed description of the characteristics of five kinds of Parameṣṭhis, reverence to whom was inculcated in Verse 49. Brahmadeva in his commentary said that, though reverence to five Parameṣṭhis is prescribed from the ordinary point of view, it is really the soul the substratum of the Parameṣṭhis which is to be meditated upon.‡

जं किंचिवि चिंतंतो णिरीहवित्ती हवे जदा साहू ।
लद्धूणय एयत्तं तदाहु तं तस्स णिच्चयं झाणं ॥५५॥§

Jaṃ kiñchivi chintanto ṇirîhavittî have jadâ sâhû,
Laddhûṇaya eyattaṃ tadâhu taṃ tassa ṇichchayaṃ jhâṇaṃ—(55).

---

* "उद्योतनमुद्योगो निर्वहणं साधनं च निस्तरणम् ।
दृगवगमचरणतपसामाख्याताराधना सद्भिः ॥"

† "सम्मत्तं सण्णाणं सच्चारित्तं हि सत्तवो चेव ।
चउरो चिट्ठहि यादि तम्हा आदा हु मे सरणं ॥"
[Verse quoted in Brahmadeva's Commentary.]

‡ "अरिहासिद्धायरियाउवज्झयासाधुपंचपरमेट्ठी ।
ते वि हु चिट्ठहि यादे तम्हा आदा हु मे सरणं ॥"
[Verse quoted in Brahmadeva's Commentary.]

§ *Sanskrit rendering:*

यत् किञ्चिदपि चिन्तयन् निरीहवृत्तिः भवति यदा साधुः।
लब्ध्वा एकत्वं तदा आहुः तत् तस्य निश्चयं ध्यानम् ॥ ५५ ॥

Yatkiñchidapi chintayan nirîhavrittiḥ bhavati yadâ sâdhuḥ,
Labdhvâ ekatvam tadâ âhuḥ tat tasya niśchayaṃ dhyânaṃ—(55).

Padapâṭha.—जदा Jadâ, when. साहू Sâhû, Sâdhu. एयत्तं Eyattaṃ, concentration. लद्धूणय Laddhûṇaya, attaining. जंकिंचिवि Jaṃkiñchivi, anything whatever. चिंतंतो Chintanto, meditating. णिरीहवित्ती Ṇirîhvaittî, void of conscious effort. हवे Have, becomes. तदा Tadâ, then. तस्स, Tassa, his. तं Taṃ, that. णिच्छयं Ṇichchayaṃ, real. झाणं Jhâṇaṃ, meditation. आहुः Âhuḥ, is called.

55. When a Sâdhu attaining concentration becomes void of conscious effort by meditating on anything whatever, that state is called real meditation.

COMMENTARY.

Brahmadeva in his commentary on this verse says that in the primary stage of meditation it is necessary to think of objects other than the ego, *e. g.*, the five Parameṣṭhis etc. to steady the mind. When the mind becomes steady by constant practice, as aforesaid, we can arrive at the second stage, where we meditate on the soul itself.* This is real meditation. In this stage, one is void of the ten kinds of external possessions and fourteen kinds of internal hindrances belonging to the mind. The external possessions are lands, houses, gold, silver, wealth, rice, male and female servants, metals other than gold and silver, and utensils. A person immersed in meditation does not at all care about the attainment of all or any of these worldly possessions. At the same time, he is bereft of delusion, knowledge of the three kinds of sexes, laughter, attachment, aversion, sorrow, fear, hatred, anger, pride, illusion and greed.† These cause the loss of equilibrium of the mind. A person being void of these can concentrate his mind upon anything, and thus attain excellent meditation.

---

* "प्राथमिकापेक्षया सविकल्पावस्थायां विषयकषायवञ्चनार्थं चित्तस्थिरीकरणार्थं पञ्चपरमेष्ठ्यादिपरद्रव्यमपि ध्येयं भवति। पश्चादभ्यासवशेन स्थिरीभूते चित्ते सति शुद्धबुद्धैकस्वभावनिजशुद्धात्मस्वरूपमेव ध्येयमित्युक्तं भवति।"

[Brahmadeva's Commentary.]

† "निष्पृहवचनेन पुनर्मिथ्यात्वं वेदत्रयं हास्यादिषट्कक्रोधादिचतुष्टयरूपचतुर्दशाभ्यन्तरपरिग्रहेण तथैव क्षेत्रवास्तुहिरण्यसुवर्णधनधान्यदासीदासकुप्यभाण्डाभिधानदशविधबहिरङ्गपरिग्रहेण च रहितं ध्यातृस्वरूपमुक्तं भवति।"

[Brahmadeva's Commentary.]

मा चिट्ठह मा जंपह मा चिंतह किंवि जेण होइ थिरो ।
अप्पा अप्पम्मि रओ इणमेव परं हवे ज्झाणं ॥५६॥*

Mâ chiṭṭhaha mâ jaṃpaha mâ chintaha kiṃvi jeṇa hoi thiro,
Appâ appammi rao iṇameva paraṃ have jjhâṇam—(56).

Padapâṭha.—किंवि Kiṃvi, anything. मा Mâ, do not. चिट्ठह Chiṭṭhaha, act. मा Mâ, do not. जंपह Jaṃpaha, talk. मा Mâ, do not. चिंतह Chintaha, think. जेण Jeṇa, by which. अप्पा Appâ, soul. अप्पम्मि Appammi, in the soul. रओ Rao, attached. थिरो Thiro, fixed. होइ Hoi, becomes. इणम् Iṇaṃ, this. एव Eva, surely. परं Paraṃ, excellent. ज्झाणं Jjhâṇaṃ, meditation. हवे Have, is.

56. Do not act, do not talk, do not think, so that the soul may be attached to and fixed in itself. This only is excellent meditation.

COMMENTARY.

To attain excellent Dhyâna (meditation), one should turn all his faculties inwards, and restrain all outward movement of the same. First of all, it is necessary to stop all actions and refrain from talk and thought of anything else. Then the soul should turn upon itself and begin to meditate on its own nature. This is Dhyâna. To reach this stage, one must first check all activities of body, mind and speech which produce disquietude of the soul, for it is impossible to arrive at the quiet stage necessary for meditation if we do not first check the disturbing elements.

तवसुदवदवं चेदा ज्झाणरहधुरंधरो हवे जम्हा ।
तम्हा तत्तियणिरदा तल्लद्धीए सदा होह ॥५७॥†

Tavasudavadavaṃ chedâ jjhâṇarahadhuraṇdharo have jamhâ,
Tamhâ tattiyaṇiradâ talladdhîe sadâ hoha—(57).

---

† *Sanskirt rendering* :--

मा चेष्टत मा जल्पत मा चिन्तयत किमपि येन भवति स्थिरः ।
आत्मा आत्मनि रतः इदमेव परं भवति ध्यानम् ॥५६॥

Mâ cheṣṭata mâ jalpata mâ chintayata kimapi yena bhavati sthiraḥ,
Âtmâ âtmani rataḥ idameva paraṃ bhavati dhyânaṃ—(56).

* *Sanskrit rendering* :

तपःश्रुतव्रतवान् चेता ध्यानरथधुरंधरः भवति यस्मात् ।
तस्मात् तत्त्रितयनिरतः तल्लब्ध्यै सदा भवत ॥५७॥

Tapaḥsrutavratavân chetâ dhyanarathadhuraṇdharaḥ bhavati yasmât,
Tasmât tattritayanirataḥ tallabdhai sadâ bhabata—(57).

Padapâṭha.—जम्हा Jamhâ, because. तवसुदवदवं Tavasudavadavaṃ, possessed of Tapa, Śruta and Vrata. चेदा Chedâ, soul. झाणरहधुरंधरो Jjhâṇarahadhurandharo, the holder of the axle of the chariot of Dhyâna. हवे Have, is. तम्हा Tamhâ, therefore. तल्लद्धीए Talladdhîe, to attain that. सदा Sadâ, always. तत्तियणिरदा Tattiyaṇiradâ, engaged in these three. होह Hoha, become.

57. As a soul which (practises) penances, (holds) vows and (has knowledge of) scriptures, becomes capable of holding the axle of the chariot of meditation, so to attain that (meditation) be always engaged in these three (*i.e.*, penances, vows and Śâstras.)

COMMENTARY.

It is said that only he who practises penances, keeps vows and acquires knowledge of scriptures, becomes capable of practising meditation by concentrating his mind on the inward soul. Therefore, it is absolutely necessary for one who wishes to practise meditation to turn himself first of all towards the practice of penances, keeping of vows and knowing the scriptures.

The twelve kinds of penances (Tapa), six external (Vâhya) and six interal (Âbhyantara) and the five kinds of Vrata have been described in Verse 35.

दव्व-संगहमिणं मुणिणाहा दोस-संचयचुदा सुदपुण्णा ।
सोधयंतु तणुसुत्तधरेण णेमिचंदमुणिणा भणियं जं ॥५८॥*

Davvasaṃgahamiṇaṃ muṇiṇâhâ dosasaṃchayachuda sudapuṇṇâ,
Sodhayantu taṇusuttadhareṇa Ṇemichandamuṇiṇâ bhaṇiyaṃ jaṃ—(58).

Padapâṭha.—तणुसुत्तधरेण Taṇusuttadhareṇa, whose knowledge of Śâstras is very little. णेमिचंदमुणिणा Nemichandamuṇiṇâ, the sage Nemichandra. जं Jaṃ, which. इणं Iṇaṃ, this. दव्वसंगहं. Davva-saṃgahaṃ, Dravyasaṃgraha. भणियं

* *Sanskrit rendering:*

द्रव्यसंग्रहमिदं मुनिनाथाः दोषसंचयच्युताः श्रुतपूर्णाः ।
शोधयन्तु तनुसूत्रधरेण नेमिचन्द्रमुनिना भणितं यत् ॥५८॥

Dravya-saṃgrahamidaṃ munninâthâḥ,
Doṣa-sañchaya-chyutâḥ śrutapûrṇâḥ;
Śodhayantu tanusûtradhareṇa,
Nemichandramuninâ bhaṇitaṃ yat—(58)

Bhaṇiyaṃ, told. सुदपुण्णा Sudapuṇṇâ, full of the (knowledge of Śâstras). दोससंचयचुदा Dosasaṃchayachudâ, void of the collection of faults. मुणिणाहा Muṇiṇâhâ, the great sages. सोधयंतु Sodhayantu, correct.

58. Let the great sages, full of the (knowledge) of Śâstras and freed from the collection of faults, correct this Dravya-saṃgraha, which is spoken by the sage Nemichandra who has little (knowledge) of the Śâstras.

COMMENTARY.

In this last verse, the author, Nemichandra Siddhânta-chakravarti, in all humility belittles himself and acknowledging that there may be defects in his work, asks the great sages to correct the same. The metre of this verse is different from the preceding ones, as it is the colophon containing the name of the work and the author.

The End.

श्रीब्रह्म-देव-विरचिता

द्रव्य-संग्रह-वृत्तिः ।

श्रीब्रह्मदेवविरचिता

द्रव्यसंग्रहवृत्तिः ।

मङ्गलाचरणम् ।

प्रणम्य परमात्मानं सिद्धं त्रैलोक्यवन्दितम् ।
स्वाभाविकचिदानन्दस्वरूपं निर्मलाव्ययम् ॥१॥
शुद्धजीवादिद्रव्याणां देशकं च जिनेश्वरम् ।
द्रव्यसंग्रहसूत्राणां वृत्तिं वक्ष्ये समासतः ॥२॥

अथ मालवदेशे धारानामनगराधिपतिराजभोजदेवाभिधानकलिकालचक्रवर्तिसम्बन्धिनः श्रीपालमण्डलेश्वरस्य सम्बन्धिन्याश्रमनामनगरे श्रीमुनिसुव्रततीर्थकरचैत्यालये शुद्धात्मद्रव्यसंवित्तिसमुत्पन्नसुखामृतरसास्वादविपरीतनारकादिदुःखभयभीतस्य परमात्मभावनोत्पन्नसुखसुधारसपिपासितस्य भेदाभेदरत्नत्रयभावनाप्रियस्य भव्यवरपुण्डरीकस्य भाण्डागाराद्यनेकनियोगाधिकारिसोमाभिधानराजश्रेष्ठिनो निमित्तं श्रीनेमिचन्द्रसिद्धान्तिदेवैः पूर्वं षड्विंशतिगाथाभिर्लघुद्रव्यसंग्रहं कृत्वा पश्चाद्विशेषतत्त्वपरिज्ञानार्थं विरचितस्य बृहद्द्रव्यसंग्रहस्याधिकारशुद्धिपूर्वकत्वेन वृत्तिः प्रारभ्यते ।

तत्रादौ "जीवमजीवं दव्वं" इत्यादिसप्तविंशतिगाथापर्यन्तं षड्द्रव्यपञ्चास्तिकायप्रतिपादकनामा प्रथमोऽधिकारः । तदनन्तरं "आसवबंधण" इत्याद्येकादशगाथापर्यन्तं सप्ततत्त्वनवपदार्थप्रतिपादनमुख्यतया द्वितीयो महाधिकारः । ततःपरं "सम्मद्दंसण णाणं" इत्यादिविंशतिगाथापर्यन्तं मोक्षमार्गकथनमुख्यत्वेन तृतीयोऽधिकारश्च । इत्यष्टाधिकपञ्चाशद्गाथाभिरधिकारत्रयं ज्ञातव्यम् ॥

तत्राप्यादौ प्रथमाधिकारे चतुर्दशगाथापर्यन्तं जीवद्रव्यव्याख्यानम् । ततः-परं "अज्जीवो पुण णेओ" इत्यादिगाथाष्टकपर्यन्तमजीवद्रव्यकथनम् । ततः-परं "एवं छब्भेयमिदं" एवं सूत्रपञ्चकपर्यन्तं पञ्चास्तिकायविवरणम् । इति प्रथमाधिकारमध्येऽन्तराधिकारत्रयमवबोद्धव्यम् ॥

तत्रापि चतुर्दशगाथासु मध्ये नमस्कारमुख्यत्वेन प्रथमगाथा । जीवादिनवाऽधिकारसूचनरूपेण "जीवो उवओगमओ" इत्यादिद्वितीयसूत्रगाथा । तदनन्तरं नवाधिकारविवरणरूपेण द्वादशसूत्राणि भवन्ति । तत्राप्यादौ जीवसिद्धयर्थं "तिक्काले चदुपाणा" इतिप्रभृतिसूत्रमेकम् , तदनन्तरं ज्ञानदर्शनोपयोगद्वयकथनार्थं "उवओगो दुवियप्पो" इत्यादिगाथात्रयम् , ततःपरममूर्त्तत्वकथनेन " वण्ण रस पंच " इत्यादिसूत्रमेकम् , ततोऽपि कर्मकर्तृत्वप्रतिपादनरूपेण "पुग्गलकम्मादीणं" इतिप्रभृतिसूत्रमेकम् , तदनन्तरं भोक्तृत्वनिरूपणार्थं "ववहारा सुहदुक्खं" इत्यादिसूत्रमेकम् , ततःपरं स्वदेहप्रमितिसिद्धयर्थं "अणुगुरुदेहपमाणो" इतिप्रभृतिसूत्रमेकम् , ततोऽपि संसारिजीवस्वरूपकथनेन "पुढविजलतेउवाऊ" इत्यादिगाथात्रयम् , तदनन्तरं "णिक्कम्मा अट्ठगुणा" इतिप्रभृतिगाथापूर्वार्धेन सिद्धस्वरूपकथनम् , उत्तरार्धेन पुनरूर्ध्वगतिस्वभावः । इति नमस्कारादिचतुर्दशगाथामेलापकेन प्रथमाधिकारे समुदायपातनिका ।

अथेदानीं गाथापूर्वार्द्धेन सम्बन्धाऽभिधेयप्रयोजनानि कथयाम्युत्तरार्द्धेन च मङ्गलार्थमिष्टदेवतानमस्कारं करोमीत्यभिप्रायं मनसि धृत्वा भगवान् सूत्रमिदं प्रतिपादयति ।

व्याख्या—'वंदे' इत्यादिक्रियाकारकसम्बन्धेन पदखण्डनारूपेण व्याख्यानं क्रियते । 'वंदे' एकदेशशुद्धनिश्चयनयेन स्वशुद्धात्माराधनलक्षणभावस्तवनेन, असद्भूतव्यवहारनयेन तत्प्रतिपादकवचनरूपद्रव्यस्तवनेन च 'वन्दे' नमस्करोमि । परमशुद्धनिश्चयनयेन पुनर्वन्द्यवन्दकभावो नास्ति । स कः कर्त्ता, अहं नेमिचन्द्रसिद्धान्तिदेवः । कथं वन्दे ? "सव्वदा" सर्वकालम् । केन ? "सिरसा" उत्तमाङ्गेन । "तं" कर्म्मतापन्नं वीतरागसर्वज्ञम् । तं किंविशिष्टम् ? 'देविंदविंदवंदं' मोक्षपदाभिलाषिदेवेन्द्रादिवन्द्यम् , "भवणालयचालीसा विंतरदेवाण होंति वत्तीसा । कप्पामरचउवीसा चंदो सूरो णरो तिरओ ॥१॥" इति गाथाकथितलक्षणेन्द्राणां शतेन वन्दितं देवेन्द्रवृन्दवन्द्यम् । "जेण" येन

भगवता किं कृतं ? "णिद्दिट्ठं" निर्दिष्टं कथितं प्रतिपादितम् । किं "जीवमजीवं दव्वं" जीवाजीवद्रव्यद्वयम् । तद्यथा,—सहजशुद्धचैतन्यादिलक्षणं जीवद्रव्यं, तद्विलक्षणं पुद्गलादिपञ्चभेदमजीवद्रव्यं च, तथैव चिच्चमत्कारलक्षणशुद्ध-जीवास्तिकायादिपञ्चास्तिकायानां, परमचिज्ज्योतिःस्वरूपशुद्धजीवादिसप्तत-त्त्वानां, निर्दोषपरमात्मादिनवपदार्थानां च स्वरूपमुपदिष्टम् । पुनरपि कथम्भूतेन भगवता ? "जिणवरवसहेण" जितमिथ्यात्वरागादित्वेन एकदेशजिनाः असं-यतसम्यग्दृष्ट्यादयस्तेषां वराः गणधरदेवास्तेषां जिनवराणां वृषभः प्रधानो जिनवरवृषभस्तीर्थंकरपरमदेवस्तेन जिनवर-वृषभेणेति ॥

अत्राध्यात्मशास्त्रे यद्यपि सिद्धपरमेष्ठिनमस्कार उचितस्तथापि व्यवहार-नयमाश्रित्य प्रत्युपकारस्मरणार्थमर्हत्परमेष्ठिनमस्कार एव कृतः । तथाचोक्तं— "श्रेयोमार्गस्य संसिद्धिः प्रसादात्परमेष्ठिनः । इत्याहुस्तद्गुणस्तोत्रं शास्त्रादौ मुनिपुङ्गवाः ॥ १ ॥" अत्र गाथापरार्द्धेन—"नास्तिकत्वपरीहारः शिष्टाचार-प्रपालनम् । पुण्यावाप्तिश्च निर्विघ्नः शास्त्रादौ तेन संस्तुतिः ॥ २ ॥" इति श्लोककथितफलचतुष्टयं समीक्षमाणा ग्रन्थकाराः शास्त्रादौ त्रिधा देवतायै त्रिधा नमस्कारं कुर्वन्ति । इत्यादिमङ्गलव्याख्यानं सूचितम् । मङ्गलमित्यु-पलक्षणम् । उक्तं च—"मंगलनिमित्तहेउं परिमाणं णाम तह य कत्तारं । वागरिय छप्पि पच्छा वक्खाणउ सत्थ—मायरिओ ॥ १ ॥" "वक्खाणउ" व्याख्यातु । स कः ? "आयरिओ" आचार्यः । कं ? "सत्थं" शास्त्रं "पच्छा" पश्चात् । किं कृत्वा पूर्वं ? "वागरिय" व्याकृत्य व्याख्याय । कान् ? "छप्पि" षडप्यधिकारान् । कथंभूतान् ? "मंगलनिमित्तहेउं परि-माणं णाम तह य कत्तारं" मङ्गलं निमित्तं हेतुं परिमाणं नाम कर्तृ संज्ञामिति । इति गाथाकथितक्रमेण मंगलाद्यधिकारषट्कमपि ज्ञातव्यम् ॥

गाथापूर्वार्द्धेन तु सम्बन्धाभिधेयप्रयोजनानि सूचितानि । कथमिति चेत् ? विशुद्धज्ञानदर्शनस्वभावपरमात्मस्वरूपादिविवरणरूपो वृत्तिग्रन्थो व्याख्यानम् । व्याख्येयं तु तत्प्रतिपादकसूत्रम् । इति व्याख्यानव्याख्येयसम्बन्धो विज्ञेयः । यदेव व्याख्येयसूत्रमुक्तं तदेवाभिधानं वाचकं प्रतिपादकं भण्यते, अनन्तज्ञाना-द्यनन्तगुणाधारपरमात्मादिस्वभावोऽभिधेयो वाच्यः प्रतिपाद्यः । इत्यभिधाना-

भिधेयस्वरूपं बोद्धव्यम् । प्रयोजनं तु व्यवहारेण षड्द्रव्यादिपरिज्ञानम्, निश्चयेन निजनिरञ्जनशुद्धात्मसंवित्तिसमुत्पन्ननिर्विकारपरमानन्दैकलक्षणसुखामृतरसास्वादरूपं स्वसंवेदनज्ञानम् । परमनिश्चयेन पुनस्तत्फलरूपा केवलज्ञानाद्यनन्तगुणाविनाभूता निजात्मोपादानसिद्धानन्तसुखावाप्तिरिति । एवं नमस्कारगाथा व्याख्याता ॥ १ ॥

अथ नमस्कारगाथायां प्रथमं यदुक्तं जीवद्रव्यं तत्सम्बन्धे नवाधिकारान् संक्षेपेण सूचयामीति अभिप्रायं मनसि सम्प्रधार्य कथनसूत्रमिति निरूपयति ।

व्याख्या । "जीवो" शुद्धनिश्चयनयेनादिमध्यान्तवर्जितस्वपरप्रकाशकाविनश्वरनिरुपाधिशुद्धचैतन्यलक्षणनिश्चयप्राणेन यद्यपि जीवति, तथाप्यशुद्धनयेनानादिकर्मबन्धवशादशुद्धद्रव्यभावप्राणैर्जीवतीति जीवः । "उवओगमओ" शुद्धद्रव्यार्थिकनयेन यद्यपि सकलविमलकेवलज्ञानदर्शनोपयोगमयस्तथाप्यशुद्धनयेन क्षायोपशमिकज्ञानदर्शननिवृत्तत्वात् ज्ञानदर्शनोपयोगमयो भवति । "अमुत्ति", यद्यपि व्यवहारेण मूर्तकर्म्माधीनत्वेन स्पर्शरसगन्धवर्णवत्या मूर्त्या सहितत्वान्मूर्त्तस्तथापि परमार्थेनामूर्त्तातीन्द्रियशुद्धबुद्धैकस्वभावत्वादमूर्त्तः । "कत्ता" यद्यपि भूतार्थनयेन निष्क्रियटङ्कोत्कीर्णज्ञायकैकस्वभावोऽयं जीवस्तथाप्यभूतार्थनयेन मनोवचनकायव्यापारोत्पादककर्म्मसहितत्वेन शुभाशुभकर्म्मकर्तृत्वात् कर्त्ता । "सदेहपरिमाणो" यद्यपि निश्चयेन सहजशुद्धलोकाकाशप्रमितासङ्ख्येयप्रदेशस्तथापि व्यवहारेणानादिकर्म्मबन्धाधीनत्वेन शरीरनामकर्मोदयजनितोपसंहारविस्ताराधीनत्वात् घटादिभाजनस्थप्रदीपवत् स्वदेहपरिमाणः । "भोत्ता" यद्यपि शुद्धद्रव्यार्थिकनयेन रागादिविकल्पोपाधिरहितस्वात्मोत्थसुखामृतभोक्ता, तथाप्यशुद्धनयेन तथाविधसुखामृतभोजनाभावाच्छुभाशुभकर्मजनितसुखदुःखभोक्तृत्वाद्भोक्ता । "संसारत्थो" यद्यपि शुद्धनिश्चयनयेन निःसंसारनित्यानन्दैकस्वभावस्तथाप्यशुद्धनयेन द्रव्यक्षेत्रकालभवभावपञ्चप्रकारसंसारे तिष्ठतीति संसारस्थः । "सिद्धो" व्यवहारेण स्वात्मोपलब्धिलक्षणसिद्धत्वप्रतिपक्षभूतकर्मोदयेन यद्यप्यसिद्धस्तथापि निश्चयनयेनानन्तज्ञानानन्त-गुणस्वभावत्वात् सिद्धः । "सो" स एवं गुणविशिष्टो जीवः । "विस्ससोढ्ढगई" यद्यपि व्यवहारेण चतुर्गतिजनककर्मोदयवशेनोर्ध्वाधस्तिर्यग्गतिस्वभावस्तथापि निश्चयेन केवलज्ञानाद्यनन्तगुणावाप्तिलक्षणमोक्षगमनकाले विस्रसा

स्वभावेनोर्द्ध्वगतिश्चेति । अत्र पदखण्डनारूपेण शब्दार्थः कथितः, शुद्धाशुद्ध-नयद्वयविभागेन नयार्थोऽप्युक्तः । इदानीं मतार्थः कथ्यते । जीवसिद्धिश्चार्वाकं प्रति, ज्ञानदर्शनोपयोगलक्षणं नैयायिकं प्रति, अमूर्त्तजीवस्थापनं भट्टचार्वाक-द्वयं प्रति, कर्मकर्तृत्वस्थापनं सांख्यं प्रति, स्वदेहप्रमितिस्थापनं नैयायिकमीमां-सकसांख्यत्रयं प्रति, कर्मभोक्तृत्वव्याख्यानं बौद्धं प्रति, संसारस्थव्याख्यानं सदा-शिवं प्रति, सिद्धत्वव्याख्यानं भट्टचार्वाकद्वयं प्रति, ऊर्द्ध्वगतिस्वभावकथनं माण्डलिकग्रन्थकारं प्रति, इति मतार्थो ज्ञातव्यः । आगमार्थः पुनः "अस्त्या-त्मानादिबद्धः" इत्यादि प्रसिद्ध एव । शुद्धनयाश्रितं जीवस्वरूपमुपादेयं, शेषं च हेयम् । इति हेयोपादेयरूपेण भावार्थोऽप्यवबोद्धव्यः । एवं शब्दनयमता-गमभावार्थो यथासम्भवं व्याख्यानकाले सर्वत्र ज्ञातव्यः । इति जीवादिनवाधि-कारसूचनसूत्रगाथा ॥२॥

अतःपरं द्वादशगाथाभिर्नवाधिकारान् विवृणोति, तत्रादौ जीवस्वरूपं कथयति ।

व्याख्या—"तिक्काले चदुपाणा" कालत्रये चत्वारः प्राणा भवन्ति । ते के "इंदिय बलमाउ आणपाणो य" अतीन्द्रियशुद्धचैतन्यप्राणात्प्रतिशत्रुपक्षभूतः क्षायोपशमिक इन्द्रियप्राणः, अनन्तवीर्यलक्षणबलप्राणादनन्तैकभागप्रमिता मनोवचनकायबलप्राणाः, अनाद्यनन्तशुद्धचैतन्यप्राणविपरीततद्विलक्षणः सादिः सान्तश्चायुः-प्राणः, उच्छ्वासपरावर्त्तोत्पन्नखेदरहितविशुद्धचित्प्राणाद्विपरीतसदृश आनपानप्राणः । "ववहारा सो जीवो" इत्थंभूतैश्चतुर्भिर्द्रव्यभावप्राणैर्यथासंभवं जीवति जीविष्यति जीवितपूर्वो वा यो व्यवहारनयात्स जीवः । द्रव्येन्द्रियादि-द्रव्यप्राणा अनुपचरितासद्भूतव्यवहारेण, भावेन्द्रियादिः क्षायोपशमिकभा-वप्राणाः पुनरशुद्धनिश्चयेन । सत्ताचैतन्यबोधादिः शुद्धभावप्राणाः निश्चयनये-नेति "णिच्छयणयदो दु चेदणा जस्स" शुद्धनिश्चयनयतः सकाशादुपादेयभूता शुद्धचेतना यस्य स जीवः, एवं

वच्छक्खभवसारिच्छ, सग्गणिरयपियराय ।
चुल्लयहंडिय पुणमडउ, नव दिट्ठंता जाय ॥ १ ॥

इति दोहककथितनवदृष्टान्तैश्चार्वाकमतानुसारिशिष्यसंबोधनार्थं जीवसिद्धिव्या-ख्यानेन गाथा गता ॥३॥

अथ गाथात्रयपर्यन्तं ज्ञानदर्शनोपयोगद्वयं कथ्यते । तत्र प्रथमगाथायां

मुख्यवृत्त्या दर्शनोपयोगव्याख्यानं करोति। यत्र मुख्यत्वमिति वदति तत्र यथासंभवमन्यदपि विवक्षितं लभ्यत इति ज्ञातव्यम् ।

व्याख्या—"उवओगो दुवियप्पो" उपयोगो द्विविकल्पः "दंसण णाणं च" निर्विकल्पकं दर्शनं सविकल्पकं ज्ञानं, च पुनः "दंसणं चदुधा" दर्शनं चतुर्धा भवति "चक्खुअचक्खू ओही दंसणमध केवलं णेयं" चक्षुर्दर्शनमचक्षुर्दर्शनमवधिदर्शनमथ अथो केवलदर्शनमिति विज्ञेयम् । तथाहि—आत्मा हि जगत्रयकालत्रयवर्त्तिसमस्तवस्तुसामान्यग्राहकसकलविमलकेवलदर्शनस्वभावस्तावत् पश्चादनादिकर्मबन्धाधीनः सन् चक्षुर्दर्शनावरणक्षयोपशमाद्बहिरङ्गद्रव्येन्द्रियालम्बनाच्च मूर्त्तसत्तासामान्यं निर्विकल्पं संव्यवहारेण प्रत्यक्षमपि निश्चयेन परोक्षरूपेणैकदेशेन यत्पश्यति तच्चक्षुर्दर्शनम् । तथैव स्पर्शनरसनघ्राणश्रोत्रेन्द्रियावरणक्षयोपशमत्वात्स्वकीयस्वकीयबहिरङ्गद्रव्येन्द्रियालम्बनाच्च मूर्त्त सत्तासामान्यं विकल्परहितं परोक्षरूपेणैकदेशेन यत्पश्यति तदचक्षुर्दर्शनम् । तथैव च मनइन्द्रियावरणक्षयोपशमात्सहकारिकारणभूताष्टदलपद्माकारद्रव्यमनोऽवलम्बनाच्च मूर्त्तामूर्त्त समस्तवस्तुगतसत्तासामान्यं विकल्परहितं परोक्षरूपेण यत्पश्यति तन्मानसमचक्षुर्दर्शनम् । स एवात्मा यदवधिदर्शनावरणक्षयोपशमान्मूर्त्तवस्तुगतसत्तासामान्यं निर्विकल्परूपेणैकदेशप्रत्यक्षेण यत्पश्यति तदवधिदर्शनम् । यत्पुनः सहजशुद्धसदानन्दैकरूपपरमात्मतत्त्वसंवित्तिप्राप्तिबलेन केवलदर्शनावरणक्षये सति मूर्त्तामूर्त्तसमस्तवस्तुगतसत्तासामान्यं विकल्परहितं सकलप्रत्यक्षरूपेणैकसमये पश्यति तदुपादेयभूतं क्षायिकं केवलदर्शनं ज्ञातव्यमिति ॥४॥

अथाष्टविकल्पं ज्ञानोपयोगं प्रतिपादयति ।

व्याख्या—" णाणं अट्ठवियप्पं" ज्ञानमष्टविकल्पं भवति । "मदिसुदओही अणाणणाणाणि" अत्राष्टविकल्पमध्ये मतिश्रुतावधयो मिथ्यात्वोदयवशाद्विपरीताभिनिवेशरूपाण्यज्ञानानि भवन्ति, तान्येव शुद्धात्मादितत्त्वविषये विपरीताभिनिवेशरहितत्वेन सम्यग्दृष्टिजीवस्य सम्यग्ज्ञानानि भवन्ति । "मणपज्जय केवलमवि" मनःपर्ययज्ञानं केवलज्ञानमप्येवमष्टविधं ज्ञानं भवति, "पच्चक्खपरोक्खभेयं च" प्रत्यक्षपरोक्षभेदं च अवधिमनःपर्ययद्वयमेकदेशप्रत्यक्षं, विभङ्गावधिरपि देशप्रत्यक्षं, केवलज्ञानं सकलप्रत्यक्षं शेषचतुष्टयं परोक्षमिति । इतो विस्तारः– आत्मा हि निश्चयनयेन सकलविमलाखण्डैकप्रत्यक्षप्रतिभासमय-

केवलज्ञानरूपस्तावत् । स च व्यवहारेणानादिकर्मबन्धप्रच्छादितः सन्मतिज्ञाना-वरणीयक्षयोपशमाद्वीर्यान्तरायक्षयोपशमाच्च बहिरङ्गपञ्चेन्द्रियमनोऽवलम्बनाच्च मूर्त्तामूर्त्तं वस्त्वेकदेशेन विकल्पाकारेण परोक्षरूपेण सांव्यवहारिकप्रत्यक्षरूपेण वा यज्जानाति तत्क्षायोपशमिकं मतिज्ञानम् । किञ्च छद्मस्थानां वीर्यान्तराय-क्षयोपशमः केवलिनां तु निरवशेषक्षयः ज्ञानचारित्राद्युत्पत्तौ सहकारी सर्वत्र ज्ञातव्यः । संव्यवहारलक्षणं कथ्यते—समीचीनो व्यवहारः संव्यवहारः । प्रवृत्तिनिवृत्तिलक्षणः संव्यवहारो भण्यते । संव्यवहारे भवं सांव्यवहारिकं प्रत्यक्षम् । यथा घटरूपमिदं मया दृष्टमित्यादि । तथैव श्रुतज्ञानावरणक्षयो-पशमान्नोइन्द्रियावलम्बनाच्च प्रकाशोपाध्यायादिबहिरङ्गसहकारिकारणाच्च मूर्त्तामूर्त्त-वस्तुलोकालोकव्याप्तिज्ञानरूपेण यदस्पष्टं जानाति तत्परोक्षं श्रुतज्ञानं भण्यते । किञ्च विशेषः—शब्दात्मकं श्रुतज्ञानं परोक्षमेव तावत्, स्वर्गापवर्गादिबहि-र्विषयपरिच्छित्तिपरिज्ञानं विकल्परूपं तदपि परोक्षं, यत्पुनरभ्यन्तरे सुखदुःख-विकल्परूपोऽहमनन्तज्ञानादिरूपोऽहमिति वा तदीषत्परोक्षम्, यच्च निश्चयभाव-श्रुतज्ञानं तच्च शुद्धात्माभिमुखसुखसंवित्तिस्वरूपं स्वसंवित्त्याकारेण सविकल्प-मपीन्द्रियमनोजनितरागादिविकल्पजालरहितत्वेन निर्विकल्पम्, अभेदनयेन तदेवात्मशब्दवाच्यं वीतरागसम्यक्चारित्राविनाभूतं केवलज्ञानापेक्षया परोक्षमपि संसारिणां क्षायिकज्ञानाभावात् क्षायोपशमिकमपि प्रत्यक्षमभिधीयते । अत्राह शिष्यः—"आद्ये परोक्ष"मिति तत्त्वार्थसूत्रे मतिश्रुतद्वयं परोक्षं भणितं तिष्ठति कथं प्रत्यक्षं भवतीति । परिहारमाह—तदुत्सर्गव्याख्यानम्, इदं पुन-रपवादव्याख्यानं, यदि तदुत्सर्गव्याख्यानं न भवति तर्हि मतिज्ञानं कथं तत्त्वार्थे परोक्षं भणितं तिष्ठति । तर्कशास्त्रे सांव्यवहारिकं प्रत्यक्षं कथं जातम् । यथा अपवादव्याख्यानेन मतिज्ञानं परोक्षमपि प्रत्यक्षज्ञानं तथा स्वात्माभिमुखं भावश्रुतज्ञानमपि परोक्षं सत्प्रत्यक्षं भण्यते । यदि पुनरेकान्तेन परोक्षं भवति तर्हि सुखदुःखादिसंवेदनमपि परोक्षं प्राप्नोति, न च तथा । तथैव च स एवात्मा अवधिज्ञानावरणीयक्षयोपशमान्मूर्त्तं वस्तु यदेकदेशप्रत्यक्षेण सविकल्पं जानाति तदवधिज्ञानम् । यत्पुनर्मनःपर्ययज्ञानावरणक्षयोपशमाद्वीर्यान्तरा-यक्षयोपशमाच्च स्वकीयमनोऽवलम्बनेन परकीयमनोगतं मूर्त्तमर्थमेकदेशप्रत्यक्षेण सविकल्पं जानाति तदिह मतिज्ञानपूर्वकं मनःपर्ययज्ञानम् । तथैव निजशुद्धा-

त्मतत्त्वसम्यक्श्रद्धानज्ञानानुचरणलक्षणैकाग्रध्यानेन केवलज्ञानावरणादिघातिचतुष्टयक्षये सति यत्समुत्पद्यते तदेव समस्तद्रव्यक्षेत्रकालभावग्राहकं सर्वप्रकारोपादेयभूतं केवलज्ञानमिति ।

अथ ज्ञानदर्शनोपयोगद्वयव्याख्यानस्य नयविभागेनोपसंहारः कथ्यते ।

व्याख्या । "अट्ठ चदु णाण दंसण सामण्णं जीवलक्खणं भणियं" अष्टविधं ज्ञानं चतुर्विधं दर्शनं सामान्यं जीवलक्षणं भणितम् । सामान्यमिति कोऽर्थः संसारिजीवमुक्तजीवविवक्षा नास्ति, अथवा शुद्धाशुद्धज्ञानदर्शनविवक्षा नास्ति । तदपि कथमितिचेद् सामान्यलक्षणमिति वचनात्, कस्मात्सामान्यं जीवलक्षणं भणितं "ववहारा" व्यवहारात् व्यवहारनयात् । अत्र केवलज्ञानदर्शनं प्रति शुद्धसद्भूतशब्दवाच्योऽनुपचरितसद्भूतव्यवहारः, छद्मस्थज्ञानदर्शनापरिपूर्णापेक्षया पुनरशुद्धसद्भूतशब्दवाच्य उपचरितसद्भूतव्यवहारः, कुमतिकुश्रुतविभङ्गत्रये पुनरुपचरितासद्भूतव्यवहारः । "सुद्धणया सुद्धं पुण दंसणं णाणं" शुद्धनिश्चयनयात्पुनः शुद्धमखण्डं केवलज्ञानदर्शनद्वयं जीवलक्षणमिति । किञ्च ज्ञानदर्शनोपयोगविवक्षायामुपयोगशब्देन विवक्षितार्थपरिच्छित्तिलक्षणोऽर्थग्रहणव्यापारो गृह्यते । शुभाशुभशुद्धोपयोगत्रयविवक्षायां पुनरुपयोगशब्देन शुभाशुभशुद्धभावनैकरूपमनुष्ठानं ज्ञातव्यमिति । अत्र सहजशुद्धनिर्विकारपरमानन्दैकलक्षणस्य साक्षादुपादेयभूतस्याक्षयसुखस्योपादानकारणत्वात्केवलज्ञानदर्शनद्वयमुपादेयमिति । एवं नैयायिकं प्रति गुणगुणिभेदैकान्तनिराकरणार्थमुपयोगव्याख्यानेन गाथात्रयं गतम् ॥ ६ ॥

अथामूर्तातीन्द्रियनिजात्मद्रव्यसंवित्तिरहितेन मूर्तपञ्चेन्द्रियविषयासक्तेन च यदुपार्जितं मूर्त्तं कर्म तदुदयेन व्यवहारेण मूर्त्तोऽपि निश्चयेनामूर्त्तो जीव इत्युपदिशति ।

व्याख्या । "वण्ण रस पञ्च गंधा दो फासा अट्ठ णिच्चया जीवे णो संति" श्वेतपीतनीलारुणकृष्णसंज्ञाः पञ्च वर्णाः; तिक्तकटुककषायाम्लमधुरसंज्ञाः पञ्च रसाः, सुगन्धदुर्गन्धसंज्ञौ द्वौ गन्धौ, शीतोष्णस्निग्धरूक्षमृदुकर्कशगुरुलघुसंज्ञा अष्टौ स्पर्शाः; "णिच्चया" शुद्धनिश्चयनयात् शुद्धबुद्धैकस्वभावे शुद्धजीवे न सन्ति । "अमुत्ति तदो" ततः कारणादमूर्त्तः, यद्यमूर्त्तस्तर्हि तस्य कथं कर्मबन्ध इति चेत् "ववहारा मुत्ति" अनुपचरितासद्भूतव्यवहारान्मूर्त्तो

यतस्तदपि कस्मात् "बंधादो" अनन्तज्ञानाद्युपलम्भलक्षणमोक्षविलक्षणादनादि-कर्मबन्धनादिति । तथा चोक्तं—कथंचिन्मूर्त्तामूर्त्तजीवलक्षणम्—"बंधं पडिए यत्तं लक्खणदो हवदि तस्स भिण्णत्तं । तम्हा असुत्तिभावो णेगंतो होदि जीवस्स । १ ।" अयमत्रार्थः—यस्यैवामूर्त्तस्यात्मनः प्राप्यभावादनादिसंसारे भ्रमितोऽयं जीवः स एवामूर्त्तो मूर्त्तपञ्चेन्द्रियविषयत्यागेन निरन्तरं ध्यातव्यः । इति भट्टचार्वाकमतं प्रत्यमूर्त्तजीवस्थापनमुख्यत्वेन सूत्रं गतम् ॥ ७ ॥

अथ निष्क्रियामूर्त्तटङ्कोत्कीर्णज्ञायकैकस्वभावेन कर्मादिकर्तृत्वरहितोऽपि जीवो व्यवहारादिनयविभागेन कर्त्ता भवतीति कथयति ।

व्याख्या । अत्र सूत्रे भिन्नप्रक्रमरूपव्यवहितसम्बन्धेन मध्यपदं गृहीत्वा व्याख्यानं क्रियते । "आदा" आत्मा "पुग्गलकम्मादीणं कत्ता ववहारदो दु" पुद्गलकर्मादीनां कर्त्ता व्यवहारतस्तु पुनः, तथाहि मनोवचनकायव्यापारक्रिया-रहितनिजशुद्धात्मतत्त्वभावनाशून्यः सन्ननुपचरितासद्भूतव्यवहारेण ज्ञानावरणा-दिद्रव्यकर्मणामादिशब्देनौदारिकवैक्रियिकाहारकशरीरत्रयाहारादिषट्पर्याप्तियो-ग्यपुद्गलपिण्डरूपनोकर्मणां तथैवोपचरितासद्भूतव्यवहारेण बहिर्विषयघटपटा-दीनां च कर्त्ता भवति । "णिच्चयदो चेदणकम्माण" निश्चयनयतश्चेतन-कर्मणां तद्यथा रागादिविकल्पोपाधिरहितनिष्क्रियपरमचैतन्यभावनारहितेन यदुपार्जितं रागाद्युत्पादकं कर्म तदुदये सति निष्क्रियनिर्मलस्वसंवित्तिमलभमानो भावकर्मशब्दवाच्यरागादिविकल्परूपचेतनकर्मणामशुद्धनिश्चयेन कर्त्ता भवति । अशुद्धनिश्चयस्यार्थः कथ्यते—कर्मोपाधिसमुत्पन्नत्वादशुद्धः, तत्काले तप्तायःपिण्ड-वत्तन्मयत्वाच्च निश्चयः, इत्युभयमेलापकेनाशुद्धनिश्चयो भण्यते । "सुद्धणया सुद्धभावाणं" शुभाशुभयोगत्रयव्यापाररहितेन शुद्धबुद्धैकस्वभावेन यदा परिणमति तदानन्तज्ञानसुखादिशुद्धभावानां छद्मस्थावस्थायां भावनारूपेण विवक्षितैकदेशशुद्धनिश्चयेन कर्त्ता, मुक्तावस्थायां तु शुद्धनयेनेति । किन्तु शुद्धाशुद्धभावानां परिणममानानामेव कर्तृत्वं ज्ञातव्यम्, न च हस्तादिव्यापार-रूपाणामिति । यतो हि नित्यनिरञ्जननिष्क्रियनिजात्मस्वरूपभावनारहितस्य कर्मादिकर्तृत्वं व्याख्यातम्, ततस्तत्रैव निजशुद्धात्मनि भावना कर्त्तव्या । एवं सांख्यमतं प्रत्येकान्ताकर्तृत्वनिराकरणमुख्यत्वेन गाथा गता ॥ ८ ॥

अथ यद्यपि शुद्धनयेन निर्विकारपरमाह्लादैकलक्षणसुखामृतस्य भोक्ता तथाप्यशुद्धनयेन सांसारिकसुखदुःखस्यापि भोक्तात्मा भवतीत्याख्याति ।

व्याख्या । "ववहारा सुहदुक्खं पुग्गलकम्मफलं पभुंजेदि" व्यवहारात्सुखदुःखरूपं पुद्गलकर्मफलं प्रभुङ्क्ते । स कः कर्त्ता "आदा" आत्मा "णिच्चयणयदो चेदणभावं आदस्स" निश्चयनयतश्चेतनभावं भुङ्क्ते "खु" स्फुटं कस्य सम्बन्धिनमात्मनः स्वस्येति । तद्यथा–आत्मा हि निजशुद्धात्मसंवित्तिसमुद्भूतपारमार्थिकसुखसुधारसभोजनमलभमान उपचरितासद्भूतव्यवहारेणेष्टानिष्टपञ्चेन्द्रियविषयजनितसुखदुःखं भुङ्क्ते तथैवानुपचरितासद्भूतव्यवहारेणाभ्यन्तरे सुखदुःखजनकं द्रव्यकर्मरूपं सातासातोदयं भुङ्क्ते । स एवाशुद्धनिश्चयनयेन हर्षविषादरूपं सुखदुःखं च भुङ्क्ते । शुद्धनिश्चयनयेन तु परमात्मस्वभावसम्यग्श्रद्धानज्ञानानुष्ठानोत्पन्नसदानन्दैकलक्षणं सुखामृतं भुङ्क्ते इति । अत्र यस्यैव स्वाभाविकसुखामृतस्य भोजनाभावादिन्द्रियसुखं भुञ्जानः सन् संसारे परिभ्रमति तदेवातीन्द्रियसुखं सर्वप्रकारेणोपादेयमित्यभिप्रायः । एवं कर्त्ता कर्मफलं न भुङ्क्ते इति बौद्धमतनिषेधार्थं भोक्तृत्वव्याख्यानरूपेण सूत्रं गतम् ॥ ९ ॥

अथ निश्चयेन लोकप्रमितासंख्येयप्रदेशमात्रोपि व्यवहारेण देहमात्रो जीव इत्यावेदयति ।

व्याख्या । "अणुगुरुदेहपमाणो" निश्चयेन स्वदेहाद्भिन्नस्य केवलज्ञानाद्यनन्तगुणराशेरभिन्नस्य निजशुद्धात्मस्वरूपस्योपलब्धेरभावात्तथैव देहममत्वमूलभूताहारभयमैथुनपरिग्रहसंज्ञाप्रभृतिसमस्तरागादिविभावानामासक्तिसद्भावाच्च यदुपार्जितं शरीरनामकर्म तदुदये सति अणुगुरुदेहप्रमाणो भवति । स कः कर्त्ता "चेदा" चेतयिता जीवः । कस्मात् "उवसंहारप्पसप्पदो" उपसंहारप्रसर्पतः शरीरनामकर्मजनितविस्तारोपसंहारधर्माभ्यामित्यर्थः । कोऽत्र दृष्टान्तः, यथा प्रदीपो महद्भाजनप्रच्छादितस्तद्भाजनान्तरं सर्वं प्रकाशयति लघुभाजनप्रच्छादितस्तद्भाजनान्तरं प्रकाशयति । पुनरपि कस्मात् "असमुहदो" असमुद्घातात् वेदनाकषायविक्रियामरणान्तिकतैजसाहारककेवलिसंज्ञसप्तसमुद्घातवर्जनात् । तथा चोक्तं सप्तसमुद्घातलक्षणम्—"वेयणकसायवेउव्वियमारणांतिओ समुद्घादो । तेजाहारो छट्ठो सत्तमउ केवलीणं तु । १ ।" तद्यथा "मूलसरीरमछंडिय उत्तरदेहस्स जीवपिंडस्स । णिग्गमणं देहादो हवदि समुद्घादयं णाम ॥ १ ॥"

तीव्रवेदनानुभवान्मूलशरीरमत्यक्त्वा आत्मप्रदेशानां बहिर्निर्गमनमिति वेदनासमुद्घातः । १ । तीव्रकषायोदयान्मूलशरीरमत्यक्त्वा परस्य घातार्थमात्मप्रदेशानां बहिर्गमनमिति कषायसमुद्घातः । २ । मूलशरीरमपरित्यज्य किमपि विकर्तुमात्मप्रदेशानां बहिर्गमनमिति विक्रियासमुद्घातः । ३ । मरणान्तसमये मूलशरीरमपरित्यज्य यत्र कुत्रचिद्बद्धमायुस्तत्प्रदेशं स्फुटितुमात्मप्रदेशानां बहिर्गमनमिति मरणान्तिकसमुद्घातः । ४ । स्वस्य मनोनिष्टजनकं किञ्चित्कारणान्तरमवलोक्य समुत्पन्नक्रोधस्य संयमनिधानस्य महामुनेर्मूलशरीरमत्यज्य सिन्दूरपुञ्जप्रभो दीर्घत्वेन द्वादशयोजनप्रमाणः सूच्यंगुलसङ्ख्येयभागमूलविस्तारो नवयोजनाग्रविस्तारः काहलाकृतिपुरुषो वामस्कन्धान्निर्गत्य वामप्रदक्षिणेन हृदये निहितं विरुद्धं वस्तु भस्मसात्कृत्य तेनैव संयमिना सह स च भस्म व्रजति द्वीपायनवत्, असावशुभस्तेजःसमुद्घातः, लोकं व्याधिदुर्भिक्षादिपीडितमवलोक्य समुत्पन्नकृपस्य परमसंयमनिधानस्य महर्षेर्मूलशरीरमत्यज्य शुभ्राकृतिः प्रागुक्तदेहप्रमाणः पुरुषो दक्षिणप्रदक्षिणेन व्याधिदुर्भिक्षादिकं स्फोटयित्वा पुनरपि स्वस्थाने प्रविशति, असौ शुभरूपस्तेजःसमुद्घातः ।५। समुत्पन्नपदपदार्थभ्रान्तेः परमर्द्धिसंपन्नस्य महर्षेर्मूलशरीरमत्यज्य शुद्धस्फटिकाकृतिरेकहस्तप्रमाणः पुरुषो मस्तकमध्यान्निर्गत्य यत्र कुत्रचिदन्तमुहूर्त्तमध्ये केवलज्ञानिनं पश्यति तद्दर्शनाच्च स्वाश्रयस्य मुनेः पदपदार्थनिश्चयं समुत्पाद्य पुनः स्वस्थाने प्रविशति, असावाहारसमुद्घातः ।६। सप्तमः केवलिनां दण्डकपाटप्रतरपूरणः सोऽयं केवलिसमुद्घातः ।७। नयविभागः कथ्यते । "ववहारा" अनुपचरितासद्भूतव्यवहारनयात् "णिच्चयणयदो असंखदेसो वा" निश्चयनयतो लोकाकाशप्रमितासंख्येयप्रदेशप्रमाणः वा शब्देन तु स्वसंवित्तिसमुत्पन्नकेवलज्ञानोत्पत्तिप्रस्तावे ज्ञानापेक्षया व्यवहारनयेन लोकालोकव्यापकः न च प्रदेशापेक्षया नैयायिकमीमांसकसांख्यमतवत् । तथैव पञ्चेन्द्रियमनोविषयविकल्परहितसमाधिकाले स्वसंवेदनलक्षणबोधसद्भावेऽपि बहिर्विषयेन्द्रियबोधाभावाज्जडः न च सर्वथा सांख्यमतवत् । तथा रागादिविभावपरिणामापेक्षया शून्योऽपि भवति न चानन्तज्ञानाद्यपेक्षया बौद्धमतवत् । किञ्च अणुमात्रशरीरशब्देनात्र उत्सेधघनांगुलासंख्येयभागप्रमितं लब्ध्यपूर्णसूक्ष्मनिगोदशरीरं ग्राह्यं न च पुद्गलपरमाणुः । गुरुशरीरशब्देन च योजनसहस्रपरिमाणं महामत्स्यशरीरं मध्यमावगाहेन मध्यमशरीराणि च । इदमत्र तात्पर्य—देहम-

मत्वनिमित्तेन देहं गृहीत्वा संसारे परिभ्रमति तेन कारणेन देहादिममत्वं त्यक्त्वा निर्मोहनिजशुद्धात्मनि भावना कर्त्तव्येति । एवं स्वदेहमात्रव्याख्यानेन गाथा गता ॥ १० ॥

अतः परं गाथात्रयेण नयविभागेन संसारिजीवस्वरूपं तदवसाने शुद्धजीवस्वरूपं च कथयति । तद्यथा—

व्याख्या । "होंति" इत्यादिव्याख्यानं क्रियते । "होंति" अतीन्द्रियामूर्त्तनिजपरमात्मस्वभावानुभूतिजनितसुखामृतरसस्वभावमलभमानास्तुच्छमपीन्द्रियसुखमभिलषन्ति छद्मस्थाः, तदासक्ताः सन्त एकेन्द्रियादिजीवानां घातं कुर्वन्ति तेनोपार्जितं यत्त्रसस्थावरनामकर्म तदुदयेन जीवा भवन्ति । कथंभूता भवन्ति "पुढविजलतेउवाऊवणप्फदी विविहथावरे इंदी" पृथिव्यप्तेजोवायुवनस्पतयः कतिसंख्योपेता विविधा आगमकथितस्वकीयस्वकीयान्तर्भेदैर्बहुविधाः स्थावरनामकर्मोदयेन स्थावरा एकेन्द्रियजातिनामकर्मोदयेन स्पर्शनेन्द्रिययुक्ता एकेन्द्रिया न केवलमित्थंभूताः स्थावरा भवन्ति । "विगतिगचदुपंचक्खा तसजीवा" द्वित्रिचतुःपञ्चाक्षास्त्रसनामकर्मोदयेन त्रसजीवा भवन्ति । ते च कथंभूताः "संखादी" शङ्खादयः स्पर्शनरसनेन्द्रियद्वययुक्ताः शङ्खशुक्तिक्रिम्यादयो द्वीन्द्रियाः, स्पर्शनरसनघ्राणेन्द्रिययुक्ताः कुन्थुपिपीलिकायूकामत्कुणादयस्त्रीन्द्रियाः, स्पर्शनरसनघ्राणचक्षुरिन्द्रियचतुष्टययुक्ता दंशमशकमक्षिकाभ्रमरादयश्चतुरिन्द्रियाः, स्पर्शनरसनघ्राणचक्षुःश्रोत्रेन्द्रियपञ्चयुक्ता मनुष्यादयः पञ्चेन्द्रिया इति । अयमत्रार्थः—विशुद्धज्ञानदर्शनस्वभावनिजपरमात्मस्वरूपभावनोत्पन्नपारमार्थिकसुखमलभमाना इन्द्रियसुखासक्ता एकेन्द्रियादिजीवानां वधं कृत्वा त्रसस्थावरा भवन्तीत्युक्तं पूर्वं तस्मात्त्रसस्थावरोत्पत्तिविनाशार्थं तत्रैव परमात्मनि भावना कर्त्तव्येति ॥११॥

तदेव त्रसस्थावरत्वं चतुर्दशजीवसमासरूपेण व्यक्तीकरोति ।

व्याख्या—"समणा अमणा" समस्तशुभाशुभविकल्पातीतपरमात्मद्रव्यविलक्षणं नानाविकल्पजालरूपं मनो भण्यते तेन सह ये वर्त्तन्ते ते समनस्काः, तद्विपरीता अमनस्का असंज्ञिनः "णेया" ज्ञेया ज्ञातव्याः । "पंचेंदिय" ते संज्ञिनस्तथैवासंज्ञिनश्च पञ्चेन्द्रियाः । एवं संज्ञ्यसंज्ञिपञ्चेन्द्रियास्तिर्यञ्च एव, नारकमनुष्यदेवाः संज्ञिपञ्चेन्द्रिया एव । "णिम्मणा परे सव्वे" निर्मनस्काः पञ्चेन्द्रियात्सकाशादपरे सर्वे द्वित्रिचतुरिन्द्रियाः "बादरसुहमे इंदी" बादरसूक्ष्मा

एकेन्द्रियास्तेऽपि यदष्टपत्रपद्माकारं द्रव्यमनस्तदाधारेण शिक्षालापोपदेशादिग्राहकं भावमनश्चेति तदुभयाभावादसंज्ञिन एव । "सव्वे पज्जत्त इदरा य" एवमुक्तप्रकारेण संज्ञ्यसंज्ञिरूपेण पञ्चेन्द्रियद्वयं द्वित्रिचतुरिन्द्रियरूपेण विकलेन्द्रियत्रयं बादरसूक्ष्मरूपेणैकेन्द्रियद्वयं चेति सप्तभेदाः । "आहारसरीरिंदिय पज्जत्ती आणपाणभासमणा । चत्तारिपंचछप्पियइंदियवियलसण्णिसण्णीणं ।" १ । इति गाथाकथितक्रमेण ते सर्वे प्रत्येकं स्वकीयस्वकीयपर्याप्तिसंभवात्सप्त पर्याप्ताः सप्तापर्याप्ताश्च भवन्ति । एवं चतुर्दशजीवसमासा ज्ञातव्यास्तेषां च "इंदियकाया ऊणिय पुण्णापुण्णे सुपुण्णगे आणा । वेइंदियादि पुण्णे सुवचिमणोसण्णि पुण्णेय । १ । दस सण्णीणं पाणा सेसे गूणंति मण्णवे ऊणा । पज्जत्ते मिदरेसु पसत्तडुगे सेसगे गूणां । २ ।" इति गाथाद्वयकथितक्रमेण यथासंभवमिन्द्रियादिदशप्राणाश्च विज्ञेयाः । अत्रैतेभ्यो भिन्नं निजशुद्धात्मतत्त्वमुपादेयमिति भावार्थः ॥ १२ ॥

अथ शुद्धपारिणामिकपरमभावग्राहकेण शुद्धद्रव्यार्थिकनयेन शुद्धबुद्धैकस्वभावा अपि जीवाः पश्चादशुद्धनयेन चतुर्दशमार्गणास्थानचतुर्दशगुणस्थानसहिता भवन्तीति प्रतिपादयति ।

व्याख्या । "मग्गणगुणठाणेहि य हवंति तह विण्णेया" यथा पूर्वसूत्रोदितचतुर्दशजीवसमासैर्भवन्ति मार्गणागुणस्थानैश्च तथा भवन्ति संभवन्तीति विज्ञेया ज्ञातव्याः । कतिसंख्योपेतैः "चउदसहि" प्रत्येकं चतुर्दशभिः । कस्मात् "असुद्धणया" अशुद्धनयात् सकाशात् । इत्थंभूताः के भवन्ति । "संसारी" सांसारिजीवाः । "सव्वे सुद्धा हु सुद्धणया" त एव सर्वे संसारिणः शुद्धाः सहजशुद्धज्ञायकैकस्वभावाः । कस्मात् शुद्धनयात् शुद्धनिश्चयनयादिति । अथागमप्रसिद्धगाथाद्वयेन गुणस्थाननामानि कथयति । "मिच्छो सासण मिस्सो अविरदसम्मोय देसविरदोय । विरयापमत्त इयरो अपुव्व अणियट्ठि सुहमोय । उवसंतखीणमोहो सजोगकेवलिजिणो अजोगी य । चउदसगुणठाणाणि य कमेण सिद्धाय णायव्वा ।" इदानीं तेषामेव गुणस्थानानां प्रत्येकं संक्षेपलक्षणं कथ्यते । तथाहि—सहजशुद्धकेवलज्ञानदर्शनरूपाखण्डैकप्रत्यक्षप्रतिभासमयनिजपरमात्मप्रभृतिषड्द्रव्यपञ्चास्तिकायसप्ततत्त्वनवपदार्थेषु मूढत्रयादिपञ्चविंशतिमलरहितं वीतरागसर्वज्ञप्रणीतनयविभागेन यस्य श्रद्धानं नास्ति

स मिथ्यादृष्टिर्भवति।१। पाषाणरेखासदृशानन्तानुबन्धिक्रोधमानमायालोभान्यत-रोदयेन प्रथममौपशमिकसम्यक्त्वात्पतितो मिथ्यात्वं नाद्यापि गच्छतीत्यन्तराल-वर्ती सासादनः।२। निजशुद्धात्मादितत्त्वं वीतरागसर्वज्ञप्रणीतं परप्रणीतं च मन्यते यः स दर्शनमोहनीयभेदमिश्रकर्मोदयेन दधिगुडमिश्रभाववत् मिश्रगुणस्थान-वर्ती भवति।३। अथ मतं—येन केनाप्येकेन मम देवेन प्रयोजनं तथा सर्वे देवा वन्दनीया न च निन्दनीया इत्यादिवैनयिकमिथ्यादृष्टिः संशयमिथ्यादृष्टिर्वा तथा मन्यते, तेन सह सम्यग्मिथ्यादृष्टेः को विशेष इति, अत्र परिहारः—"स सर्वदेवेषु सर्वसमयेषु च भक्तिपरिणामेन येन केनाप्येकेन मम पुण्यं भविष्य-तीति मत्वा संशयरूपेण भक्तिं कुरुते निश्चयो नास्ति। मिश्रस्य पुनरुभयत्र निश्चयोऽस्तीति विशेषः। स्वाभाविकानन्तज्ञानाद्यनन्तगुणाधारभूतं निजपरमात्म-द्रव्यमुपादेयम्, इन्द्रियसुखादिपरद्रव्यं हि हेयमित्यर्हत्सर्वज्ञप्रणीतनिश्चयव्यव-हारनयसाध्यसाधकभावेन मन्यते परं किन्तु भूमिरेखादिसदृशक्रोधादिद्वितीय-कषायोदयेन मारणनिमित्तं तलवरगृहीततस्करवदात्मनिन्दादिसहितः सन्निन्द्रि-यसुखमनुभवतीत्यविरतसम्यग्दृष्टेर्लक्षणम्।४। यः पूर्वोक्तप्रकारेण सम्यग्दृष्टिः सन् भूमिरेखादिसमानक्रोधादिद्वितीयकषायोदयाभावे सत्यभ्यन्तरे निश्चयनयेनैकदेश-रागादिरहितस्वाभाविकसुखानुभूतिलक्षणेषु बहिर्विषये पुनरेकदेशहिंसानृतास्ते-याब्रह्मपरिग्रहनिवृत्तिलक्षणेषु "दंसणवयसामाइयपोसहसचित्तराइभत्तेय। बंभा-रंभपरिग्गह अणुमण उद्दिट्ठ देशविरदेदे।" इति गाथाकथितैकादशनिल-येषु वर्त्तते स पञ्चमगुणस्थानवर्त्ती श्रावको भवति।५। स एव सद्दृष्टिर्धूलि-रेखादिसदृशक्रोधादितृतीयकषायोदयाभावे सत्यभ्यन्तरे निश्चयनयेन रागाद्युपा-धिरहितस्वशुद्धात्मसंवित्तिसमुत्पन्नसुखामृतानुभवलक्षणेषु बहिर्विषयेषु पुनः सामस्त्येन हिंसानृतस्तेयब्रह्मपरिग्रहनिवृत्तिलक्षणेषु च पञ्चमहाव्रतेषु वर्त्तते यदा तदा दुःस्वप्नादिव्यक्ताव्यक्तप्रमादसहितोऽपि षष्ठगुणस्थानवर्ती प्रमत्तसंयतो भवति।६। स एव जलरेखादिसदृशसंज्वलनकषायमन्दोदये सति निष्प्रमाद-शुद्धात्मसंवित्तिमलजनकव्यक्ताव्यक्तप्रमादरहितः सन्सप्तमगुणस्थानवर्ती अप्र-मत्तसंयतो भवति।७। स एवातीतसंज्वलनकषायमन्दोदये सत्यपूर्वपरमाह्ला-दैकसुखानुभूतिलक्षणापूर्वकरणोपशमकक्षपकसंज्ञोऽष्टमगुणस्थानवर्त्ती भवति।८। दृष्टश्रुतानुभूतभोगाकाङ्क्षादिरूपसमस्तसङ्कल्पविकल्परहितनिजनिश्चलपर-

मात्मतत्त्वैकाग्रध्यानपरिणामेन कृत्वा येषां जीवानामेकसमये ये परस्परं पृथक्कर्त्तुं नायान्ति ते वर्णसंस्थानादिभेदेऽप्यनिवृत्तिकरणौपशमिकक्षपकसंज्ञा द्वितीयकषायाद्येकविंशतिभेदभिन्नचारित्रमोहप्रकृतीनामुपशमक्षपणसमर्था नवमगुणस्थानवर्त्तिनो भवन्ति । ९ । सूक्ष्मपरमात्मतत्त्वभावनाबलेन सूक्ष्मक्लिष्टगतलोभकषायस्योपशमकाः क्षपकाश्च दशमगुणस्थानवर्त्तिनो भवन्ति । १० । परमोपशममूर्त्तिनिजात्मस्वभावसंवित्तिबलेन सकलोपशान्तमोहा एकादशगुणस्थानवर्त्तिनो भवन्ति । ११ । उपशमश्रेणिविलक्षणेन क्षपकश्रेणिमार्गेण निष्कषायशुद्धात्मभावनाबलेन क्षीणकषाया द्वादशगुणस्थानवर्त्तिनो भवन्ति ।१२ । मोहक्षपणानन्तरमन्तमुंहूर्त्तकालं स्वशुद्धात्मसंवित्तिलक्षणैकत्ववितर्कविचारद्वितीयशुक्लध्याने स्थित्वा तदन्त्यसमये ज्ञानावरणदर्शनावरणान्तरायत्रयं युगपदेकसमयेन निर्मूल्य मेघपञ्जरविनिर्गतदिनकर इव सकलविमलकेवलज्ञानकिरणैर्लोकालोकप्रकाशकास्त्रयोदशगुणस्थानवर्त्तिनो जिनभास्करा भवन्ति । १३ । मनोवचनकायवर्गणालम्बनकर्मादाननिमित्तात्मप्रदेशपरिस्पन्दलक्षणयोगरहिताश्चतुर्दशगुणस्थानवर्त्तिनोऽयोगिजिना भवन्ति । १४ । ततश्च निश्चयरत्नत्रयात्मककारणभूतसमयसारसंज्ञेन परमयथाख्यातचारित्रेण चतुर्दशगुणस्थानातीताः ज्ञानावरणाद्यष्टकर्मरहिताः सम्यक्त्वाद्यष्टगुणान्तर्भूतनिर्नामगोत्राद्यनन्तगुणाः सिद्धा भवन्ति । अत्राह शिष्यः—केवलज्ञानोत्पत्तौ मोक्षकारणभूतरत्नत्रयपरिपूर्णतायां सत्यां तस्मिन्नेव क्षणे मोक्षेण भाव्यं सयोग्य-योगिजिनगुणस्थानद्वये कालो नास्तीति । परिहारमाह—यथाख्यातचारित्रं जातं परं किन्तु परमयथाख्यातं नास्ति । अत्र दृष्टान्तः । यथा चौरव्यापाराभावेऽपि पुरुषस्य चौरसंसर्गो दोषं जनयति तथा चारित्रविनाशकचारित्रमोहोदयाभावेऽपि सयोगिकेवलिनां निष्क्रियशुद्धात्माचरणविलक्षणो योगत्रयव्यापारश्चारित्रमलं जनयति, योगत्रयगते पुनरयोगिजिने चरमसमयं विहाय शेषाघातिकर्मतीव्रोदयश्चारित्रमलं जनयति, चरमसमये तु मन्दोदये सति चारित्रमलाभावान्मोक्षं गच्छति । इतिचतुर्दशगुणस्थानव्याख्यानं गतम् ।

इदानीं मार्गणाः कथ्यन्ते। "गइ इंदियं च काये जोए वेए कसाय णाणे य । संयम दंसण लेस्सा भविआ सम्मत्तसण्णि आहारे ।" इति गाथाकथितक्रमेण गत्यादिचतुर्दशमार्गणा ज्ञातव्याः। तद्यथा—स्वात्मोपलब्धिसिद्धिविलक्षणा नारकतिर्य-

मनुष्यदेवगतिभेदेन चतुर्विधा गतिमार्गणा भवति । १ । अतीन्द्रियशुद्धात्मतत्त्वप्रतिपक्षभूता ह्येकद्वित्रिचतुःपञ्चेन्द्रियभेदेन पञ्चप्रकारेन्द्रियमार्गणा । २ । अशरीरात्मतत्त्वविसदृशी पृथिव्यप्तेजोवायुवनस्पतित्रसकायभेदेन षड्भेदा कायमार्गणा । ३ । निर्व्यापारशुद्धात्मपदार्थविलक्षणमनोवचनकाययोगभेदेन त्रिधा योगमार्गणा, अथवा विस्तरेण सत्यासत्योभयानुभयभेदेन चतुर्विधो मनोयोगो वचनयोगश्च, औदारिकौदारिकमिश्रवैक्रियिकवैक्रियिकमिश्राहारकाहारकमिश्रकार्मणकायभेदेन सप्तविधो काययोगश्चेति समुदायेन पञ्चदशविधा वा योगमार्गणा । ४ । वेदोदयोद्भवरागादिदोषरहितपरमात्मद्रव्याद्भिन्ना स्त्रीपुंनपुंसकभेदेन त्रिधा वेदमार्गणा । ५ । निष्कषायशुद्धात्मस्वभावप्रतिकूलक्रोधलोभमायामानभेदेन चतुर्विधा कषायमार्गणा, विस्तरेण कषायनोकषायभेदेन पञ्चविंशतिविधा वा । ६ । मत्यादिसंज्ञापञ्चकं कुमत्याद्यज्ञानत्रयं चेत्यष्टविधा ज्ञानमार्गणा । ७ । सामायिकच्छेदोपस्थापनपरिहारविशुद्धिसूक्ष्मसांपराययथाख्यातभेदेन चारित्रं पञ्चविधम्, संयमासंयमस्तथैवासंयमश्चेति प्रतिपक्षद्वयेन सह सप्तप्रकारा संयममार्गणा । ८ । चक्षुरचक्षुरवधिकेवलदर्शनभेदेन चतुर्विधा दर्शनमार्गणा । ९ । कषायोदयरञ्जितयोगप्रवृत्तिविसदृशपरमात्मद्रव्यप्रतिपन्थिनी कृष्णनीलकापोततेजः-पद्मशुक्लभेदेन षड्विधा लेश्यामार्गणा । १० । भव्याभव्यभेदेन द्विविधा भव्यमार्गणा । ११ । अत्राह शिष्यः शुद्धपारिणामिकपरमभावरूपशुद्धनिश्चयेन गुणस्थानमार्गणास्थानरहिता जीवा इत्युक्तं पूर्वम्, इदानीं पुनर्भव्याभव्यरूपेण मार्गणामध्येऽपि पारिणामिकभावो भणित इति पूर्वापरविरोधः । अत्र—परिहारमाह—पूर्वं शुद्धपारिणामिकभावापेक्षया गुणस्थानमार्गणानिषेधः कृतः, इदानीं पुनर्भव्याभव्यत्वद्वयमशुद्धपारिणामिकभावरूपं मार्गणामध्येऽपि घटते । ननु—शुद्धाशुद्धभेदेन पारिणामिकभावो द्विविधो नास्ति किन्तु शुद्ध एव । नैवं—यद्यपि सामान्यरूपेणोत्सर्गव्याख्यानेन शुद्धपारिणामिकभावः कथ्यते तथाप्यपवादव्याख्यानेनाशुद्धपारिणामिकभावोऽप्यस्ति । तथाहि—"जीवभव्याभव्यत्वानि च" इति तत्त्वार्थसूत्रे त्रिधा पारिणामिकभावो भणितः, तत्र—शुद्धचैतन्यरूपं जीवत्वमविनश्वरत्वेन शुद्धद्रव्याश्रितत्वाच्छुद्धद्रव्यार्थिकसंज्ञः शुद्धपारिणामिकभावो भण्यते, यत्पुनः कर्मजनितदशप्राणरूपं जीवत्वं, भव्यत्वम्, अभव्यत्वं चेति त्रयं, तद्विनश्वरत्वेन पर्यायाश्रितत्वात्प-

र्यायार्थिकसंज्ञस्त्वशुद्धपारिणामिकभाव उच्यते । अशुद्धत्वं कथमिति चेत्—यद्यप्येतदशुद्धपारिणामिकत्रयं व्यवहारेण संसारिजीवेऽस्ति तथापि "सव्वे सुद्धा हु सुद्धणया" इति वचनाच्छुद्धनिश्चयेन नास्ति त्रयं, मुक्तजीवे पुनः सर्वथैव नास्ति, इति हेतोरशुद्धत्वं भण्यते । तत्र शुद्धाशुद्धपारिणामिकमध्ये शुद्धपारिणामिकभावो ध्यानकाले ध्येयरूपो भवति ध्यानरूपो न भवति, कस्मात् ? ध्यानपर्यायस्य विनश्वरत्वात्, शुद्धपारिणामिकस्तु द्रव्यरूपत्वादविनश्वरः, इति भावार्थः । औपशमिकक्षायोपशमिकक्षायिकसम्यक्त्वभेदेन त्रिधा सम्यक्त्वमार्गणा मिथ्यादृष्टिसासादनमिश्रसंज्ञविपक्षत्रयभेदेन सह षड्विधा ज्ञातव्या । १२ । संज्ञित्वासंज्ञित्वविसदृशपरमात्मस्वरूपाद्भिन्ना संज्ञ्यसंज्ञिभेदेन द्विधा संज्ञिमार्गणा । १३ । आहारकानाहारकजीवभेदेनाहारकमार्गणापि द्विधा । १४ । इति चतुर्दशमार्गणास्वरूपं ज्ञातव्यम् । एवं "पुढविजलतेउ वाऊ" इत्यादिगाथाद्वयेन, तृतीयगाथापादत्रयेण च "गुणजीवापज्जत्ती पाणासण्णायमग्गणा उया । उवओगो विय कमसो वीसं तु परूवणा भणिया ।" इति गाथाप्रभृतिकथितस्वरूपं धवलजयधवलमहाधवलप्रबन्धाभिधानसिद्धान्तत्रयबीजपदं सूचितम् । "सव्वे सुद्धा हु सुद्धणया" । इति शुद्धात्मतत्त्वप्रकाशकं तृतीयगाथाचतुर्थपादेन पञ्चास्तिकायप्रवचनसारसमयसाराभिधानप्राभृतत्रयस्यापि बीजपदं सूचितमिति । अत्र गुणस्थानमार्गणादिमध्ये केवलज्ञानदर्शनद्वयं क्षायिकसम्यक्त्वमनाहारकशुद्धात्मस्वरूपं च साक्षादुपादेयं, यत्पुनश्च शुद्धात्मसम्यक्श्रद्धानज्ञानानुचरणलक्षणं कारणसमयसारस्वरूपं तत्तस्यैवोपादेयभूतस्य विवक्षितैकदेशशुद्धनयेन साधकत्वात्पारम्पर्येणोपादेयं, शेषं तु हेयमिति । यच्चाध्यात्मग्रन्थस्य बीजपदभूतं शुद्धात्मस्वरूपमुक्तं तत्पुनरुपादेयमेव । अनेन प्रकारेण जीवाधिकारमध्ये शुद्धाशुद्धजीवकथनमुख्यत्वेन सप्तमस्थले गाथात्रयं गतम् ॥ १३ ॥

अथेदानीं गाथापूर्वार्द्धेन सिद्धस्वरूपमुत्तरार्द्धेन पुनरूर्ध्वगतिस्वभावं च कथयति ।

व्याख्या । सिद्धाः सिद्धा भवन्तीति क्रियाध्याहारः । किंविशिष्टाः "णिक्कम्मा अट्ठगुणा किंचूणा चरमदेहदो" निष्कर्माणोऽष्टगुणाः किञ्चिदूनाश्चरमदेहतः सकाशादिति सूत्रपूर्वार्द्धेन सिद्धस्वरूपमुक्तम् । ऊर्ध्वगमनं कथ्यते "लोयग्गठिदा णिच्चा उप्पादवयेहि संजुत्ता" ते च सिद्धा लोकाग्रस्थिता नित्या उत्पादव्य-

याभ्यां संयुक्ताः । अतो विस्तरः । कर्मारिविध्वंसकस्वशुद्धात्मसंवित्तिबलेन ज्ञानावरणादिमूलोत्तरगतसमस्तकर्मप्रकृतिविनाशकत्वादष्टकर्मरहिताः "सम्मत्त-णाणदंसणवीरियसुहुमं तहेव अवगहणं । अगुरुलहुअव्वाबाहं अठ्ठगुणा हुंति सिद्धाणं ।" इति गाथाकथितक्रमेण तेषामष्टकर्मरहितानामष्टगुणाः कथ्यन्ते । तथाहि केवलज्ञानादिगुणास्पदनिजशुद्धात्मैवोपादेय इति रुचिरूपं निश्चयसम्यक्त्वं यत्पूर्वं तपश्चरणावस्थायां भावितं तस्य फलभूतं समस्तजीवादितत्त्वविषये विपरीताभिनिवेशरहितपरिणतिरूपं परमक्षायिकसम्यक्त्वं भण्यते । पूर्वं छद्मस्थावस्थायां भावितस्य निर्विकारस्वसंवेदनज्ञानस्य फलभूतं युगपल्लोकालोकसमस्तवस्तुगतविशेषपरिच्छेदकं केवलज्ञानम् । निर्विकल्पस्वशुद्धात्मसत्तावलोकनरूपं यत्पूर्वं दर्शनं भावितं तस्यैव फलभूतं युगपल्लोकालोकसमस्तवस्तुगतसामान्यग्राहकं केवलदर्शनम् । कस्मिंश्चित्स्वरूपचलनकारणे जाते सति घोरपरीषहोपसर्गादौ निजनिरञ्जनपरमात्मध्याने पूर्वं धैर्यमवलम्बितं तस्यैव फलभूतमनन्तपदार्थपरिच्छित्तिविषये खेदरहितत्वमनन्तवीर्यम् । सूक्ष्मातीन्द्रियकेवलज्ञानविषयत्वात्सिद्धस्वरूपस्य सूक्ष्मत्वं भण्यते । एकदीपप्रकाशे नानादीपप्रकाशवदेकसिद्धक्षेत्रे सङ्करव्यतिकरदोषपरिहारेणानन्तसिद्धावकाशदानसामर्थ्यमवगाहनगुणो भण्यते । यदि सर्वथा गुरुत्वं भवति तदा लोहपिण्डवदधःपतनं, यदि च सर्वथा लघुत्वं भवति तदा वाताहतार्कतूलवत्सर्वदैव भ्रमणमेव स्यान्न च तथा तस्मादगुरुलघुत्वगुणोऽभिधीयते । सहजशुद्धस्वरूपानुभवसमुत्पन्नरागादिविभावरहितसुखामृतस्य यदेकदेशसंवेदनं कृतं पूर्वं तस्यैव फलभूतमव्याबाधमनन्तसुखं भण्यते । इति मध्यमरुचिशिष्यापेक्षया सम्यक्त्वादिगुणाष्टकं भणितम् । मध्यमरुचिशिष्यं प्रति पुनर्विशेषभेदनयेन निर्गतित्वं, निरिन्द्रियत्वं, निष्कायत्वं, निर्योगत्वं, निर्वेदत्वं, निष्कषायत्वं, निर्नामत्वं, निर्गोत्रत्वं, निरायुषत्वमित्यादिविशेषगुणास्तथैवास्तित्ववस्तुत्वप्रमेयत्वादिसामान्यगुणाः स्वागमाविरोधेनानन्ता ज्ञातव्याः । संक्षेपरुचिशिष्यं प्रति पुनर्विवक्षिताभेदनयेनानन्तज्ञानादिचतुष्टयम्, अनन्तज्ञानदर्शनसुखत्रयं, केवलज्ञानदर्शनद्वयं, साक्षादभेदनयेन शुद्धचैतन्यमेवैको गुण इति । पुनरपि कथंभूताः सिद्धाः चरमशरीरात् किञ्चिदूना भवन्ति तत् किञ्चिदूनत्वं शरीरोपाङ्गजनितनासिकादिच्छिद्राणामपूर्णत्वे सति यस्मिन्नेव क्षणे सयोगिचरमसमये त्रिंशत्प्रकृत्युदय-

विच्छेदमध्ये शरीरोपाङ्गनामकर्मविच्छेदो जातस्तस्मिन्नेव क्षणे जातमिति ज्ञातव्यम् । कश्चिदाह यथा प्रदीपस्य भाजनाद्यावरणे गते प्रकाशस्य विस्तारो भवति तथा देहाभावे लोकप्रमाणेन भाव्यमिति । तत्र परिहारमाह—प्रदीप-संबन्धी योऽसौ प्रकाशविस्तारः पूर्वं स्वभावेनैव तिष्ठति पश्चादावरणं जातं जीवस्य तु लोकमात्रासंख्येयप्रदेशत्वं स्वभावो भवति यस्तु प्रदेशानां संबन्धी विस्तारः स स्वभावो न भवति कस्मादिति चेत् पूर्वं लोकमात्रप्रदेशा विस्तीर्णा निरावरणास्तिष्ठन्ति पश्चात् प्रदीपवदावरणं जातमेव । तन्न किन्तु पूर्वमेवा-नादिसन्तानरूपेण शरीरेणावृतास्तिष्ठन्ति ततः कारणात्प्रदेशानां संहारो न भवति, विस्तारश्च शरीरनामकर्माधीन एव न च स्वभावस्तेन कारणेन शरीरा-भावे विस्तारो न भवति । अपरमप्युदाहरणं दीयते—यथा हस्तचतुष्टयप्रमाण-वस्त्रं पुरुषेण मुष्टौ बद्धं तिष्ठति पुरुषाभावे सङ्कोचविस्तारौ वा न करोति; निष्पत्तिकाले सार्द्रं मृन्मयभाजनं वा शुष्कं सज्जलाभावे सति; तथा जीवोऽपि पुरुषस्थानीयजलस्थानीयशरीराभावे विस्तारसंकोचौ न करोति। यत्रैव मुक्तस्तत्रैव तिष्ठतीति ये केचन वदन्ति तन्निषेधार्थं पूर्वप्रयोगादसङ्गत्वाद्बन्धच्छेदात्तथा गति-परिणामाच्चेति हेतुचतुष्टयेन तथैवाविद्धकुलालचक्रवद् व्यपगतलेपालाम्बुव-देरण्डबीजवदग्निशिखावच्चेति दृष्टान्तचतुष्टयेन च स्वभावोर्ध्वगमनं ज्ञातव्यं तच्च लोकाग्रपर्यन्तमेव न च परतो धर्मास्तिकायाभावादिति । नित्या इति विशेषणं तु मुक्तात्मनां कल्पशतप्रमितकाले गते जगति शून्ये जाते सति पुनरागमनं भवतीति सदाशिववादिनो वदन्ति तन्निषेधार्थं विज्ञेयम् । उत्पादव्ययसंयुक्तत्वं विशेषणं सर्वथैवापरिणामित्वनिषेधार्थमिति । किञ्च विशेषः निश्चलाविनश्व-रशुद्धात्मस्वरूपाद्भिन्न सिद्धानां नारकादिगतिषु भ्रमणं नास्ति कथमुत्पादव्यय-त्वमिति । तत्र परिहारः । आगमकथितागुरुलघुषट्स्थानपतितहानिवृद्धिरूपेण येऽर्थपर्यायास्तदपेक्षया अथवा येन येनोत्पादव्ययध्रौव्यरूपेण प्रतिक्षणं ज्ञेय-पदार्थाः परिणमन्ति तत्परिच्छित्त्याकारेणानीहितवृत्त्या सिद्धज्ञानमपि परिणमति तेन कारणेनोत्पादव्ययत्वम् , अथवा व्यञ्जनपर्यायापेक्षया संसारपर्यायवि-नाशः, सिद्धपर्यायोत्पादः, शुद्धजीवद्रव्यत्वेन ध्रौव्यमिति । एवं नयविभागेन नवाधिकारैर्जीवद्रव्यं ज्ञातव्यम् , अथवा तदेव बहिरात्मान्तरात्मपरमात्मभेदेन त्रिधा भवति । तद्यथा—स्वशुद्धात्मसंवित्तिसमुत्पन्नवास्तवसुखात्प्रतिपक्षभूते-

नेन्द्रियसुखेनासक्तो बहिरात्मा, तद्विलक्षणोऽन्तरात्मा । अथवा देहरहितनिजशुद्धात्मद्रव्यभावनालक्षणभेदज्ञानरहितत्वेन देहादिपरद्रव्येष्वेकत्वभावनापरिणतो बहिरात्मा, तस्मात्प्रतिपक्षभूतोऽन्तरात्मा । अथवा हेयोपादेयविचारकचित्तनिर्दोषपरमात्मनो भिन्ना रागादयो दोषाः शुद्धचैतन्यलक्षण आत्मन्युक्तलक्षणेषु चित्तदोषात्मसु त्रिषु वीतरागसर्वज्ञप्रणीतेषु अन्येषु वा पदार्थेषु येस्य परस्परसापेक्षनयविभागेन श्रद्धानं ज्ञानं च नास्ति स बहिरात्मा, तस्माद्विसदृशोऽन्तरात्मेति रूपेण बहिरात्मान्तरात्मनोर्लक्षणं ज्ञातव्यम् । परमात्मलक्षणं कथ्यते—सकलविमलकेवलज्ञानेन येन कारणेन समस्तं लोकालोकं जानाति व्याप्नोति तेन कारणेन विष्णुर्भण्यते । परब्रह्मसंज्ञनिजशुद्धात्मभावनासमुत्पन्नसुखामृततृप्तस्य सत उर्वशीरम्भातिलोत्तमाभिर्देवकन्याभिरपि यस्य ब्रह्मचर्यव्रतं न खण्डितं स परमब्रह्म भण्यते । केवलज्ञानादिगुणैश्वर्ययुक्तस्य सतो देवेन्द्रादयोऽपि तत्पदाभिलाषिणः सन्तो यस्याज्ञां कुर्वन्ति स ईश्वराभिधानो भवति । केवलज्ञानशब्दवाच्यं गतं ज्ञानं यस्य स सुगतः, अथवा शोभनमविनश्वरं मुक्तिपदं गतः सुगतः । "शिवं परमकल्याणं निर्वाणं ज्ञानमक्षयम् । प्राप्तं मुक्तिपदं येन स शिवः परिकीर्त्तितः ।" इति श्लोककथितलक्षणः शिवः । कामक्रोधादिदोषजयेनानन्तज्ञानादिगुणसहितो जिनः । इत्यादिपरमागमकथिताष्टोत्तरसहस्रसंख्यनामवाच्यः परमात्मा ज्ञातव्यः । एवमेतेषु त्रिविधात्मसु मध्ये मिथ्यादृष्टिभव्यजीवे बहिरात्मा व्यक्तिरूपेण तिष्ठति, अन्तरात्मपरमात्मद्वयं शक्तिरूपेण भाविनैगमनयापेक्षया व्यक्तिरूपेण च । अभव्यजीवेपुनर्बहिरात्मा व्यक्तिरूपेण अन्तरात्मपरमात्मद्वयं शक्तिरूपेणैव न च भाविनैगमनयेनेति । यद्यभव्यजीवे परमात्मा शक्तिरूपेण वर्त्तते तर्हि कथमभव्यत्वमिति चेत् परमात्मशक्तेः केवलज्ञानादिरूपेण व्यक्तिर्न भविष्यतीत्यभव्यत्वं शक्तिः पुनः शुद्धनयेनोभयत्र समाना । यदि पुनः शक्तिरूपेणाप्यभव्यजीवे केवलज्ञानं नास्ति तदा केवलज्ञानावरणं न घटते । भव्याभव्यद्वयं पुनरशुद्धनयेनेति भावार्थः । एवं यथा मिथ्यादृष्टिसंज्ञे बहिरात्मनि नयविभागेन दर्शितमात्मत्रयं तथा शेषगुणस्थानेष्वपि । तद्यथा—बहिरात्मावस्थायामन्तरात्मपरमात्मद्वयं शक्तिरूपेण भाविनैगमनयेन व्यक्तिरूपेण च विज्ञेयम्, अन्तरात्मावस्थायां तु बहिरात्मा भूतपूर्वन्यायेन घृतघटवत्, परमात्मस्वरूपं तु शक्तिरूपेण भाविनैगमनयेन व्यक्तिरूपेण च । परमात्मावस्थायां

पुनरन्तरात्मबहिरात्मद्वयं भूतपूर्वनयेनेति । अथ त्रिधात्मानं गुणस्थानेषु योजयति । मिथ्या सासादनमिश्रगुणस्थानत्रये तारतम्यन्यूनाधिकभेदेन बहिरात्मा ज्ञातव्यः, अविरतगुणस्थाने तद्योग्याशुभलेश्यापरिणतो जघन्यान्तरात्मा, क्षीणकषायगुणस्थाने पुनरुत्कृष्टः, अविरतक्षीणकषाययोर्मध्ये मध्यमः, सयोग्ययोगिगुणस्थानद्वये विवक्षितैकदेशशुद्धनयेन सिद्धसदृशः परमात्मा, सिद्धस्तु साक्षात्परमात्मेति । अत्र बहिरात्मा हेयः, उपादेयभूतस्यानन्तसुखसाधकत्वादन्तरात्मोपादेयः, परमात्मा पुनः साक्षादुपादेय इत्यभिप्रायः । एवं षड्द्रव्यपञ्चास्तिकायप्रतिपादकप्रथमाधिकारमध्ये नमस्कारादिचतुर्दशगाथाभिर्नवभिरन्तस्थलैर्जीवद्रव्यकथनरूपेण प्रथमोऽन्तराधिकारः समाप्तः ॥ १४ ॥

अतःपरं यद्यपि शुद्धबुद्धैकस्वभावं परमात्मद्रव्यमुपादेयं भवति तथापि हेयरूपस्याजीवद्रव्यस्य गाथाष्टकेन व्याख्यानं करोति । कस्मादिति चेत्—हेयतत्त्वपरिज्ञाने सति पश्चादुपादेयस्वीकारो भवतीति हेतोः । तद्यथा—

व्याख्या "अज्जीवो पुण ग्णेओ" अजीवः पुनर्ज्ञेयः । सकलविमलकेवलज्ञानदर्शनद्वयं शुद्धोपयोगः, मतिज्ञानादिरूपो विकलोऽशुद्धोपयोग इति द्विविधोपयोगः, अव्यक्तसुखदुःखानुभवनरूपा कर्मफलचेतना, तथैव मतिज्ञानादिमनःपर्ययपर्यन्तमशुद्धोपयोग इति, स्वेहापूर्वेष्टानिष्टविकल्परूपेण विशेषरागद्वेषपरिणमनं कर्मचेतना, केवलज्ञानरूपा शुद्धचेतना इत्युक्तलक्षणोपयोगश्चेतना च यत्र नास्ति स भवत्यजीव इति विज्ञेयः । पुनः पश्चाज्जीवाधिकारानन्तरं "पुग्गल धम्मो अधम्म आयासं कालो" स च पुद्गलधर्माधर्माकाशकालद्रव्यभेदेन पञ्चधा । पूरणगलनस्वभावत्वात्पुद्गल इत्युच्यते । गतिस्थित्यवगाहवर्त्तनालक्षणा धर्माधर्माकाशकालाः, "पुग्गल मुत्तो" पुद्गलोमूर्त्तः । कस्मात् "रूवादिगुणो" रूपादिगुणसहितो यतः । "अमुत्ति सेसा दु" रूपादिगुणाभावादमूर्त्ता भवन्ति पुद्गलाच्छेषाश्चत्वार इति । तथाहि यथा अनन्तज्ञानदर्शनसुखवीर्यगुणचतुष्टयं सर्वजीवसाधारणं तथा रूपरसगन्धस्पर्शगुणचतुष्टयं सर्वपुद्गलसाधारणं, यथा च शुद्धबुद्धैकस्वभावसिद्धजीवे अनन्तचतुष्टयमतीन्द्रियं तथैव शुद्धपुद्गलपरमाणुद्रव्ये रूपादिचतुष्टयमतीन्द्रियं, यथा रागादिस्नेहगुणेन कर्मबन्धावस्थायां ज्ञानादिचतुष्टयस्याशुद्धत्वं तथा स्निग्धरूक्षत्वगुणेन द्व्यणुकादिबन्धावस्थायां रूपादि-

चतुष्टयस्याशुद्धत्वं, यथा निस्नेहनिजपरमात्मभावनाबलेन रागादिस्निग्धत्वविनाशे सत्यनन्तचतुष्टयस्य शुद्धत्वं तथा जघन्यगुणानां बन्धो न भवतीति वचनात्परमाणुद्रव्ये स्निग्धरूक्षत्वगुणस्य जघन्यत्वे सति रूपादिचतुष्टयस्य शुद्धत्वमवबोद्धव्यमित्यभिप्रायः ॥१५॥

अथ पुद्गलद्रव्यस्य विभावव्यञ्जनपर्यायान्प्रतिपादयति ।

व्याख्या—शब्दबन्धसौक्ष्म्यस्थौल्यसंस्थानभेदतमश्छायातपोद्योतसहिताः पुद्गलद्रव्यस्य पर्याया भवन्ति । अथ विस्तारः—भाषात्मकोऽभाषात्मकश्च द्विविधः शब्दः । तत्राक्षरानक्षरात्मकभेदेन भाषात्मको द्विधा भवति । तत्राप्यक्षरात्मकः संस्कृतप्राकृतापभ्रंशपैशाचिकादिभाषाभेदेनार्यम्लेच्छमनुष्यादिव्यवहारहेतुर्बहुधा । अनक्षरात्मकस्तु द्वीन्द्रियादितिर्यग्जीवेषु सर्वज्ञदिव्यध्वनौ च । अभाषात्मकोऽपि प्रायोगिकवैश्रसिकभेदेन द्विविधः । "ततं वीणादिकं ज्ञेयं विततं पटहादिकम् । घनं तु कांस्यतालादि वंशादि सुषिरं विदुः ।" इति श्लोककथितक्रमेण प्रयोगे भवः प्रायोगिकश्चतुर्धा भवति । विश्रसा स्वभावेन भवो वैश्रसिको मेघादिप्रभो बहुधा । किञ्च शब्दातीतनिजपरमात्मभावनाच्युतेन शब्दादिमनोज्ञामनोज्ञपञ्चेन्द्रियविषयासक्तेन च जीवेन यदुपार्जितं सुस्वरदुःस्वरनामकर्म तदुदयेन यद्यपि जीवे शब्दो दृश्यते तथापि स जीवसंयोगेनोत्पन्नत्वाद् व्यवहारेण जीवशब्दो भण्यते, निश्चयेन पुनः पुद्गलस्वरूप एवेति । बन्धः कथ्यते—मृत्पिण्डादिरूपेण योऽसौ बहुधा बन्धः स केवलः पुद्गलबन्धः, यस्तु कर्मनोकर्मरूपः स जीवपुद्गलसंयोगबन्धः । किञ्च विशेषः—कर्मबन्धपृथग्भूतस्वशुद्धात्मभावनारहितजीवस्यानुपचरितासद्भूतव्यवहारेण द्रव्यबन्धः, तथैवाशुद्धनिश्चयेन योऽसौ रागादिरूपो भावबन्धः कथ्यते सोऽपि शुद्धनिश्चयनयेन पुद्गलबन्ध एव । बिल्वाद्यपेक्षया बदरादीनां सूक्ष्मत्वं, परमाणोः साक्षादिति । बदराद्यपेक्षया बिल्वादीनां स्थूलत्वं, जगद्व्यापिनी महास्कन्धे सर्वोत्कृष्टमिति । समचतुरस्रन्यग्रोधसात्विककुब्जवामनहुण्डभेदेन षट्प्रकारसंस्थानं यद्यपि व्यवहारनयेन जीवस्यास्ति तथाप्यसंस्थानाच्चिच्चमत्कारपरिणतेर्भिन्नत्वान्निश्चयेन पुद्गलसंस्थानमेव । यदपि जीवादन्यत्र वृत्तत्रिकोणचतुष्कोणादिव्यक्ताव्यक्तरूपं बहुधा संस्थानं तदपि पुद्गल एव । गोधूमादिचूर्णरूपेण घृतखण्डादिरूपेण बहुधा भेदो ज्ञातव्यः । दृष्टिप्रतिबन्धकोऽन्धकारस्तम इति भण्यते । वृक्षाद्याश्रयरूपा मनु-

ष्यादिप्रतिबिम्बरूपा च छाया विज्ञेया । उद्योतश्चन्द्रविमाने खद्योतादितिर्यग्जीवेषु च भवति । आतप आदित्यविमाने अन्यत्रापि सूर्यकान्तमणिविशेषादौ पृथ्वीकाये ज्ञातव्यः । अयमत्रार्थः— यथा जीवस्य शुद्धनिश्चयेन स्वात्मोपलब्धिलक्षणे सिद्धस्वरूपे स्वभावव्यञ्जनपर्याये विद्यमानेऽप्यनादिकर्मबन्धवशात् स्निग्धरूक्षस्थानीयरागद्वेषपरिणामे सति स्वाभाविकपरमानन्दैकलक्षणस्वास्थ्यभावभ्रष्टस्य नरनारकादिविभावव्यञ्जनपर्याया भवन्ति तथा पुद्गलस्यापि निश्चयनयेन शुद्धपरमाण्ववस्थालक्षणे स्वभावव्यञ्जनपर्याये सत्यपि स्निग्धरूक्षत्वाद्बन्धो भवतीति वचनाद्रागद्वेषस्थानीयबन्धयोग्यस्निग्धरूक्षत्वपरिणामे सत्युक्तलक्षणाच्छब्दादन्येऽप्यथागमोक्तलक्षणा आकुञ्चनप्रसारणदधिदुग्धादयो विभावव्यञ्जनपर्याया ज्ञातव्याः । एवमजीवाधिकारमध्ये पूर्वसूत्रोदितरूपादिगुणचतुष्टययुक्तस्य तथैवात्र सूत्रोदितशब्दादिपर्यायसहितस्य संक्षेपेणाणुस्कन्धभेदभिन्नस्य पुद्गलद्रव्यस्य व्याख्यानमुख्यत्वेन प्रथमस्थले गाथाद्वयं गतम् ॥ १६ ॥

अथ धर्मद्रव्यमाख्याति ।

व्याख्या । गतिपरिणतानां धर्मो जीवपुद्गलानां गमनसहकारिकारणं भवति । दृष्टान्तमाह—तोयं यथा मत्स्यानाम् । स्वयं तिष्ठतो नैव स नयति तानिति । तथाहि —यथा सिद्धो भगवानमूर्त्तोऽपि निष्क्रियस्तथैवाप्रेरकोऽपि सिद्धवदनन्तज्ञानादिगुणस्वरूपोऽहमित्यादिव्यवहारेण सविकल्पसिद्धभक्तियुक्तानां निश्चयेन निर्विकल्पसमाधिरूपस्वकीयोपादानकारणपरिणतानां भव्यानां सिद्धगतेः सहकारिकारणं भवति । तथा निष्क्रियोऽमूर्त्तो निष्प्रेरकोऽपि धर्मास्तिकायः स्वकीयोपादानकारणेन गच्छतां जीवपुद्गलानां गतेः सहकारिकारणं भवति । लोकप्रसिद्धदृष्टान्तेन तु मत्स्यादीनां जलादिवदित्यभिप्रायः ॥ एवं धर्मद्रव्यव्याख्यानरूपेण गाथा गता ॥ १७ ॥

अथाधर्मद्रव्यमुपदिशति ।

व्याख्या । स्थानयुक्तानामधर्मः पुद्गलजीवानां स्थितेः सहकारिकारणं भवति । तत्र दृष्टान्तः—छाया यथा पथिकानाम् । स्वयं गच्छतो जीवपुद्गलान्स नैव धरतीति । तद्यथा—स्वसंवित्तिसमुत्पन्नसुखामृतरूपं परमस्वास्थ्यं यद्यपि निश्चयेन स्वरूपे स्थितिकारणं भवति तथा "सिद्धोऽहं सुद्धोऽहं अणंतणाणादिगुणसमिद्धोऽहं । देहपमाणो णिच्चो असंखदेसो अमुत्तोय ।" इति गाथाकथितसि-

द्धभक्तिरूपेणेह पूर्वं सविकल्पावस्थायां सिद्धोऽपि यथा भव्यानां बहिरङ्गसहकारिकारणं भवति तथैव स्वकीयोपादानकारणेन स्वयमेव तिष्ठतां जीवपुद्गलानामधर्मद्रव्यं स्थितेः सहकारिकारणम् । लोकव्यवहारेण तु छायावद्वा पृथिवीवद्वेति सूत्रार्थः ॥ एवमधर्मद्रव्यकथनेन गाथा गता ॥ १८ ॥

अथाकाशद्रव्यमाह ।

व्याख्या । जीवादीनामवकाशदानयोग्यमाकाशं विजानीहि हे शिष्य ! किं विशिष्टं "जेण्हं" जिनस्येदं जैनं, जिनेन प्रोक्तं वा जैनम् । तच्च लोकालोकाकाशभेदेन द्विविधमिति । इदानीं विस्तारः—सहजशुद्धसुखामृतरसास्वादेन परमसमरसीभावेन भरितावस्थेषु केवलज्ञानाद्यनन्तगुणाधारभूतेषु लोकाकाशप्रमितासंख्येयस्वकीयशुद्धप्रदेशेषु यद्यपि निश्चयनयेन सिद्धास्तिष्ठन्ति, तथाप्युपचरितासद्भूतव्यवहारेण मोक्षशिलायां तिष्ठन्तीति भण्यते इत्युक्तोऽस्ति । स च ईदृशो मोक्षो यत्र प्रदेशे परमध्यानेनात्मा स्थितः सन् कर्मरहितो भवति, तत्रैव भवति नान्यत्र । ध्यानप्रदेशे कर्मपुद्गलान् त्यक्त्वा ऊर्ध्वगमनस्वभावेन गत्वा मुक्तात्मानो यतो लोकाग्रे तिष्ठन्तीति तत उपचारेण लोकाग्रमपि मोक्षः प्रोच्यते । यथा तीर्थभूतपुरुषसेवितस्थानमपि भूमिजलादिरूपमुपचारेण तीर्थं भवति । यथा तथैव सर्वद्रव्याणि यद्यपि निश्चयनयेन स्वकीयप्रदेशेषु तिष्ठन्ति तथाप्युपचरितासद्भूतव्यवहारेण लोकाकाशे तिष्ठन्तीत्यभिप्रायो भगवतां श्रीनेमिचन्द्रसिद्धान्तदेवानामिति ॥ १९ ॥

तमेव लोकाकाशं विशेषेण द्रढयति ।

व्याख्या । धर्माधर्मकालपुद्गलजीवाश्च सन्ति यावत्याकाशे स लोकः । तथा चोक्तं—लोक्यन्ते दृश्यन्ते जीवादिपदार्था यत्र स लोक इति । तस्माल्लोकाकाशात्परतो बहिर्भागे पुनरनन्ताकाशमलोक इति । अत्राह सोमाभिधानो राजश्रेष्ठी । हे भगवन् ! केवलज्ञानस्यानन्तभागप्रमितमाकाशद्रव्यं तस्याप्यनन्तभागे सर्वमध्यमप्रदेशे लोकस्तिष्ठति । स चानादिनिधनः केनापि पुरुषविशेषेण न कृतो न हतो न धृतो न च रक्षितः । तथैवासंख्यातप्रदेशस्तत्रासंख्यातप्रदेशे लोकेऽनन्तजीवास्तेभ्योऽप्यनन्तगुणाः पुद्गलाः, लोकाकाशप्रमितासंख्येयकालाणुद्रव्याणि, प्रत्येकं लोकाकाशप्रमाणं धर्माधर्मद्वयमित्युक्तलक्षणाः पदार्थाः कथमवकाशं लभन्त इति । भगवानाह—एकप्रदीपप्रकाशे नानाप्रदीप-

प्रकाशवदेकगूढरसनागगद्याणके बहुसुवर्णवद्भस्मघटमध्ये सूचिकोष्ट्रदुग्धवदित्यादिदृष्टान्तेन विशिष्टावगाहनशक्तिवशादसंख्यातप्रदेशेऽपि लोकेऽवस्थानमवगाहो न विरुध्यते । यदि पुनरित्थंभूतावगाहनशक्तिर्न भवति तर्ह्यसंख्यातप्रदेशेष्वसंख्यातपरमाणूनामेव व्यवस्थानं, तथा सति सर्वे जीवा यथा शुद्धनिश्चयेन शक्तिरूपेण निरावरणाः शुद्धबुद्धैकस्वभावास्तथा व्यक्तिरूपेण व्यवहारनयेनापि न च तथा प्रत्यक्षविरोधादागमविरोधाच्चेति । एवमाकाशद्रव्यप्रतिपादनरूपेण सूत्रद्वयं गतम् ॥ २० ॥

अथ निश्चयव्यवहारकालस्वरूपं कथयति ।

व्याख्या । "दव्वपरिवट्टरूवो जो" द्रव्यपरिवर्त्तरूपो यः "सो कालो हवेइ ववहारो" स कालो भवति व्यवहाररूपः । स च कथंभूतः "परिणामादी लक्खो" परिणामक्रियापरत्वापरत्वेन लक्ष्यत इति परिणामादिलक्ष्यः । इदानीं निश्चयकालः कथ्यतेः—"वट्टणलक्खो य परमट्ठो" वर्त्तनालक्षणश्च परमार्थकाल इति । तद्यथा—जीवपुद्गलयोः परिवर्त्तो नवजीर्णपर्यायस्तस्य या समयघटिकादिरूपा स्थितिः स्वरूपं यस्य स भवति द्रव्यपर्यायरूपो व्यवहारकालः । तथाचोक्तं संस्कृतप्राभृतेन—"स्थितिः कालसंज्ञका" तस्य पर्यायस्य संबन्धिनी याऽसौ समयघटिकादिरूपा स्थितिः सा व्यवहारकालसंज्ञा भवति न च पर्याय इत्यभिप्रायः । यत एव पर्यायसंबन्धिनी स्थितिर्व्यवहारकालसंज्ञां भजते तत एव जीवपुद्गलसंबन्धिनीपरिणामेन पर्यायेण तथैव देशान्तरचलनरूपया गोदोहनपाकादिपरिस्पन्दलक्षणरूपया वा क्रियया तथैव दूरासन्नचलनकालकृतपरत्वापरत्वेन च लक्ष्यते ज्ञायते यः स परिणामक्रियापरत्वापरत्वलक्षण इत्युच्यते । अथ द्रव्यरूपनिश्चयकालमाह । स्वकीयोपादानरूपेण स्वयमेव परिणममानानां पदार्थानां कुम्भकारचक्रस्याधस्तनशिलावत्, शीतकालाध्ययने अग्निवत्, पदार्थपरिणतेर्यत्सहकारित्वं सा वर्त्तना भण्यते । सैव लक्षणं यस्य स वर्त्तनालक्षणः कालाणुद्रव्यरूपो निश्चयकालः, इति व्यवहारकालस्वरूपं निश्चयकालस्वरूपं च विज्ञेयम् । कश्चिदाह "समयरूप एव निश्चयकालस्तस्मादन्यः कालाणुद्रव्यरूपो निश्चयकालो नास्त्यदर्शनात् ।" तत्रोत्तरं दीयते—समयस्तावत्कालस्तस्यैव पर्यायः, स कथं पर्याय इति चेत् पर्यायस्योत्पन्नप्रध्वंसित्वात् । तथाचोक्तं "समउप्पन्न पधंसी" स च पर्यायो द्रव्यं विना न भवति, पश्चात्तस्य समयरूपपर्याय-

कालस्योपादानकारणभूतं द्रव्यं तेनापि कालरूपेण भाव्यम् । इन्धनाग्निसहकारिकारणोत्पन्नस्यौदनपर्यायस्य तन्दुलोपादानकारणवत्, अथ कुम्भकारचक्रचीवरादिबहिरङ्गनिमित्तोत्पन्नस्य मृन्मयघटपर्यायस्य मृत्पिण्डोपादानकारणवत्, अथवा नरनारकादिपर्यायस्य जीवोपादानकारणवदिति । तदपि कस्मादुपादानकारणसदृशं कार्यं भवतीति वचनात् । अथ मतं "समयादिकालपर्यायाणां कालद्रव्यमुपादानकारणं न भवति; किन्तु समयोत्पत्तौ मन्दगतिपरिणतपुद्गलपरमाणुस्तथा निमेषकालोत्पत्तौ नयनपुटविघटनं, तथैव घटिकाकालपर्यायोत्पत्तौ घटिकासामग्रीभूतजलभाजनपुरुषहस्तादिव्यापारो, दिवसपर्याये तु दिनकरबिम्बमुपादानकारणमिति नैवम् । यथा तन्दुलोपादानकारणोत्पन्नस्य सदोदनपर्यायस्य शुक्लकृष्णादिवर्णा, सुरभ्यसुरभिगन्ध—स्निग्धरुक्षादिस्पर्श—मधुरादिरसविशेषरूपा गुणा दृश्यन्ते । तथा पुद्गलपरमाणुनयनपुटविघटनजलभाजनपुरुषव्यापारादिदिनकरबिम्बरूपैः पुद्गलपर्यायैरुपादानभूतैः समुत्पन्नानां समयनिमिषघटिकादिकालपर्यायाणामपि शुक्लकृष्णादिगुणाः प्राप्नुवन्ति न च तथा । उपादानकारणसदृशं कार्यमिति वचनात् किं बहुना । योऽसावनाद्यनिधनतस्थैवामूर्त्तो नित्यः समयाद्युपादानकारणभूतोऽपि समयादिविकल्परहितः कालाणुद्रव्यरूपः स निश्चयकालो, यस्तु सादिसान्तसमयघटिकाप्रहरादिविवक्षितव्यवहारविकल्परूपस्तस्यैव द्रव्यकालस्य पर्यायभूतो व्यवहारकाल इति । अयमत्र भावः—यद्यपि काललब्धिवशेनानन्तसुखभाजनो भवति जीवस्तथापि विशुद्धज्ञानदर्शनस्वभावनिजपरमात्मतत्त्वस्य सम्यक्श्रद्धानज्ञानानुष्ठानसमस्तबहिर्द्रव्येच्छानिवृत्तिलक्षणतपश्चरणरूपा या निश्चयचतुर्विधाराधना सैव तत्रोपादानकारणं ज्ञातव्यं न च कालस्तेन स हेय इति ॥ २१ ॥

अथ निश्चयकालस्यावस्थानक्षेत्रं द्रव्यगणनां च प्रतिपादयति ।

व्याख्या । "लोयायपदेसे इक्केक्के जे ट्ठिया हु इक्केक्का" लोकाकाशप्रदेशेष्वेकैकेषु ये स्थिता एकैकसंख्योपेता "हु" स्फुटं क इव "रयणाणं रासीमिव" परस्परतादात्म्यपरिहारेण रत्नानां राशिरिव । "ते कालाणू "तेकालाणवः । कति संख्योपेताः । "असंखदव्वाणि" लोकाकाशप्रमितासंख्येयद्रव्याणीति । तथाहि—यथाङ्गुलिद्रव्यस्य यस्मिन्नेव क्षणे वक्रपर्यायोत्पत्तिस्तस्मिन्नेव क्षणे पूर्वप्राञ्जलपर्यायविनाशोऽङ्गुलिरूपेण ध्रौव्यमिति द्रव्यसिद्धिः । यथैव च

केवलज्ञानादिव्यक्तिरूपेण कार्यसमयसारस्योत्पादो निर्विकल्पसमाधिरूपकारणसमयसारस्य विनाशस्तदुभयाधारपरमात्मद्रव्यत्वेन ध्रौव्यमिति वा द्रव्यसिद्धिः । तथा कालाणोरपि मन्दगतिपरिणतपुद्गलपरमाणुना व्यक्तीकृतस्य कालाणूपादानकारणोत्पन्नस्य य एव वर्त्तमानसमयस्योत्पादः स एवातीतसमयापेक्षया विनाशस्तदुभयाधारकालाणुद्रव्यत्वेन ध्रौव्यमित्युत्पादव्ययध्रौव्यात्मककालद्रव्यसिद्धिः । लोकबहिर्भागे कालाणुद्रव्याभावात्कथमाकाशद्रव्यस्य परिणतिरिति चेत् अखण्डद्रव्यत्वादेकदेशदण्डाहतकुम्भकारचक्रभ्रमणवत्, तथैवैकदेशमनोहरस्पर्शनेन्द्रियविषयानुभवसर्वाङ्गसुखवत्, लोकमध्यस्थितकालाणुद्रव्यधारणैकदेशेनापि सर्वत्र परिणमनं भवतीति कालद्रव्यं शेषद्रव्याणां परिणतेः सहकारिकारणं भवति । कालद्रव्यस्य किं सहकारिकारणमिति ! यथाकाशद्रव्यमशेषद्रव्याणामाधारः स्वस्यापि, तथा कालद्रव्यमपि परेषां परिणतिसहकारिकारणं स्वस्यापि । अथ मतं यथा कालद्रव्यं स्वस्योपादानकारणं परिणतेः सहकारिकारणं च भवति तथा सर्वद्रव्याणि, कालद्रव्येण किं प्रयोजनमिति । नैवम् । यदि पृथग्भूतसहकारिकारणेन प्रयोजनं नास्ति तर्हि सर्वद्रव्याणां साधारणगतिस्थित्यवगाहनविषये धर्माधर्माकाशद्रव्यैरपि सहकारिकारणभूतैः प्रयोजनं नास्ति । किञ्च कालस्य घटिकादिवसादिकार्यं प्रत्यक्षेण दृश्यते धर्मादीनां पुनरागमकथनमेव । प्रत्यक्षेण किमपि कार्यं न दृश्यते ततस्तेषामपि कालद्रव्यस्येवाभावः प्राप्नोति । ततश्च जीवपुद्गलद्रव्यद्वयमेव । स चागमविरोधः । किञ्च सर्वद्रव्याणां परिणतिसहकारित्वं कालस्यैव गुणः, घ्राणेन्द्रियस्य रसास्वादनमिवान्यद्रव्यस्य गुणोऽन्यद्रव्यस्य कर्त्तुं नायाति द्रव्यसंकरदोषप्रसंगादिति । कश्चिदाह—यावत्कालेनैकाकाशप्रदेशं परमाणुरतिक्रामति ततस्तावत्कालेन समयो भवतीत्युक्तमागमे एकसमयेन चतुर्दशरज्जुगमने यावंत आकाशप्रदेशास्तावन्तः समया प्राप्नुवन्ति। परिहारमाह—एकाकाशप्रदेशातिक्रमेण यत्समयव्याख्यानं कृतं तन्मन्दगत्यपेक्षया, यत्पुनरेकसमये चतुर्दशरज्जुगमनव्याख्यानं तत्पुनः शीघ्रगत्यपेक्षया । तेन कारणेन चतुर्दशरज्जुगमनेऽप्येकसमयः । तत्र दृष्टान्तः—कोऽपि देवदत्तो योजनशतं मन्दगत्या दिनशतेन गच्छति । स एव विद्याप्रभावेण शीघ्रगत्या दिनेनैकेनापि गच्छति तत्र किं दिनशतं भवति । किन्त्वेक एव दिवसः । तथा चतुर्दशरज्जुगमनेऽपि शीघ्रगमनेनैक एव समयः । किञ्च स्वयं विषयानुभवरहितोऽप्ययं

जीवः परकीयविषयानुभवं दृष्टं श्रुतं च मनसि स्मृत्वा यद्विषयाभिलाषं करोति तदपध्यानं भण्यते तत्प्रभृतिसमस्तविकल्पजालरहितं स्वसंवित्तिसमुत्पन्नसहजानन्दैकलक्षणसुखरसास्वादसहितं यत्तद्वीतरागचारित्रं भवति । यत्पुनस्तदविनाभूतं तन्निश्चयसम्यक्त्वं चेति भण्यते । तदेव कालत्रयेऽपि मुक्तिकारणम् ; कालस्तु तदभावे सहकारिकारणमपि न भवति सतः स हेय इति । तथाचोक्तं "किं पल्लविएण बहुणा जे सिद्धा णरबरा गए काले । सिद्धिहंहि जेवि भविया तं जाणह सम्ममाहप्पं" इदमत्र तात्पर्यं–कालद्रव्यमन्यद्वा परमागमाविरोधेन विचारणीयं परं किन्तु वीतरागसर्वज्ञवचनं प्रमाणमिति मनसि निश्चित्य विवादो न कर्त्तव्यः । कस्मादिति चेत्–विवादे रागद्वेषौ भवतस्ततश्च संसारवृद्धिरिति ॥ २२ ॥

एवं कालद्रव्य - व्याख्यानमुख्यतया पञ्चमस्थले सूत्रद्वयं गतम् । इत्यष्टगाथासमुदायेन पञ्चभिः स्थलैरजीवद्रव्यव्याख्यानेन द्वितीयान्तराधिकारः समाप्तः ।

अतःपरं सूत्रपञ्चकपर्यन्तं पञ्चास्तिकायव्याख्यानं करोति । तत्रादौ गाथापूर्वार्द्धेन षड्द्रव्यव्याख्यानोपसंहार उत्तरार्धेन तु पञ्चास्तिकायव्याख्यानप्रारम्भः कथ्यते ।

व्याख्या । "एवं छब्भेयमिदं जीवाजीवप्पभेददो दव्वं उत्तं" एवं पूर्वोक्तप्रकारेण षड्भेदमिदं जीवाजीवप्रभेदतः साकाशाद् द्रव्यमुक्तं कथितं प्रतिपादितम् । "कालविजुत्तं णायव्वा पंच अत्थिकाया दु" तदेव षड्विधं द्रव्यं कालेन वियुक्तं रहितं ज्ञातव्याः पञ्चास्तिकायास्तु पुनरिति ॥ २३ ॥

पञ्चेति संख्या ज्ञाता तावदिदानीमस्तित्वं कायत्वं च निरूपयति ।

व्याख्या । "संति जदो तेणेदे अत्थीति भणंति जिणवरा" सन्ति विद्यन्ते यत एते जीवाद्याकाशपर्यन्ताः पञ्च तेन कारणेनैतेऽस्तीति भणन्ति जिणवराः सर्वज्ञाः । "जम्हा काया इव बहुदेसा तम्हा काया य" यस्मात्काया इव बहुप्रदेशास्तस्मात्कारणात्कायाश्च भणंति जिनवराः । "अत्थिकाया य" एवं न केवलं पूर्वोक्तप्रकारेणास्तित्वेन युक्ता अस्तिसंज्ञास्तथैव कायत्वेन युक्ताः कायसंज्ञा भवन्ति किन्तूभयमेलापकेनास्तिकायसंज्ञाश्च भवन्ति । इदानीं संज्ञालक्षणप्रयोजनादिभेदेऽप्यस्तित्वेन सहाभेदं दर्शयति । तथाहि शुद्धजीवास्तिकाये सिद्धत्वलक्षणः शुद्धद्रव्यव्यञ्जनपर्यायः, केवलज्ञानादयो विशेषगुणाः अस्तित्ववस्तुत्वागुरुलघुत्वादयः सामान्यगुणाश्च । तथैवाव्याबाधानन्तसुखाद्यनन्तगुणव्यक्तिरूपस्य कार्यसमयसारस्योत्पादो रागादिविभावरहितपरमस्वास्थ्यरूपस्य

कारणसमयसारस्य व्ययस्तदुभयाधारभूतपरमात्मद्रव्यत्वेन ध्रौव्यमित्युक्तलक्षणै-र्गुणपर्यायैरुत्पादव्ययध्रौव्यैश्च सह मुक्तावस्थायां संज्ञालक्षणप्रयोजनादिभेदेऽपि सत्तारूपेण प्रदेशरूपेण च भेदो नास्ति । कस्मादिति चेत्—मुक्तात्मसत्तायां गुणपर्यायाणामुत्पादव्ययध्रौव्याणां चास्तित्वं सिद्ध्यति, गुणपर्यायोत्पादव्यय-ध्रौव्यसत्तायाश्च मुक्तात्मास्तित्वं सिद्ध्यतीति परस्परसाधितसिद्धत्वादिति । कायत्वं कथ्यते—बहुप्रदेशप्रचयं दृष्ट्वा यथा शरीरं कायो भण्यते तथानन्त-ज्ञानादिगुणाधारभूतानां लोकाकाशप्रमितासंख्येयशुद्धप्रदेशानां प्रचयं समूहं संघातं मेलापकं दृष्ट्वा मुक्तात्मनि कायत्वं भण्यते । यथा शुद्धगुणपर्यायोत्पाद-व्ययध्रौव्यैः सह मुक्तात्मनः सत्तारूपेण निश्चयेनाभेदो दर्शितस्तथा यथासंभवं संसारिजीवेषु पुद्गलधर्माधर्माकाशकालेषु च द्रष्टव्यः । कालद्रव्यं विहाय कायत्वं चेति सूत्रार्थः ॥२४॥

अथ कायत्वव्याख्याने पूर्वं यत्प्रदेशास्तित्वं सूचितं तस्य विशेषव्याख्यानं करोतीत्येका पातनिका, द्वितीया तु कस्य द्रव्यस्य कियन्तः प्रदेशा भवन्तीति प्रतिपादयति ।

व्याख्या । "होंति असंखा जीवे धम्माधम्मे" भवन्ति लोकाकाशप्रमिता-संख्येयप्रदेशाः प्रदीपवदुपसंहारविस्तारयुक्तेऽप्येकजीवे, नित्यं स्वभावविस्तीर्ण-योर्धर्माधर्मयोरपि । "अणंत आयासे" अनन्तप्रदेशा आकाशे भवन्ति । "मुत्ते तिविह पदेसा" मूर्ते पुद्गलद्रव्ये संख्यातासंख्यातानन्ताणूनां पिण्डाः स्कन्धास्त एव त्रिविधाः प्रदेशा भण्यन्ते न च क्षेत्रप्रदेशाः । कस्मात् पुद्गल-स्यानन्तप्रदेशक्षेत्रेऽवस्थानाभावादिति । "कालस्सेगो" कालाणुद्रव्यस्यैक एव प्रदेशः । "ण तेण सो काओ" तेन कारणेन स कायो न भवति । कालस्यैक-प्रदेशत्वविषये युक्तिं प्रदर्शयति । तद्यथा—किञ्चिदूनचरमशरीरप्रमाणस्य सिद्धत्वपर्यायस्योपादानकारणभूतं शुद्धात्मद्रव्यं तत्पर्यायप्रमाणमेव । यथा वा मनुष्यदेवादिपर्यायोपादानकारणभूतं संसारिजीवद्रव्यं तत्पर्यायप्रमाणमेव, तथा कालद्रव्यमपि समयरूपस्य कालपर्यायस्य विभागेनोपादानकारणभूतमवि-भाग्येकप्रदेश एव भवति । अथवा मन्दगत्या गच्छतः पुद्गलपरमाणोरेकाका-शप्रदेशपर्यन्तमेव कालद्रव्यं गतेः सहकारिकारणं भवति ततो ज्ञायते तदप्येक-प्रदेशमेव । कश्चिदाह—पुद्गलपरमाणोर्गतिसहकारिकारणं धर्मद्रव्यं तिष्ठति,

कालस्य किमायातम् । नैवं वक्तव्यं—कर्मद्रव्ये गतिसहकारिकारणे विद्यमानेऽपि मत्स्यानां जलवन्मनुष्याणां शकटारोहणादिवत्सहकारिकारणानि बहून्यपि भवन्तीति । अथ मतं कालद्रव्यं पुद्गलानां गतिसहकारिकारणं कुत्र भणित-मास्ते । तदुच्यते । "पुग्गलकरणा जीवा खंधा खलु काल करणादु" इत्युक्तं श्रीकुन्दकुन्दाचार्यदेवैः पञ्चास्तिकायप्राभृते । अस्यार्थः कथ्यते । धर्मद्रव्ये विद्यमानेऽपि जीवानां कर्मनोकर्मपुद्गला गतेः सहकारिकारणं भवन्ति, अणु-स्कन्धभेदभिन्नपुद्गलानां तु कालद्रव्यमित्यर्थः ॥२५॥

अथैकप्रदेशस्यापि पुद्गलपरमाणोरुपचारेण कायत्वमुपदिशति ।

व्याख्या—"एयपदेसो वि अणू णाणाखंधप्पदेसदो होदि बहुदेसो" एकप्रदेशोऽपि पुद्गलपरमाणुर्नानास्कन्धरूपबहुप्रदेशतः सकाशाद्बहुप्रदेशो भवति । "उवयारा" उपचाराद् व्यवहारनयात् "तेण य काओ भणंति सव्वण्हु" तेन कारणेन कायमिति सर्वज्ञा भणन्तीति । तथाहि—यथायं परमात्मा शुद्धनिश्चयनयेन द्रव्यरूपेण शुद्धस्तथैकोऽप्यनादिकर्मबन्धवशात्स्निग्धरूक्षस्था-नीयरागद्वेषाभ्यां परिणम्य नरनारकादिविभावपर्यायरूपेण व्यवहारेण बहुविधो भवति । तथा पुद्गलपरमाणुरपि स्वभावेनैकोऽपि शुद्धोऽपि रागद्वेषस्थानीयबन्ध-योग्यस्निग्धरूक्षगुणाभ्यां परिणम्य द्व्यणुकादिस्कन्धरूपविभावपर्यायैर्बहुविधो बहुप्रदेशो भवति तेन कारणेन बहुप्रदेशलक्षणकायत्वकारणत्वादुपचारेण कायो भण्यते । अथ मतं—यथा—पुद्गलपरमाणोर्द्रव्यरूपेणैकस्यापि द्व्यणुकादि-स्कन्धपर्यायरूपेण बहुप्रदेशरूपं कायत्वं जातं तथा कालाणोरपि द्रव्येणैकस्यापि पर्यायेण कायत्वं भवतीति । तत्र परिहारः—स्निग्धरूक्षहेतुकस्य बन्धस्याभावान्न भवति । तदपि कस्मात् । स्निग्धरूक्षत्वं पुद्गलस्यैव धर्मो यतः कारणादिति । अणुत्वं पुद्गलसंज्ञा, कालस्याणुसंज्ञा कथमिति चेत् तत्रोत्तरम्—अणुशब्देन व्यवहारेण पुद्गला उच्यन्ते निश्चयेन तु वर्णादिगुणानां पूरणगलनयोगात्पुद्गला इति वस्तुवृत्या पुनरणुशब्दः सूक्ष्मवाचकः । तद्यथा परमेण प्रकर्षेणाणुः अणुकोऽर्थः सूक्ष्म इति व्युत्पत्त्या परमाणुः स च सूक्ष्मवाचकोऽणुशब्दो निर्विभागपुद्गलविवक्षायां पुद्गलाणुवदिति । अविभागिकालद्रव्यविवक्षायां तु कालाणुं कथयतीत्यर्थः ॥२६॥

अथ प्रदेशलक्षणमुपलक्षयति ।

व्याख्या । "जावदियं आयासं अविभागी पुग्गलाणुवट्टद्धं तं खु पदेसं जाणे" यावत्प्रमाणमाकाशमविभागिपुद्गलपरमाणुना विष्टब्धं व्याप्तं तदाकाशं खु स्फुटं प्रदेशं जानीहि हे शिष्य । कथंभूतं "सव्वाणुट्ठाणदाणरिहं" सर्वाणूनां सर्वपरमाणूनां सूक्ष्मस्कन्धानां च स्थानदानस्यावकाशदानस्यार्हं योग्यं समर्थमिति । यत एवेत्थंभूतावगाहनशक्तिरस्त्याकाशस्य तत एवासंख्यातप्रदेशेऽपि लोके अनन्तानन्तजीवास्तेभ्योऽप्यनन्तगुणपुद्गला अवकाशं लभन्ते । तथा चोक्तं जीवपुद्गलविषयेऽवकाशदानसामर्थ्यम् "एगणिगोदशरीरे जीवादव्वप्पमाणदोदिट्ठा । सिद्धेहि अणंतगुणा सव्वेण वितीदकालेण ॥ १ ॥ उग्गाढगाढणिचिदो पुग्गलकाए हि सव्वदो लोगो । सुहुमे हि बादरे हि य णंताणंतेहिं विविहेहिं ।२।" अथ मतं मूर्त्तपुद्गलानां भेदो भवतु नास्ति विरोधः । अमूर्त्ताखण्डस्याकाशद्रव्यस्य कथं विभागकल्पनेति । तन्न रागाद्युपाधिरहितस्वसंवेदनप्रत्यक्षभावनोत्पन्नसुखामृतरसास्वादतृप्तस्य मुनियुगलस्यावस्थानक्षेत्रमेकमनेकं वा । यद्येकं तर्हि द्वयोरेकत्वं प्राप्नोति न च तथा । भिन्नं चेत्तदा निर्विभागद्रव्यस्यापि विभागकल्पनमायातं घटाकाशपटाकाशमित्यादिवदिति ॥२७॥

एवं सूत्रपञ्चकेन पञ्चास्तिकायप्रतिपादकनामा तृतीयोऽन्तराधिकारः ॥

इति श्रीनेमिचन्द्रसैद्धान्तदेवविरचिते द्रव्यसंग्रहग्रन्थे नमस्कारादिसप्तविंशतिगाथाभिरन्तराधिकारत्रयसमुदायेन षड्द्रव्यपञ्चास्तिकायप्रतिपादकनामा प्रथमाधिकारः समाप्तः ॥

अतःपरं पूर्वोक्तषड्द्रव्याणां चूलिकारूपेण विस्तरव्याख्यानं क्रियते । तद्यथा—

परिणामि—जीव—मुत्तं, सपदेसं एय—खेत्त—किरियाय ।
णिच्चं कारण—कत्ता, सव्वगदमिदरं हि यपवेसे ॥१॥
दुण्णिय एयं एयं , पंच—त्तिय एय दुण्णि चउरो य ।
पंच य एयं एयं, एदेसं एय उत्तरं णेयं ॥२॥

व्याख्या । "परिणामि" इत्यादिव्याख्यानं क्रियते । परिणामपरिणामिनौ जीवपुद्गलौ स्वभावविभावपर्यायाभ्यां कृत्वा, शेषचत्वारि द्रव्याणि विभावव्यञ्जनपर्यायाभावान्मुख्यवृत्त्यापुनरपरिणामीनीति । "जीव" शुद्धनिश्चयनयेन विशुद्ध-

ज्ञानदर्शनस्वभावं शुद्धचैतन्यं प्राणशब्देनोच्यते तेन जीवतीति जीवः । व्यवहारनयेन पुनः कर्मोदयजनितद्रव्यभावरूपैश्चतुर्भिः प्राणैर्जीवति, जीविष्यति, जीवितपूर्वो वा जीवः । पुद्गलादिपञ्चद्रव्याणि पुनरजीवरूपाणि । "मुत्तं" शुद्धात्मनो विलक्षणस्पर्शरसगन्धवर्णवती मूर्त्तिरुच्यते, तत्सद्भावान्मूर्त्तः पुद्गलः । जीवद्रव्यं पुनरनुपचरितासद्भूतव्यवहारेण मूर्त्तमपि शुद्धनिश्चयनयेनामूर्त्तम्, धर्माधर्माकाशकालद्रव्याणि चामूर्त्तानि । "सपदेसं" लोकमात्रप्रमितासंख्येयप्रदेशलक्षणं जीवद्रव्यमादिं कृत्वा पञ्चद्रव्याणि पञ्चास्तिकायसंज्ञानि सप्रदेशानि । कालद्रव्यं पुनर्बहुप्रदेशत्वलक्षणकायत्वाभावादप्रदेशम् । "एय" द्रव्यार्थिकनयेन धर्माधर्माकाशद्रव्याण्येकानि भवन्ति । जीवपुद्गलकालद्रव्याणि पुनरनेकानि भवन्ति । "खेत्त" सर्वद्रव्याणामवकाशदानसामर्थ्यात् क्षेत्रमाकाशमेकम् । शेषपञ्चद्रव्याण्यक्षेत्राणि । "किरियाय" क्षेत्रात्क्षेत्रान्तरगमनरूपा परिस्पन्दवती चलनवती क्रिया सा विद्यते ययोस्तौ क्रियावन्तौ जीवपुद्गलौ । धर्माधर्माकाशकालद्रव्याणि पुनर्निष्क्रियाणि । "णिच्चं" धर्माधर्माकाशकालद्रव्याणि यद्यप्यर्थपर्यायत्वेनानित्यानि, तथापि मुख्यवृत्त्या विभावव्यञ्जनपर्यायाभावान्नित्यानि, द्रव्यार्थिकनयेन च जीवपुद्गलद्रव्ये पुनर्यद्यपि द्रव्यार्थिकनयापेक्षया नित्ये तथाप्यगुरुलघुपरिणतिस्वरूपस्वभावपर्यायापेक्षया विभावव्यञ्जनपर्यायापेक्षया चानित्ये । "कारण" पुद्गलधर्माधर्माकाशकालद्रव्याणि व्यवहारनयेन जीवस्य शरीरवाङ्मनःप्राणापानादिगतिस्थित्यवगाहवर्त्तनाकार्याणि कुर्वन्तीति कारणानि भवन्ति । जीवद्रव्यं पुनर्यद्यपि गुरुशिष्यादिरूपेण परस्परोपग्रहं करोति तथापि पुद्गलादिपञ्चद्रव्याणां किमपि न करोतीत्यकारणम् । "कत्ता" शुद्धपरिणामिकपरमभावग्राहकेण शुद्धद्रव्यार्थिकनयेन यद्यपि बन्धमोक्षद्रव्यभावरूपपुण्यपापघटपटादीनामकर्त्ता जीवस्तथाप्यशुद्धनिश्चयेन शुभाशुभोपयोगाभ्यां परिणतः सन् पुण्यपापबन्धयोः कर्त्ता फलभोक्ता भवति । विशुद्धज्ञानदर्शनस्वभावनिजशुद्धात्मद्रव्यस्य सम्यक्श्रद्धानज्ञानानुष्ठानरूपेण शुद्धोपयोगेन तु परिणतः सन् मोक्षस्यापि कर्त्ता तत्फलभोक्ता चेति । शुभाशुभशुद्धपरिणामानां परिणमनमेव कर्तृत्वं सर्वत्र ज्ञातव्यमिति । पुद्गलादिपञ्चद्रव्याणां च स्वकीयस्वकीयपरिणामेन परिणमनमेव कर्तृत्वम् । वस्तुवृत्त्या पुनः पुण्यपापादिरूपेणाकर्तृत्वमेव । "सव्वंग" लोकालोकव्याप्त्यपेक्षया सर्वगतमाकाशं भण्यते । लोकव्याप्त्य-

पेक्षया धर्माधर्मौ च । जीवद्रव्यं पुनरेकजीवापेक्षया लोकपूरणावस्थां विहायासवगतं, नानाजीवापेक्षया सर्वगतमेव भवति, पुद्गलद्रव्यं पुनर्लोकरूपमहास्कन्धापेक्षया सर्वगतं, शेष पुद्गलापेक्षया सर्वगतं न भवति, कालद्रव्यं पुनरेककालाणुद्रव्यापेक्षया सर्वगतं न भवति, लोकप्रदेशप्रमाणनानाकालाणुविवक्षया लोके सर्वगतं भवति । "इदरंहि यपवेसे" यद्यपि सर्वद्रव्याणि व्यवहारेणैकक्षेत्रावगाहेनान्योन्यप्रवेशेन तिष्ठन्ति तथापि निश्चयनयेन चेतनादिस्वकीयस्वरूपं न त्यजन्तीति ॥ अत्र षड् द्रव्येषु मध्ये वीतरागचिदानन्दैकादिगुणस्वभावं शुभाशुभमनोवचनकायव्यापार रहितं निजशुद्धात्मद्रव्यमेवोपादेयमिति भावार्थः ॥

अत ऊर्द्ध्वं पुनरपि षड्द्रव्याणां मध्ये हेयोपादेयस्वरूपं विशेषेण विचारयति । तत्र शुद्धनिश्चयनयेन शक्तिरूपेण शुद्धबुद्धैकस्वभावत्वात्सर्वे जीवा उपादेया भवन्ति । व्यक्तिरूपेण पुनः पञ्चपरमेष्ठिन एव । तत्राप्यर्हत्सिद्धद्वयमेव । तत्रापि निश्चयेन सिद्ध एव । परमनिश्चयेन तु भोगाकाङ्क्षादिरूपसमस्तविकल्पजालरहितपरमसमाधिकाले सिद्धसदृशः स्वशुद्धात्मैवोपादेयः शेषद्रव्याणि हेयानीति तात्पर्यम् । शुद्धबुद्धैकस्वभाव इति कोऽर्थः ? मिथ्यात्वरागादिसमस्तविभावरहितत्वेन शुद्ध इत्युच्यते केवलज्ञानाद्यनन्तगुणसहितत्वाद्बुद्धः । इति शुद्धबुद्धैकलक्षणं सर्वत्र ज्ञातव्यम् । इति षड्द्रव्यचूलिका समाप्ता । चूलिकाशब्दार्थः कथ्यते—चूलिका विशेषव्याख्यानम्, अथवा उक्तानुक्तव्याख्यानम्, उक्तानुक्तसंकीर्णव्याख्यानं चेति ॥

अतः परं जीवपुद्गलपर्यायरूपाणामास्रवादिसप्तपदार्थानामेकादशगाथापर्यन्तं व्याख्यानं करोति । तत्रादौ "आसवबंधण" इत्याद्यधिकारसूत्रगाथैका, तदनन्तरमास्रवपदार्थव्याख्यानरूपेण "आसबदि जेण" इत्यादि गाथात्रयं, ततःपरं बन्धव्याख्यानकथनेन "वज्झदि कम्म" इति प्रभृतिगाथाद्वयं, ततोऽपि संवरकथनरूपेण "चेदणपरिणामो" इत्यादि सूत्रद्वयं, ततश्च निर्जराप्रतिपादनरूपेण "जह कालेण तवेण य" इति प्रभृतिसूत्रमेकं, तदनन्तरं मोक्षस्वरूपकथनेन "सव्वस्स कम्मणो" इत्यादि सूत्रमेकं, ततश्च पुण्यपापद्वयकथनेन "सुहासुह" इत्यादि सूत्रमेकं चेत्येकादशगाथाभिः स्थलसप्तकसमुदायेन द्वितीयाधिकारे समुदायपातनिका ।

अत्राह शिष्यः—यद्येकान्तेन जीवाजीवौ परिणामिनौ भवतस्तदा संयोग-

पर्यायरूप एक एव पदार्थः, यदि पुनरेकान्तेनापरिणामिनौ भवतस्तदा जीवाजीवद्रव्यरूपौ द्वावेव पदार्थौ, तत आस्रवादि सप्तपदार्थाः कथं घटन्त इति । तत्रोत्तरं—कथंचित्परिणामित्वाद् घटन्ते । कथंचित्परिणामित्वमिति कोऽर्थः ? यथा स्फटिकमणिविशेषो यद्यपि स्वभावेन निर्मलस्तथापि जपापुष्पाद्युपाधिजनितंपर्यायान्तरपरिणतिं गृह्णाति । यद्यप्युपाधिं गृह्णाति तथापि निश्चयेन शुद्धस्वभावं न त्यजति तथा जीवोऽपि यद्यपि शुद्धद्रव्यार्थिकनयेन सहजशुद्धचिदानन्दैकस्वभावस्तथाप्यनादिकर्मबन्धपर्यायवशेन रागादिपरद्रव्योपाधिपर्यायं गृह्णाति । यद्यपि परपर्यायेण परिणमति तथापि निश्चयेन शुद्धस्वरूपं न त्यजति । पुद्गलोऽपि तथेति । परस्परसापेक्षत्वं कथंचित्परिणामित्वशब्दस्यार्थः । एवं कथंचित्परिणामित्वे सति जीवपुद्गलसंयोगपरिणतिनिर्वृत्तत्वादास्रवादिसप्तपदार्थां घटन्ते । ते च पूर्वोक्तजीवाजीवाभ्यां सह नव भवन्ति तत एव नव पदार्थाः । पुण्यपापपदार्थद्वयस्याभेदनयेन कृत्वा पुण्यपापयोर्बन्धपदार्थस्य वा मध्ये अन्तर्भावविवक्षया सप्ततत्त्वानि भण्यन्ते । हे भगवन्, यद्यपि कथंचित्परिणामित्वबलेन भेदप्रधानपर्यायार्थिकनयेन नवपदार्थाः सप्ततत्त्वानि वा सिद्धानि तथापि तैः किं प्रयोजनम् । यथैवाभेदनयेन पुण्यपापपदार्थद्वयस्यान्तर्भावो जातस्तथैव विशेषाभेदनयविवक्षायामास्रवादिपदार्थानामपि जीवाजीवद्वयमध्येऽन्तर्भावे कृते जीवाजीवौ द्वावेव पदार्थाविति । तत्र परिहारः—हेयोपादेयतत्त्वपरिज्ञानप्रयोजनार्थमास्रवादिपदार्थाः व्याख्येया भवन्ति । तदेव कथयति—उपादेयतत्त्वमक्षयानन्तसुखं, तस्य कारणं मोक्षो, मोक्षस्य कारणं संवरनिर्जराद्वयं, तस्य कारणं विशुद्धज्ञानदर्शनस्वभावनिजात्मतत्त्वसम्यक्श्रद्धानज्ञानानुचरणलक्षणं निश्चयरत्नत्रयस्वरूपं, तत्साधकं व्यवहाररत्नत्रयरूपं चेति । इदानीं हेयतत्त्वं कथ्यते—आकुलत्वोत्पादकं नारकादिदुःखं निश्चयेनेन्द्रियसुखं च हेयतत्त्वम् । तस्य कारणं संसारः, संसारकारणमास्रवबंधपदार्थद्वयं, तस्य कारणं पूर्वोक्तव्यवहारनिश्चयरत्नत्रयाद्विलक्षणं मिथ्यादर्शनज्ञानचारित्रत्रयमिति । एवं हेयोपादेयतत्त्वव्याख्याने कृते सति सप्ततत्त्वनवपदार्थाः स्वयमेव सिद्धाः ।

इदानीं कस्य पदार्थस्य कः कर्त्तेति कथ्यते—निजनिरञ्जनशुद्धात्मभावनोत्पन्नपरमानन्दैकलक्षणसुखामृतरसास्वादपराङ्मुखो बहिरात्मा भण्यते । स

चास्रवबन्धपापपदार्थत्रयस्य कर्त्ता भवति । क्वापि काले पुनर्मन्दमिथ्यात्वमन्दकषायोदये सति भोगाकाङ्क्षादिनिदानबन्धेन भाविकाले पापानुबन्धिपुण्यपदार्थस्यापि कर्त्ता भवति । यस्तु पूर्वोक्तबहिरात्मनो विलक्षणः सम्यग्दृष्टिः स संवरनिर्जरामोक्षपदार्थत्रयस्य कर्त्ता भवति । रागादिविभावरहितपरमसामायिके यदा स्थातुं समर्थो न भवति तदा विषयकषायोत्पन्नदुर्ध्यानवञ्चनार्थं संसारस्थितिच्छेदं कुर्वन् पुण्यानुबन्धितीर्थंकरनामप्रकृत्यादिविशिष्टपुण्यपदार्थस्य कर्त्ता भवति । कर्तृत्वविषयं नयविभागः कथ्यते । मिथ्यादृष्टेर्जीवस्य पुद्गलद्रव्यपर्यायरूपाणामास्रवबन्धपुण्यपापपदार्थानां कर्तृत्वमनुपचरितासद्भूतव्यवहारेण, जीवभावपर्यायरूपाणां पुनरशुद्धनिश्चयनयेनेति । सम्यग्दृष्टेस्तु संवरनिर्जरामोक्षपदार्थानां द्रव्यरूपाणां यत्कर्तृत्वं तदप्यनुचरितासद्भूतव्यवहारेण, जीवभावपर्यायरूपाणां तु विवक्षितैकदेशशुद्धनिश्चयनयेनेति । परमशुद्धनिश्चयेन तु ''ण वि उप्पज्जइ, ण विमरइ, बंधु न मोक्खु करेइ । जिउ परमत्थें जोइया, जिणवरु एम भणेइ इति ।'' वचनाद्बन्धमोक्षौ न स्तः । स च पूर्वोक्तविवक्षितैकदेशशुद्धनिश्चय आगमभाषया किं भण्यते—स्वशुद्धात्मसम्यक्श्रद्धानज्ञानानुचरणरूपेण भविष्यतीति भव्यः, एवंभूतस्य भव्यत्वसंज्ञस्य पारिणामिकभावस्य संबन्धिनी व्यक्तिर्भण्यते । अध्यात्मभाषया पुनर्द्रव्यशक्तिरूपशुद्धपारिणामिकभावविषये भावना भण्यते, पर्यायनामान्तरेण निर्विकल्पसमाधिर्वाशुद्धोपयोगादिकं वेति । यत एव भावना मुक्तिकारणं तत एव शुद्धपारिणामिकभावो ध्येयरूपो भवति ध्यानभावनारूपो न भवति । कस्मादिति चेत्—ध्यानभावनापर्यायो विनश्वरः स च द्रव्यरूपत्वादविनश्वर इति । इदमत्र तात्पर्यं—मिथ्यात्वरागादिविकल्पजालरहितनिजशुद्धात्मभावनोत्पन्नसहजानन्दैकलक्षणसुखसंवित्तिरूपा च भावना मुक्तिकारणं भवति । तां च कोऽपि जनः केनापि पर्यायनामान्तरेण भणतीति । एवं पूर्वोक्तप्रकारेणानेकान्तव्याख्यानेनास्रवबन्धपुण्यपापपदार्थाः जीवपुद्गलसंयोगपरिणामरूपविभावपर्यायेणोत्पद्यन्ते । संवरनिर्जरामोक्षपदार्थाः पुनर्जीवपुद्गलसंयोगपरिणामविनाशोत्पन्नेन विवक्षितस्वभावपर्यायेणेति स्थितम् ॥

तद्यथा—

व्याख्या । ''आसव'' निरास्रवस्वसंवित्तिविलक्षणशुभाशुभपरिणामेन शुभाशुभकर्मागमनमास्रवः । ''बंधण'' बन्धातीतशुद्धात्मोपलम्भभावनाच्युत-

जीवस्य कर्मप्रदेशैः सह संश्लेषो बन्धः। "संवर" कर्मास्रवनिरोधसमर्थस्वसंवित्तिपरिणतजीवस्य शुभाशुभकर्मागमनसंवरणं संवरः। "णिज्जर" शुद्धोपयोगभावनासामर्थ्येन नीरसीभूतकर्मपुद्गलानामेकदेशगलनं निर्जरा। "मोक्खो" जीवपुद्गलसंश्लेषरूपबन्धस्य विघटने समर्थः स्वशुद्धात्मोपलब्धिपरिणामो मोक्ष इति। "सपुण्णपावा जे" पुण्यपापसहिता ये "ते वि समासेण पभणामो" यथा जीवाजीवपदार्थौ व्याख्यातौ पूर्वं तथा तानप्यास्रवादिपदार्थान् समासेन संक्षेपेण प्रभणामो वयं, ते च कथंभूताः "जीवाजीवविसेसा" जीवाजीवविशेषाः। विशेषा इत्यस्य कोऽर्थः पर्यायाः। चैतन्या अशुद्धपरिणामा जीवस्य, अचेतनाः कर्मपुद्गलपर्याया अजीवस्येत्यर्थः। एवमधिकारसूत्रगाथा गता ॥२८॥

अथ गाथात्रयेणास्रवव्याख्यानं क्रियते, तत्रादौ भावास्रवद्रव्यास्रवस्वरूपं सूचयति।

व्याख्या। "आसवदि जेण कम्मं परिणामेणप्पणो स विण्णेओ भावासवो" आस्रवति कर्म येन परिणामेनात्मनः स विज्ञेयो भावास्रवः। कर्मास्रवनिर्मूलनसमर्थशुद्धात्मभावनाप्रतिपक्षभूतेन येन परिणामेनास्रवति कर्म कस्यात्मनः स्वस्य स परिणामो भावास्रवो विज्ञेयः। स च कथंभूतः "जिणुत्तो" जिनेन वीतरागसर्वज्ञेनोक्तः। "कम्मासवणं परो होदि" कर्मास्रवणं परो भवति ज्ञानावरणादिद्रव्यकर्मणामास्रवणमागमनं परः, पर इति कोऽर्थः—भावास्रवादन्यो भिन्नो भावास्रव निमित्तेन तैलम्रक्षितानां धूलिसमागम इव द्रव्यास्रवो भवतीति। ननु "आस्रवति येन कर्म" तेनैव पदेन द्रव्यास्रवो लब्धः, पुनरपि कर्मास्रवणं परो भवतीति द्रव्यास्रवव्याख्यानं किमर्थमिति यदुक्तं त्वया तन्न। येन परिणामेन किं भवति आस्रवति कर्म तत्परिणामस्य सामर्थ्यं दर्शितं न च द्रव्यास्रवव्याख्यानमिति भावार्थः ॥२९॥

अथ भावास्रवस्वरूपं विशेषेण कथयति।

व्याख्या। "मिच्छत्ताविरदिपमादजोगकोहादओ" मिथ्यात्वाविरतिप्रमादयोगक्रोधादयः। अभ्यन्तरे वीतरागनिजात्मतत्त्वानुभूतिरुचिविषये विपरीताभिनिवेशजनकं बहिर्विषये तु परकीयशुद्धात्मतत्त्वप्रभृतिसमस्तद्रव्येषु विपरीताभिनिवेशोत्पादकं च मिथ्यात्वं भण्यते। अभ्यन्तरे निजपरमात्मस्वरूपभाव-

नोत्पन्नपरमसुखामृतरतिविलक्षणा बहिर्विषये पुनरव्रतरूपाचेत्यविरतिः । अभ्यन्तरे निष्प्रमादशुद्धात्मानुभूतिचलनरूपः बहिर्विषये तु मूलोत्तरगुणमलजनकश्चेति प्रमादः । निश्चयेन निष्क्रियस्यापि परमात्मानो व्यवहारेण वीर्यान्तरायक्षयोपशमोत्पन्नो मनोवचनकायवर्गणावलम्बनः कर्मादानहेतुभूत आत्मप्रदेशपरिस्पन्दो योग इत्युच्यते । अभ्यन्तरे परमोपशममूर्त्तिकेवलज्ञानाद्यनन्तगुणस्वभावपरमात्मस्वरूपक्षोभकारकः बहिर्विषयें तु परेषां संबन्धित्वेन क्रूरत्वाद्यावेशरूपाः क्रोधादयश्चेत्युक्तलक्षणाः पञ्चास्रवाः "अथ" अथो "विण्णेया" विज्ञेया ज्ञातव्याः । कतिभेदास्ते "पण पण पणदश तिय चदु कमसो भेदा दु" पञ्चपञ्चपञ्चदशत्रिचतुर्भेदाः क्रमशो भवन्ति पुनः । तथाहि "एयंत बुद्धदरसी विवरीओ बंभतावसो विणओ । इंदो विय संसइदो मक्कडिओ चैव अण्णाणी इति गाथाकथितलक्षणं पञ्चविधं मिथ्यात्वम् । हिंसानृतस्तेयाब्रह्मपरिग्रहाकाङ्क्षारूपेणाविरतिरपि पञ्चविधा । अथवा मनःसहितपञ्चेन्द्रियप्रवृत्तिपृथिव्यादिषट्कायविराधनाभेदेन द्वादशविधा । "विकहा तहय कसाया इंदिय णिद्दाय तहय पणयो य । चदु चदु पणमेगेगं हुंति पमादाहु पण्णरसा ।" इति गाथाकथितक्रमेण पञ्चदश प्रमादाः । मनोवचनकायव्यापारभेदेन त्रिविधो योगः, विस्तारेण पञ्चदशभेदो वा । क्रोधमानमायालोभभेदेन कषायाश्चत्वारः, कषायनोकषायभेदेन पञ्चविंशतिविधा वा । एते सर्वे भेदाः-कस्य संबन्धिनः "पुव्वस्स" पूर्वसूत्रोदितभावास्रवस्येत्यर्थः ॥३०॥

अथ द्रव्यास्रवस्वरूपमुद्योतयति ।

व्याख्या । "णाणावरणादीणं" सहजशुद्धकेवलज्ञानमभेदेन केवलज्ञानाद्यनन्तगुणाधारभूतं ज्ञानशब्दवाच्यं परमात्मानं वा आवृणोतीति ज्ञानावरणं, तदादिर्येषां तानि ज्ञानावरणादीनि तेषां ज्ञानावरणादीनां "जोग्गं" योग्यं "जं पुग्गलं समासवदि" स्नेहाभ्यक्तशरीराणां धूलिरेणुसमागम इव निष्कषायशुद्धात्मसंवित्तिच्युतजीवानां कर्मवर्गणारूपं यत्पुद्गलद्रव्यं समास्रवति "दव्वासवो स णेओ" द्रव्यास्रवः स विज्ञेयः । "अणेयभेओ" स च ज्ञानदर्शनावरणीयवेदनीयमोहनीयायुर्नामगोत्रान्तरायसंज्ञानामष्टमूलप्रकृतीनां भेदेन, तथैव "पण णव दु अट्ठवीसा चउ तियणवदीय दोण्णि पंचेव । बावण्णहीण बियसयपयडिविणासेण होंति ते सिद्धा ।" इति गाथाकथितक्रमेणाष्टचत्वारिंशद-

धिकशतसंख्याप्रमितोत्तरप्रकृतिभेदेन तथा चासंख्येयलोकप्रमितपृथिवीकाय-नामकर्माद्युत्तरोत्तरप्रकृतिरूपेणानेकभेद इति "जिणक्खादो" जिनख्यातो जिनप्रणीत इत्यर्थः ।।३१।। एवमास्रवव्याख्यानगाथात्रयेण प्रथमस्थलं गतम् ।

अतःपरं सूत्रद्वयेन बन्धव्याख्यानं क्रियते । तत्रादौ गाथापूर्वार्धेन भाव-बन्धमुत्तरार्धेन तु द्रव्यबन्धस्वरूपमावेदयति ।

व्याख्या । "बज्झदि कम्मं जेण दु चेदणभावेण भावबंधो सो" बध्यते कर्म येन चेतनभावेन स भावबन्धो भवति । समस्तकर्मबन्धविध्वंसनसमर्था-खण्डैकप्रत्यक्षप्रतिभासमयपरमचैतन्यविलासलक्षणज्ञानगुणस्य, अभेदनयेना-नन्तज्ञानादिगुणाधारभूतपरमात्मनो वा संबन्धिनी या तु निर्मलानुभूतिस्तद्वि-पक्षभूतेन मिथ्यात्वरागादिपरिणतिरूपेण वाऽशुद्धचेतनभावेन परिणामेन बध्यते ज्ञानावरणादि कर्म येन भावेन स भावबन्धो भण्यते । "कम्मादपदेसाणं अण्णोण्णपवेसणं इदरो" कर्मात्मप्रदेशानामन्योन्यप्रवेशनमितरः । तेनैव भाव-बन्धनिमित्तेन कर्मप्रदेशानामात्मप्रदेशानां च क्षीरनीरवदन्योन्यं प्रवेशनं संश्लेषो द्रव्यबन्ध इति ।।३२।।

अथ तस्यैव बन्धस्य गाथापूर्वार्धेन प्रकृतिबन्धादिभेदचतुष्टयं कथयति, उत्तरार्धेन तु प्रकृतिबन्धादीनां कारणं चेति ।

व्याख्या । "पयडिट्ठिदिअणुभागप्पदेसभेदा दु चदुविधो बंधो" प्रकृति-स्थित्यनुभागप्रदेशभेदाच्चतुर्विधो बन्धो भवति । तथाहि ज्ञानावरणीयस्य कर्मणः का प्रकृतिः ? देवतामुखवस्त्रमिव ज्ञानप्रच्छादनता । दर्शनावरणीयस्य का प्रकृतिः । राजदर्शनप्रतिषेधकप्रतीहारवद्दर्शनप्रच्छादनता । सातासातवेदनीयस्य का प्रकृतिः ? मधुलिप्तखड्गधारास्वादनवदल्पसुखबहुदुःखोत्पादकता । मोहनीयस्य का प्रकृतिः ? मद्यपानवद्धेयोपादेयविचारविकलता । आयुःकर्मणः का प्रकृतिः ? निगडवद्गत्यन्तरगमननिवारणता । नामकर्मणः का प्रकृतिः ? चित्रकारपुरुषव-न्नानारूपकरणता । गोत्रकर्मणः का प्रकृतिः ? गुरुलघुभाजनकारककुम्भकार-वदुच्चनीचगोत्रकरणता । अन्तरायकर्मणः का प्रकृतिः ? भाण्डागारिकवद्दानादि-विघ्नकरणतेति । तथाचोक्तं—"पडपडिहारसिमज्जाहडिचित्तकुलालभंडयारीणं । जह एदेसिं भावा तहविह कम्मा मुणेयव्वा ।" इति दृष्टान्ताष्टकेन प्रकृति-बन्धो ज्ञातव्यः ।। अजागोमहिष्यादिदुग्धानां प्रहरद्वयादिस्वकीयमधुररसावस्थान-

पर्यन्तं यथा स्थितिर्भण्यते तथा जीवप्रदेशेष्वपि यावत्कालं कर्मसम्बन्धेन स्थितिस्तावत्कालं स्थितिबन्धो ज्ञातव्यः । यथा च तेषामेव दुग्धानां तारतम्येन रसगतशक्तिविशेषोऽनुभागो भण्यते तथा जीवप्रदेशस्थितकर्मस्कन्धानामपि सुखदुःखदानसमर्थशक्तिविशेषोऽनुभागबन्धो विज्ञेयः । सा च घातिकर्मसम्बन्धिनी शक्तिर्लतादार्वस्थिपाषाणभेदेन चतुर्धा । तथैवाशुभाऽघातिकर्मसम्बन्धिनी निम्बकाञ्जीरविषहालाहलरूपेण । शुभाघातिकर्मसम्बन्धिनी पुनर्गुडखण्डशर्करामृतरूपेण चतुर्धा भवति । एकैकात्मप्रदेशे सिद्धानन्तैकभागसंख्या अभव्यानन्तगुणप्रमिता अनन्तानन्तपरमाणवः प्रतिक्षणबन्धमायान्तीति प्रदेशबन्धः । इदानीं बन्धकारणं कथ्यते । "जोगा पयडिपदेसा ठिदिअणुभागा कसायदो होंति ।" योगात्प्रकृतिप्रदेशौ स्थित्यनुभागौ कषायतो भवत इति । तथाहि निश्चयेन निष्क्रियाणामपि शुद्धात्मप्रदेशानां व्यवहारेण परिस्पन्दनहेतुर्योगः, तस्मात्प्रकृतिप्रदेशबन्धद्वयं भवति । निर्दोषपरमात्मभावनाप्रतिबन्धकक्रोधादिकषायोदयात् स्थित्यनुभागबंधद्वयं भवतीति । आस्रवे बन्धे च मिथ्यात्वाविरत्यादिकारणानि समानानि को विशेष इति चेत् नैवं—प्रथमक्षणे कर्मस्कन्धानामागमनमास्रवः, आगमनानन्तरं द्वितीयक्षणादौ जीवप्रदेशेष्ववस्थानं बन्ध इति भेदः । यत एव योगकषायाद्बन्धचतुष्टयं भवति तत एव बन्धविनाशार्थं योगकषायत्यागेन निजशुद्धात्मनि भावना कर्त्तव्येति तात्पर्यम् ॥३३॥ एवं बन्धव्याख्यानेन सूत्रद्वयेन द्वितीयं स्थलं गतम् ।

अत ऊर्ध्वं गाथाद्वयेन संवरपदार्थः कथ्यते । तत्र प्रथमगाथायां भावसंवरद्रव्यसंवरस्वरूपं निरूपयति ।

व्याख्या । "चेदणपरिणामो जो कम्मस्सासवणिरोहणे हेऊ सो भावसंवरो खलु" चेतनपरिणामो यः कर्थंभूतः कर्मास्रवनिरोधने हेतुः स भावसंवरो भवति खलु निश्चयेन । "दव्वासवरोहणे अण्णो" द्रव्यकर्मास्रवनिरोधने सत्यन्यो द्रव्यसंवर इति । तद्यथा—निश्चयेन स्वतः सिद्धत्वात्परकारणनिरपेक्षः, स चैवाविनश्वरत्वान्नित्यः परमोद्योतस्वभावत्वात्स्वपरप्रकाशनसमर्थः, अनाद्यनन्तत्वादादिमध्यान्तमुक्तः, दृष्टश्रुतानुभूतभोगाकाङ्क्षारूपनिदानबन्धादिसमस्तरागादिविभावमलरहितत्वादत्यन्तनिर्मलः, परमचैतन्यविलासलक्षणत्वाच्चिदुच्छलननिर्भरः, स्वाभाविकपरमानन्दैकलक्षणत्वात्परमसुखमूर्त्तिः, निरास्रवसहज-

स्वभावत्वात्सर्वकर्मसंवरहेतुरित्युक्तलक्षणः परमात्मा तत्स्वभावेनोत्पन्नो योऽसौ शुद्धचेतनपरिणामः स भावसंवरो भवति । यस्तु भावसंवरात्कारणभूतादुत्पन्नः कार्यभूतो नवतरद्रव्यकर्मागमनाभावः स द्रव्यसंवर इत्यर्थः ॥

अथ संवरविषयनयविभागः कथ्यते । तथा हि मिथ्यादृष्ट्यादिक्षीणकषायपर्यन्तमुपर्युपरि मन्दत्वात्तारतम्येन तावदशुद्धनिश्चयो वर्त्तते । तस्य मध्ये पुनर्गुणस्थानभेदेन शुभाशुभशुद्धानुष्ठानरूपयोगत्रयव्यापारस्तिष्ठति । तदुच्यते—मिथ्यादृष्टिसासादनमिश्रगुणस्थानेषूपर्युपरि मन्दत्वेनाशुभोपयोगो वर्त्तते, ततोऽप्यसंयतसम्यग्दृष्टिश्रावकप्रमत्तसंयतेषु पारम्पर्येण शुद्धोपयोगसाधक उपर्युपरि तारतम्येन शुभोपयोगो वर्त्तते, तदनन्तरमप्रमत्तादिक्षीणकषायपर्यन्तं जघन्यमध्यमोत्कृष्टभेदेन विवक्षितैकदेशशुद्धनयरूपशुद्धोपयोगो वर्त्तते, तत्रैवं मिथ्यादृष्टिगुणस्थाने संवरो नास्ति, सासादनादिगुणस्थानेषु "सोलसपणवीसणभं दसचउछक्केक्कबंधवो छिन्ना । दुगतीसचदुरपुव्वे पणसोलहजोगिणो एक्को ॥" इति बन्धविच्छेदत्रिभङ्गीकथितक्रमेणोपर्युपरि प्रकर्षेण संवरो ज्ञातव्य इति । अशुद्धनिश्चयमध्ये मिथ्यादृष्ट्यादिगुणस्थानेषूपयोगत्रयं व्याख्यातं, तत्राशुद्धनिश्चये शुद्धोपयोगः कथं घटत इति चेत्तत्रोत्तरं—शुद्धोपयोगे शुद्धबुद्धैकस्वभावो निजात्मा ध्येयस्तिष्ठति तेन कारणेन शुद्धध्येयत्वाच्छुद्धावलम्बनत्वाच्छुद्धात्मस्वरूपसाधकत्वाच्च शुद्धोपयोगो घटते । स च संवरशब्दवाच्यः शुद्धोपयोगः संसारकारणभूतमिथ्यात्वरागाद्यशुद्धपर्यायवदशुद्धो न भवति तथैव फलभूतकेवलज्ञानलक्षणशुद्धपर्यायवत् शुद्धोऽपि न भवति किन्तु ताभ्यामशुद्धशुद्धपर्यायाभ्यां विलक्षणं शुद्धात्मानुभूतिरूपनिश्चयरत्नत्रयात्मकं मोक्षकारणमेकदेशव्यक्तिरूपमेकदेशनिरावरणं च तृतीयमवस्थान्तरं भण्यते ।

कश्चिदाह—केवलज्ञानं सकलनिरावरणं शुद्धं तस्य कारणेनापि सकलनिरावरणेन शुद्धेन भाव्यम्, उपादानकारणसदृशं कार्यं भवतीति वचनात् । तत्रोत्तरं दीयते—युक्तमुक्तं भवता परं किन्तूपादानकारणमपि षोडशवर्णिकासुवर्णकार्यस्याधस्तनवर्णिकोपादानकारणवत्, मृन्मयकलशकार्यस्य मृत्पिण्डस्थासकोशकुशूलोपादानकारणवदिति च कार्यादेकदेशेन भिन्नं भवति । यदि पुनरेकान्तेनोपादानकारणस्य कार्येण सहाभेदो भेदो वा भवति तर्हि पूर्वोक्तसुवर्णमृत्तिकादृष्टान्तद्वयवत्कार्यकारणभावो न घटते ततः किं सिद्धं—एकदेशेन निराव-

णत्वेन क्षायोपशमिकज्ञानलक्षणमेकदेशव्यक्तिरूपं विवक्षितैकदेशे शुद्धनयेन संवरशब्दवाच्यं शुद्धोपयोगस्वरूपं मुक्तिकारणं भवति । यच्च लब्ध्यपर्याप्तसूक्ष्मनिगोदजीवे नित्योद्घाटं निरावरणं ज्ञानं श्रूयते तदपि सूक्ष्मनिगोदसर्वजघन्यक्षयोपशमापेक्षया निरावरणं न च सर्वथा । कस्मादिति चेत्—तदावरणे जीवाभावः प्राप्नोति । वस्तुत उपरितनक्षायोपशमिकज्ञानापेक्षया केवलज्ञानापेक्षया च तदपि सावरणं संसारिणां क्षायिकज्ञानाभावाच्च क्षायोपशमिकमेव । यदि पुनर्लोचनपटलस्यैकदेशनिरावरणवत्केवलज्ञानांशरूपं भवति तर्हि तेनैकदेशेनापि लोकालोकप्रत्यक्षतां प्राप्नोति न च तथा दृश्यते । किन्तु प्रचुरमेघप्रच्छादितादित्यबिम्बवन्निबिडलोचनपटलवद्वा स्तोकं प्रकाशयतीत्यर्थः ॥

अथ क्षयोपशमलक्षणं कथ्यते । सर्वप्रकारेणात्मगुणप्रच्छादिकाः कर्मशक्तयः सर्वघातिस्पर्द्धकानि भण्यन्ते, विवक्षितैकदेशेनात्मगुणप्रच्छादिकाः शक्तयो देशघातिस्पर्द्धकानि भण्यन्ते, सर्वघातिस्पर्द्धकानामुदयाभाव एव क्षयस्तेषामेवास्तित्वमुपशम उच्यते सर्वघात्युदयाभावलक्षणक्षयेण सहित उपशमः तेषामेकदेशघातिस्पर्द्धकानामुदयश्चेति समुदायेन क्षयोपशमो भण्यते । क्षयोपशमे भवः क्षायोपशमिको भावः । अथवा देशघातिस्पर्द्धकोदये सति जीव एकदेशेन ज्ञानादिगुणं लभते यत्र स क्षायोपशमिको भावः । तेन किं सिद्धं—पूर्वोक्तसूक्ष्मनिगोदजीवे ज्ञानावरणीयदेशघातिस्पर्द्धकोदये सत्येकदेशेन ज्ञानगुणं लभ्यते तेन कारणेन तत् क्षायोपशमिकं ज्ञानं न च क्षायिकं कस्मादेकदेशोदयसद्भावादिति । अयमत्रार्थः—यद्यपि पूर्वोक्तं शुद्धोपयोगलक्षणं क्षायोपशमिकं ज्ञानं मुक्तिकारणं भवति तथापि ध्यातृपुरुषेण यदेव सकलनिरावरणमखण्डैकसकलविमलकेवलज्ञानलक्षणं परमात्मस्वरूपं तदेवाहं न च खण्डज्ञानरूप इति भावनीयम् । इति संवरतत्त्वव्याख्यानविषये नयविभागो ज्ञातव्य इति ॥ ३४ ॥

अथ संवरकारणभेदान् कथयतीत्येका पातनिका, द्वितीया तु कैः कृत्वा संवरो भवतीति पृष्टे प्रत्युत्तरं ददातीति, पातनिकाद्वयं मनसि धृत्वा सूत्रमिदं प्रतिपादयति भगवान् ।

व्याख्या । 'वदसमिदीगुत्तीओ' व्रतसमितिगुप्तयः "धम्माणुपिहा" धर्मस्तथैवानुप्रेक्षाः "परीसहजओ य" परीसहजयश्च "चारित्तं बहुभेयं" चारित्रं बहुभेदयुक्तं "णायव्वा भावसंवरविसेसा" एते सर्वे मिलिता भावसंवरविशेषा

भेदा ज्ञातव्याः । अथ विस्तरः—निश्चयेन विशुद्धज्ञानदर्शनस्वभावनिजात्मतत्त्वभावनोत्पन्नसुखसुधास्वादबलेन समस्तशुभाशुभरागादिविकल्पनिवृत्तिर्व्रतम्, व्यवहारेण तत्साधकं हिंसानृतस्तेयाब्रह्मपरिग्रहाच्च यावज्जीवनिवृत्तिलक्षणं पञ्चविधं व्रतम् । निश्चयेनानन्तज्ञानादिस्वभावे निजात्मनि सम् सम्यक् समस्तरागादिविभावपरित्यागेन तल्लीनतच्चिन्तनतन्मयत्वेन अयनं गमनं परिणमनं समितिः, व्यवहारेण तद्बहिरङ्गसहकारिकारणभूताचारादिचरणग्रन्थोक्ता ईर्याभाषैषणादाननिक्षेपोत्सर्गसंज्ञाः पञ्च समितयः । निश्चयेन सहजशुद्धात्मभावनालक्षणे गूढस्थाने संसारकारणरागादिभयात्स्वस्यात्मनो गोपनं प्रच्छादनं झम्पनं प्रवेशनं रक्षणं गुप्तिः, व्यवहारेण बहिरङ्गसाधनार्थं मनोवचनकायव्यापारनिरोधो गुप्तिः । निश्चयेन संसारे पतन्तमात्मानं धरतीति विशुद्धज्ञानदर्शनलक्षणनिजशुद्धात्मभावनात्मको धर्मः, व्यवहारेण तत्साधनार्थं देवेन्द्रनरेन्द्रादिवन्द्यपदे धरतीत्युत्तमक्षमामार्दवार्जवसत्यशौचसंयमतपस्त्यागाकिञ्चन्यब्रह्मचर्यलक्षणो दशप्रकारो धर्मः ।

द्वादशानुप्रेक्षाः कथ्यन्ते—अध्रुवाशरणसंसारैकत्वान्यत्वशुचित्वास्रवसंवरनिर्जरालोकबोधिदुर्लभधर्मानुचिन्तनमनुप्रेक्षाः । ताश्च कथ्यन्ते । तद्यथा—द्रव्यार्थिकनयेन टङ्कोत्कीर्णज्ञायकैकस्वभावत्वेनाविनश्वरस्वभावनिजपरमात्मद्रव्याद्न्यद् भिन्नं यज्जीवसंबन्धे अशुद्धनिश्चयनयेन रागादिविभावरूपं भावकर्म, अनुपमचरितासद्भूतव्यवहारेण द्रव्यकर्मनोकर्मरूपं च तथैव तत्स्वस्वामिभावसम्बन्धेन गृहीतं यच्चेतनं वनितादिकम्, अचेतनं सुवर्णादिकं तदुभयमिश्रं चेत्युक्तलक्षणं तत्सर्वमध्रुवमिति भावयितव्यम् । तद्भावनासहितपुरुषस्य तेषां वियोगेऽपि सत्युच्छिष्टेष्विव ममत्वं न भवति तत्र ममत्वाभावादविनश्वरनिजपरमात्मानमेव भेदाभेदरत्नत्रयभावनया भावयति, यादृशमविनश्वरमात्मानं भावयति तादृशमेवाक्षयानन्तसुखस्वभावं मुक्तात्मानं प्राप्नोति । इत्यध्रुवानुप्रेक्षा गता ।

अथ निश्चयरत्नत्रयपरिणतं स्वशुद्धात्मद्रव्यं तद्बहिरङ्गसहकारिकारणभूतं पञ्चपरमेष्ठ्याराधनञ्च शरणम्, तस्माद्बहिर्भूता ये देवेन्द्रचक्रवर्तिसुभटकोटिभटपुत्रादिचेतना गिरिदुर्गभूविवरमणिमन्त्राज्ञाप्रासादौषधादयः पुनरचेतनास्तदुभयात्मका मिश्राश्च मरणकालादौ महाटव्यां व्याघ्रगृहीतमृगबालस्यैव महासमुद्रे पोतच्युतपक्षिण इव शरणं न भवन्तीति विज्ञेयम् । तद्विज्ञाय भोगा-

कांक्षारूपनिदानबन्धादिनिरालम्बने स्वसंवित्तिसमुत्पन्नसुखामृतसालम्बने स्वशुद्धात्मन्येवावलम्बनं कृत्वा भावनां करोति । यादृशं शरणभूतमात्मानं भावयति तादृशमेव सर्वकालशरणभूतं शरणागतवज्रपञ्जरसदृशं निजशुद्धात्मानं प्राप्नोति। इत्यशरणानुप्रेक्षा व्याख्याता ॥

अथ शुद्धात्मद्रव्यादितराणि सपूर्वापूर्वमिश्रपुद्गलद्रव्याणि ज्ञानावरणादिद्रव्यकर्मरूपेण शरीरपोषणार्थाशनपानादिपञ्चेन्द्रियविषयरूपेण चानन्तवारान् गृहीत्वा विमुक्तानीति द्रव्यसंसारः । स्वशुद्धात्मद्रव्यसंबन्धिसहजशुद्धलोकाकाशप्रमितासंख्येयप्रदेशेभ्यो भिन्ना ये लोकक्षेत्रप्रदेशास्तत्रैकैकं प्रदेशं व्याप्यानन्तवारान् यत्र न जातो न मृतोऽयं जीवः स कोऽपि प्रदेशो नास्तीति क्षेत्रसंसारः । शुद्धात्मानुभूतिरूपनिर्विकल्पसमाधिकालं विहाय प्रत्येकं दशकोटाकोटिसागरेण प्रमितोत्सर्पिण्यवर्पिण्येकैकसमये नानापरावर्त्तनकालेनानन्तवारानयं जीवो यत्र न जातो न मृतः स समयो नास्तीति कालसंसारः । अभेदरत्नत्रयात्मकसमाधिबलेन सिद्धगतौ स्वात्मोपलब्धिलक्षणसिद्धपर्यायरूपेण योऽसावुत्पादो भवस्तं विहाय नारकतिर्यङ्मनुष्यभवेषु तथैव देवभवेषु च निश्चयरत्नत्रयभावनारहितभोगाकांक्षानिदानपूर्वकद्रव्यतपश्चरणरूपजिनदीक्षाबलेन नवग्रैवेयकपर्यन्तं "सक्को सक्कमहिस्सी दक्खिणइंदा य लोयवाला य । लोयंतिया य देवा तच्छ चुदा णिव्वुदिं जंति ॥" इति गाथाकथितपदानि तथागमनिषिद्धान्यन्यपदानि च त्यक्त्वा भवविध्वंसकनिजशुद्धात्मभावनारहितो भवोत्पादकमिथ्यात्वरागादिभावनासहितश्च सन्नयं जीवोऽनन्तवारान् जीवितो मृतश्चेति भवसंसारो ज्ञातव्यः ।

अथ भावसंसारः कथ्यते । तद्यथा—सर्वजघन्यप्रकृतिबन्धप्रदेशबन्धनिमित्तानि सर्वजघन्यमनोवचनकायपरिस्पन्दरूपाणि श्रेण्यसंख्येयभागप्रमितानि चतुःस्थानपतितानि सर्वजघन्ययोगस्थानानि भवन्ति । तथैव सर्वोत्कृष्टप्रकृतिबन्धप्रदेशबन्धनिमित्तानि सर्वोत्कृष्टमनोवचनकायव्यापाररूपाणि तद्योग्यश्रेण्यसंख्येयभागप्रमितानि चतुःस्थानपतितानि सर्वोत्कृष्टयोगस्थानानि च भवन्ति । तथैव सर्वजघन्यस्थितिबन्धनिमित्तानि सर्वजघन्यकषायाध्यवसायस्थानानि तद्योग्यासंख्येयलोकप्रमितानि षट्स्थानपतितानि च भवन्ति । तथैव च सर्वोत्कृष्टकषायाध्यवसायस्थानानि तान्यप्यसंख्येयलोकप्रमितानि

षट्स्थानपतितानि च भवन्ति । तथैव सर्वजघन्यानुभागबन्धनिमित्तानि सर्वजघन्यानुभागाध्यवसायस्थानानि तान्यप्यसंख्येयलोकप्रमितानि षट्स्थानपतितानि भवन्ति । तथैव च सर्वोत्कृष्टानुभागबन्धनिमित्तानि सर्वोत्कृष्टानुभागाध्यवसायस्थानानि तान्यप्यसंख्येयलोकप्रमितानि षट्स्थानपतितानि च विज्ञेयानि । तेनैव प्रकारेण स्वकीयस्वकीयजघन्योत्कृष्टयोर्मध्ये तारतम्येन मध्यमानि च भवन्ति । तथैव जघन्यादुत्कृष्टपर्यन्तानि ज्ञानावरणादिमूलोत्तरप्रकृतीनां स्थितिबन्धस्थानानि च । तानि सर्वाणि परमागमकथितानुसारेणानन्तवारान् भ्रमितान्यनेन जीवेन परं किन्तु पूर्वोक्तसमस्तप्रकृतिबन्धादीनां सद्भावविनाशकारणानि विशुद्धज्ञानदर्शनस्वभावनिजपरमात्मतत्त्वसम्यक्श्रद्धानज्ञानानुचरणरूपाणि यानि सम्यग्दर्शनज्ञानचारित्राणि तान्येव न लब्धानि । इति भावसंसारः ।

एवं पूर्वोक्तप्रकारेण द्रव्यक्षेत्रकालभवभावरूपं पञ्चप्रकारं संसारं भावयतोऽस्य जीवस्य संसारातीतस्वशुद्धात्मसंवित्तिनाशकेषु संसारवृद्धिकारणेषु मिथ्यात्वाविरतिप्रमादकषाययोगेषु परिणामो न जायते, किन्तु संसारातीतसुखास्वादे रतो भूत्वा स्वशुद्धात्मसंवित्तिबलेन संसारविनाशकनिजनिरञ्जनपरमात्मन्येव भावनां करोति । ततश्च यादृशमेव परमात्मानं भावयति तादृशमेव लब्ध्वा संसारविलक्षणे मोक्षेऽनन्तकालं तिष्ठतीति । अयं तु विशेषः—नित्यनिगोदजीवान् विहाय पञ्चप्रकारसंसारव्याख्यानं ज्ञातव्यम् । कस्मादिति चेत्—नित्यनिगोदजीवानां कालत्रयेऽपि त्रसत्वं नास्तीति । तथा चोक्तं—"संति अणंता जीवा जेहिं ण पत्तो तसाण परिणामो । भावकलङ्कसुपउरा णिगोदवासं ण मुंचंति ॥" अनुपममद्वितीयमनादिमिथ्यादृशोऽपि भरतपुत्रास्त्रयोविंशत्यधिकनवशतपरिमाणास्ते च नित्यनिगोदवासिनः क्षपितकर्माण इन्द्रगोपाः संजातास्तेषां च पुञ्जीभूतानामुपरि भरतहस्तिन्या पादो दत्तस्ततस्ते मृत्वापि वर्द्धनकुमारादयो भरतपुत्रा जातास्ते च केनचिदपि सह न वदन्ति । ततो भरतेन समवसरणे भगवान् पृष्टो भगवता च प्राकृतनं वृत्तान्तं कथितम् । तच्छ्रुत्वा ते तपो गृहीत्वा क्षणस्तोककालेन मोक्षं गताः । आचाराराधनाटिप्पणे कथितमास्ते । इति संसारानुप्रेक्षा गता ॥

अथैकत्वानुप्रेक्षा कथ्यते । तद्यथा—निश्चयरत्नत्रयैकलक्षणैकत्वभावनापरि-

णतस्यास्य जीवस्य निश्चयनयेन सहजानन्दसुखाद्यनन्तगुणाधारभूतं केवलज्ञानमेवैकं सहजं शरीरम् । शरीरं कोऽर्थः स्वरूपं न च सप्तधातुमयौदारिकशरीरम् । तथैवार्त्तरौद्रदुर्ध्यानविलक्षणपरमसामायिकलक्षणैकत्वभावनापरिणतं निजात्मतत्त्वमेवैकं सदा शाश्वतं परमहितकारि न च पुत्रकलत्रगोत्रादिः । तेनैव प्रकारेण परमोपेक्षासंयमलक्षणैकत्वभावनासहितः स्वशुद्धात्मपदार्थ एक एवाविनश्वरहितकारी परमोऽर्थः न च सुवर्णाद्यर्थः । तथैव निर्विकल्पसमाधिसमुत्पन्ननिर्विकारपरमानन्दैकलक्षणानाकुलत्वस्वभावात्मसुखमेवैकं सुखं न चाकुलत्वोत्पादकेन्द्रियसुखमिति । कस्मादिदं देहबन्धुजनसुवर्णाद्यर्थेन्द्रियसुखादिकं जीवस्य निश्चयेन निराकृतमिति चेत् यतो मरणकाले जीव एक एव गत्यन्तरं गच्छति न च देहादीनि । तथैव रोगव्याप्तिकाले विषयकषायादिदुर्ध्यानरहितः स्वशुद्धात्मैकसहायो भवति । तदपि कथमिति चेत् ? यदि चरमदेहो भवति तर्हि केवलज्ञानादिव्यक्तिरूपं मोक्षं नयति, अचरमदेहस्य तु संसारस्थितिं स्तोकां कृत्वा देवेन्द्राद्यभ्युदयसुखं दत्वा च पश्चात् पारम्पर्येण मोक्षं प्रापयतीत्यर्थः । तथा चोक्तं—"सग्गं तवेण सव्वो, वि पावए किंतु झाणजोयेण । जो पावइ सो पावइ, परं भवे सासयं सोक्खं ॥" एवमेकत्वभावनाफलं ज्ञात्वा निरन्तरं निजशुद्धात्मैकत्वभावना कर्त्तव्या । इत्येकत्वानुप्रेक्षा गता ॥

अथान्यत्वानुप्रेक्षां कथयति । तथा हि—पूर्वोक्तानि यानि देहबन्धुजनसुवर्णाद्यर्थेन्द्रियसुखादीनि कर्माधीनत्वे विनश्वराणि तथैव हेयभूतानि च, तानि सर्वाणि टङ्कोत्कीर्णज्ञायकैकस्वभावत्वेन नित्यात्सर्वप्रकारोपादेयभूतान्निर्विकारपरमचैतन्यचिच्चमत्कारस्वभावान्निजपरमात्मपदार्थान्निश्चयनयेनान्यानि भिन्नानि। तेभ्यः पुनरात्माप्यन्यो भिन्न इति । अयमत्र भावः—एकत्वानुप्रेक्षायामेकोऽहमित्यादिविधिरूपेण व्याख्यानं, अन्यत्वानुप्रेक्षायां तु देहादयो मत्सकाशादन्ये मदीया न भवन्तीति निषेधरूपेण । इत्येकत्वान्यत्वानुप्रेक्षायां विधिनिषेधरूप एव विशेषस्तात्पर्यं तदेव । इत्यन्यत्वानुप्रेक्षा समाप्ता ॥

अतः परमशुचित्वानुप्रेक्षा कथ्यते । तद्यथा—सर्वाशुचिशुक्रशोणितकारणोत्पन्नत्वात्तथैव "वसासृग्मांसमेदोऽस्थिमज्जाशुक्राणि धातवः" इत्युक्ताशुचिसप्तधातुमयत्वेन तथा नासिकादिनवरन्ध्रद्वारैरपि स्वरूपेणाशुचित्वात्तथैव मूत्रपुरीषाद्यशुचिमलानामुत्पत्तिस्थानत्वाच्चाशुचिरयं देहः । न केवलमशुचिकारणत्वे-

नाशुचिः स्वरूपेणाशुच्युत्पादकत्वेन चाशुचिः । शुचि सुगन्धमाल्यवस्त्रादीना-मशुचित्वोत्पादकत्वाच्चाशुचिः । इदानीं शुचित्वं कथ्यते—सहजशुद्धकेवल-ज्ञानादिगुणानामाधारभूतत्वात्स्वयं निश्चयेन शुचिरूपत्वाच्च परमात्मैव शुचिः । "जीवो बह्माजीवह्मि चेव चरिया हविज्ज जो जदिणो । तं जाण बह्मचेरं विमु-क्कपरदेहभत्तीए ।" इति गाथाकथितनिर्मलब्रह्मचर्यं तत्रैव निजपरमात्मनि स्थितानामेव लभ्यते । तथैव "ब्रह्मचारी सदा शुचि" रितिवचनात्तथाविधब्रह्मचा-रिणामेव शुचित्वं न च कामक्रोधादिरतानां जलस्नानादिशौचेऽपि । तथैव च— "जन्मना जायते शूद्रः क्रियया द्विज उच्यते । श्रुतेन श्रोत्रियो ज्ञेयो ब्रह्मचर्येण ब्राह्मणः ॥" इति वचनात्त एव निश्चयशुद्धाः ब्राह्मणः । तथा चोक्तं नारायणेन युधिष्ठिरं प्रति विशुद्धात्मनदीस्नानमेव परमशुचित्वकारणं न च लौकिकगङ्गा-दितीर्थे स्नानादिकम् । "आत्मा नदी संयमतोयपूर्णा सत्यावहा शीलतटा दयो-र्मिः । तत्राभिषेकं कुरु पाण्डुपुत्र न वारिणा शुद्ध्यति चान्तरात्मा ॥" इत्यशुचित्वानुप्रेक्षा गता ॥

अत ऊर्ध्वमास्रवानुप्रेक्षा कथ्यते । समुद्रे सच्छिद्रपोतवदयं जीव इन्द्रि-याद्यास्रवैः संसारसागरे पततीति वार्त्तिकम् । अतीन्द्रियस्वशुद्धात्मसंवित्तिविल-क्षणानि स्पर्शनरसनघ्राणचक्षुःश्रोत्राणीन्द्रियाणि भण्यन्ते । परमोपशममूर्त्ति-परमात्मस्वभावस्य क्षोभोत्पादकाः क्रोधमानमायालोभकषाया अभिधीयन्ते । रागादिविकल्पनिवृत्तिरूपायाः शुद्धात्मानुभूतेः प्रतिकूलानि हिंसानृतस्तेयाब्र-ह्मपरिग्रहप्रवृत्तिरूपाणि पञ्चाव्रतानि । निष्क्रियनिर्विकारात्मतत्त्वाद्विपरीता मनोवचनकायव्यापाररूपाः परमागमोक्ताः सम्यक्त्वक्रिया मिथ्यात्वक्रियेत्या-दिपञ्चविंशतिक्रियाः उच्यन्ते । इन्द्रियकषायाव्रतक्रियारूपास्रवाणां स्वरूपमेत-द्विज्ञेयम् । यथा समुद्रेऽनेकरत्नभाण्डपूर्णस्य सच्छिद्रपोतस्य जलप्रवेशे पातो भवति न च वेलापत्तनं प्राप्नोति । तथा सम्यग्दर्शनज्ञानचारित्रलक्षणामूल्यरत्न-भाण्डपूर्णजीवपोतस्य पूर्वोक्तास्रवद्वारैः कर्मजलप्रवेशे सति संसारसमुद्रे पातो भवति न च केवलज्ञानाव्याबाधसुखाद्यनन्तगुणरत्नपूर्णमुक्तिवेलापत्तनं प्राप्नोतीति । एवमास्रवगतदोषानुचिन्तनमास्रवानुप्रेक्षा ज्ञातव्येति ॥

अथ संवरानुप्रेक्षा कथ्यते—यथा तदेव जलपात्रं छिद्रस्य झम्पने सति जलप्रवेशाभावे निर्विघ्नेन वेलापत्तनं प्राप्नोति; तथा जीवजलपात्रं निजशुद्धात्म-

संवित्तिबलेन इन्द्रियाद्यास्रवच्छिद्राणां झम्पने सति कर्मजलप्रवेशाभावे निर्विघ्नेन केवलज्ञानाद्यनन्तगुणरत्नपूर्णमुक्तिवेलापत्तनं प्राप्नोतीति । एवं संवरगतगुणानुचिन्तनं संवरानुप्रेक्षा ज्ञातव्या ।। ८ ।।

अथ निर्जरानुप्रेक्षां प्रतिपादयति । यथा कोऽप्यजीर्णदोषेण मलसञ्चये जाते सत्याहारं त्यक्त्वा किमपि हरीतक्यादिकं मलपाचकमग्निदीपकं चौषधं गृह्णाति । तेन च मलपाकेन मलानां पातने गलने निर्जरणे सति सुखी भवति । तथायं भव्यजीवोऽप्यजीर्णजनकाहारस्थानीयमिथ्यात्वरागाद्यज्ञानभावेन कर्ममलसञ्चये सति मिथ्यात्वरागादिकं त्यक्त्वा परमौषधस्थानीयं जीवितमरणलाभालाभसुखदुःखादिसमभावनाप्रतिपादकं कर्ममलपाचकं शुद्धध्यानाग्निदीपकं च जिनवचनौषधं सेवते । तेन च कर्ममलानां गलने निर्जरणे सति सुखी भवति । किञ्च यथा कोऽपि धीमानजीर्णकाले यद्दुःखजातं तदजीर्णे गतेऽपि न विस्मरति ततश्चाजीर्णजनकाहारं परिहरति तेन च सर्वदैव सुखी भवति । तथा विवेकिजनोऽपि "आर्त्ता नरा धर्मपरा भवन्ति" इति वचनाद्दुःखोत्पत्तिकाले ये धर्मपरिणामा जायन्ते तान् दुःखे गतेऽपि न विस्मरति । ततश्च निजपरमात्मानुभूतिबलेन निर्जरार्थं दृष्टश्रुतानुभूतभोगाकाङ्क्षादिविभावपरिणामपरित्यागरूपैः संवेगवैराग्यपरिणामैर्वर्त्तत इति । संवेगवैराग्यलक्षणं कथ्यते—"धम्मे य धम्मफलम्हि दंसणे य हरिसो य हुंति संवेगो । संसारदेहभोगेसु विरत्तभावो य वैरग्गं ।" इति निर्जरानुप्रेक्षा गता ।। ९ ।।

अथ लोकानुप्रेक्षां प्रतिपादयति । तद्यथा—अनन्तानन्ताकाशबहुमध्यप्रदेशे घनोदधिघनवाततनुवाताभिधानवायुत्रयवेष्टितानादिनिधनाकृत्रिमनिश्चलासंख्यातप्रदेशो लोकोऽस्ति । तस्याकारः कथ्यते—अधोमुखार्द्धमुरजस्योपरि पूर्णे मुरजे स्थापिते यादृशाकारो भवति तादृशाकारः परं किन्तु मुरजो वृत्तो लोकस्तु चतुष्कोण इति विशेषः । अथवा प्रसारितपादस्य कटितटन्यस्तहस्तस्य चोर्ध्वस्थितपुरुषस्य यादृशाकारो भवति तादृशः । इदानीं तस्यैवोत्सेधायामविस्ताराः कथ्यन्ते—चतुर्दशरज्जुप्रमाणोत्सेधस्तथैव दक्षिणोत्तरेण सर्वत्र सप्तरज्जुप्रमाणायामो भवति । पूर्वपश्चिमेन पुनरधोविभागे सप्तरज्जुविस्तारः । ततश्चाधोभागात् क्रमहानिरूपेण हीयते यावन्मध्यलोक एकरज्जुप्रमाणविस्तारो भवति । ततो मध्यलोकादूर्ध्वं क्रमवृद्ध्या वर्द्धते यावद्ब्रह्मलोकान्ते रज्जुपञ्चकविस्तारो भवति ।

ततश्चोर्ध्वं पुनरपि हीयते यावल्लोकान्ते रज्जुप्रमाणविस्तारो भवति। तस्यैव लोकस्य पुनरुदूखलस्य मध्याधोभागे छिद्रे कृते सति निक्षिप्तवंशनालिकेव चतुष्कोणा त्रसनाडी भवति। सा चैकरज्जुविष्कम्भा चतुर्दशरज्जूत्सेधा विज्ञेया। तस्यास्त्वधोभागे सप्तरज्जवोऽधोलोकसंबन्धिन्यः। ऊर्ध्वभागे मध्यलोकोत्सेधसंबन्धिलक्षयोजनप्रमाणमेरूत्सेधः सप्तरज्जव ऊर्ध्वलोकसंबन्धिन्यः ॥

अतः परमधोलोकः कथ्यते। अधोभागे मेरोराधारभूता रत्नप्रभाख्या प्रथमपृथिवी। तस्याधोऽधः प्रत्येकमेकैकरज्जुप्रमाणमाकाशं गत्वा यथाक्रमेण शर्करावालुकापङ्कधूमतमोमहातमःसंज्ञा षड् भूमयो भवन्ति। तस्मादधोभागे रज्जुप्रमाणं क्षेत्रं भूमिरहितं निगोदादिपञ्चस्थावरभृतं च तिष्ठति। रत्नप्रभादिपृथिवीनां प्रत्येकं घनोदधिघनवाततनुवातत्रयमाधारभूतं भवतीति विज्ञेयम्। कस्यां पृथिव्यां कति नरकबिलानि सन्तीति प्रश्ने यथाक्रमेण कथयति तासु त्रिंशत्पञ्चविंशतिपञ्चदशदशत्रिपञ्चोनैकनरकशतसहस्राणि पञ्च चैव यथाक्रमम् ८४०००००। अथ रत्नप्रभादिपृथिवीनां क्रमेण पिण्डस्य प्रमाणं कथयति। पिण्डस्य कोऽर्थः मन्द्रत्वस्य बाहुल्यस्येति। अशीतिसहस्राधिकैकलक्षं तथैव द्वात्रिंशदष्टाविंशतिचतुर्विंशतिषोडशाष्टसहस्रप्रमितानि योजनानि ज्ञातव्यानि। तिर्यग्विस्तारस्तु चतुर्दिग्भागे यद्यपि त्रसनाड्यपेक्षयैकरज्जुप्रमाणस्तथापि त्रसरहितबहिर्भागे लोकान्तप्रमाणमिति। तथाचोक्तं "भुवामन्ते स्पृशन्तीनां लोकान्तं सर्वदिक्षु च"। अत्र विस्तारेण तिर्यग्विस्तारपर्यन्तमन्द्रत्वेन मन्दरावगाहयोजनसहस्रबाहुल्या मध्यमलोके या चित्रा पृथिवी तिष्ठति तस्या अधोभागे षोडशसहस्रबाहुल्यः खरभागस्तिष्ठति। तस्मादप्यधश्चतुरशीतियोजनसहस्रबाहुल्यः पङ्कभागस्तिष्ठति। ततोऽप्यधोभागे अशीतिसहस्रबाहुल्यो अब्बहुलभागस्तिष्ठत्येवं रत्नप्रभा पृथिवी त्रिभेदा ज्ञातव्या। तत्र खरभागेऽसुरकुलं विहाय नवप्रकारभवनवासिदेवानां तथैव राक्षसकुलं विहाय सप्तप्रकारव्यन्तरदेवानां आवासा ज्ञातव्या इति। पङ्कभागे पुनरसुराणां राक्षसानां चेति। अब्बहुलभागे नारकास्तिष्ठन्ति।

तत्र बहुभूमिकप्रासादवदधोऽधः सर्वपृथिवीषु स्वकीयस्वकीयबाहुल्यात् सकाशादध उपरि चैकैकयोजनसहस्रं विहाय मध्यभागे भूमिक्रमेण पटलानि भवन्ति त्रयोदशैकादशनवसप्तपञ्चत्र्येकसंख्यानि, तान्येव सर्वसमुदायेन पुनरे-

कोनपञ्चाशत्प्रमितानि । पटलानि कोऽर्थः ? प्रस्तारा इन्द्रका अन्तर्भूमय इति । तत्र रत्नप्रभायां सीमन्तसंज्ञे प्रथमपटलविस्तारे नृलोकवत् यत्संख्येययोजनविस्तारवत् मध्यबिलं तस्येन्द्रकसंज्ञा । तस्यैव चतुर्दिग्विभागे प्रतिदिशं पङ्क्तिरूपेणासंख्येययोजनविस्ताराण्येकोनपञ्चाशद्बिलानि । तथैव विदिक्चतुष्टये प्रतिदिशं पङ्क्तिरूपेण यान्यष्टचत्वारिंशद्बिलानि तान्यप्यसंख्यातयोजनविस्ताराणि । तेषामपि श्रेणीबद्धसंज्ञा । दिग्विदिगष्टकान्तरेषु पङ्क्तिरहितत्वेन पुष्पप्रकरवत्कानिचित्संख्येययोजनविस्ताराणि कानिचिदसंख्येययोजनविस्ताराणि यानि तिष्ठन्ति तेषां प्रकीर्णकसंज्ञा । इतीन्द्रकश्रेणीबद्धप्रकीर्णकरूपेण त्रिधा नरका भवन्ति । इत्यनेन क्रमेण प्रथम पटलव्याख्यानं विज्ञेयम् । तथैव पूर्वोक्तैकोनपञ्चाशत्पटलेष्वयमेव व्याख्यानक्रमः किन्त्वष्टश्रेणिष्वेकैकपटलं प्रत्येकैकं हीयते यावत्सप्तमपृथिव्यां चतुर्दिग्भागेष्वेकं बिलं तिष्ठति ॥

रत्नप्रभादिनरकदेहोत्सेधः कथ्यते प्रथमपटले हस्तत्रयम् ततः क्रमवृद्धिवशात्त्रयोदशपटले सप्तचापानि हस्तत्रयमङ्गुलषट्कं चेति । ततो द्वितीयपृथिव्यादिषु चरमेन्द्रकेषु द्विगुणद्विगुणे क्रियमाणे सप्तमपृथिव्यां चापशतपञ्चकं भवति । उपरितने नरके य उत्कृष्टोत्सेधः सोऽधस्तने नरके विशेषाधिको जघन्यो भवति, तथैव पटलेषु च ज्ञातव्यः । आयुःप्रमाणं कथ्यते । प्रथमपृथिव्यां प्रथमे पटले जघन्येन दशवर्षसहस्राणि तत आगमोक्तक्रमवृद्धिवशादन्तपटले सर्वोत्कर्षेणैकसागरोपमम् । ततः परं द्वितीयपृथिव्यादिषु क्रमेण त्रिसप्तदशसप्तदशद्वाविंशतित्रयस्त्रिंशत्सागरोपमम्रुत्कृष्टजीवितम् । यच्च प्रथमपृथिव्यामुत्कृष्टं तद्द्वितीयायां समयाधिकं जघन्यं, तथैव पटलेषु च । एवं सप्तमपृथिवीपर्यन्तं ज्ञातव्यम् । स्वशुद्धात्मसंवित्तिलक्षणनिश्चयरत्नत्रयविलक्षणैस्तीव्रमिथ्यात्वदर्शनज्ञानचरित्रैः परिणतानामसंज्ञिपञ्चेन्द्रियसरठपक्षिसर्पसिंहस्त्रीणां क्रमेण रत्नप्रभादिषु षट्पृथिवीषु गमनशक्तिरस्ति सप्तम्यां तु कर्मभूमिजमनुष्याणां मत्स्यानामेव । किञ्च यदि कोऽपि निरन्तरं नरके गच्छति तदा पृथिवीक्रमेणाष्टसप्तषट्पञ्चचतुस्त्रिद्विसंख्यवारानेव । किन्तु सप्तमनरकादागताः पुनरप्येकवारं तत्रान्यत्र वा नरके गच्छन्तीति नियमः । नरकादागता जीवा बलदेववासुदेवप्रतिवासुदेवचक्रवर्तिसंज्ञाः शलाकापुरुषाः न भवन्ति । चतुर्थपञ्चमषष्ठसप्तमनरकेभ्यः समागताः क्रमेण तीर्थकरचरमदेहभावसंयतश्रावका न भवन्ति । तर्हि किं

भवन्ति ? "णिरयादो णिस्सीरिदो णरतिरएकम्मसण्णिपज्जत्तो । गव्वभवे उप्पज्जदि सत्तमणिरयादुतिरिएव" ॥

इदानीं नारकदुःखानि कथ्यन्ते । तद्यथा—विशुद्धज्ञानदर्शनस्वभावनिजपरमात्मतत्त्वसम्यक्श्रद्धानज्ञानानुष्ठानभावनोत्पन्ननिर्विकारपरमानन्दैकलक्षणसुखामृतरसास्वादरहितैः पञ्चेन्द्रियविषयसुखास्वादलम्पटैर्मिथ्यादृष्टिजीवैर्यदुपार्जितं नरकायुर्नरकगत्यादिपापकर्म तदुदयेन नरके समुत्पद्य पृथिवीचतुष्टये तीव्रोष्णदुःखं, पञ्चम्यां पुनरुपरितनत्रिभागे तीव्रोष्णदुःखमधोभागे तीव्रशीतदुःखं षष्ठीसप्तम्योरतिशीतोत्पन्नदुःखमनुभवन्ति । तथैव छेदनभेदनक्रकचविदारणयन्त्रपीडनशूलारोहणादितीव्रदुःखं सहन्ते । तथा चोक्तं—"अच्छिणिमीलणमित्तं णत्थि सुहं दुःखमेव अणुबद्धं । णिरये णेरयियाणं अहोणिसं पच्चमाणाणं ।" प्रथमपृथिवीत्रयपर्यन्तमसुरोदीरितं चेति । एवं ज्ञात्वा नारकदुःखविनाशार्थं भेदाभेदरत्नत्रयभावना कर्त्तव्या । संक्षेपेणाधोलोकव्याख्यानं ज्ञातव्यम् ॥

अतः परं तिर्यग्लोकः कथ्यते—जम्बूद्वीपादिशुभनामानो द्वीपाः, लवणोदादिशुभनामानः समुद्राश्च द्विगुणद्विगुणविस्तारेण पूर्वं पूर्वं परिवेष्ट्य वृत्ताकाराः स्वयम्भूरमणपर्यन्तास्तिर्यग्विस्तारेण विस्तीर्णास्तिष्ठन्ति यतस्तेन कारणेन तिर्यग्लोको भण्यते, मध्यलोकश्च । तद्यथा—तेषु सार्द्धतृतीयोद्धारसागरोपमलोमच्छेदप्रमितेष्वसंख्यातद्वीपसमुद्रेषु मध्ये जम्बूद्वीपस्तिष्ठति । स च जम्बूवृक्षोपलक्षितो मध्यभागस्थितमेरुपर्वतसहितो वृत्ताकारलक्षयोजनप्रमाणस्तद्द्विगुणविष्कम्भेण योजनलक्षद्वयप्रमाणेन वृत्ताकारेण बहिर्भागे लवणसमुद्रेण वेष्टितः । सोऽपि लवणसमुद्रस्तद्द्विगुणविस्तारेण योजनलक्षचतुष्टयप्रमाणेन वृत्ताकारेण बहिर्भागे धातकीखण्डद्वीपेन वेष्टितः । सोऽपि धातकीखण्डद्वीपस्तद्द्विगुणविस्तारेण योजनाष्टलक्षप्रमाणेन बहिर्भागे कालोदकसमुद्रेण वेष्टितः । सोऽपि कालोदकसमुद्रस्तद्द्विगुणविस्तारेण षोडशयोजनलक्षप्रमाणेन वृत्ताकारेण बहिर्भागे पुष्करद्वीपेन वेष्टितः । इत्यादिद्विगुणद्विगुणविष्कम्भः स्वयम्भूरमणद्वीपस्वयम्भूरमणसमुद्रपर्यन्तो ज्ञातव्यः । यथा जम्बूद्वीपलवणसमुद्रविष्कम्भद्वयसमुदायाद्योजनलक्षत्रयप्रमितात्सकाशाद्धातकीखण्ड एकलक्षेणाधिकस्तथैवासंख्येयद्वीपसमुद्रविष्कम्भेभ्यः स्वयम्भूरमणसमुद्रविष्कम्भ एकलक्षेणाधिको ज्ञातव्यः । एवमुक्तलक्षणेष्वसंख्ये-

यद्वीपसमुद्रेषु व्यन्तरदेवानां पर्वताद्युपरिगता आवासाः, अधोभूभागगतानि भवनानि, तथैव द्वीपसमुद्रादिगतानि पुराणि च, परमागमोक्तभिन्नलक्षणानि। तथैव खरभागपङ्कभागस्थितप्रतरासंख्येयप्रमाणासंख्येयव्यन्तरदेवावासाः, तथैव द्वासप्ततिलक्षाधिककोटिसप्तप्रमितभवनवासिदेवसंबन्धिभवनान्यकृत्रिमजिनचैत्यालयसहितानि भवन्ति। एवमतिसंक्षेपेण तिर्यग्लोको व्याख्यातः ॥

अथ तिर्यग्लोकमध्यस्थितो मनुष्यलोको व्याख्यायते—तन्मध्यस्थितजम्बूद्वीपे सप्तक्षेत्राणि भण्यन्ते। दक्षिणदिग्विभागादारभ्य भरतहैमवतहरिविदेहरम्यकहैरण्यवतैरावतसंज्ञानि सप्त क्षेत्राणि भवन्ति। क्षेत्राणि कोऽर्थः ? वर्षा वंशा जनपदा इत्यर्थः। तेषां क्षेत्राणां विभागकारकाः षट् कुलपर्वताः कथ्यन्ते—दक्षिणदिग्भागमादीकृत्य हिमवन्महाहिमवन्निषधनीलरुक्मिशिखरिसंज्ञा भरतादिसप्तक्षेत्राणामन्तरेषु पूर्वापरायताः षट् कुलपर्वता भवन्ति। पर्वता इति कोऽर्थः। वर्षधरपर्वताः सीमापर्वता इत्यर्थः। तेषां पर्वतानामुपरि क्रमेण ह्रदाः कथ्यन्ते । पद्ममहापद्मतिगिञ्छकेशरिमहापुण्डरीकपुण्डरीकसंज्ञा अकृत्रिमा षट् ह्रदा भवन्ति। ह्रदा इति कोऽर्थः ? सरोवराणीत्यर्थः। तेभ्यः पद्मादिषड्ह्रदेभ्यः सकाशादागमकथितक्रमेण निर्गता याश्चतुर्दश नद्यस्ताः कथ्यन्ते। तथाहि —हिमवत्पर्वतस्थपद्मनाममहाह्रदार्धकोशावगाहक्रोशार्धाधिकषट्योजनप्रमाणविस्तारपूर्वतोरणद्वारेण निर्गत्य तत्पर्वतस्यैवोपरि पूर्वदिग्विभागेन योजनशतपञ्चकं गच्छति ततो गङ्गाकूटसमीपे दक्षिणेन व्यावृत्य भूमिस्थकुण्डे पतति तस्माद् दक्षिणद्वारेण निर्गत्य भरतक्षेत्रमध्यमभागस्थितस्य दीर्घत्वेन पूर्वापरसमुद्रस्पर्शिनो विजयार्द्धस्य गुहाद्वारेण निर्गत्य तत आर्यखण्डार्द्धभागे पूर्वेण व्यावृत्य प्रथमावगाहापेक्षया दशगुणेन गव्यूतिपञ्चकावगाहेन तथैव प्रथमविष्कम्भापेक्षया दशगुणेन योजनार्द्धसहितद्विषष्टियोजनप्रमाणविस्तारेण च पूर्वसमुद्रे प्रविष्टा गङ्गा। तथा गङ्गावत्सिन्धुरपि तस्मादेव हिमवत्पर्वतस्थपद्मह्रदात्पर्वतस्यैवोपरि पश्चिमद्वारेण निर्गत्य पश्चाद्दक्षिणदिग्विभागेनागत्य विजयार्द्धगुहाद्वारेण निर्गत्यार्यखण्डार्द्धभागे पश्चिमेन व्यावृत्य पश्चिमसमुद्रे प्रविष्टेति। एवं दक्षिणदिग्विभागसमागतगङ्गासिन्धुभ्यां पूर्वापरायतेन विजयार्द्धपर्वतेन च षट्खण्डीकृतं भरतक्षेत्रम् ॥

अथ महाहिमवत्पर्वतस्थमहापद्मह्रदाद्दक्षिणदिग्विभागेन हैमवतक्षेत्रमध्ये

समागत्य तत्रस्थनाभिगिरिपर्वतं योजनार्धेनास्पृशन्ती तस्यैवार्धे प्रदक्षिणं कृत्वा रोहित्पूर्वसमुद्रं गता। तथैव हिमवत्पर्वतस्थितपद्मह्रदादुत्तरेणागत्य तमेव नाभिगिरिं योजनार्धेनास्पृशन्ती तस्यैवार्द्धप्रदक्षिणं कृत्वा रोहितास्या पश्चिमसमुद्रं गता। इति रोहिद्रोहितास्यासंज्ञं नदीद्वन्द्वं हैमवतसंज्ञजघन्यभोगभूमिक्षेत्रे ज्ञातव्यम्। अथ निषधपर्वतस्थिततिगिञ्छनामह्रदाद्दक्षिणेनागत्य नाभिगिरिपर्वतं योजनार्धेनास्पृशन्ती तस्यैवार्धप्रदक्षिणं कृत्वा हरित्पूर्वसमुद्रं गता। तथैव महाहिमवत्पर्वतस्थमहापद्मनामह्रदादुत्तरदिग्विभागेनागत्य तमेव नाभिगिरिं योजनार्धेनास्पृशन्ती तस्यैवार्धप्रदक्षिणं कृत्वा हरिकान्ता नाम नदी पश्चिमसमुद्रं गता। इति हरिद्धरिकान्तासंज्ञं नदीद्वयं हरिसंज्ञमध्यमभोगभूमिक्षेत्रे विज्ञेयम्। अथ नीलपर्वतस्थितकेसरिनामह्रदाद्दक्षिणेनागत्योत्तरकुरुसंज्ञोत्कृष्टभूमिक्षेत्रे मध्येन गत्वा मेरुसमीपे गजदन्तपर्वतं भित्त्वा च प्रदक्षिणेन योजनार्धेन मेरुं विहाय पूर्वभद्रशालवनस्य मध्येन पूर्वविदेहस्य च मध्ये शीतानामनदी पूर्वसमुद्रं गता। तथैव निषधपर्वतस्थिततिगिञ्छह्रदादुत्तरदिग्विभागेनागत्य देवकुरुसंज्ञोत्तमभोगभूमिक्षेत्रमध्येन गत्वा मेरुसमीपे गजदन्तपर्वतं भित्वा च प्रदक्षिणेन योजनार्धेन मेरुं विहाय पश्चिमभद्रशालवनस्य मध्येन पश्चिमविदेहस्य च मध्येन शीतोदा पश्चिमसमुद्रं गता। एवं शीताशीतोदासंज्ञं नदीद्वयं विदेहाभिधाने कर्मभूमिक्षेत्रे ज्ञातव्यम्। यत्पूर्वं गङ्गासिन्धुनदीद्वयस्य विस्तारावगाहप्रमाणं भणितं तदेव क्षेत्रे क्षेत्रे नदीयुगलं प्रति विदेहपर्यन्तं द्विगुणं द्विगुणं ज्ञातव्यम्। अथ गङ्गा चतुर्दशसहस्रपरिवारनदीसहिता, सिन्धुरपि तथा, तद्द्विगुणसंख्यानं रोहिद्रोहितास्याद्वयम्, ततोऽपि द्विगुणसंख्यानं हरिद्धरिकान्ताद्वयमिति। तथा षड्विंशत्यधिकयोजनशतपञ्चकमेकोनविंशतिभागीकृतैकयोजनस्य भागषट्कं च यद्दक्षिणोत्तरेण कर्मभूमिसंज्ञभरतक्षेत्रस्य विष्कम्भप्रमाणं तद्द्विगुणं हिमवत्पर्वते, तस्माद्द्विगुणं हैमवतक्षेत्रे, इत्यादि द्विगुणं द्विगुणं विदेहपर्यन्तं ज्ञातव्यम्। तथा पद्मह्रदो योजनसहस्रायामस्तदर्द्धविष्कम्भो दशयोजनावगाहो योजनैकप्रमाणपद्मविष्कम्भस्तस्मान्महापद्मो द्विगुणस्तस्मादपि तिगिञ्छो द्विगुण इति॥

अथ यथा भरते हिमवत्पर्वताभिर्गतं गङ्गासिन्धुद्वयं, तथोत्तरे कर्मभूमिसंज्ञैरावतक्षेत्रे शिखरिपर्वताभिर्गतं रक्तारक्तोदानदीद्वयम्। यथा च हैमवतसंज्ञे

जघन्यभोगभूमिक्षेत्रे महाहिमवद्धिमवन्नामपर्वतद्वयात्क्रमेण निर्गतं रोहितरोहितास्यानदीद्वयं, तथोत्तरे हैरण्यवतसंज्ञजघन्यभोगभूमिक्षेत्रे शिखरिरुक्मिसंज्ञपर्वतद्वयात्क्रमेण निर्गतं सुवर्णकूलारूप्यकूलानदीद्वयम् । तथैव यथा हरिसंज्ञमध्यमभोगभूमिक्षेत्रे । निषधमहाहिमवन्नामपर्वतद्वयात्क्रमेण निर्गतं हरिद्धरिकान्तानदीद्वयं, तथोत्तरे रम्यकसंज्ञमध्यमभोगभूमिक्षेत्रे रुक्मनीलनामपर्वतद्वयात्क्रमेण निर्गतं नारीनरकान्तानदीद्वयमिति विज्ञेयम् । सुषमसुषमादिषट्कालसंबन्धिपरमागमोक्तायुरुत्सेधादिसहिता दशसागरोपमकोटिकोटिप्रमितावसर्पिणी तथोत्सर्पिणी च यथा भरते वर्त्तते तथैवैरावते च । अयन्तु विशेषः भरतम्लेच्छखण्डेषु विजयार्धनगेषु च चतुर्थकालसमयाद्यन्ततुल्यकालोऽस्ति नापरः । किं बहुना यथा खट्वाया एकभागे ज्ञाते द्वितीयभागस्तथैव ज्ञायते तथैव जम्बूद्वीपस्य क्षेत्रपर्वतनदीह्रदादीनां यदेव दक्षिणविभागे व्याख्यानं तदुत्तरेऽपि विज्ञेयम् ।

अथ देहममत्वमूलभूतमिथ्यात्वरागादिविभावरहिते केवलज्ञानदर्शनसुखाद्यनन्तगुणसहिते च निजपरमात्मद्रव्ये यया सम्यग्दर्शनज्ञानचारित्रभावनया कृत्वा विगतदेहा देहरहिताः सन्तो मुनयः प्राचुर्येण यत्र मोक्षं गच्छन्ति स विदेहो भण्यते । तस्य जम्बूद्वीपस्य मध्यमवर्त्तिनः किमपि विवरणं क्रियते । तद्यथा—नवनवतिसहस्रयोजनोत्सेध एकसहस्रावगाह आदौ भूमितले दशयोजनसहस्रप्रवृत्तविस्तार उपर्युपरि पुनरेकादशांशहानिक्रमेण हीयमानत्वे सति मस्तके योजनसहस्रविस्तार आगमोक्ताकृत्रिमचैत्यालयदेववनदेवावासाद्यागमकथितानेकाश्चर्यसहितो विदेहक्षेत्रमध्ये महामेरुर्नाम पर्वतोऽस्ति । स च गजो जातस्तस्मान्मेरुगजात्सकाशादुत्तरमुखे दन्तद्वयाकारेण यन्निर्गतं पर्वतद्वयं तस्य गजदन्तद्वयसंज्ञेति, तथोत्तरे भागे नीलपर्वते लग्नं तिष्ठति । तयोर्मध्ये यत्त्रिकोणाकारक्षेत्रमुत्तमभोगभूमिरूपं तस्योत्तरकुरुसंज्ञा । तस्य च मध्ये मेरोरीशानदिग्विभागे शीतानीलपर्वतयोर्मध्ये परमागमवर्णितानाद्यकृत्रिमपार्थिवो जम्बूवृक्षस्तिष्ठति । तस्या एव शीताया उभयतटे यमलगिरिसंज्ञं पर्वतद्वयं विज्ञेयम् । तस्मात्पर्वतद्वयाद्दक्षिणभागे कियन्तमध्वानं गत्वा शीतानदीमध्ये अन्तरान्तरेण पद्मादिह्रदपञ्चकमस्ति । तेषां ह्रदानामुभयपार्श्वयोः प्रत्येकं सुवर्णरत्नमयजिनगृह मण्डिता लोकानुयोगव्याख्यानेन दश दश सुवर्णपर्वता भवन्ति । तथैव

निश्चयव्यवहाररत्नत्रयाराधकोत्तमपात्रपरमभक्तिदत्ताहारदानफलेनोत्पन्नानां तिर्यग्मनुष्याणां स्वशुद्धात्मभावनोत्पन्ननिर्विकारसदानन्दैकलक्षणसुखामृतरसास्वादविलक्षणस्य । चक्रवर्त्तिभोगसुखादप्यधिकस्य विविधपञ्चेन्द्रियभोगसुखस्य प्रदायका ज्योतिर्गृहप्रदीपतुर्यभोजनवस्त्रमाल्यभाजनभूषणरागमदोत्पादकरसाङ्गसंज्ञा दशप्रकारकल्पवृक्षाः भोगभूमिक्षेत्रं व्याप्य तिष्ठन्तीत्यादिपरमागमोक्तप्रकारेणानेकाश्चर्याणि ज्ञातव्यानि । तस्मादेव मेरुगजाद्दक्षिणदिग्विभागेन गजदन्तद्वयमध्ये देवकुरुसंज्ञमुत्तमभोगभूमिक्षेत्रमुत्तरकुरुवद्विज्ञेयम् ॥

तस्मादेव मेरुपर्वतात्पूर्वस्यां दिशि पूर्वापरेण द्वाविंशतिसहस्रयोजनविष्कम्भं सवेदिकं भद्रशालवनमस्ति । तस्मात्पूर्वदिग्भागे कर्मभूमिसंज्ञः पूर्वविदेहोऽस्ति । तत्र नीलकुलपर्वताद्दक्षिणभागे शीतानद्या उत्तरभागे मेरोः प्रदक्षिणेन यानि क्षेत्राणि तिष्ठन्ति तेषां विभागः कथ्यते । तथाहि—मेरोः पूर्वदिशाभागे या पूर्वभद्रशालवनवेदिका तिष्ठति तस्याः पूर्वदिग्भागे प्रथमं क्षेत्रं भवति, तदनन्तरं दक्षिणोत्तरायतो वक्षारनामा पर्वतो भवति, तदनन्तरं क्षेत्रं तिष्ठति, ततोऽप्यनन्तरं विभङ्गा नदी भवति, ततोऽपि क्षेत्रं, तस्मादपि वक्षारपर्वतस्तिष्ठति, ततश्च क्षेत्रं, ततोऽपि विभङ्गा नदी, तदनन्तरं क्षेत्रं, ततः परं वक्षारपर्वतोऽस्ति, तदनन्तरं क्षेत्रं, ततो विभङ्गा नदी, ततश्च क्षेत्रं, ततो वक्षारपर्वतस्ततः क्षेत्रं, तदनन्तरं पूर्वसमुद्रसमीपे यद्देवारण्यं तस्य वेदिका चेति नवभित्तिभिरष्टक्षत्राणि ज्ञातव्यानि । तेषां क्रमेण नामानि कथ्यन्ते—कच्छा १ सुकच्छा २ महाकच्छा ३ कच्छावती ४ आवर्त्ता ५ लाङ्गलावर्त्ता ६ पुष्कला ७ पुष्कलावती ८ चेति । इदानीं क्षेत्रमध्यस्थितनगरीणां नामानि कथ्यन्ते । क्षेमा १ क्षेमपुरी २ रिष्टा ३ रिष्टपुरी ४ खड्गा ५ मञ्जूषा ६ औषधी ७ पुण्डरीकिणी ८ चेति ॥

अत ऊर्ध्वं शीताया दक्षिणविभागे निषधपर्वतादुत्तरविभागे यान्यष्टक्षेत्राणि तानि कथ्यन्ते । तद्यथा—पूर्वोक्ता या देवारण्यवेदिका तस्याः पश्चिमभागे क्षेत्रमस्ति, तदनन्तरं वक्षारपर्वतस्ततः परं क्षेत्रं, ततो विभङ्गा नदी, ततश्च क्षेत्रं, तस्माद्वक्षारपर्वतस्ततश्च क्षेत्रं, ततो विभङ्गा नदी ततः क्षेत्रं, ततो वक्षारपर्वतः, ततः क्षेत्रं, ततो विभङ्गा नदी, तदनन्तरं क्षेत्रं, ततो वक्षारपर्वतस्ततः क्षेत्रं, ततो मेरुदिग्भागे पूर्वभद्रशालवनवेदिका भवतीति नवभित्तिमध्येऽष्टौ क्षेत्राणि ज्ञातव्यानि । इदानीं तेषां क्रमेण नामानि कथ्यन्ते—वच्छा १,

सुवच्छा २, महावच्छा ३, वच्छावती ४, रम्या ५, रम्यका ६, रमणीया ७, मङ्गलावती ८ चेति । इदानीं तन्मध्यस्थितनगरीणां नामानि कथ्यन्ते—सुसीमा १, कुण्डला २, अपराजिता ३, प्रभाकरी ४, अङ्का ५, पद्मा ६, शुभा ७, रत्नसंचया ८ चेति, इति पूर्वविदेहक्षेत्रविभागव्याख्यानं समाप्तम् ॥

अथ मेरोः पश्चिमदिग्भागे पूर्वापरद्वाविंशतिसहस्रयोजनविष्कम्भो पश्चिमभद्रशालवनानन्तरं पश्चिमविदेहस्तिष्ठति । तत्र निषधपर्वतादुत्तरविभागे शीतोदानद्या दक्षिणभागे यानि क्षेत्राणि तेषां विभाग उच्यते । तथाहि—मेरुदिग्भागे या पश्चिमभद्रशालवनवेदिका तिष्ठति तस्याः पश्चिमभागे क्षेत्रं भवति, ततो दक्षिणोत्तरायतो वक्षारपर्वतस्तिष्ठति, तदनन्तरं क्षेत्रं, ततो विभङ्गा नदी, ततश्च क्षेत्रं, ततो वक्षारपर्वतस्ततः परं क्षेत्रं, ततो विभङ्गा नदी, ततः क्षेत्रं, ततो वक्षारपर्वतस्ततः क्षेत्रं, तदनन्तरं पश्चिमसमुद्रसमीपे यद्भूतारण्यवनं तिष्ठति तस्य वेदिका चेति नवभित्तिषु मध्येऽष्टौ क्षेत्राणि भवन्ति । तेषां नामानि कथ्यन्ते । पद्मा १, सुपद्मा २, महापद्मा ३, पद्मकावती ४, शंखा ५, नलिना ६, कुमुदा ७, सलिला ८ चेति । तन्मध्यस्थितनगरीणां नामानि कथयन्ति—अश्वपुरी १, सिंहपुरी २, महापुरी ३, विजयापुरी ४, अरजापुरी ५, विरजापुरी ६, अशोकापुरी ७, विशोकापुरी ८ चेति ॥

अत ऊर्ध्वं शीतोदाया उत्तरभागे नीलकुलपर्वताद्दक्षिणे भागे यानि क्षेत्राणि तिष्ठन्ति तेषां विभागभेदं कथयति । पूर्वभणिता या भूतारण्यवनवेदिका तस्याः पूर्वभागे क्षेत्रं भवति । तदनन्तरं वक्षारपर्वतस्तदनन्तरं क्षेत्रं, ततो विभङ्गा नदी, ततः क्षेत्रं, ततो वक्षारपर्वतः, ततश्च क्षेत्रं, ततश्च विभङ्गा नदी, ततोऽपि क्षेत्रं, ततो वक्षारपर्वतस्ततः क्षेत्रं, ततो विभङ्गा नदी, ततः क्षेत्रं, ततश्च वक्षारपर्वतस्ततः क्षेत्रं, ततो मेरुदिशाभागे पश्चिमभद्रशालवनवेदिका चेति नवभित्तिषु मध्येऽष्टौ क्षेत्राणि भवन्ति । तेषां क्रमेण नामानि कथ्यन्ते—वप्रा १, सुवप्रा २, महावप्रा ३, वप्रकावती ४, गन्धा ५, सुगन्धा ६, गन्धिला ७, गन्धमालिनी ८ चेति । तन्मध्यस्थितनगरीणां नामानि कथ्यन्ते । विजया १, वैजयन्ती २, जयन्ती ३, अपराजिता ४, चक्रपुरी ५, खड्गपुरी ६, अयोध्या ७, अवध्या ८ चेति ॥

अथ भरतक्षेत्रे यथा गङ्गासिन्धुनदीद्वयेन विजयार्धपर्वतेन च म्लेच्छ-

खण्डपञ्चकमार्यखण्डं चेति षट् खण्डानि जातानि । तथैव तेषु द्वात्रिंशत्क्षेत्रेषु गङ्गासिन्धुसमाननदीद्वयेन विजयार्धपर्वतेन च प्रत्येकं षट्खण्डानि ज्ञातव्यानि । अयं तु विशेषः । एतेषु सर्वदैव चतुर्थकालादिसमानकालः, उत्कर्षेण पूर्वकोटि-जीवितं, पञ्चशतधनुरुत्सेधश्चेति विज्ञेयम् । पूर्वप्रमाणं कथ्यते । "पुव्वस्स दु परिमाणं सदरिं खलु सदसहस्सकोडीउ । छप्पण्णं च सहस्सा बोधव्वा वास-गणनाउ ॥" इति संक्षेपेण जम्बूद्वीपव्याख्यानं समाप्तम् ॥

तदनन्तरं यथा सर्वद्वीपेषु सर्वसमुद्रेषु च द्वीपसमुद्रमर्यादाकारिका योजना-ष्टकोत्सेधावज्रवेदिकास्ति तथा जम्बूद्वीपेऽप्यस्तीति विज्ञेयम् । तद्बहिर्भागे योजनलक्षद्वयवलयविष्कम्भअगाधकमथितषोडशसहस्रयोजनजलोत्सेधाद्यनेका-श्चर्यसहितो लवणसमुद्रोऽस्ति । तस्मादपि बहिर्भागे योजनलक्षचतुष्टयवलय-विष्कम्भो धातकीखण्डद्वीपोऽस्ति । तत्र च दक्षिणभागे लवणोदधिकालोदधि-समुद्रद्वयवेदिकास्पर्शी दक्षिणोत्तरायामःसहस्रयोजनविष्कभः शतचतुष्टयोत्सेध इक्ष्वाकारनामपर्वतोऽस्ति । तथोत्तरविभागेऽपि । तेन पर्वतद्वयेन खण्डीकृतं पूर्वापरधातकीखण्डद्वयं ज्ञातव्यम् । तत्र पूर्वधातकीखण्डद्वीपमध्ये चतुरशीति-सहस्रयोजनोत्सेधः सहस्रयोजनावगाहः क्षुल्लकमेरुरस्ति । तथा पश्चिमधातकी-खण्डेऽपि । यथा जम्बूद्वीपमहामेरौ भरतादिक्षेत्रहिमवदादिपर्वतगङ्गादिनदीपद्मा-दिह्रदानां दक्षिणोत्तरेण व्याख्यानं कृतं तथात्र पूर्वधातकीखण्डमेरौ पश्चिम-धातकीखण्डमेरौ च ज्ञातव्यम् । अत एव जम्बूद्वीपापेक्षया संख्यां प्रति द्विगु-णानि भवन्ति भरतक्षेत्राणि, न च विस्तारायामापेक्षया । कुलपर्वताः पुनर्वि-स्तारापेक्षयैव द्विगुणा नत्वायामं प्रति । तत्र धातकीखण्डद्वीपे यथा चक्रस्या-रास्तथाकाराः कुलपर्वता भवन्ति । यथा चाराणां विवराणि छिद्राणि मध्या-न्यभ्यन्तरे सङ्कीर्णानि बहिर्भागे विस्तीर्णानि तथा क्षेत्राणि ज्ञातव्यानि ॥

इत्थंभूतं धातकीखण्डद्वीपमष्टलक्षयोजनवलयविष्कम्भः कालोदकसमुद्रः परिवेष्ट्य तिष्ठति । तस्माद्बहिर्भागे योजनलक्षाष्टकं गत्वा पुष्करद्वीपस्य वल-याकारेण चतुर्दिशाभागे मानुषोत्तरनामा पर्वतस्तिष्ठति । तत्र पुष्करार्धेऽपि धातकीखण्डद्वीपवद्दक्षिणोत्तरेणेक्ष्वाकारनामपर्वतद्वयं पूर्वापरेण क्षुल्लकमेरुद्वयं च । तथैव भरतादिक्षेत्रविभागश्च बोद्धव्यः । परं किन्तु जम्बूद्वीपभरतादिसंख्या-पेक्षया भरतक्षेत्रादिद्विगुणत्वं न च धातकीखण्डापेक्षया । कुलपर्वतानां तु

धातकीखण्डकुलपर्वतापेक्षया द्विगुणो विष्कम्भ आयामश्च । उत्सेधप्रमाणं पुनर्दक्षिणभागे विजयार्धपर्वते योजनानि पञ्चविंशतिः, हिमवति पर्वते शतं, महाहिमवति द्विशतं, निषधे चतुःशतं, तथोत्तरभागे च । मेरुसमीपगजदन्तेषु शतपञ्चकं, नदीसमीपे वक्षारेषु चान्यनिषधनीलसमीपे चतुःशतं च, शेषपर्वतानां च मेरुं त्यक्त्वा यदेव जम्बूद्वीपे भणितं तदेवार्धतृतीयद्वीपेषु च विज्ञेयम् । तथा नामानि च क्षेत्रपर्वतनदीदेशनगरादीनां तान्येव । तथैव क्रोशद्वयोत्सेधा पञ्चशतधनुर्विस्तारा पद्मरागरत्नमयी वनादीनां वेदिका सर्वत्र समानेति । अत्रापि चक्राकारवत्पर्वता आरविवरसंस्थानानि क्षेत्राणि ज्ञातव्यानि । मानुषोत्तरपर्वतादभ्यन्तरभाग एव मनुष्यास्तिष्ठन्ति न च बहिर्भागे । तेषां च जघन्यजीवितमन्तर्मुहूर्तप्रमाणम्, उत्कर्षेण पल्यत्रयं, मध्ये मध्यमविकल्पा बहवस्तथा तिरश्चां च । एवमसंख्येयद्वीपसमुद्रविस्तीर्णतिर्यग्लोकमध्येऽर्धतृतीयद्वीपप्रमाणः संक्षेपेण मनुष्यलोको व्याख्यातः ॥

अथ मानुषोत्तरपर्वतसकाशाद्बहिर्भागे स्वयम्भूरमणद्वीपार्धं परिक्षिप्य योऽसौ नागेन्द्रनामा पर्वतस्तस्मात्पूर्वभागे ये संख्यातीता द्वीपसमुद्रास्तिष्ठन्ति तेषु यद्यपि व्यन्तरा निरन्तरा इति वचनाद् व्यन्तरदेवावासास्तिष्ठन्ति तथापि पल्यप्रमाणायुषां तिरश्चां संबन्धिनी जघन्यभोगभूमिरिति ज्ञेयम् । नागेन्द्रपर्वताद्बहिर्भागे स्वयम्भूरमणद्वीपार्धे समुद्रे च पुनर्विदेहवत्सर्वदैव कर्मभूमिश्चतुर्थकालश्च । परं किन्तु मनुष्या न सन्ति । एवमुक्तलक्षणतिर्यग्लोकस्य तदनन्तरं मध्यमभागवर्तिनो मनुष्यलोकस्य च प्रतिपादनेन संक्षेपेण मध्यमलोकव्याख्यानं समाप्तम् । अथ मनुष्यलोके द्विहीनशतचतुष्टयं तिर्यग्लोके तु नन्दीश्वरकुण्डलरुचकाभिधानद्वीपत्रयेषु क्रमेण द्विपञ्चाशच्चतुष्टयचतुष्टयसंख्याश्चाकृत्रिमाः स्वतन्त्रजिनगृहा ज्ञातव्याः ॥

अत ऊर्ध्वं ज्योतिर्लोकः कथ्यते । तद्यथा—चन्द्रादित्यग्रहनक्षत्राणि प्रकीर्णतारकाश्चेति ज्योतिष्कदेवाः पञ्चविधा भवन्ति । तेषां मध्येऽस्माद्भूमितलादुपरि नवत्यधिकसप्तशतयोजनान्याकाशे गत्वा तारकविमानाः सन्ति, ततोऽपि योजनदशकं गत्वा सूर्यविमानाः, ततः परमशीतियोजनानि गत्वा चन्द्रविमानाः, ततोऽपि त्रैलोक्यसारकथितक्रमेण योजनचतुष्टयं गते अश्विन्यादिनक्षत्रविमानाः, ततःपरं योजनचतुष्टयं गत्वा बुधविमानाः, ततःपरं योजनत्रयं गत्वा शुक्रवि-

मानाः, ततो योजनत्रये गते बृहस्पतिविमानाः, ततो योजनत्रयानन्तरं मङ्गलविमानाः, ततोऽपि योजनत्रयानन्तरं शनैश्चरविमाना इति । तथा चोक्तं "णउदुत्तरसत्तसया दस सीदी चउदुगं तु तिचउक्कं । तारारविससिरिक्खा बुहभग्गवअंगिरारसणी ।" ते च ज्योतिष्कदेवा अर्धतृतीयद्वीपेषु निरन्तरं मेरोः प्रदक्षिणेन परिभ्रमणगतिं कुर्वन्ति । तत्र घटिकाप्रहरदिवसादिरूपः स्थूलव्यवहारकालः समयनिमिषादिसूक्ष्मव्यवहारकालवत् यद्यप्यनादिनिधनेन समयघटिकादिविवक्षितविकल्परहितेन कालाणुद्रव्यरूपेण निश्चयकालेनोपादानभूतेन जन्यते तथापि चन्द्रादित्यादिज्योतिष्कदेवविमानगमनागमनेन कुम्भकारेण निमित्तभूतेन मृत्पिण्डोपादानजनितघट इव व्यज्यते प्रकटीक्रियते ज्ञायते तेन कारणेनोपचारेण ज्योतिष्कदेवकृत इत्यभिधीयते । निश्चयकालस्तु तद्विमानगतिपरिणतेर्बहिरङ्गसहकारिकारणं भवति कुम्भकारचक्रभ्रमणस्याधस्तनशिलावदिति ॥

इदानीमर्धतृतीयद्वीपेषु चन्द्रादित्यसंख्या कथ्यते । तथाहि—जम्बूद्वीपे चन्द्रद्वयं सूर्यद्वयं च, लवणोदे चतुष्टयं, धातकीखण्डद्वीपे द्वादश चन्द्रादित्याश्च, कालोदकसमुद्रे द्विचत्वारिंशच्चन्द्रादित्याश्च, पुष्करार्धे द्वीपे द्वासप्ततिचन्द्रादित्याश्चेति । ततःपरं भरतैरावतस्थितजम्बूद्वीपचन्द्रसूर्ययोः किमपि विवरणं क्रियते । तद्यथा—जम्बूद्वीपाभ्यन्तरे योजनानामशीतिशतं बहिर्भागे लवणसमुद्रसंबन्धे त्रिंशदधिकशतत्रयमिति समुदायेन दशोत्तरयोजनशतपञ्चकं चारक्षेत्रं भण्यते तच्चन्द्रादित्ययोरेकमेव । तत्र भरतेन बहिर्भागे तस्मिंश्चारक्षेत्रे सूर्यस्य चतुरशीतिशतसंख्या मार्गा भवन्ति, चन्द्रस्य पञ्चदशैव । तत्र जम्बूद्वीपाभ्यन्तरे कर्कटसङ्क्रान्तिदिने दक्षिणायनप्रारम्भे निषधपर्वतस्योपरि प्रथममार्गे सूर्यः प्रथमोदयं करोति । यत्र सूर्यविमानस्थं निर्दोषपरमात्मनो जिनेश्वरस्याकृत्रिमं जिनबिम्बं प्रत्यक्षेण दृष्ट्वा अयोध्यानगरीस्थितो निर्मलसम्यक्त्वानुरागेण भरतचक्री पुष्पाञ्जलिमुत्क्षिप्यार्घं ददातीति । तन्मार्गस्थितभरतक्षेत्रादित्यस्यैरावतादित्येन सह तथापि चन्द्रस्य चन्द्रेण सह यदन्तरं भवति तद्विशेषेणागमतो ज्ञातव्यम् ॥

अथ " सदभिस भरणी अद्दा सादी असलेस जेट्ठमवरवरा । रोहिणिविसहपुणव्वसु तिउत्तरा मज्झिमा सेसा । " इति गाथाकथितक्रमेण यानि जघन्योत्कृष्टमध्यनक्षत्राणि तेषु मध्ये कस्मिन्नक्षत्रे कियन्ति दिनान्यादित्यस्तिष्ठतीति । "इंदु रवी दो रिक्खा सत्तट्ठियपंचगयणखंडहिया । अहियहिदरिक्ख-

खंडा इंदुरविअ्गत्थण्णमुहत्ता । " इत्यनेन गाथासूत्रेणागमकथितक्रमेण पृथक्-पृथगानीय मेलापके कृते सति षडधिकषष्टियुतत्रिशतसंख्यदिनानि भवन्ति । तस्य दिनसमूहार्धस्य यदा द्वीपाभ्यन्तराद्दक्षिणेन बहिर्भागेषु दिनकरो गच्छति तदा दक्षिणायनसंज्ञा; यदा पुनः समुद्रात्सकाशादुत्तरेणाभ्यन्तरमार्गेषु समायाति तदोत्तरायणसंज्ञेति । तत्र यदा द्वीपाभ्यन्तरे प्रथममार्गपरिधौ कर्कटसंक्रान्तिदिने दक्षिणायनप्रारम्भे तिष्ठत्यादित्यस्तदा चतुर्णवतिसहस्रपञ्चविंशत्यधिकपञ्चयोजनशतप्रमाण उत्कर्षेणादित्यविमानस्य पूर्वापरेणातपविस्तारो ज्ञेयः । तत्र पुनरष्टादशमुहूर्त्तैर्दिवसो भवति द्वादशमुहूर्त्तैं रात्रिरिति । ततः क्रमेणातपहानौ सत्यां मुहूर्त्तद्वयस्यैकषष्टिभागीकृतस्यैको भागो दिवसमध्ये दिनं प्रति हीयते यावल्लवणसमुद्रेऽवसानमार्गे माघमासे मकरसंक्रान्तावुत्तरायणदिवसे त्रिषष्टिसहस्राधिकषोडशयोजनप्रमाणो जघन्येनादित्यविमानस्य पूर्वापरेणातपविस्तारो भवति । तथैव द्वादशमुहूर्त्तैर्दिवसो भवत्यष्टादशमुहूर्त्तैं रात्रिश्चेति । शेषं विशेष व्याख्यानं लोकविभागादौ विज्ञेयम् ।

ये तु मनुष्यक्षेत्राद्बहिर्भागे ज्योतिष्कविमानास्तेषां चलनं नास्ति । ते च मानुषोत्तरपर्वताद्बहिर्भागे पञ्चाशत्सहस्राणि योजनानां गत्वा वलयाकारं पङ्क्तिक्रमेण पूर्वक्षेत्रं परिवेष्ट्य तिष्ठन्ति । तत्र प्रथमवलये चतुश्चत्वारिंशदधिकशतप्रमाणाश्चन्द्रास्तथादित्याश्चान्तरान्तरेण तिष्ठन्ति । ततः परं योजनलक्षे लक्षे गते तेनैव क्रमेण वलयं भवति । अयन्तु विशेषः—वलये वलये चन्द्रचतुष्टयं सूर्यचतुष्टयं च वर्धते यावत्पुष्करार्धबहिर्भागे वलयाष्टकमिति । ततः पुष्करसमुद्रप्रवेशे वेदिकायाः सकाशद्धिपञ्चाशत्सहस्रप्रमितयोजनानि जलमध्ये प्रविश्य यत्पूर्वं चत्वारिंशदधिकशतप्रमाणं प्रथमवलयं व्याख्यातं तस्माद्द्विगुणसंख्यानं प्रथमवलयं भवति । तदनन्तरं पूर्ववद्योजनलक्षे लक्षे गते वलयं भवति चन्द्रचतुष्टयस्य सूर्यचतुष्टयस्य च वृद्धिरित्यनेनैव क्रमेण स्वयम्भूरमणसमुद्रबहिर्भागवेदिकापर्यन्तं ज्योतिष्कदेवानामवस्थानं बोद्धव्यम् । एते च प्रतरासंख्येयभागप्रमिता असंख्येया ज्योतिष्कविमाना अकृत्रिमसुवर्णमयरत्नमयजिनचैत्यालयमण्डिता ज्ञातव्याः । इति संक्षेपेण ज्योतिष्कलोकव्याख्यानं समाप्तम् ॥

अथानन्तरमूर्ध्वलोकः कथ्यते । तथाहि सौधर्मैशानसनत्कुमारमाहेन्द्रब्रह्मब्रह्मोत्तरलान्तवकापिष्टशुक्रमहाशुक्रशतारसहस्रारानतप्राणतारणाच्युतसंज्ञाः षो-

दश स्वर्गास्ततोऽपि नव ग्रैवेयकसंज्ञास्ततश्च नवानुदिशसंज्ञं नवविमानसंख्यमेकपटलं ततोऽपि पञ्चानुत्तरसंज्ञं पञ्चविमानसंख्यमेकपटलं चेत्युक्तक्रमेणोपर्युपरि वैमानिकदेवास्तिष्ठन्तीति वार्त्तिकं सङ्ग्रहवाक्यं समुदायकथनमिति यावत्। आदिमध्यान्तेषु द्वादशाष्टचतुर्योजनवृत्तविष्कम्भा चत्वारिंशत्प्रमितयोजनोत्सेधा या मेरुचूलिका तिष्ठति तस्योपरि कुरुभूमिजमर्त्यवालाग्रान्तरितः पुनश्च ऋजुविमानमस्ति। तदादिं कृत्वा चूलिकासहितलक्षयोजनप्रमाणं मेरूत्सेधमानमर्द्धाधिकैकरज्जुप्रमाणं यदाकाशक्षेत्रं तत्पर्यन्तं सौधर्मैशानसंज्ञं स्वर्गयुगलं तिष्ठति। ततः परमर्द्धाधिकैकरज्जुपर्यन्तं सनत्कुमारमाहेन्द्रसंज्ञं स्वर्गयुगलं भवति, तस्मादर्द्धरज्जुप्रमाणाकाशपर्यन्तं ब्रह्मब्रह्मोत्तराभिधानं स्वर्गयुगलमस्ति, ततोऽप्यर्द्धरज्जुपर्यन्तं लान्तवकापिष्टनामस्वर्गयुगलमस्ति, ततश्चार्द्धरज्जुपर्यन्तं शुक्रमहाशुक्राभिधानं स्वर्गद्वयं ज्ञातव्यम्, तदनन्तरमर्द्धरज्जुपर्यन्तं शतारसहस्रारसंज्ञं स्वर्गयुगलं भवति, ततोऽप्यर्द्धरज्जुपर्यन्तमानतप्राणतनामस्वर्गयुगलं, ततः परमर्द्धरज्जुपर्यन्तमाकाशं यावदारणाच्युताभिधानं स्वर्गद्वयं ज्ञातव्यमिति। तत्र प्रथमयुगलद्वये स्वकीयस्वकीयस्वर्गनामानश्चत्वार इन्द्रा विज्ञेयाः, मध्ययुगलचतुष्टये पुनः स्वकीयस्वकीयप्रथमस्वर्गाभिधान एकैक एवेन्द्रो भवति, उपरितनयुगलद्वयेऽपि स्वकीयस्वकीयस्वर्गनामानश्चत्वार इन्द्रा भवन्तीति समुदायेन षोडशस्वर्गेषु द्वादशेन्द्रा ज्ञातव्याः। षोडशस्वर्गादूर्ध्वमेकरज्जुमध्ये नवग्रैवेयकनवानुदिशपञ्चानुत्तरविमानवासिदेवास्तिष्ठन्ति। ततः परं तत्रैव द्वादशयोजनेषु गतेष्वष्टयोजनबाहुल्या मनुष्यलोकवत्पञ्चाधिकचत्वारिंशल्लक्षयोजनविस्तारा मोक्षशिला भवति। तस्योपरि घनोदधिघनवाततनुवातत्रयमस्ति। तत्र तनुवातमध्ये लोकान्ते केवलज्ञानाद्यनन्तगुणसहिताः सिद्धास्तिष्ठन्ति॥

इदानीं स्वर्गपटलसंख्या कथ्यते—सौधर्मैशानयोरेकत्रिंशत्, सनत्कुमारमाहेन्द्रयोः सप्त, ब्रह्मब्रह्मोत्तरयोश्चत्वारि, लान्तवकापिष्टयोर्द्वयम्, शुक्रमहाशुक्रयोः पटलमेकम्, शतारसहस्रारयोरेकम्, आनतप्राणतयोस्त्रयम्, आरणाच्युतयोस्त्रयमिति। नवसु ग्रैवैयकेषु नवकं, नवानुदिशेषु पुनरेकं, पञ्चानुत्तरेषु चैकमिति समुदायेनोपर्युपरि त्रिषष्टिपटलानि ज्ञातव्यानि। तथा चोक्तं "इगतीससत्तचत्तारिदोण्णिएक्केक्कछक्कचदुकप्पे। तित्तियएक्केकिंदयणामा उडुआदि तेवट्ठी॥"

अतः परं प्रथमपटलव्याख्यानं क्रियते । ऋजु विमानं यदुक्तं पूर्वं मेरुचूलिकाया उपरि तस्य मनुष्यक्षेत्रप्रमाणविस्तारस्येन्द्रकसंज्ञा । तस्य चतुर्दिग्भागेष्वसंख्येययोजनविस्ताराणि पङ्क्तिरूपेण सर्वद्वीपसमुद्रेषूपरि प्रतिदिशं यानि त्रिषष्टिविमानानि तिष्ठन्ति तेषां श्रेणीबद्धसंज्ञा । यानि च पङ्क्तिरहितपुष्पप्रकरवद्विदिक्चतुष्टये तिष्ठन्ति तेषां संख्येयासंख्येययोजनविस्ताराणां प्रकीर्णकसंज्ञेति समुदायेन प्रथमपटललक्षणं ज्ञातव्यम् । तत्र पूर्वापरदक्षिणश्रेणित्रयविमानानि । तन्मध्ये विदिग्द्वयविमानानि च सौधर्मसंबन्धीनि भवन्ति, शेषविदिग्द्वयविमानानि च पुनरीशानसंबन्धीनि । अस्मात्पटलादुपरि जिनदृष्टमानेन संख्येयान्यसंख्येयानि योजनानि गत्वा तेनैव क्रमेण द्वितीयादिपटलानि भवन्ति । अयं च विशेषः—श्रेणीचतुष्टये पटले पटले प्रतिदिशमेकैकविमानं हीयते यावत्पञ्चानुत्तरपटले चतुर्दिक्ष्वेकैकविमानं तिष्ठति । एते सौधर्मादिविमानाश्चतुरशीतिलक्षसप्तनवतिसहस्रत्रयोविंशतिप्रमिता अकृत्रिमसुवर्णमयजिनगृहमण्डिता ज्ञातव्या इति ॥

अथ देवानामायुःप्रमाणं कथ्यते । भवनवासिषु जघन्येन दशवर्षसहस्राणि, उत्कर्षेण पुनरसुरकुमारेषु सागरोपमम्, नागकुमारेषु पल्यत्रयं, सुपर्णे सार्धद्वयं; द्वीपकुमारे द्वयं, शेषकुलषट्के सार्धपल्यमिति । व्यन्तरे जघन्येन दशवर्षसहस्राणि, उत्कर्षेण पल्यमधिकमिति । ज्योतिष्कदेवे जघन्येन पल्याष्टमविभागः, उत्कर्षेण चन्द्रे लक्षवर्षाधिकं पल्यं, सूर्ये सहस्राधिकं पल्यं, शेषज्योतिष्कदेवानामागमानुसारेणेति । अथ सौधर्मेशानयोर्जघन्येन साधिकपल्यं, उत्कर्षेण साधिकसागरोपमद्वयं, सनत्कुमारमाहेन्द्रयोः साधिकसागरोपमसप्तकं, ब्रह्मब्रह्मोत्तरयोः साधिकसागरोपमदशकं, लान्तवकापिष्ठयोः साधिकानि चतुर्दशसागरोपमानि, शुक्रमहाशुक्रयोः षोडश साधिकानि, शतारसहस्रारयोरष्टादश साधिकानि, आनतप्राणतयोर्विंशतिरेव, आरणाच्युतयोर्द्वाविंशतिरिति । अतः परमच्युतादूर्ध्वं कल्पातीतनवग्रैवेयकेषु द्वाविंशतिसागरोपमप्रमाणादूर्ध्वमेकैकसागरोपमे वर्धमाने सत्येकत्रिंशत्सागरोपमाण्यवसाननवग्रैवेयके भवन्ति । नवानुदिशपटले द्वात्रिंशत्, पञ्चानुत्तरपटले त्रयस्त्रिंशत्, उत्कृष्टायुःप्रमाणं ज्ञातव्यम् । तदायुः सौधर्मादिषु स्वर्गेषु यदुत्कृष्टं तत्परस्मिन्

परस्मिन् स्वर्गे सर्वार्थसिद्धिं विहाय जघन्यं चेति । शेषं विशेषव्याख्यानं त्रिलोकसारादौ बोद्धव्यम् ॥

किञ्च आदिमध्यान्तमुक्ते शुद्धबुद्धैकस्वभावे परमात्मनि सकलविमलकेवलज्ञानलोचनेनादर्शे बिम्बानीव शुद्धात्मादिपदार्था लोक्यन्ते दृश्यन्ते ज्ञायन्ते परिच्छिद्यन्ते यतस्तेन कारणेन स एव निश्चयलोकस्तस्मिन्निश्चयलोकाख्ये स्वकीयशुद्धपरमात्मनि अवलोकनं वा स निश्चयलोकः । "सस्साओ य तिलेस्सा इंदियवसदा य अत्तरुद्दाणि । णाणं च दुप्पउत्तं मोहो पावप्पदो होदि । " इति गाथोदितविभावपरिणाममादिं कृत्वा समस्तशुभाशुभसंकल्पविकल्पत्यागेन निजशुद्धात्मभावनोत्पन्नपरमाह्लादैकसुखामृतरसास्वादानुभवनेन च या भावना सैव निश्चयलोकानुप्रेक्षा । शेषा पुनर्व्यवहारेणेत्येवं संक्षेपेण लोकानुप्रेक्षाव्याख्यानं समाप्तम् ॥

अथ दुर्लभानुप्रेक्षां कथयति । तथाहि एकेन्द्रियविकलेन्द्रियपञ्चेन्द्रियसंज्ञिपर्याप्तमनुष्यदेशकुलरूपेन्द्रियपटुत्वनिर्व्याध्यायुष्कवरबुद्धिसद्धर्मश्रवणग्रहणधारणश्रद्धानसंयमविषयसुखव्यावर्त्तनक्रोधादिकषायनिवर्त्तनेषु परं परं दुर्लभेषु कथंचित्काकतालीयकन्यायेन लब्धेष्वपि तल्लब्धिरूपबोधे फलभूतस्वशुद्धात्मसंवित्त्यात्मकनिर्मलधर्मध्यानशुक्लध्यानरूपः परमसमाधिर्दुर्लभः । कस्मादिति चेत्तत्प्रतिबन्धकमिथ्यात्वविषयकषायनिदानबन्धादिविभावपरिणामानां प्रबलत्वादिति । तस्मात्स एव निरन्तरं भावनीयः । तद्भावनारहितानां पुनरपि संसारे पतनमिति । तथा चोक्तम्—"इत्यतिदुर्लभरूपां बोधिं लब्ध्वा यदिप्रमादी स्यात् । संसृतिभीमारण्ये भ्रमति वराको नरः सुचिरम् । " पुनश्चोक्तं मनुष्यभवदुर्लभत्वम्—"अशुभपरिणामबहुलता लोकस्य विपुलता महामहती । योनिविपुलता च कुरुते सुदुर्लभां मानुषीं योनिम् । " बोधिसमाधिलक्षणं कथ्यते—सम्यग्दर्शनज्ञानचारित्राणामप्राप्तप्रापणं बोधिस्तेषामेव निर्विघ्नेन भवान्तरप्रापणं समाधिरिति । एवं संक्षेपेण दुर्लभानुप्रेक्षा समाप्ता ।

अथ धर्मानुप्रेक्षां कथयति । तद्यथा—संसारे पतन्तं जीवमुद्धृत्य नागेन्द्रनरेन्द्रदेवेन्द्रादिवन्द्ये अव्याबाधानन्तसुखाद्यनन्तगुणलक्षणे मोक्षपदे धरतीति धर्मः । तस्य च भेदाः कथ्यन्ते—अहिंसालक्षणः सागारानगारलक्षणो वा उत्तमक्षमादिलक्षणो वा निश्चयव्यवहाररत्नत्रयात्मको वा शुद्धात्मसंवित्त्यात्मकमोहक्षोभ-

रहितात्मपरिणामो वा धर्मः । अस्य धर्मस्यालाभेऽतीतानन्तकाले "णिच्चेदरधाउ-सत्तय तरुदस वियलेदियासु छब्बेव । सुरणिरयतिरियचउरो चउदस मणुयेसु सदसहस्सा ।" इति गाथाकथितचतुरशीतियोनिलक्षेषु मध्ये परमस्वास्थ्य-भावनोत्पन्ननिर्व्याकुलपारमार्थिकसुखविलक्षणानि पञ्चेन्द्रियसुखाभिलाषजनि-तव्याकुलत्वोत्पादकानि दुःखानि सहमानः सन् भ्रमितोऽयं जीवो यदा पुनरेवं-गुणविशिष्टस्य धर्मस्य लाभो भवति तदा राजाधिराजमहाराजार्द्धमाण्डलिक-महामाण्डलिकबलदेववासुदेवकामदेवसकलचक्रवर्त्तिदेवेन्द्रगणधरदेवतीर्थकरपर-मदेवप्रथमकल्याणत्रयपर्यन्तं विविधाभ्युदयसुखं प्राप्य पश्चादभेदरत्नत्रयभावना-बलेनाक्षयानन्तसुखादिगुणास्पदमर्हत्पदं सिद्धपदं च लभते । तेन कारणेन धर्म एव परमरसरसायनं निधिनिधानं कल्पवृक्षः कामधेनुश्चिन्तामणिरिति । किं बहुना ये जिनेश्वरप्रणीतं धर्मं प्राप्य दृढमतयो जातास्त एव धन्याः। तथाचोक्तम्—"धन्या ये प्रतिबुद्धा धर्मे खलु जिनवरैः समुपदिष्टे । ये प्रतिपन्ना धर्मं स्वभावनोपस्थि-तमनीषाः ।" इति संक्षेपेण धर्मानुप्रेक्षा समाप्ता ॥

इत्युक्तलक्षणा अनित्याशरणसंसारैकत्वान्यत्वाशुचित्वास्रवसंवरनिर्जरालो-कबोधिदुर्लभधर्मतत्त्वानुचिन्तनसंज्ञा निरास्रवस्वशुद्धात्मतत्त्वपरिणतिरूपस्य संव-रस्य कारणभूता द्वादशानुप्रेक्षाः समाप्ताः ॥

अथ परीषहजयः कथ्यते—क्षुत्पिपासाशीतोष्णदंशमशकनाग्न्यारतिस्त्रीच-र्यानिषद्याशय्याक्रोशवधयाचनालाभरोगतृणस्पर्शमलसत्कारपुरस्कारप्रज्ञाज्ञानदर्श-नानीति द्वाविंशतिपरीषहा विज्ञेयाः । तेषां क्षुधादिवेदनानां तीव्रोदयेऽपि सुखदुःखजीवितमरणलाभालाभनिन्दाप्रशंसादिसमतारूपपरमसामायिकेन नव-तरशुभाशुभकर्मसंवरणचिरन्तनशुभाशुभकर्मनिर्जरणसमर्थेनायं निजपरमात्म-भावनासंजातनिर्विकारनित्यानन्दलक्षणसुखामृतसंवित्तेरचलनं स परीषह-जय इति ॥

अथ चारित्रं कथयति । शुद्धोपयोगलक्षणनिश्चयरत्नत्रयपरिणते स्वशुद्धात्म-स्वरूपे चरणमवस्थानं चारित्रम् । तच्च तारतम्यभेदेन पञ्चविधम् । तथाहि—सर्वे जीवाः केवलज्ञानमया इति भावनारूपेण समतालक्षणं सामायिकम्, अथवा परमस्वास्थ्यबलेन युगपत्समस्तशुभाशुभसङ्कल्पविकल्पत्यागरूपसमाधि-लक्षणं वा, निर्विकारस्वसंवित्तिबलेन रागद्वेषपरिहाररूपं वा, स्वशुद्धात्मानुभू-

तिबलेनार्त्तरौद्रपरित्यागरूपं वा, समस्तसुखदुःखादिमध्यस्थरूपं वेति । अथ छेदोपस्थापनं कथयति—यदा युगपत्समस्तविकल्पत्यागरूपे परमसामायिके स्थातुमशक्तोऽयं जीवस्तदा समस्तहिंसानृतस्तेयाब्रह्मपरिग्रहेभ्यो विरतिर्व्रतमित्यनेन पञ्चप्रकारविकल्पभेदेन व्रतच्छेदेन रागादिविकल्परूपसावद्येभ्यो निवर्त्य निजशुद्धात्मन्यात्मानमुपस्थापयतीति छेदोपस्थापनम् । अथवा छेदे व्रतखण्डे सति निर्विकारसंवित्तिरूपनिश्चयप्रायश्चित्तेन तत्साधकबहिरङ्गव्यवहारप्रायश्चित्तेन वा स्वात्मन्युपस्थापनं छेदोपस्थापनमिति । अथ परिहारविशुद्धिं कथयति—"तीसं वासा जम्मे वासपहुत्तं च तित्थयरमूले । पच्चक्खाणं पढिदो संझूण-दुगाऊपविहारो ।" इति गाथाकथितक्रमेण मिथ्यात्वरागादिविकल्पमलानां प्रत्याख्यानेन परिहारेण विशेषेण स्वात्मनः शुद्धिर्नैर्मल्यं परिहारविशुद्धिश्चारित्रमिति । अथ सूक्ष्मसाम्परायचारित्रं कथयति । सूक्ष्मातीन्द्रियनिजशुद्धात्मसंवित्तिबलेन सूक्ष्मलोभाभिधानसाम्परायस्य कषायस्य यत्र निरवशेषोपशमनं क्षपणं वा तत्सूक्ष्मसाम्परायचारित्रमिति । अथ यथाख्यातचारित्रं कथयति—यथा सहजशुद्धस्वभावत्वेन निष्कम्पत्वेन निष्कषायमात्मस्वरूपं तथैवाख्यातं कथितं यथाख्यातचारित्रमिति ॥

इदानीं सामायिकादिचारित्रपञ्चकस्य गुणस्थानस्वामित्वं कथयति । प्रमत्ताप्रमत्तापूर्वानिवृत्तिसंज्ञगुणस्थानचतुष्टये सामायिकचारित्रं भवति छेदोपस्थापनञ्च, परिहारविशुद्धिस्तु प्रमत्ताप्रमत्तगुणस्थानद्वये, सूक्ष्मसांपरायचारित्रं पुनरेकस्मिन्नेव सूक्ष्मसाम्परायगुणस्थाने, यथाख्यातचारित्रमुपशान्तकषायक्षीणकषायसयोगिजिनायोगिजिनाभिधानगुणस्थानचतुष्टये भवतीति । अथ संयमप्रतिपक्षं कथयति संयमासंयमसंज्ञं दार्शनिकाद्येकादशभेदभिन्नं देशचारित्रमेकस्मिन्नेव पञ्चमगुणस्थाने ज्ञातव्यम् । असंयमस्तु मिथ्यादृष्टिसासादनमिश्राविरतसम्यग्दृष्टिसंज्ञगुणस्थानचतुष्टये भवति । इति चारित्रव्याख्यानं समाप्तम् ॥

एवं व्रतसमितिगुप्तिधर्मद्वादशानुप्रेक्षापरीषहजयचारित्राणां भावसंवरकारणभूतानां यद्व्याख्यानं कृतं, तत्र निश्चयरत्नत्रयसाधकव्यवहाररत्नत्रयरूपस्य शुभोपयोगस्य प्रतिपादकानि यानि वाक्यानि तानि पापास्रवसंवरकारणानि ज्ञातव्यानि । यानि तु व्यवहाररत्नत्रयसाध्यस्य शुद्धोपयोगलक्षण-

निश्चयरत्नत्रयस्य प्रतिपादकानि तानि पुण्यपापद्वयसंवरकारणानि भवन्तीति ज्ञातव्यम् । अत्राह सोमनामराजश्रेष्ठी । भगवन्नेतेषु व्रतादिसंवरकारणेषु मध्ये संवरानुप्रेक्षैव सारभूता, सा चैव संवरं करिष्यति किं विशेषप्रपञ्चेनेति । भगवानाह—त्रिगुप्तिलक्षणनिर्विकल्पसमाधिस्थानां यतीनां तथैव पूर्यते तत्रा-समर्थानां पुनर्बहुप्रकारेण संवरप्रतिभूतो मोहो विजृम्भते तेन कारणेन व्रतादि-विस्तरं कथयन्त्याचार्याः ॥३५॥ "असिदिसदं किरियाणं अक्किरियाणं तु होइ चुलसीदी । सत्तठ्ठी अण्णाणी वेणइया हुंति वत्तीसा । जोगा पयडिप-देसा ठिदिअणुभागा कसायदो हुंति । अपरिणिदुच्छिन्नेसु यबंधठ्ठिदिकारणं नत्थि ।" एवं संवरतत्त्वव्याख्याने सूत्रद्वयेन तृतीयं स्थलं गतम् ॥

अथ सम्यग्दृष्टिजीवस्य संवरपूर्वकं निर्जरातत्त्वं कथयति ।

व्याख्या । 'णेया' इत्यादिव्याख्यानं क्रियेत—"णेया" ज्ञातव्या का "णिज्जरा" भावनिर्जरा । सा का निर्विकारपरमचैतन्यचिच्चमत्कारानुभूतिसञ्जा-तसहजानन्दस्वभावसुखामृतरसास्वादरूपो भाव इत्यध्याहारः । "जेण भावेण" येन भावेन जीवपरिणामेन किं भवति "सडदि" विशीर्यते पतति गलति विनश्यति किं कर्तृ "कम्मपुग्गलं" कर्मारिविध्वंसकस्वकीयशुद्धात्मनो विल-क्षणं कर्मपुद्गलद्रव्यं कथंभूतं "भुत्तरसं" स्वोदयकालं प्राप्य सांसारिकसुख-दुःखरूपेण भुक्तरसं दत्तफलं केन कारणभूतेन गलति "जह कालेण" स्वकाल-पच्यमानाम्रफलवत्सविपाकनिर्जरापेक्षया, अभ्यन्तरे निजशुद्धात्मसंवित्तिपरि-णामस्य बहिरङ्गसहकारिकारणभूतेन काललब्धिसंज्ञेन यथाकालेन न केवलं यथाकालेन "तवेण य" अकालपच्यमानानामाम्रादिफलवदविपाकनिर्जरापेक्षया अभ्यन्तरेण समस्तपरद्रव्येच्छानिरोधलक्षणेन बहिरङ्गेणान्तस्तत्त्वसंवित्तिसाधक-संभूतेनानशनादिद्वादशविधेन तपसा चेति "तस्सडणं" कर्म्मणो गलनं यच्च सा द्रव्यनिर्जरा । ननु पूर्वं यदुक्तं 'सडदि' तेनैव द्रव्यनिर्जरा लब्धा पुनरपि सडनं किमर्थं भणितम् ? तत्रोत्तरं—तेन सडदिशब्देन निर्मलात्मानुभूतिग्रहणभाव-निर्जराभिधानपरिणामस्य सामर्थ्यमुक्तं न च द्रव्यनिर्जरेति । "इदि" इति द्रव्यभावरूपेण निर्ज्जरा द्विविधा भवति ॥

अत्राह शिष्यः—सविपाकनिर्जरा नरकादिगतिष्वज्ञानिनामपि दृश्यते सज्ञानिनामेवेति नियमो नास्ति । तत्रोत्तरं—अत्रैव मोक्षकारणं या संवर-

पूर्विका निर्जरा सैव ग्राह्या । या पुनरज्ञानिनां निर्जरा सा गजस्नानवन्निष्फला । यतः स्तोकं कर्म निर्जरयति बहुतरं बध्नाति तेन कारणेन सा न ग्राह्या । यातु सरागसद्दृष्टीनां निर्जरा सा यद्यप्यशुभकर्मविनाशं करोति तथापि संसारस्थितिं स्तोकां कुरुते । तद्भवे तीर्थकरप्रकृत्यादिविशिष्टपुण्यबन्धकारणं भवति पारम्पर्येण मुक्तिकारणं चेति । वीतरागसद्दृष्टीनां पुनः पुण्यपापद्वयविनाशे तद्भवेऽपि मुक्तिकारणमिति । उक्तं च श्रीकुन्दकुन्दाचार्यदेवैः "जं अण्णाणी कम्मं खवेदि भवसदसहस्सकोडीहिं । तं णाणी तिहिं गुत्तो खवेदि उस्सासमित्तेण ।" कश्चिदाह— सद्दृष्टीनां वीतरागविशेषणं किमर्थं रागादयो हेया मदीया न भवन्तीति भेदविज्ञाने जाते सति रागानुभवेऽपि ज्ञानमात्रेण मोक्षो भवतीति । तत्र परिहारः । अन्धकारे पुरुषद्वयम् एकः प्रदीपहस्तस्तिष्ठति । अन्यः पुनरेकः प्रदीपरहितस्तिष्ठति । स च कूपे पतनं सर्पादिकं वा न जानाति तस्य विनाशे दोषो नास्ति । यस्तु प्रदीपहस्तस्तस्य कूपपतनादिविनाशे प्रदीपफलं नास्ति । यस्तु कूपपतनादिकं त्यजति तस्य प्रदीपफलमस्ति । तथा कोऽपि रागादयो हेया मदीया न भवन्तीति भेदविज्ञानं न जानाति स कर्मणा बध्यते तावत्, अन्यः कोऽपि रागादिभेदविज्ञाने जातेऽपि यावतांशेन रागादिकमनुभवति तावतांशेन सोऽपि बध्यत एव, तस्यापि रागादिभेदविज्ञानफलं नास्ति । यस्तु रागादिभेदविज्ञाने जाते सति रागादिकं त्यजति तस्य भेदविज्ञानफलमस्तीति ज्ञातव्यम् । तथा चोक्तं—"चक्खुस्स दंसणस्स य सारो सप्पादिदोसपरिहारो । चक्खू होदि णिरत्थं दट्ठूण विलेपडंतस्स" ॥ ३६ ॥ एवं निर्जराव्याख्याने सूत्रेणैकेन चतुर्थस्थलं गतम् ॥

अथ मोक्षतत्त्वमावेदयति ।

व्याख्या । यद्यपि सामान्येन निरवशेषनिराकृतकर्ममलकलङ्कस्याशरीरस्यात्मन आत्यन्तिकस्वाभाविकाचिन्त्याद्भुतानुपमसकलविमलकेवलज्ञानाद्यनन्तगुणास्पदमवस्थान्तरं मोक्षो भण्यते तथापि विशेषेण भावद्रव्यरूपेण द्विधा भवतीति वार्त्तिकम् । तद्यथा—"णेओ स भावमोक्खो" णेयो ज्ञातव्यः स भावमोक्षः । स कः "अप्पणो हु परिणामो" निश्चयरत्नत्रयात्मककारणसमयसाररूपो "हु" स्फुटमात्मनः परिणामः । कथंभूतः "सव्वस्स कम्मणो जो खयहेदू" सर्वस्य द्रव्यभावरूपमोहनीयादिघातिचतुष्टयकर्मणो यः क्षयहेतुरिति । द्रव्यमोक्षं

कथयति । "दव्वविमोक्खो" अयोगिचरमसमये द्रव्यविमोक्षो भवति कोऽसौ "कम्मपुधभावो" टङ्कोत्कीर्णशुद्धबुद्धैकस्वभावपरमात्मन आयुरादिशेषाघातिकर्मणामपि य आत्यन्तिकपृथग्भावो विश्लेषो विघटनमिति ॥

तस्य मुक्तात्मनः सुखं कथ्यते । "आत्मोपादानसिद्धं स्वयमतिशयवद्वीतबाधं विशालं वृद्धिह्रासव्यपेतं विषयविरहितं निष्प्रतिद्वन्द्वभावम् । अन्यद्द्रव्यानपेक्षं निरुपममभितं शाश्वतं सर्वकालमुत्कृष्टानन्तसारं परमसुखमतस्तस्य सिद्धस्य जातम् ।" कश्चिदाह—इन्द्रियसुखमेव सुखं मुक्तात्मनामिन्द्रियशरीराभावे पूर्वोक्तमतीन्द्रियसुखं कथं घटत इति । तत्रोत्तरं दीयते—सांसारिकसुखं तावत् स्त्रीसेवादिपञ्चेन्द्रियविषयप्रभवमेव, यत्पुनः पञ्चेन्द्रिय विषयव्यापाररहितानां निर्व्याकुलचित्तानां पुरुषाणां सुखं तदतीन्द्रियसुखमत्रैव दृश्यते । पञ्चेन्द्रियमनोजनितविकल्पजालरहितानां निर्विकल्पसमाधिस्थानां परमयोगिनां रागादिरहितत्वेन स्वसंवेद्यमात्मसुखं तद्विशेषेणातीन्द्रियम् । यच्च भावकर्मद्रव्यकर्मरहितानां सर्वप्रदेशाह्लादैकपारमार्थिकपरमानन्दपरिणतानां मुक्तात्मनामतीन्द्रियसुखं तदत्यन्तविशेषेण ज्ञातव्यम् । अत्राह शिष्यः—संसारिणां निरन्तरं कर्मबन्धोऽस्ति, तथैवोदयोऽप्यस्ति, शुद्धात्मभावनाप्रस्तावो नास्ति, कथं मोक्षो भवतीति ? तत्र प्रत्युत्तरं । यथा शत्रोः क्षीणावस्थां दृष्ट्वा कोऽपि धीमान् पर्यालोचयत्ययं मम हनने प्रस्तावस्ततः पौरुषं कृत्वा शत्रुं हन्ति तथा कर्मणामप्येकरूपावस्था नास्ति ह्रीयमानस्थित्यनुभागत्वेन कृत्वा यदा लघुत्वं क्षीणत्वं भवति तदा धीमान् भव्य आगमभाषया "खयउवसमियविसोही देसणपाउग्गकरणलद्धी य । चत्तारि वि सामण्णाकरणं सम्मत्तचारित्ते ।" इति गाथाकथितलब्धिपञ्चकसंज्ञेनाध्यात्मभाषया निजशुद्धात्माभिमुखपरिणामसंज्ञेन च निर्मलभावनाविशेषखड्गेन पौरुषं कृत्वा कर्मशत्रुं हन्तीति । यत्पुनरन्तः कोटाकोटीप्रमितकर्मस्थितिरूपेण तथैव लतादारुस्थानीयानुभागरूपेण च कर्मलघुत्वे जातेऽपि सत्ययं जीव आगमभाषया अधःप्रवृत्तिकरणापूर्वकरणानिवृत्तिकरणसंज्ञामध्यात्मभाषया स्वशुद्धात्माभिमुखपरिणतिरूपां कर्महननबुद्धिं कृत्वा कापि कालेन करिष्यतीति तद्भव्यत्वगुणस्यैव लक्षणं ज्ञातव्यमिति । अन्यदपि दृष्टान्तनवकं मोक्षविषये ज्ञातव्यम्—"रयणदीवदिणयरदहिउ, दुद्धउ धाउपाहाणु । सुण्णुरुप्पफलिहउ अगणि, णव दिट्ठंता जाणि ।" नन्वनादिकाले मोक्षं गच्छतां जीवानां

जगच्छून्यं भविष्यतीति ? तत्र परिहारः यथा—भाविकालसमयानां क्रमेण गच्छतां यद्यपि भाविकालसमयराशेः स्तोकत्वं भवति तथाप्यवसानं नास्ति। तथा मुक्तिं गच्छतां जीवानां यद्यपि जीवराशेः स्तोकत्वं भवति तथाप्यवसानं नास्ति। इति चेत्तर्हि पूर्वकाले बहवोऽपि जीवा मोक्षं गता इदानीं जगतः शून्यत्वं न दृश्यते। किञ्चाभव्यानामभव्यसमानभव्यानां च मोक्षो नास्ति कथं शून्यत्वं किं भविष्यतीति ॥ ३७ ॥ एवं संक्षेपेण मोक्षतत्त्वव्याख्यानेनैकसूत्रेण पञ्चमं स्थलं गतम्।

अत ऊर्ध्वं षष्ठस्थले गाथापूर्वार्धेन पुण्यपापपदार्थद्वयस्वरूपमुत्तरार्धेन च पुण्यपापप्रकृतिसंख्यां कथयामीत्यभिप्रायं मनसि धृत्वा भगवान् सूत्रमिदं प्रतिपादयति।

व्याख्या। "पुण्णं पावं हवंति खलु जीवा" चिदानन्दैकसहजशुद्धस्वभावत्वेन पुण्यपापबन्धमोक्षादिपर्यायरूपविकल्परहिता अपि सन्तानागतानादिकर्मबन्धपर्यायेण पुण्यं पापं च भवन्ति खलु स्फुटं जीवाः। कथंभूताः सन्तः "सुहअसुहभावजुत्ता" "उद्वम मिथ्यात्वविषं भावय दृष्टिं च कुरु परां भक्तिम्। भाव नमस्काररतो ज्ञाने युक्तो भव सदापि। पञ्चमहाव्रतरक्षां कोपचतुष्कस्य निग्रहं परमम्। दुर्दान्तेन्द्रियविजयं तपःसिद्धिविधौ कुरूद्योगम्।" इत्यार्याद्वयकथितलक्षणेन शुभोपयोगभावेन परिणामेन तद्विलक्षणेनाशुभोपयोगपरिणामेन च युक्ताः परिणताः। इदानीं पुण्यपापभेदान् कथयति "सादं सुहाउ णामं गोदं पुण्णं" सद्वेद्यशुभायुर्नामगोत्राणि पुण्यं भवति "पराणि पावं च" तस्मादपराणि कर्माणि पापं चेति। तद्यथा—सद्वेद्यमेकं, तिर्यग्मनुष्यदेवायुस्त्रयं, सुभगयशःकीर्त्तितीर्थकरत्वादिनामप्रकृतीनां सप्तत्रिंशत्, तथोच्चैर्गोत्रमिति समुदायेन द्विचत्वारिंशत्संख्याः पुण्यप्रकृतयो विज्ञेयाः। शेषा द्व्यशीतिपापमिति। तत्र "दर्शनविशुद्धिर्विनयसंपन्नता शीलव्रतेष्वनतिचारोऽभीक्ष्णज्ञानोपयोगसंवेगौ शक्तितस्त्यागतपसी साधुसमाधिर्वैयावृत्त्यकरणमर्हदाचार्यबहुश्रुतप्रवचनभक्तिरावश्यकापरिहाणिर्मार्गप्रभावना प्रवचनवत्सलत्वमिति तीर्थकरत्वस्य" इत्युक्तलक्षणषोडशभावनोत्पन्नतीर्थकरनामकर्मैवं त्रिशिष्टं पुण्यम्। षोडशभावनासु मध्ये परमागमभाषया "मूढत्रयं मदाश्चाष्टौ तथानायतनानि षट्। अष्टौ शङ्कादयश्चेति दृग्दोषाः पञ्चविंशतिः।"

इति श्लोककथितपञ्चविंशतिमलरहिता तथाध्यात्मभाषया निजशुद्धात्मोपादेयरुचिरूपा सम्यक्त्वभावनैव मुख्येति विज्ञेयम् । सम्यग्दृष्टेर्जीवस्य पुण्यपापद्वयमपि हेयम् । कथं पुण्यं करोतीति ? तत्र युक्तिमाह । यथा कोऽपि देशान्तरस्थमनोहरस्त्रीसमीपादागतपुरुषाणां तदर्थं दानसन्मानादिकं करोति तथा सम्यग्दृष्टिरप्युपादेयरूपेण स्वशुद्धात्मानमेव भावयति चारित्रमोहोदयात्तत्रासमर्थः सन् निर्दोषपरमात्मस्वरूपाणामर्हत्सिद्धानां तदाराधकाचार्योपाध्यायसाधूनां च परमात्मपदप्राप्त्यर्थं विषयकषायवञ्चनार्थं च दानपूजादिना गुणस्तवनादिना वा परमभक्तिं करोति तेन भोगाकाङ्क्षादिनिदानरहितपरिणामेन कुटुम्बिनां पलालमिव अनीहितवृत्त्या विशिष्टपुण्यमास्रवति तेन च स्वर्गे देवेन्द्रलोकान्तिकादिवीभूतिं प्राप्य विमानपरीवारादिसंपदं जीर्णतृणमिव गणयन् पञ्चमहाविदेहेषु गत्वा पश्यति । किं पश्यतीति चेत्—तदिदं समवसरणं, त एते वीतरागसर्वज्ञाः, त एते भेदाभेदरत्नत्रयाराधका गणधरदेवादयो ये पूर्वं श्रूयन्ते त इदानीं प्रत्यक्षेण दृष्टा इति मत्वा विशेषेण दृढधर्ममतिर्भूत्वा चतुर्थगुणस्थानयोग्यामात्मनो विरतावस्थामपरित्यजन् भोगानुभवेऽपि सति धर्मध्यानेन कालं नीत्वा स्वर्गादागत्य तीर्थकरादिपदे प्राप्तेऽपि पूर्वभवभावितविशिष्टभेदज्ञानवासनाबलेन मोहं न करोति ततो जिनदीक्षां गृहीत्वा पुण्यपापरहितनिजपरमात्मध्यानेन मोक्षं गच्छतीति । मिथ्यादृष्टिस्तु तीव्रनिदानबन्धपुण्येन भोगं प्राप्य पश्चादर्द्धचक्रवर्तिरावणादिवन्नरकं गच्छतीति । एवमुक्तलक्षणपुण्यपापपदार्थद्वयेन सह पूर्वोक्तानि सप्ततत्त्वान्येव नव पदार्था भवन्तीति ज्ञातव्यम् ।

इति श्रीनेमिचन्द्रसैद्धान्तिकदेवविरचिते द्रव्यसङ्ग्रहग्रन्थे "आसवबंधण" इत्याद्येका सूत्रगाथा तदनन्तरं गाथादशकेन स्थलषट्कंचेति समुदायेनैकादशसूत्रैः सप्ततत्त्वनवपदार्थप्रतिपादकनामा द्वितीयाधिकारः समाप्तः ॥ २ ॥

अत ऊर्ध्वं विंशतिगाथापर्यन्तं मोक्षमार्गं कथयति । तत्रादौ "सम्मद्दंसण" इत्याद्यष्टगाथाभिर्निश्चयमोक्षमार्गव्यवहारमोक्षमार्गं प्रतिपादकमुख्यत्वेन प्रथमोऽन्तराधिकारस्ततः परम् "दुविहं पि मोक्खहेउं" इति प्रभृतिद्वादशसूत्रैर्ध्यातृध्येयध्यानफलकथनमुख्यत्वेन द्वितीयोन्तराधिकारः ! तृतीयाधिकारे समुदायेन पातनिका ।

अथ प्रथमतः सूत्रपूर्वार्धेन व्यवहारमोक्षमार्गमुत्तरार्धेन च निश्चयमोक्षमार्गं निरूपयति ।

व्याख्या । "सम्मद्दंसणणाणं चरणं मोक्खस्स कारणं जाणे ववहारा" सम्यग्दर्शनज्ञानचारित्रत्रयं मोक्षस्य कारणं हे शिष्य जानीहि व्यवहारनयात् । "णिच्चयदो तत्तियमइओ णिओ अप्पा" निश्चयतस्तत्त्रितयमयो निजात्मेति । तथा हि—वीतरागसर्वज्ञप्रणीतषड्द्रव्यपञ्चास्तिकायसप्ततत्त्वनवपदार्थसम्यक्श्रद्धानज्ञानव्रताद्यनुष्ठानविकल्परूपो व्यवहारमोक्षमार्गः । निजनिरञ्जनशुद्धात्मतत्त्वसम्यक्श्रद्धानज्ञानानुचरणैकाग्र्यपरिणतिरूपो निश्चयमोक्षमार्गः । अथवा धातुपाषाणेऽग्निवत्साधको व्यवहारमोक्षमार्गः, सुवर्णस्थानीयनिर्विकारस्वोपलब्धिसाध्यरूपो निश्चयमोक्षमार्गः । एवं संक्षेपेण व्यवहारनिश्चयमोक्षमार्गलक्षणं ज्ञातव्यमिति । ३९ ।

अथाभेदेन सम्यग्दर्शनज्ञानचारित्राणि स्वशुद्धात्मैव तेन कारणेन निश्चयेनात्मैव निश्चयमोक्षमार्ग इत्याख्याति । अथवा पूर्वोक्तमेव निश्चयमोक्षमार्गं प्रकारान्तरेण दृढयति ।

व्याख्या । "रयणत्तयं ण वट्टइ अप्पाणं मुयतु अण्णदवियम्हि" रत्नत्रयं न वर्त्तते स्वकीयशुद्धात्मानं मुक्त्वा अन्याचेतने द्रव्ये । "तम्हा तत्तियमइओ होदि हु मोक्खस्स कारणं आदा" तस्मात्तत्त्रितयमयआत्मैव निश्चयेन मोक्षस्य कारणं भवतीति जानीहि । अथ विस्तारः—रागादिविकल्पोपाधिरहितचिच्चमत्कारभावनोत्पन्नमधुररसास्वादसुखोऽहमिति । निश्चयरूपं सम्यग्दर्शनं तस्यैव सुखस्य समस्तविभावेभ्यः स्वसंवेदनज्ञानेन पृथक् परिच्छेदनं सम्यग्ज्ञानं, तथैव दृष्टश्रुतानुभूतभोगाकाङ्क्षाप्रभृतिसमस्तापध्यानरूपमनोरथजनितसंकल्पविकल्पजालत्यागेन तत्रैव सुखे रतस्य सन्तुष्टस्य तृप्तस्यैकाकारपरमसमरसीभावेन द्रवीभूतचित्तस्य पुनः पुनः स्थिरीकरणं सम्यक्चारित्रकम् । इत्युक्तलक्षणं निश्चयरत्नत्रयं शुद्धात्मानं विहायान्यत्रघटपटादिबहिर्द्रव्ये न वर्त्तते यतस्ततः कारणादभेदेन येनानेकद्रव्यात्मकैकप्रपानकवत्तदेव सम्यग्दर्शनं, तदेव सम्यग्ज्ञानं, तदेव चारित्रं तदेव स्वात्मतत्त्वमित्युक्तलक्षणं निजशुद्धात्मानमेव मुक्तिकारणं जानीहि ॥ ४० ॥

एवं प्रथमस्थले सूत्रद्वयेन निश्चयव्यवहारमोक्षमार्गस्वरूपं संक्षेपेण

व्याख्याय तदनन्तरं द्वितीयस्थले गाथाषट्कपर्यन्तं सम्यक्त्वादित्रयं क्रमेण विवृणोति । तत्रादौ सम्यक्त्वमाह ।

व्याख्या। "जीवादीसद्दहणं सम्मत्तं" वीतरागसर्वज्ञप्रणीतशुद्धजीवादितत्त्वविषये चलमलिनावगाढरहितत्वेन श्रद्धानं रुचिर्निश्चय इदमेवेत्थमेवेति निश्चयबुद्धिः सम्यग्दर्शनम् । "रूवमप्पणो तं तु" तच्चाभेदनयेन रूपं स्वरूपं तु पुनः कस्यात्मन आत्मपरिणाम इत्यर्थः । तस्य सामर्थ्यमाहात्म्यं दर्शयति । "दुरभिणिवेसविमुक्कं णाणं सम्मं खु होदि सदि जम्हि" यस्मिन् सम्यक्त्वे सति ज्ञानं सम्यग् भवति स्फुटं कथम्भूतं सम्यग्भवति "दुरभिणिवेसविमुक्कं" चलितप्रतिपत्तिगच्छत्तृणस्पर्शशुक्तिकाशकलरजतविज्ञानसदृशं संशयविभ्रमविमोहैर्मुक्तं रहितमित्यर्थः ।

इतो विस्तारः—सम्यक्त्वे सति ज्ञानं सम्यग्भवतीति यदुक्तं तस्य विवरणं क्रियते । तथाहि—गौतमाग्निभूतिवायुभूतिनामानो विप्राः पञ्चपञ्चशतब्राह्मणोपाध्याया वेदचतुष्टयं, ज्योतिष्कव्याकरणादिषडङ्गानि, मनुस्मृत्याद्यष्टादशस्मृतिशास्त्राणि तथा भारताद्यष्टादशपुराणानि मीमांसान्यायविस्तर इत्यादिलौकिकसर्वशास्त्राणि यद्यपि जानन्ति तथापि तेषां हि ज्ञानं सम्यक्त्वं विना मिथ्याज्ञानमेव । यदा पुनः प्रसिद्धकथान्यायेन श्रीवीरवर्द्धमानस्वामितीर्थकरपरमदेवसमवसरणे मानस्तम्भावलोकनमात्रादेवागमभाषया दर्शनचारित्रमोहनीयोपशमक्षयसंज्ञेनाध्यात्मभाषया स्वशुद्धात्माभिमुखपरिणामसंज्ञेन च कालादिलब्धिविशेषेण मिथ्यात्वं विलयं गतं तदा तदेव मिथ्याज्ञानं सम्यग्ज्ञानं जातम् । ततश्च "जयति भगवान्" इत्यादि नमस्कारं कृत्वा जिनदीक्षां गृहीत्वा कचलोचानन्तरमेव चतुर्ज्ञानसप्तर्द्धिसम्पन्नास्त्रयोऽपि गणधरदेवाः संजाताः । गौतमस्वामी भव्योपकारार्थं द्वादशाङ्गश्रुतरचनां कृतवान् । पश्चान्निश्चयरत्नत्रयभावनाबलेन त्रयोऽपि मोक्षं गताः । शेषाः पञ्चदशशतप्रमितब्राह्मणा जिनदीक्षां गृहीत्वा यथासम्भवं स्वर्गं मोक्षं च गताः । अभव्यसेनः पुनरेकादशाङ्गधारकोऽपि सम्यक्त्वं विना मिथ्याज्ञानी सञ्जात इति । एवं सम्यक्त्वमाहात्म्येन ज्ञानतपश्चरणव्रतोपशमध्यानादिकं मिथ्यारूपमपि सम्यग्भवति । तदभावे विषयुक्तदुग्धमिव सर्वं वृथेति ज्ञातव्यम् ।

१०

तच्च सम्यक्त्वं पञ्चविंशतिमलरहितं भवति । तद्यथा—देवतामूढलोकमूढ-समयमूढभेदेन मूढत्रयं भवति । तत्र क्षुधाद्यष्टादशदोषरहितमनन्तज्ञानाद्यनन्त-गुणसहितं वीतरागसर्वज्ञदेवतास्वरूपमजानन् ख्यातिपूजालाभरूपलावण्यसौभाग्यपुत्रकलत्रराज्यादिविभूतिनिमित्तं रागद्वेषोपहतार्त्तरौद्रपरिणतक्षेत्रपालचण्डिकादिमिथ्यादेवानां यदाराधनं करोति जीवस्तद्देवतामूढत्वं भण्यते । न च ते देवाः किमपि फलं प्रयच्छन्ति । कथमिति चेत् ? रावणेन रामस्वामिलक्ष्मीधरविनाशार्थं बहुरूपिणी विद्या साधिता, कौरवैस्तु पाण्डवनिर्मूलनार्थं कात्यायनी विद्या साधिता, कंसेन च नारायणविनाशार्थं बह्व्योऽपि विद्याः समाराधिता-स्ताभिः कृतं न किमपि रामस्वामिपाण्डवनारायणानाम् । तैस्तु यद्यपि मिथ्या-देवता नानुकूलितास्तथापि निर्मलसम्यक्त्वोपार्जितेन पूर्वकृतपुण्येन सर्वं निर्विघ्नं जातमिति । अथ लोकमूढत्वं कथयति । गङ्गादिनदीतीर्थस्नानसमुद्रस्नानप्रातः-स्नानजलप्रवेशमरणाग्निप्रवेशमरणगोग्रहणादिमरणभूम्यग्निवटवृक्षपूजादीनि पुण्य-कारणानि भवन्तीति यद्वदन्ति तल्लोकमूढत्वं विज्ञेयम् । अथ समयमूढत्वमाह । अज्ञानिजनचित्तचमत्कारोत्पादकं ज्योतिष्कमन्त्रवादादिकं दृष्ट्वा वीतरागसर्वज्ञप्रणीतसमयं विहाय कुदेवागमलिङ्गिनां भयाशास्नेहलोभैर्धर्मार्थं प्रणामविनयपूजा-पुरस्कारादिकरणं समयमूढत्वमिति । एवमुक्तलक्षणं मूढत्रयं सरागसम्यग्दृष्ट्य-वस्थायां परिहरणीयमिति । त्रिगुप्तावस्थालक्षणवीतरागसम्यक्त्वप्रस्तावे पुनर्निजनिरञ्जननिर्दोषपरमात्मैव देव इति निश्चयबुद्धिर्देवतामूढरहितत्वं विज्ञेयम् । तथैव मिथ्यात्वरागादिरूपमूढभावत्यागेन स्वशुद्धात्मन्येवावस्थानं लोकमूढर-हितत्वं विज्ञेयम् । तथैव च समस्तशुभाशुभसङ्कल्पविकल्परूपपरभावत्यागेन निर्विकारतात्त्विकपरमानन्दैकलक्षणपरमसमरसीभावेन तस्मिन्नेव सम्यग्रूपेणायनं गमनं परिणमनं समयमूढरहितत्वं बोद्धव्यम् । इति मूढत्रयं व्याख्यातम् ।

अथ मदाष्टस्वरूपं कथ्यते । विज्ञानैश्वर्यज्ञानतपःकुलजातिरूपसंज्ञं मदाष्टकं सरागसम्यग्दृष्टिभिस्त्याज्यमिति । वीतरागसम्यग्दृष्टीनां पुनर्मानकषायादुत्पन्न-मदमात्सर्यादिसमस्तविकल्पजालपरिहारेण ममकाराहङ्काररहिते शुद्धात्मनि भावनैव मदाष्टकत्याग इति । ममकाराहङ्कारलक्षणं कथयति । कर्मजनितदेहपुत्रकलत्रादौ ममेदमिति ममकारस्तत्रैवाभेदेन गौरस्थूलादिदेहोऽहं राजाहमित्य-हङ्कारलक्षणमिति ।

अथानायतनषट्कं कथयति । मिथ्यादेवो, मिथ्यादेवाराधका, मिथ्यातपो, मिथ्यातपस्वी, मिथ्यागमो, मिथ्यागमधरा पुरुषाश्चेत्युक्तलक्षणमनायतनषट्कं सरागसम्यग्दृष्टीनां त्याज्यं भवतीति । वीतरागसम्यग्दृष्टीनां पुनः समस्तदोषायतनभूतानां मिथ्यात्वविषयकषायरूपायतनानां परिहारेण केवलज्ञानाद्यनन्तगुणायतनभूते स्वशुद्धात्मनि निवास एवानायतनसेवापरिहार इति । अनायतनशब्दस्यार्थः कथ्यते । सम्यक्त्वादिगुणानामायतनं गृहमावास आश्रय आधारकरणं निमित्तमायतनं भण्यते तद्विपक्षभूतमनायतनमिति ।

अतः परं शङ्काद्यष्टमलत्यागं कथयति । निःशङ्काद्यष्टगुणप्रतिपालनमेव शङ्काद्यष्टमलत्यागो भण्यते । तद्यथा—रागादिदोषा अज्ञानं वाऽसत्यवचनकारणं तदुभयमपि वीतरागसर्वज्ञानां नास्ति ततः कारणात्तत्प्रणीते हेयोपादेयतत्त्वे मोक्षे मोक्षमार्गे च भव्यैः संशयः सन्देहो न कर्त्तव्यः । तत्र शङ्कादिदोषपरिहारविषये पुनरञ्जनचौरकथा प्रसिद्धा । तत्रैव विभीषणकथा । तथाहि—सीताहरणप्रघट्टके रावणस्य रामलक्ष्मणाभ्यां सह सङ्ग्रामप्रस्तावे विभीषणेन विचारितं रामस्तावदष्टमबलदेवो लक्ष्मणश्चाष्टमो वासुदेवो रावणश्चाष्टमः प्रतिवासुदेव इति । तस्य च प्रतिवासुदेवस्य वासुदेवहस्तेन मरणमिति जैनागमे पठितमास्ते तन्मिथ्या न भवतीति निःशङ्को भूत्वा त्रैलोक्यकण्टकं रावणं स्वकीयज्येष्ठभ्रातरं त्यक्त्वा त्रिंशदक्षौहिणीप्रमितचतुरङ्गबलेन सह स रामस्वामिपार्श्वे गत इति । तथैव देवकीवसुदेवद्वयं निःशङ्कं ज्ञातव्यम् । तथाहि—यदा देवकीबालकस्य मारणनिमित्तं कंसेन प्रार्थना कृता तदा ताभ्यां पर्यालोचितं मदीयः पुत्रो नवमो वासुदेवो भविष्यति तस्य हस्तेन जरासिन्धुनाम्नो नवमप्रतिवासुदेवस्य कंसस्यापि मरणं भविष्यतीति जैनागमे भणितं तिष्ठतीति, तथैवातिमुक्तभट्टारकैरपि कथितमिति निश्चित्य कंसाय स्वकीयं बालकं दत्तम् । तथा शेषभव्यैरपि जिनागमे शङ्का न कर्त्तव्येति । इदं व्यवहारेण सम्यक्त्वस्य व्याख्यानम् । निश्चयेन पुनस्तस्यैव व्यवहारनिःशङ्कागुणस्य सहकारित्वेनेहलोकात्राणागुप्तिमरणव्याधिवेदनाकस्मिकाभिधानभयसप्तकं मुक्त्वा घोरोपसर्गपरीषहप्रस्तावेऽपि शुद्धोपयोगलक्षणनिश्चयरत्नत्रयभावनैव निःशङ्कगुणो ज्ञातव्य इति ।

अथ निष्काङ्क्षितागुणं कथयति। इहलोकपरलोकाशारूपभोगाकाङ्क्षानिदानत्यागेन केवलज्ञानाद्यनन्तगुणव्यक्तिरूपमोक्षार्थं ज्ञानपूजातपश्चरणाद्यनुष्ठान-

करणं निष्काङ्क्षागुणो भण्यते । तथानन्तमतीकन्याकथा प्रसिद्धा । द्वितीया च सीतामहादेवीकथा । सा कथ्यते । सीता यदा लोकापवादपरिहारार्थं दिव्ये शुद्धा जाता तदा रामस्वामिना दत्तं पट्टमहादेवीविभूतिपदं त्यक्त्वा सकलभूषणानगारकेवलिपादमूले कृतान्तवक्रादिराजभिस्तथा बहुराज्ञीभिश्च सह जिनदीक्षां गृहीत्वा शशिप्रभाधार्मिकासमुदायेन सह ग्रामपुरखेटकादिविहारेण भेदाभेदरत्नत्रयभावनया द्विषष्टिवर्षाणि जिनसमयप्रभावनां कृत्वा पश्चादवसाने त्रयस्त्रिंशद्दिवसपर्यन्तं निर्विकारपरमात्मभावनासहितं संन्यासं कृत्वाऽच्युताभिधानषोडशस्वर्गे प्रतीन्द्रतां याता ततश्च निर्मलसम्यक्त्वफलं दृष्ट्वा धर्मानुरागेण नरके रावणलक्ष्मणयोः संबोधनं कृत्वेदानीं स्वर्गे तिष्ठति। अग्रे स्वर्गादागत्य सकलचक्रवर्त्ती भविष्यति । तौ च रावणलक्ष्मीधरौ तस्य पुत्रौ भविष्यतः । ततश्च तीर्थंकरपादमूले पूर्वभवान्तरं दृष्ट्वा पुत्रद्वयेन सह परिवारेण च सह जिनदीक्षां गृहीत्वा भेदाभेदरत्नत्रयभावनया पञ्चानुत्तरविमाने त्रयोऽप्यहमिन्द्रा भविष्यन्ति । तस्मादागत्य रावणस्तीर्थंकरो भविष्यति, सीता च गणधर इति, लक्ष्मीधरो धातकीखण्डद्वीपे तीर्थंकरो भविष्यति । इति व्यवहारनिष्काङ्क्षितागुणो विज्ञातव्यः । निश्चयेन पुनस्तस्यैव व्यवहारनिष्काङ्क्षागुणस्य सहकारित्वेन दृष्टश्रुतानुभूतपञ्चेन्द्रियभोगत्यागेन निश्चयरत्नत्रयभावनोत्पन्नपारमार्थिकस्वात्मोत्थसुखामृतरसे चित्तसन्तोषः स एव निष्काङ्क्षा गुण इति ।

अथ निर्विचिकित्सागुणं कथयति । भेदाभेदरत्नत्रयाराधकभव्यजीवानां दुर्गन्धबीभत्सादिकं दृष्ट्वा धर्मबुद्धया कारुण्यभावेन वा यथायोग्यं विचिकित्सापरिहरणं द्रव्यनिर्विचिकित्सागुणो भण्यते । यत्पुनर्जैनसमये सर्वं समीचीनं परं किन्तु वस्त्रप्रावरणं जलस्नानादिकं च न कुर्वन्ति तदेव दूषणमित्यादिकुत्सितभावस्य विशिष्टविवेकबलेन परिहरणं सा निर्विचिकित्सा भण्यते । अस्य व्यवहारनिर्विचिकित्सागुणस्य विषय उद्दायनमहाराजकथा रुक्मिणीमहादेवीकथा चागमप्रसिद्धा ज्ञातव्येति । निश्चयेन पुनस्तस्यैव व्यवहारनिर्विचिकित्सागुणस्य बलेन समस्तद्वेषादिविकल्परूपकल्लोलमालात्यागेन निर्मलात्मानुभूतिलक्षणे निजशुद्धात्मनि व्यवस्थानं निर्विचिकित्सागुण इति ।

इतः परममूढदृष्टिगुणकथां कथयति । वीतरागसर्वज्ञप्रणीतागमार्थाद्बहिर्भूतैः कुदृष्टिभिर्यत्प्रणीतं धातुवादखन्यवादहरमेखलक्षुद्रविद्याव्यन्तरविकुर्वणादिकमज्ञा-

निजनचित्तचमत्कारोत्पादकं दृष्ट्वा श्रुत्वा च योऽसौ मूढभावेन धर्मबुद्धया तत्र रुचिं भक्तिं न कुरुते स एव व्यवहारेऽमूढदृष्टिरुच्यते। तत्र चोत्तरमथुरायां उदुरुलिभट्टारकरेवतीश्राविकाचन्द्रप्रभनामविद्याधरब्रह्मचारिसम्बन्धिनी कथा प्रसिद्धेति । निश्चयेन पुनस्तस्यैव व्यवहारमूढदृष्टिगुणस्य प्रसादेनान्तस्तत्त्वबहिस्तत्त्वनिश्चये जाते सति समस्तमिथ्यात्वरागादिशुभाशुभसङ्कल्पविकल्पेष्टात्मबुद्धिमुपादेयबुद्धिं हितबुद्धिं ममत्वभावं त्यक्त्वा त्रिगुप्तिरूपेण विशुद्धज्ञानदर्शनस्वभावे निजात्मनि यन्निश्चलावस्थानं तदेवामूढदृष्टित्वमिति। सङ्कल्पविकल्पलक्षणं कथ्यते। पुत्रकलत्रादौ बहिर्द्रव्ये ममेदमितिकल्पना सङ्कल्पः, अभ्यन्तरे सुख्यहं दुःख्यहमिति हर्षविषादकारणं विकल्प इति। अथवा वस्तुवृत्त्या सङ्कल्प इति कोऽर्थो विकल्प इति तस्यैव पर्यायः ॥

अथोपगूहनगुणं कथयति। भेदाभेदरत्नत्रयभावनारूपो मोक्षमार्गः स्वभावेन शुद्ध एव तावत्, तत्राज्ञानिजननिमित्तेन तथैवाशक्तजननिमित्तेन च धर्मस्य पैशून्यं दूषणमपवादो दुष्प्रभावना यदा भवति तदागमाविरोधेन यथाशक्त्यार्थेन धर्मोपदेशेन वा यद्धर्मार्थं दोषस्य झम्पनं निवारणं क्रियते तद्व्यवहारनयेनोपगूहनं भण्यते। तत्र मायाब्रह्मचारिणा पार्श्वभट्टारकप्रतिमालग्नरत्नहरणे कृते सत्युपगूहनविषये जिनदत्तश्रेष्ठिकथा प्रसिद्धेति। अथवा रुद्रजनन्या ज्येष्ठासंज्ञाया लोकापवादे जाते सति यद्दोषझम्पनं कृतं तत्र चेलिनीमहादेवीकथेति। तथैव निश्चयेन पुनस्तस्यैव व्यवहारोपगूहनगुणस्य सहकारित्वेन निजनिरञ्जननिर्दोषपरमात्मनः प्रच्छादका ये मिथ्यात्वरागादिदोषास्तेषां तस्मिन्नेव परमात्मनि सम्यक्श्रद्धानज्ञानानुष्ठानरूपं यद्ध्यानं तेन प्रच्छादनं विनाशनं गोपनं झम्पनं तदेवोपगूहनमिति ॥

अथ स्थितीकरणं कथयति। भेदाभेदरत्नत्रयधारकस्य चातुर्वर्णसङ्घस्य मध्ये यदा कोऽपि दर्शनचारित्रमोहोदयेन दर्शनं ज्ञानं चारित्रं वा परित्यक्तुं वाञ्छति तदागमाविरोधेन यथाशक्त्या धर्मश्रवणेन वा अर्थेन वा सामर्थ्येन वा केनाप्युपायेन यद्धर्मे स्थिरत्वं क्रियते तद्व्यवहारेण स्थितीकरणमिति। तत्र च पुष्पडालतपोधनस्य स्थिरीकरणप्रस्तावे वारिषेणकुमारकथागमप्रसिद्धेति। निश्चयेन पुनस्तेनैव व्यवहारेण स्थितीकरणगुणेन धर्मदृढत्वे जाते सति दर्शनचारित्रमोहोदयजनितसमस्तमिथ्यात्वरागादिविकल्पजालत्यागेन निजपरमात्मस्वभावभावनोत्प-

परमानन्दैकलक्षणसुखामृतरसास्वादेन तन्मयतन्मयपरमसमरसीभावेन चित्त-स्थितीकरणमेव स्थितीकरणमिति ।

अथ वात्सल्याभिधानं सप्तमाङ्गं प्रतिपादयति । बाह्याभ्यन्तररत्नत्रयाधारे चतुर्विधसङ्घे वत्से धेनुवत्पञ्चेन्द्रियविषयनिमित्तं पुत्रकलत्रसुवर्णादिस्नेहवद्वा यदकृत्रिमस्नेहकरणं तद्व्यवहारेण वात्सल्यं भण्यते । तत्र च हस्तिनागपुराधिप-तिपद्मराजसंबन्धिना बलिनामदुष्टमन्त्रिणा निश्चयव्यवहाररत्नत्रयाराधकाकम्प-नाचार्यप्रभृतिसप्तशतयतीनामुपसर्गे क्रियमाणे सति विष्णुकुमारनाम्ना निश्चय-व्यवहारमोक्षमार्गाराधकपरमयतिना विकुर्वणर्द्धिप्रभावेण वामनरूपं कृत्वा बलि-मन्त्रिपार्श्वे पादत्रयप्रमाणभूमिप्रार्थनं कृत्वा पश्चादेकः पादो मेरुमस्तके दत्तो द्वितीयो मानुषोत्तरपर्वते तृतीयपादस्यावकाशो नास्तीति वचनच्छलेन मुनिवा-त्सल्यनिमित्तं बलिमन्त्री बद्ध इत्येका तावदागमप्रसिद्धा कथा । द्वितीया च दशपुरनगराधिपतेर्वज्रकर्णनाम्नः । उज्जयिनीनगराधिपतिना सिंहोदरमहाराजेन जैनोऽयं मम नमस्कारं न करोतीति मत्वा दशपुरनगरं परिवेष्ट्य घोरोपसर्गे क्रियमाणे भेदाभेदरत्नत्रयभावनाप्रियेण रामस्वामिना वज्रकर्णवात्सल्यनिमित्तं सिंहोदरो बद्ध इति रामायणमध्ये प्रसिद्धेयं वात्सल्यकथेति । निश्चयवात्सल्यं पुनस्तस्यैव व्यवहारवात्सल्यगुणस्य सहकारित्वेन धर्मे दृढत्वे जाते सति मिथ्या-त्वरागादिसमस्तशुभाशुभबहिर्भावेषु प्रीतिं त्यक्त्वा रागादिविकल्पोपाधिरहित-परमस्वास्थ्यसंवित्तिसञ्जातसदानन्दैकलक्षणसुखामृतरसास्वादं प्रति प्रीतिकरण-मेवेति सप्तमाङ्गं व्याख्यातम् ॥

अथाष्टमाङ्गं नाम प्रभावनागुणं कथयति । श्रावकेन दानपूजादिना तपोधनेन च तपःश्रुतादिना जैनशासनप्रभावना कर्त्तव्येति व्यवहारेण प्रभावनागुणो ज्ञातव्यः । तत्र पुनरुत्तरमथुरायां जिनसमयप्रभावनशीलायां उरविल्लामहा-देव्याः प्रभावननिमित्तमुपसर्गे जाते सति वज्रकुमारनाम्ना विद्याधरश्रमणेनाकाशे जैनरथभ्रमणेन प्रभावना कृतेत्येका आगमप्रसिद्धा कथा । द्वितीया तु जिनस-मयप्रभावनाशीलवप्रामहादेवीनामस्वकीयजनन्या निमित्तं स्वस्य धर्मानुरागेण च हरिषेणनामदशमचक्रवर्तिना तद्भवमोक्षगामिना जिनसमयप्रभावनार्थमुत्तुङ्ग-तोरणजिनचैत्यालयमण्डितं सर्वभूमितलं कृतमिति रामायणे प्रसिद्धेयं कथा । निश्चयेन पुनस्तस्यैव व्यवहारप्रभावनागुणस्य बलेन मिथ्यात्वविषयकषायप्रभृति-

समस्तविभावपरिणामरूपपरसमयानां प्रभावं हत्वा शुद्धोपयोगलक्षणस्वसंवेदनज्ञानेन विशुद्धज्ञानदर्शनस्वभावनिजशुद्धात्मनः प्रकाशनमनुभवनमेव प्रभावनेति ॥

एवमुक्तप्रकारेण मूढत्रयमदाष्टकषडनायतनशङ्काद्यष्टमलरहितं शुद्धजीवादितत्त्वार्थश्रद्धानलक्षणं सरागसम्यक्त्वाभिधानं व्यवहारसम्यक्त्वं विज्ञेयम् । तथैव तेनैव व्यवहारसम्यक्त्वेन पारम्पर्येण साध्यं शुद्धोपयोगलक्षणनिश्चयरत्नत्रयभावनोत्पन्नपरमाह्लादैकरूपसुखामृतरसास्वादनमेवोपादेयमिन्द्रियसुखादिकं च हेयमिति रुचिरूपं वीतरागचारित्राविनाभूतं वीतरागसम्यक्त्वाभिधानं निश्चयसम्यक्त्वं च ज्ञातव्यमिति । अत्र व्यवहारसम्यक्त्वमध्ये निश्चयसम्यक्त्वं किमर्थं व्याख्यातमिति चेद् व्यवहारसम्यक्त्वेन निश्चयसम्यक्त्वं साध्यत इति साध्यसाधकभावज्ञापनार्थमिति ॥

इदानीं येषां जीवानां सम्यग्दर्शनग्रहणात्पूर्वमायुर्बन्धो नास्ति तेषां व्रताभावेऽपि नरनारकादिकुत्सितस्थानेषु जन्म न भवतीति कथयति । "सम्यग्दर्शनशुद्धा नारकतिर्यङ्नपुंसकस्त्रीत्वानि । दुष्कुलविकृताल्पायुर्दरिद्रतां च व्रजन्ति नाव्रतिकाः । १ ।" इतः परं मनुष्यगतिसमुत्पन्नसम्यग्दृष्टेः प्रभावं कथयति । "ओजस्तेजोविद्यावीर्ययशोवृद्धिविजयविभवसनाथाः । उत्तमकुला महार्था मानवतिलका भवन्ति दर्शनपूताः ॥" अथ देवगतौ पुनः प्रकीर्णकदेववाहनदेवकिल्बिषदेवनीचदेवत्रयं विहायान्येषु महर्द्धिकदेवेषूत्पद्यते सम्यग्दृष्टिः । इदानीं सम्यक्त्वग्रहणात्पूर्वंदेवायुष्कं विहाय ये बद्धायुष्कास्तान् प्रति सम्यक्त्वमाहात्म्यं कथयति । "हेट्ठिमछप्पुढवीणं जोइसवणभवणसव्वइत्थीणं । पुण्णिदरे णहि सम्मो ण सासणो णारयापुण्णे ॥" तमेवार्थं प्रकारान्तरेण कथयति "ज्योतिर्भावनभौमेषु षट्स्वधः श्वभ्रभूमिषु । तिर्यक्षु नृसुरस्त्रीषु सद्दृष्टिर्नैव जायते ॥" अथौपशमिकवेदकक्षायिकाभिधानसम्यक्त्वत्रयमध्ये कस्यां गतौ कस्य सम्यक्त्वस्य सम्भवोऽस्तीति कथयति "सौधर्मादिष्वसंख्याब्दायुष्कतिर्यक्षु नृष्वपि । रत्नप्रभावनौ च स्यात्सम्यक्त्वत्रयमङ्गिनाम् ॥" कर्मभूमिजपुरुषे च त्रयं सम्भवति बद्धायुष्के लब्धायुष्केऽपि । किन्त्वौपशमिकमपर्याप्तावस्थायां महर्द्धिकदेवेष्वेव । "शेषेषु देवतिर्यक्षु षट्स्वधः श्वभ्रभूमिषु । द्वौ वेदकोपश-

मकौ स्यातां पर्याप्तदेहिनाम् ।१।" इति निश्चयव्यवहाररत्नत्रयात्मकमोक्षमार्गावयविनः प्रथमावयवभूतस्य सम्यक्त्वस्य व्याख्यानेन गाथा गता ॥ ४१ ॥

अथ रत्नत्रयात्मकमोक्षमार्गद्वितीयावयवरूपस्य सम्यग्ज्ञानस्य स्वरूपं प्रतिपादयति ।

व्याख्या । "संसयविमोहविब्भमविवज्जियं" संशयः शुद्धात्मतत्त्वादि प्रतिपादकमागमज्ञानं किं वीतरागसर्वज्ञप्रणीतं भविष्यति ? परसमयप्रणीतं वेति संशयः । तत्र दृष्टान्तः—स्थाणुर्वा पुरुषो वेति । विमोहः परस्परसापेक्षनयद्वयेन द्रव्यगुणपर्यायादिपरिज्ञानाभावो विमोहः । तत्र दृष्टान्तः—गच्छत्तृणस्पर्शवद्दिग्मोहवद्वा । विभ्रमोऽनेकान्तात्मकवस्तुनो नित्यक्षणिकैकान्तादिरूपेण ग्रहणं विभ्रमः । तत्र दृष्टान्तः—शुक्तिकायां रजतविज्ञानवत् । इत्युक्तलक्षणसंशयविमोहविभ्रमैर्वर्जितं "अप्पपरसरूवस्स गहणं" सहजशुद्धकेवलज्ञानदर्शनस्वभावस्वात्मरूपस्य ग्रहणं परिच्छेदनं परिच्छित्तिस्तथा परद्रव्यस्य च भावकर्मद्रव्यकर्मनोकर्मरूपस्य जीवसम्बन्धिनस्तथैव पुद्गलादिपञ्चद्रव्यरूपस्य परकीयजीवरूपस्य च परिच्छेदनं यत्तत् "सम्मंणाणं" सम्यग्ज्ञानं भवति । तच्च कथंभूतं "सायारं" घटोऽयं पटोऽयमित्यादिग्रहणव्यापाररूपेण साकारं सविकल्पं व्यवसायात्मकं निश्चयात्मकमित्यर्थः । पुनश्च किंविशिष्टं "अणेयभेयं च" अनेकभेदं च पुनरिति ॥

तस्य भेदाः कथ्यन्ते । मतिश्रुतावधिमनःपर्ययकेवलज्ञानभेदेन पञ्चधा । अथवा श्रुतज्ञानाऽपेक्षया द्वादशाङ्गमङ्गबाह्यं चेति द्विभेदम् । द्वादशाङ्गानां नामानि कथ्यन्ते । आचारं, सूत्रकृतं, स्थानं, समवायनामधेयं, व्याख्याप्रज्ञप्तिः, ज्ञातृकथा, उपासकाध्ययनं, अन्तकृतदशं, अनुत्तरोपपादिकदशं, प्रश्नव्याकरणं, विपाकसूत्रं, दृष्टिवादश्चेति । दृष्टिवादस्य च परिकर्मसूत्रप्रथमानुयोगपूर्वगतचूलिकाभेदेन पञ्च भेदाः कथ्यन्ते । तत्र चन्द्रसूर्यजम्बूद्वीपसागरव्याख्याप्रज्ञप्तिभेदेन परिकर्म पञ्चविधं भवति। सूत्रमेकभेदमेव । प्रथमानुयोगोऽप्येकभेदः । पूर्वगतं पुनरुत्पादपूर्वं, अग्रायणीयं, वीर्यानुप्रवादं, अस्तिनास्तिप्रवादं, ज्ञानप्रवादं, सत्यप्रवादं, आत्मप्रवादं, कर्मप्रवादं, प्रत्याख्यानं, विद्यानुवादं, कल्याणनामधेयं, प्राणानुवादं, क्रियाविशालं, लोकसंज्ञं, पूर्वं, चेति चतुर्दशभेदम् । जलगतस्थल-

गताकाशगतहरमेखलादिमायास्वरूपशाकिन्यादिरूपपरावर्त्तनभेदेन चूलिका पञ्चविधा चेति संक्षेपेण द्वादशाङ्गव्याख्यानम्। अङ्गबाह्यं पुनः सामायिकं, चतुर्विंशतिस्तवं, वन्दना, प्रतिक्रमणं, वैनयिकं, कृतिकर्म, दशवैकालिकम् उत्तराध्ययनं, कल्पव्यवहारः, कल्पाकल्पं, महाकल्पं, पुण्डरीकं, महापुण्डरीकं, अशीतिकं चेति चतुर्दशप्रकीर्णकसंज्ञं बोद्धव्यमिति।

अथवा वृषभादिचतुर्विंशतितीर्थङ्करभरतादिद्वादशचक्रवर्त्तिविजयादिनवबलदेवत्रिपिष्टादिनववासुदेवसुग्रीवादिनवप्रतिवासुदेवसम्बन्धित्रिषष्टिपुरुषपुराणभेदभिन्नः प्रथमानुयोगो भण्यते। उपासकाध्ययनादौ श्रावकधर्मम्, आचाराराधनादौ यतिधर्मं च यत्र मुख्यत्वेन कथयति स चरणानुयोगो भण्यते। त्रिलोकसारजिनान्तरलोकविभागादिग्रन्थव्याख्यानं करणानुयोगो विज्ञेयः। प्राभृततत्त्वार्थसिद्धान्तादौ यत्र शुद्धाशुद्धजीवादिषड्द्रव्यादीनां मुख्यवृत्त्या व्याख्यानं क्रियते स द्रव्यानुयोगो भण्यते। इत्युक्तलक्षणानुयोगचतुष्टयरूपेण चतुर्विधं श्रुतज्ञानं ज्ञातव्यम्। अनुयोगोऽधिकारः परिच्छेदः प्रकरणमित्याद्येकोऽर्थः। अथवा षड्द्रव्यपञ्चास्तिकायसप्ततत्त्वनवपदार्थेषु मध्ये निश्चयनयेन स्वकीयशुद्धात्मद्रव्यं, स्वशुद्धजीवास्तिकायो, निजशुद्धात्मतत्त्वं, निजशुद्धात्मपदार्थ उपादेयः। शेषं च हेयमिति संक्षेपेण हेयोपादेयभेदेन द्विधा व्यवहारज्ञानमिति॥

इदानीं तेनैव विकल्परूपव्यवहारज्ञानेन साध्यं निश्चयज्ञानं कथ्यते। तथाहि—रागात् परकलत्रादिवाञ्छारूपं, द्वेषात् परवधबन्धच्छेदादिवाञ्छारूपं च मदीयापध्यानं कोऽपि न जानातीति मत्वा स्वशुद्धात्मभावनासमुत्पन्नसदानन्दैकलक्षणसुखामृतरसनिर्मलजलेन चित्तशुद्धिमकुर्वाणः सन्नयं जीवो बहिरङ्गबकवेषेण यल्लोकरञ्जनां करोति तन्मायाशल्यं भण्यते। निजनिरञ्जननिर्दोषपरमात्मैवोपादेय इति रुचिरूपसम्यक्त्वाद्विलक्षणं मिथ्याशल्यं भण्यते। निर्विकारपरमचैतन्यभावनोत्पन्नपरमाह्लादैकरूपसुखामृतरसास्वादमलभमानोयं जीवो दृष्टश्रुतानुभूतभोगेषु यन्नियतं निरन्तरं चित्तं ददाति तन्निदानशल्यमभिधीयते। इत्युक्तलक्षणशल्यत्रयविभावपरिणामप्रभृतिसमस्तशुभाशुभसङ्कल्पविकल्परहितेन परमस्वास्थ्यसंवित्तिसमुत्पन्नतात्त्विकपरमानन्दैकलक्षणसुखामृत-

तृप्तेन स्वेनात्मना स्वस्य सम्यग्निर्विकल्परूपेण वेदनं परिज्ञानमनुभवनमिति निर्विकल्पस्वसंवेदनज्ञानमेव निश्चयज्ञानं भण्यते ॥

अत्राह शिष्यः । इत्युक्तप्रकारेण प्राभृतग्रन्थे यन्निर्विकल्पस्वसंवेदनज्ञानं भण्यते, तन्न घटते । कस्मादिति चेत् तदुच्यते । सत्तावलोकरूपं चक्षुरादि-दर्शनं यथा जैनमते निर्विकल्पं कथ्यते, तथा बौद्धमते ज्ञानं निर्विकल्पकं भण्यते । परं किन्तु तन्निर्विकल्पमपि विकल्पजनकं भवति । जैनमते तु विकल्प-स्योत्पादकं भवत्येव न । किन्तु स्वरूपेणैव सविकल्पमिति । तथैव स्वपरप्रका-शकं चेति । तत्र परिहारः । कथंचित् सविकल्पकं निर्विकल्पकं च । तथाहि—यथा विषयानन्दरूपं स्वसंवेदनं रागसंवित्तिविकल्परूपेण सविकल्पमपि शेषा-नीहितसूक्ष्मविकल्पानां सद्भावेऽपि सति तेषां मुख्यत्वं नास्ति तेन कारणेन निर्विकल्पमपि भण्यते । तथा स्वशुद्धात्मसंवित्तिरूपं वीतरागस्वसंवेदनज्ञान-मपि स्वसंवित्त्याकारैकविकल्पेन सविकल्पमपि बहिर्विषयानीहितसूक्ष्मविकल्पानां सद्भावेऽपि सति तेषां मुख्यत्वं नास्ति तेन कारणेन निर्विकल्पमपि भण्यते । यत एवेहापूर्वस्वसंवित्त्याकारान्तर्मुखप्रतिभासेऽपि बहिर्विषयानीहितसूक्ष्मा-विकल्पा अपि सन्ति तत एव कारणात् स्वपरप्रकाशकं च सिद्धम् । इदं तु सविकल्पकनिर्विकल्पकस्य तथैव स्वपरप्रकाशकस्य ज्ञानस्य च व्याख्यानं यद्या-गमाध्यात्मतर्कशास्त्रानुसारेण विशेषेण व्याख्यायते तदा महान् विस्तारो भवति । स चाध्यात्मशास्त्रत्वान्न कृत इति ।

एवं रत्नत्रयात्मकमोक्षमार्गावयविनो द्वितीयावयवभूतस्य ज्ञानस्य व्याख्या-नेन गाथा गता ॥ ४२ ॥

अथ निर्विकल्पसत्ताग्राहकं दर्शनं कथयति ॥

व्याख्या । "जं सामण्णं गहणं भावाणं" यत् सामान्येन सत्तावलोकनेन ग्रहणं परिच्छेदनं भावानां पदार्थानां; किं कृत्वा "णेव कट्टुमायारं" नैव कृत्वा कं आकारं विकल्पं; तदपि किं कृत्वा ? "अविसेसिदूण अट्ठे" अविशेष्याविभेद्यार्थान्; केन रूपेण ? शुक्लोऽयं, कृष्णोऽयं, दीर्घोऽयं, ह्रस्वोऽयं, घटोऽयं, पटोऽयमित्यादि "दंसणमिदि भण्णये समये" तत्सत्तावलोकं दर्शनमिति भण्यते समये परमागमे । नेदमेव तत्त्वार्थश्रद्धानलक्षणं सम्यग्दर्शनं वक्तव्यम् । कस्मा-

दिति चेत्—तत्र श्रद्धानं विकल्परूपमिदं तु निर्विकल्पं यतः । अयमत्र भावः—यदा कोऽपि किमप्यवलोकयति पश्यति; तदा यावत् विकल्पं न करोति तावत् सत्तामात्रग्रहणं दर्शनं भण्यते । पश्चाच्छुक्लादिविकल्पे जाते ज्ञानमिति ॥ ४३ ॥

अथ छद्मस्थानां ज्ञानं सत्तावलोकनदर्शनपूर्वकं भवति, मुक्तात्मानं युगपदिति प्रतिपादयति ॥

व्याख्या । "दंसणपुव्वं णाणं छदुमत्थाणं" सत्तावलोकनदर्शनपूर्वकं ज्ञानं भवति छद्मस्थानां संसारिणाम् । कस्मात् "ण दुण्णि उवओग जुगवं जम्हा" ज्ञानदर्शनोपयोगद्वयं युगपन्न भवति यस्मात्, "केवलिणाहे जुगवं तु ते दोवि" केवलिनाथे तु युगपत्तौ ज्ञानदर्शनोपयोगौ द्वौ भवत इति ।

अथ विस्तरः । चक्षुरादीन्द्रियाणां स्वकीयस्वकीयक्षयोपशमानुसारेण तद्योग्यदेशस्थितरूपादिविषयाणां ग्रहणमेव सन्निपातः सम्बन्धः सन्निकर्षो भण्यते । न च नैयायिकमतवच्चक्षुरादीन्द्रियाणां स्वरूपादिस्वकीयस्वकीयविषयपार्श्वे गमन इति सन्निकर्षो वक्तव्यः । स एव सम्बन्धो लक्षणं यस्य तल्लक्षणं यन्निर्विकल्पं सत्तावलोकनदर्शनं तत्पूर्वं शुक्लमिदमित्याद्यवग्रहादिविकल्परूपमिन्द्रियानिन्द्रियजनितं मतिज्ञानं भवति । इत्युक्तलक्षणमतिज्ञानपूर्वकं तु धूमादग्निविज्ञानवदर्थादर्थान्तरग्रहणरूपं लिङ्गजं, तथैव घटादिशब्दश्रवणरूपं शब्दजं चेति द्विविधं श्रुतज्ञानं भवति । अथावधिज्ञानं पुनरवधिदर्शनपूर्वकमिति । ईहामतिज्ञानपूर्वकं तु मनःपर्ययज्ञानं भवति ।

अत्र श्रुतज्ञानमनःपर्ययज्ञानजनकं यदवग्रहेहादिरूपं मतिज्ञानं भणितम्, तदपि दर्शनपूर्वकत्वादुपचारेण दर्शनं भण्यते, यतस्तेन कारणेन श्रुतज्ञानमनःपर्ययज्ञानद्वयमपि दर्शनपूर्वकं ज्ञातव्यमिति । एवं छद्मस्थानां सावरणक्षयोपशमिकज्ञानसहितत्वात् दर्शनपूर्वकं ज्ञानं भवति । केवलिनां तु भगवतां निर्विकारस्वसंवेदनसमुत्पन्ननिरावरणक्षायिकज्ञानसहितत्वान्निर्मेघादित्ये युगपदातपप्रकाशवद्दर्शनं ज्ञानं च युगपदेवेति विज्ञेयम् । छद्मस्था इति कोऽर्थः ? छद्मशब्देन ज्ञानदर्शनावरणद्वयं भण्यते, तत्र तिष्ठन्तीति छद्मस्थाः । एवं तर्काभिप्रायेण सत्तावलोकनदर्शनं व्याख्यातम् ।

अत ऊर्ध्वं सिद्धान्ताभिप्रायेण कथ्यते । तथाहि उत्तरज्ञानोत्पत्तिनिमित्तं

यत् प्रयत्नं तद्रूपं यत् स्वस्यात्मनः परिच्छेदनमवलोकनं तद्दर्शनं भण्यते । तदनन्तरं यद्बहिर्विषये विकल्परूपेण पदार्थग्रहणं तज्ज्ञानमिति वार्त्तिकम् । यथा कोऽपि पुरुषो घटविषयविकल्पं कुर्वन्नास्ते, पश्चात् पटपरिज्ञानार्थं चित्ते जाते सति घटविकल्पाद्व्यावर्त्त्य यत् स्वरूपे प्रयत्नमवलोकनं परिच्छेदनं करोति तद्दर्शनमिति । तदनन्तरं पटोऽयमिति निश्चयं यद्बहिर्विषयरूपेण पदार्थग्रहणविकल्पं करोति तद् ज्ञानं भण्यते ।

अत्राह शिष्यः—यद्यात्मग्राहकं दर्शनं, परग्राहकं ज्ञानं भण्यते; तर्हि यथा नैयायिकमते ज्ञानमात्मानं न जानाति; तथा जैनमतेऽपि ज्ञानमात्मानं न जानातीति दूषणं प्राप्नोति । अत्र परिहारः । नैयायिकमते ज्ञानं पृथग्दर्शनं पृथगिति गुणद्वयं नास्ति; तेन कारणेन तेषामात्मपरिज्ञानाभावदूषणं प्राप्नोति । जैनमते पुनर्ज्ञानगुणेन परद्रव्यं जानाति, दर्शनगुणेनात्मानं च जानातीत्यात्मपरिज्ञानाभावदूषणं न प्राप्नोति । कस्मादिति चेत् यथैकोऽप्यग्निर्दहतीति दाहकः, पचतीति पाचको, विषयभेदेन द्विधा भिद्यते । तथैवाभेदनयेनैकमपि चैतन्यं भेदनयविवक्षायां यदात्मग्राहकत्वेन प्रवृत्तं तदा तस्य दर्शनमिति संज्ञा, पश्चात् यच्च परद्रव्यग्राहकत्वेन प्रवृत्तं तस्य ज्ञानसंज्ञेति विषयभेदेन द्विधा भिद्यते । किं च यदि सामान्यग्राहकं दर्शनं विशेषग्राहकं ज्ञानं भण्यते, तदा ज्ञानस्य प्रमाणत्वं न प्राप्नोति । कस्मादिति चेत् वस्तुग्राहकं प्रमाणं; वस्तु च सामान्यविशेषात्मकं; ज्ञानेन पुनर्वस्त्वेकदेशो विशेष एव गृहीतो; न च वस्तु । सिद्धान्तेन पुनर्निश्चयेन गुणगुणिनोरभिन्नत्वात् संशयविमोहविभ्रमरहितवस्तुज्ञानस्वरूपात्मैव प्रमाणम् । स च प्रदीपवत् स्वपरगतं सामान्यं विशेषं च जानाति । तेन कारणेनाभेदेन तस्यैव प्रमाणत्वमिति ।

अथ मतं—यदि दर्शनं बहिर्विषये न प्रवर्त्तते तदान्धवत् सर्वजनानामन्धत्वं प्राप्नोतीति । नैवं वक्तव्यम् । बहिर्विषये दर्शनाभावेऽपि ज्ञानेन विशेषेण सर्वं परिच्छिनत्तीति । अयं तु विशेषः दर्शनेनात्मनि गृहीते सत्यात्माविनाभूतं ज्ञानमपि गृहीतं भवति; ज्ञाने च गृहीते सति ज्ञानविषयभूतं बहिर्वस्त्वपि गृहीतं भवतीति । यथोक्तं भवता यद्यात्मग्राहकं दर्शनं भण्यते, तर्हि "जं सामण्णं गहणं भावाणं तद्दंसणमिति" गाथार्थः कथं घटते । तत्रोत्तरं सामान्यग्रहणमात्मग्रहणं तद्दर्शनम् । कस्मादिति चेत्—आत्मा वस्तुपरिच्छित्तिं कुर्वन्निदं जानामीदं न

जानामीति विशेषपक्षपातं न करोति; किन्तु सामान्येन वस्तु परिच्छिनत्ति। तेन कारणेन सामान्यशब्देनात्मा भण्यत इति गाथार्थः ।

किं बहुना यदि कोऽपि तर्कार्थं सिद्धान्तार्थं च ज्ञात्वैकान्तदुराग्रहत्यागेन नयविभागेन मध्यस्थवृत्त्या व्याख्यानं करोति, तदा द्वयमपि घटत इति। कथमिति चेत्— तर्के मुख्यवृत्त्या परसमयव्याख्यानं, तत्र यदा कोऽपि परसमयी पृच्छति जैनागमे दर्शनं ज्ञानं चेति गुणद्वयं जीवस्य कथ्यते तत्कथं घटत इति। तदा तेषामात्मग्राहकं दर्शनमिति कथिते सति ते न जानन्ति । पश्चादाचार्यैस्तेषां प्रतीत्यर्थं स्थूलव्याख्यानेन बहिर्विषये यत् सामान्यपरिच्छेदनं तस्य सत्तावलोकनदर्शनसंज्ञा स्थापिता, यच्च शुक्लमिदमित्यादिविशेषपरिच्छेदनं तस्य ज्ञानसंज्ञा स्थापितेति दोषो नास्ति। सिद्धान्ते पुनः स्वसमयव्याख्यानं मुख्यवृत्त्या। तत्र सूक्ष्मव्याख्याने क्रियमाणे सत्याचार्यैरात्मग्राहकं दर्शनं व्याख्यातमित्यत्रापि दोषो नास्ति ।

अत्राह शिष्यः—सत्तावलोकनदर्शनस्य ज्ञानेन सह भेदो ज्ञातस्तावदिदानीं यत्तत्त्वार्थश्रद्धानरूपं सम्यग्दर्शनं वस्तुविचाररूपं सम्यग्ज्ञानं तयोर्विशेषो न ज्ञायते। कस्मादिति चेत् सम्यग्दर्शने पदार्थनिश्चयोऽस्ति, तथैव सम्यग्ज्ञाने च को विशेष इति। अत्र परिहारः। अर्थग्रहणपरिच्छित्तिरूपः क्षयोपशमविशेषो ज्ञानं भण्यते, तत्रैव भेदनयेन वीतरागसर्वज्ञप्रणीतशुद्धात्मादितत्त्वेष्विदमेवेत्थमेवेति निश्चयसम्यक्त्वमिति। अविकल्परूपेणाभेदनयेन पुनर्यदेव सम्यग्ज्ञानं तदेव सम्यक्त्वमिति। कस्मादिति चेत्—अतत्त्वे तत्त्वबुद्धिरदेवे देवबुद्धिरधर्मे धर्मबुद्धिरित्यादिविपरीताभिनिवेशरहितस्य ज्ञानस्यैव सम्यग्विशेषणवाच्योऽवस्थाविशेषः सम्यक्त्वं भण्यते यतः कारणात् ।

यदि भेदो नास्ति तर्हि कथमावरणद्वयमिति चेत्—तत्रोत्तरम्। येन कर्मणार्थपरिच्छित्तिरूपः क्षयोपशमः प्रच्छाद्यते तस्य ज्ञानावरणसंज्ञा, तस्यैव क्षयोपशमविशेषस्य यत् कर्म पूर्वोक्तलक्षणं विपरीताभिनिवेशमुत्पादयतिं तस्य मिथ्यात्वसंज्ञेति भेदनयेनावरणभेदः। निश्चयनयेन पुनरभेदविवक्षायां कर्मत्वं प्रत्यावरणद्वयमप्येकमेव विज्ञातव्यम्। एवं दर्शनपूर्वकं ज्ञानं भवतीति व्याख्यानरूपेण गाथा गता ॥ ४४ ॥

अथ सम्यग्दर्शनज्ञानपूर्वकं रत्नत्रयात्मकमोक्षमार्गतृतीयावयवभूतं स्वशुद्धात्मानुभूतिरूपशुद्धोपयोगलक्षणवीतरागचारित्रस्य पारम्पर्येण साधकं सरागचारित्रं प्रतिपादयति ।

व्याख्या । अस्यैव सरागचारित्रस्यैकदेशावयवभूतं देशचारित्रं तावत्कथ्यते । तद्यथा–मिथ्यात्वादिसप्तप्रकृत्युपशमक्षयोपशमक्षये सति, अध्यात्मभाषया निजशुद्धात्माभिमुखपरिणामे वा सति शुद्धात्मभावनोत्पन्ननिर्विकारवास्तवसुखामृतमुपादेयं कृत्वा संसारशरीरभोगेषु योऽसौ हेयबुद्धिः सम्यग्दर्शनशुद्धः स चतुर्थगुणस्थानवर्त्ती व्रतरहितो दर्शनिको भण्यते । यश्च प्रत्याख्यानावरणसंज्ञद्वितीयकषायक्षयोपशमे जाते सति पृथिव्यादिपञ्चस्थावरवधे प्रवृत्तोऽपि यथाशक्त्या त्रसवधे निवृत्तः स पञ्चमगुणस्थानवर्त्ती श्रावको भण्यते ।

तस्यैकादशभेदाः कथ्यन्ते । तथाहि—सम्यक्त्वपूर्वकत्वेन मद्यमांसमधुत्यागोदुम्बरपञ्चकपरिहाररूपाष्टमूलगुणसहितः सन् संग्रामादिवृत्तोऽपि पापाद्धर्यादिभिर्निष्प्रयोजनजीवघातादौ निवृत्तः प्रथमो दर्शनिकश्रावको भण्यते । स एव सर्वथा त्रसवधे निवृत्तः सन् पञ्चाणुव्रतगुणव्रतत्रयशिक्षाव्रतचतुष्टयसहितो द्वितीयव्रतिकसंज्ञो भवति । स एव त्रिकालसामायिके प्रवृत्तः तृतीयः, प्रोषधोपवासे प्रवृत्तश्चतुर्थः, सचित्तपरिहारेण पञ्चमः, दिवा–ब्रह्मचर्येण षष्ठः, सर्वथा ब्रह्मचर्येण सप्तमः, आरम्भादिसमस्तव्यापारनिवृत्तोऽष्टमः, वस्त्रप्रावरणं विहायान्यसर्वपरिग्रहनिवृत्तो नवमः, गृहव्यापारादिसर्वसावद्यानुमतनिवृत्तो दशमः, उद्दिष्टाहारनिवृत्त एकादशम इति । एतेष्वेकादशश्रावकेषु मध्ये प्रथमषट्कं तारतम्येन जघन्यम्, ततश्च त्रयं मध्यमम्, ततो द्वयमुत्तममिति सङ्क्षेपेण दर्शनिकश्रावकाद्येकादशभेदाः ज्ञातव्याः ॥

अथैकदेशचारित्रव्याख्यानानन्तरं सकलचारित्रमुपदिशति । "असुहादो विणिवित्ती सुहे पवित्ती य जाण चारित्तं" अशुभान्निवृत्तिः शुभे प्रवृत्तिश्चापि जानीहि चारित्रम् । तच्च कथम्भूतं—"वदसमिदिगुत्तिरूवं ववहारणया दु जिणभणियं" व्रतसमितिगुप्तिरूपं व्यवहारनयाज्जिनैरुक्तमिति । तथाहि—प्रत्याख्यानावरणसंज्ञतृतीयकषायक्षयोपशमे सति "विसयकसाओगाढोदुस्सुदिदुचित्तदुठ्ठगोठ्ठिजुदो । उग्गो उमग्गपरो उवओगो जस्स सो असुहे ॥" इति

गाथाकथितलक्षणादशुभोपयोगान्निवृत्तिस्तद्विलक्षणे शुभोपयोगे प्रवृत्तिश्च हे शिष्य चारित्रं जानीहि । तच्चाचाराराधनादिचरणशास्त्रोक्तप्रकारेण पञ्चमहाव्रत-पञ्चसमितित्रिगुप्तिरूपमप्यपहृतसंयमाख्यं शुभोपयोगलक्षणं सरागचारित्राभि-धानं भवति । तत्र योऽसौ बहिर्विषये पञ्चेन्द्रियविषयादिपरित्यागः स उपच-रितासद्भूतव्यवहारेण, यश्चाभ्यन्तरे रागादिपरिहारः स पुनरशुद्धनिश्चयेनेति नयविभागो ज्ञातव्यः । एवं निश्चयचारित्रसाधकं व्यवहारचारित्रं व्याख्या-तमिति ॥ ४५ ॥

अथ तेनैव व्यवहारचारित्रेण साध्यं निश्चयचारित्रं निरूपयति ।

व्याख्या । "तं" तत् "परमं" परमोपेक्षालक्षणं निर्विकारस्वसंवित्त्यात्मक-शुद्धोपयोमाविनाभूतं परमं "सम्मचारित्तं" सम्यक्चारित्रं ज्ञातव्यम् । तत्किं— "बहिरब्भंतरकिरियारोहो" निष्क्रियनित्यनिरञ्जनविशुद्धज्ञानदर्शनस्वभावस्य निजात्मनः प्रतिपक्षभूतस्य बहिर्विषये शुभाशुभवचनकायव्यापाररूपस्य तथैवा-भ्यन्तरे शुभाशुभमनोविकल्परूपस्य च क्रियाव्यापारस्य योऽसौ निरोधस्त्यागः स च किमर्थं "भवकारणप्पणासट्ठं" पञ्चप्रकारभवातीतनिर्दोषपरमात्मनो विलक्षणस्य भवस्य संसारस्य व्यापारकारणभूतो योऽसौ शुभाशुभकर्मास्रवस्त-स्य प्रणाशार्थं विनाशार्थमिति । इत्युभयक्रियानिरोधलक्षणचारित्रं कस्य भवति ? "णाणिस्स" निश्चयरत्नत्रयात्मकाभेदज्ञानिनः । पुनरपि किं विशिष्टं "जं जिणुत्तं" यज्जिनेन वीतरागसर्वज्ञेनोक्तमिति ॥ ४६ ॥

एवं वीतरागसम्यक्त्वज्ञानाविनाभूतं निश्चयरत्नत्रयात्मकनिश्चयमोक्षमार्गे तृतीयावयवरूपं वीतरागचारित्रं व्याख्यातम् ॥ इति द्वितीयस्थले गाथाषट्कं गतम् ।

एवं मोक्षमार्गप्रतिपादकतृतीयाधिकारमध्ये निश्चयव्यवहारमोक्षमार्ग-संक्षेपकथनेन सूत्रद्वयम्, तदनन्तरं तस्यैव मोक्षमार्गस्यावयवभूतानां सम्यग्दर्श-नज्ञानचारित्राणां विशेषविवरणरूपेण सूत्रषट्कं चेति स्थलद्वयसमुदायेनाष्ट-गाथाभिः प्रथमोऽन्तराधिकारः समाप्तः ॥

अतःपरं ध्यानध्यातृध्येयध्यानफलकथनमुख्यत्वेन प्रथमस्थले गाथात्रयम्, ततः परं पञ्चपरमेष्ठिव्याख्यानरूपेण द्वितीयस्थले गाथापञ्चकम्, ततश्च तस्यैव

ध्यानस्योपसंहाररूपविशेषव्याख्यानेन तृतीयस्थले सूत्रचतुष्टयमिति स्थलत्रय-समुदायेन द्वादशसूत्रेषु द्वितीयान्तराधिकारे समुदायपातनिका। तथा हि—निश्चयव्यवहारमोक्षमार्गसाधकध्यानाभ्यासं कुरुत यूयमित्युपदिशति ।

व्याख्या । " दुविहं पि मोक्खहेउं झाणे पाउणदि जं मुणी णियमा" द्विविधमपि मोक्षहेतुं ध्यानेन प्राप्नोति यस्मात् मुनिर्नियमात् । तद्यथा—निश्चयरत्नत्रयात्मकं निश्चयमोक्षहेतुं निश्चयमोक्षमार्गं, तथैव व्यवहाररत्नत्रयात्मकं व्यवहारमोक्षहेतुं व्यवहारमोक्षमार्गं च यं साध्यसाधकभावेन कथितवान् पूर्वं तद्द्विविधमपि निर्विकारस्वसंवित्त्यात्मकपरमध्यानेन मुनिः प्राप्नोति यस्मात्कारणात् "तम्हा पयत्तचित्ता जूयं झाणं समब्भसन्ह" तस्मात् प्रयत्नचित्ताः सन्तो हे भव्या यूयं ध्यानं सम्यगभ्यसत । तथा हि तस्मात्कारणाद्दृष्टश्रुतानुभूतनानामनोरथरूपसमस्तशुभाशुभरागादिविकल्पजालं त्यक्त्वा परमस्वास्थ्यसमुत्पन्नसहजानन्दैकलक्षणसुखामृतरसास्वादानुभवे स्थित्वा च ध्यानाभ्यासं कुरुत यूयमिति ॥ ४७ ॥

अथ ध्यातृपुरुषलक्षणं कथयति ।

व्याख्या । "मा मुज्झह मा रज्जह मा दुस्सह" समस्तमोहरागद्वेषजनितविकल्पजालरहितनिजपरमात्मतत्त्वभावनासमुत्पन्नपरमानन्दैकलक्षणसुखामृतरसात्सकाशादुद्गता संजाता तत्रैव परमात्मसुखास्वादे लीना तन्मया या तु परमकला परमसंवित्तिस्तत्र स्थित्वा हे भव्या मोहरागद्वेषान्मा कुरुत; केषु विषयेषु " इट्ठणिट्ठअत्थेसु " स्रग्वनिताचन्दनताम्बूलादय इष्टेन्द्रियार्थाः, अहिविषकण्टकशत्रुव्याधिप्रभृतयः पुनरनिष्टेन्द्रियार्थास्तेषु यदि किं "थिरमिच्छह जइ चित्तं " तत्रैव परमात्मानुभवे स्थिरं निश्चलं चित्तं यदीच्छत यूयं किमर्थं "विचित्तझाणप्पसिद्धीए " विचित्रं नानाप्रकारं यद्ध्यानं तत्प्रसिद्ध्यै निमित्तं अथवा विगतं चित्तं चित्तोद्भवशुभाशुभविकल्पजालं यत्र तद्विचित्तं ध्यानं तदर्थमिति ।

इदानीं तस्यैव ध्यानस्य तावदागमभाषया विचित्रभेदाः कथ्यन्ते । तथा हि—इष्टवियोगानिष्टसंयोगव्याधिप्रतीकारभोगनिदानेषु वाञ्छारूपं चतुर्विधमार्त्तध्यानम् । तच्च तारतम्येन मिथ्यादृष्ट्यादिषट्गुणस्थानवर्त्तिजीवसम्भवम् । यद्यपि मिथ्यादृष्टीनां तिर्यग्गतिकारणं भवति तथापि बद्धायुष्कं विहाय सम्य-

ग्दृष्टीनां न भवति । कस्मादिति चेत्—स्वशुद्धात्मैवोपादेय इति विशिष्टभावनाबलेन तत्कारणभूतसंक्लेशाभावादिति ।

अथ रौद्रध्यानं कथ्यते । हिंसानन्दमृषानन्दस्तेयानन्दविषयसंरक्षणानन्दप्रभवं रौद्रं चतुर्विधम् । तारतम्येन मिथ्यादृष्ट्यादिपञ्चमगुणस्थानवर्त्तिजीवसम्भवम् । तच्च मिथ्यादृष्टीनां नरकगतिकारणमपि बद्धायुष्कं विहाय सम्यग्दृष्टीनां तत्कारणं न भवति । तदपि कस्मादितिचेत्—निजशुद्धात्मतत्त्वमेवोपादेयं विशिष्टभेदज्ञानबलेन तत्कारणभूततीव्रसंक्लेशाभावादिति ॥

अतः परमार्त्तरौद्रपरित्यागलक्षणमाज्ञापायविपाकसंस्थानविचयसंज्ञचतुर्भेदभिन्नं, तारतम्यवृद्धिक्रमेणासंयतसम्यग्दृष्टिदेशविरतप्रमत्तसंयताप्रमत्ताभिधानचतुर्गुणस्थानवर्त्तिजीवसम्भवं, मुख्यवृत्त्या पुण्यबन्धकारणमपि परम्परया मुक्तिकारणं चेति धर्मध्यानं कथ्यते । तथाहि—स्वयं मन्दबुद्धित्वेऽपि विशिष्टोपाध्यायाभावेऽपि शुद्धजीवादिपदार्थानां सूक्ष्मत्वेऽपि सति "सूक्ष्मं जिनोदितं वाक्यं हेतुभिर्यन्न हन्यते । आज्ञासिद्धं तु तद्ग्राह्यं नान्यथावादिनो जिनाः ॥" इति श्लोककथितक्रमेण पदार्थनिश्चयकरणमाज्ञाविचयध्यानं भण्यते । तथैव भेदाभेदरत्नत्रयभावनाबलेनास्माकं परेषां वा कदा कर्मणामपायो विनाशो भविष्यतीति चिन्तनमपायविचयं ज्ञातव्यम् । शुद्धनिश्चयेन शुभाशुभकर्मविपाकरहितोऽप्ययं जीवः पश्चादनादिकर्मबन्धवशेन पापस्योदयेन नारकादिदुःखविपाकफलमनुभवति, पुण्योदयेन देवादिसुखविपाकमनुभवतीति विचारणं विपाकविचयं विज्ञेयम् । पूर्वोक्तलोकानुप्रेक्षाचिन्तनं संस्थानविचयम् । इति चतुर्विधं धर्मध्यानं भवति ॥

अथ पृथक्त्ववितर्कवीचारं, एकत्ववितर्कवीचारं सूक्ष्मक्रियाप्रतिपातिसंज्ञं व्युपरतक्रियानिवृत्तिसंज्ञं चेति भेदेन चतुर्विधं शुक्लध्यानं कथयति । तद्यथा—पृथक्त्ववितर्कवीचारं तावत्कथ्यते । द्रव्यगुणपर्यायाणां भिन्नत्वं पृथक्त्वं भण्यते, स्वशुद्धात्मानुभूतिलक्षणं भावश्रुतं तद्वाचकमन्तर्जल्पवचनं वा वितर्को भण्यते, अनीहितवृत्त्यार्थान्तरपरिणमनं वचनाद्वचनान्तरपरिणमनं मनोवचनकाययोगेषु योगाद्योगान्तरपरिणमनं वीचारो भण्यते । अयमत्रार्थः—यद्यपि ध्याता पुरुषः स्वशुद्धात्मसंवेदनं विहाय बहिश्चिन्तां न करोति तथापि यावतांशेन स्वरूपे

स्थिरत्वं नास्ति तावतांशेनानीहितवृत्त्या विकल्पाः स्फुरन्ति, तेन कारणेन पृथक्त्ववितर्कवीचारं ध्यानं भण्यते। तच्चोपशमश्रेणिविवक्षायामपूर्वोपशमकानिवृत्युपशमकसूक्ष्मसाम्परायकोपशमकोपशान्तकषायपर्यन्तगुणस्थानचतुष्टये भवति। क्षपकश्रेण्यां पुनरपूर्वकरणक्षपकानिवृत्तिकरणक्षपकसूक्ष्मसाम्परायक्षपकाभिधानगुणस्थानत्रये चेति प्रथमं शुक्लध्यानं व्याख्यातम्।

निजशुद्धात्मद्रव्ये वा निर्विकारात्मसुखसंवित्तिपर्याये वा निरुपाधिस्वसंवेदनगुणे वा यत्रैकस्मिन् प्रवृत्तं तत्रैव वितर्कसंज्ञेन स्वसंवित्तिलक्षणभावश्रुतबलेन स्थिरीभूय वीचारं गुणद्रव्यपर्यायपरावर्त्तनं करोति यत्तदेकत्ववितर्कवीचारसंज्ञं क्षीणकषायगुणस्थानसम्भवं द्वितीयं शुक्लध्यानं भण्यते। तेनैव केवलज्ञानोत्पत्तिरिति। अथ सूक्ष्मकायक्रियाव्यापाररूपं च तदप्रतिपाति च सूक्ष्मक्रियाप्रतिपातिसंज्ञं तृतीयं शुक्लध्यानम्। तच्चोपचारेण सयोगिकेवलिजिने भवतीति। विशेषेणोपरता निवृत्ता क्रिया यत्र तद्व्युपरतक्रियं च तदनिवृत्ति चानिवर्त्तकं च तद्व्युपरतक्रियानिवृत्तिसंज्ञं चतुर्थं शुक्लध्यानं व्याख्यातम्। अध्यात्मभाषया पुनः सहजशुद्धपरमचैतन्यशालिनि निर्भरानन्दमालिनि भगवति निजात्मन्युपादेयबुद्धिं कृत्वा पश्चादनन्तज्ञानोऽहमनन्तसुखोऽहमित्यादिभावनारूपमभ्यन्तरधर्मध्यानमुच्यते। पञ्चपरमेष्ठिभक्त्यादितदनुकूलशुभानुष्ठानं पुनर्बहिरङ्गधर्मध्यानं भवति। तथैव स्वशुद्धात्मनि निर्विकल्पसमाधिलक्षणं शुक्लध्यानमिति। अथवा "पदस्थं मन्त्रवाक्यस्थं पिण्डस्थं स्वात्मचिन्तनम्। रूपस्थं सर्वचिद्रूपं रूपातीतं निरञ्जनम्॥१॥" इति श्लोककथितक्रमेण विचित्रध्यानं ज्ञातव्यमिति॥

अथ ध्यानप्रतिबन्धकानां मोहरागद्वेषाणां स्वरूपं कथ्यते। शुद्धात्मादितत्त्वेषु विपरीताभिनिवेशजनको मोहो दर्शनमोहो मिथ्यात्वमिति यावत्। निर्विकारस्वसंवित्तिलक्षणवीतरागचारित्रप्रच्छादकचारित्रमोहो रागद्वेषौ भण्यते। चारित्रमोहो रागद्वेषौ कथं भण्यते? इति चेत्—कषायमध्ये क्रोधमानद्वयं द्वेषाङ्गं, मायालोभद्वयं रागाङ्गं, नोकषायमध्ये तु स्त्रीपुंनपुंसकवेदत्रयं हास्यरतिद्वयं च रागाङ्गं, अरतिशोकद्वयं भयजुगुप्साद्वयं च द्वेषाङ्गमिति ज्ञातव्यम्। अत्राह शिष्यः—रागद्वेषादयः किं कर्मजनिताः किं जीवजनिता इति। तत्रोत्तरं—स्त्रीपुरुषसंयोगोत्पन्नपुत्र इव सुधाहरिद्रासंयोगोत्पन्नवर्णविशेष इवोभयसंयोगजनिता इति। पश्चान्नयविवक्षावशेन विवक्षितैकदेशशुद्धनिश्चयेन कर्म-

जनिता भण्यन्ते । तथैवाशुद्धनिश्चयेन जीवजनिता इति । स चाशुद्धनिश्चयः शुद्धनिश्चयापेक्षया व्यवहार एव । अथ मतं–साक्षाच्छुद्धनिश्चयनयेन कस्यैत इति पृच्छामो वयम् । तत्रोत्तरं—साक्षाच्छुद्धनिश्चयेन स्त्रीपुरुषसंयोगरहित-पुत्रस्येव, सुधाहरिद्रासंयोगरहितरङ्गविशेषस्येव तेषामुत्पत्तिरेव नास्ति कथमुत्तरं प्रयच्छाम इति ॥४८॥ एवं ध्यातृव्याख्यानमुख्यत्वेन तद्ध्यानेन विच्चित्रध्यान-कथनेन च सूत्रं गतम् ॥

अत ऊर्ध्वं पदस्थं ध्यानं मन्त्रवाक्यस्थं यदुक्तं तस्य विवरणं कथयति ।

व्याख्या ।—"पणतीस" "णमो अरिहंताणं, णमो सिद्धाणं, णमो आय-रियाणं, णमो उवज्झायाणं, णमो लोए सव्वसाहूणं" एतानि पञ्चत्रिंशदक्ष-राणि सर्वपादानि भण्यन्ते । "सोल" 'अरिहंत सिद्ध आचार्य उवज्झाय साहू' एतानि षोडशाक्षराणि नामपदानि भण्यन्ते । "छ" 'अरिहन्तसिद्ध एतानि षडक्षराणि अर्हत्सिद्धयोर्नामपदे द्वे भण्येते । "पण" 'अ सि आ उ सा' एतानि पञ्चाक्षराणि आदिपदानि भण्यन्ते । "चदु" "अरिहंत" इदमक्षर-चतुष्टयमर्हतो नामपदम् । "दुगं" सिद्ध इत्यक्षरद्वयं सिद्धस्य नामपदम् । "एगं च" 'अ' इत्येकाक्षरर्हभत आदिपदम् । अथवा 'ओं' एकाक्षरं पञ्चपरमेष्ठि-नामादिपदम् । तत्कथमिति चेत् "अरिहंता असरीरा आयरिया तह उवज्झया मुणिणो । पढमक्खरनिप्पण्णो उंकारो पंच परमेट्ठी । इति गाथाकथित-प्रथमाक्षराणां 'समानः सवर्णे दीर्घीभवति' 'परश्च लोपम्' 'उवर्णे ऊ' इति स्वरसन्धिविधानेन ओं—शब्दो निष्पद्यते । कस्मादिति—"जवह ज्झाएह" एतेषां पदानां सर्वमन्त्रवादपदेषु मध्ये सारभूतानां इहलोकपरलोकेष्टफलप्रदान-समर्थं ज्ञात्वा पश्चादनन्तज्ञानादिगुणस्मरणरूपेण वचनोच्चारणेन च जापं कुरुत । तथैव शुभोपयोगरूपत्रिगुप्तावस्थायां मौनेन ध्यायत । पुनरपि कथम्भूतांम् "परमेट्ठिवाचयाणं" 'अरिहंत' इति पदवाचकमनन्तज्ञानादिगुणयुक्तोऽर्हद्वाच्योऽ-भिधेय इत्यादिरूपेण पञ्चपरमेट्ठिवाचकानां । "अण्णं च गुरूवएसेण" अन्यदपि द्वादशसहस्रप्रमितपञ्चनमस्कारग्रन्थकथितक्रमेण लघुसिद्धचक्रं, बृहत्सिद्धचक्र-मित्यादिदेवार्चनविधानं भेदाभेदरत्नत्रयाराधकगुरुप्रसादेन ज्ञात्वा ध्यातव्यम् । इति पदस्थध्यानस्वरूपं व्याख्यातम् ॥४९॥

एवमनेन प्रकारेण "गुप्तेन्द्रियमनो ध्यात ध्येयं वस्तु यथास्थितम् ।

एकाग्रचिन्तनं ध्यानं फलं संवरनिर्जरौ ॥" इति श्लोककथितलक्षणानां ध्यातृध्येयध्यानफलानां संक्षेपव्याख्यानरूपेण गाथात्रयेण द्वितीयान्तराधिकारे प्रथमं स्थलं गतम् ।

अतः परं रागादिविकल्पोपाधिरहितनिजपरमात्मपदार्थभावनोत्पन्नसदानन्दैकलक्षणसुखामृतरसास्वादतृप्तिरूपस्य निश्चयध्यानस्य परम्परया कारणभूतं यच्छुभोपयोगलक्षणं व्यवहारध्यानं तद्ध्येयभूतानां पंचपरमेष्ठीनां मध्ये तावदर्हत्स्वरूपं कथयामीत्येका पातनिका । द्वितीया तु पूर्वसूत्रोदितसर्वपदनामपदादिपदानां वाचकभूतानां वाच्या ये पञ्चपरमेष्ठिनस्तद्व्याख्याने क्रियमाणे प्रथमतस्तावज्जिनस्वरूपं निरूपयामि । अथवा तृतीया पातनिका पदस्थपिण्डस्थरूपस्थध्यानत्रयस्य ध्येयभूतमर्हत्सर्वज्ञस्वरूपं दर्शयामीति पातनिकात्रयं मनसि धृत्वा भगवान् सूत्रमिदं प्रतिपादयति ।

व्याख्या । "णट्ठचदुघाइकम्मो" निश्चयरत्नत्रयात्मकशुद्धोपयोगध्यानेन पूर्वं घातिकर्ममुख्यभूतमोहनीयस्य विनाशनात्तदनन्तरं ज्ञानदर्शनावरणान्तरायसंज्ञयुगपद्घातित्रयविनाशकत्वाच्च प्रणष्टचतुर्घातिकर्मा । "दंसणसुहणाणवीरियमईओ" तेनैव घातिकर्माभावेन लब्धानन्तचतुष्टयत्वात् सहजशुद्धाविनश्वरदर्शनज्ञानसुखवीर्यमयः । "सुहदेहत्थो" निश्चयेनाशरीरोऽपि व्यवहारेण सप्तधातुरहितदिवाकरसहस्रभासुरपरमौदारिकशरीरत्वात् शुभदेहस्थः । "सुद्धो" "क्षुधा तृषा भयं द्वेषो रागो मोहश्च चिन्तनम् । जरा रुजा च मृत्युश्च खेदः स्वेदो मदोऽरतिः ।१। विस्मयो जननं निद्रा विषादोऽष्टादश स्मृताः । एतैर्दोषैर्विनिर्मुक्तः सोऽयमाप्तो निरञ्जनः ॥२॥" इति श्लोकद्वयकथिताष्टादशदोषरहितत्वात् शुद्धः । "अप्पा" एवं गुणविशिष्ट आत्मा । "अरिहो" अरिशब्दवाच्यमोहनीयस्य, रजःशब्दवाच्यज्ञानदर्शनावरणद्वयस्य, रहस्यशब्दवाच्यान्तरायस्य च हननाद्विनाशात्सकाशात् इन्द्रादिविनिर्मितां गर्भावतरणजन्माभिषेकनिःक्रमणकेवलज्ञानोत्पत्तिनिर्वाणाभिधानपञ्चमहाकल्याणरूपां पूजामर्हति योग्यो भवति तेन कारणेन अर्हन् भण्यन्ते । "विचिंतज्जो" इत्युक्तविशेषणैर्विशिष्टमाप्तागमप्रभृतिग्रन्थकथितवीतरागसर्वज्ञाद्यष्टोत्तरसहस्रनामानमर्हतं जिनभट्टारकं पदस्थपिंडस्थरूपस्थध्याने स्थित्वा विशेषेण चिन्तयत ध्यायत हे भव्या यूयमिति ।

अत्रावसरे भट्टचार्वाकमतं गृहीत्वा शिष्यः पूर्वपक्षं करोति। नास्ति सर्वज्ञोऽनुपलब्धेः। खरविषाणवत्। तत्र प्रत्युत्तरं—किमत्र देशेऽत्र काले अनुपलब्धिः, सर्वदेशे काले वा। यद्यत्र देशेऽत्र काले नास्ति तदा सम्मत एव। अथ सर्वदेशकाले नास्तीति भण्यते तज्जगत्त्रयं कालत्रयं सर्वज्ञरहितं कथं ज्ञातं भवता। ज्ञातं चेत्तर्हि भवानेव सर्वज्ञः। अथ न ज्ञातं तर्हि निषेधः कथं क्रियते। तत्र दृष्टान्तः—यथा कोऽपि निषेधको घटस्याधारभूतं घटरहितं भूतलं चक्षुषा दृष्ट्वा पश्चाद्वदत्यत्र भूतले घटो नास्तीति युक्तम्। यस्तु चक्षूरहितस्तस्य पुनरिदं वचनमयुक्तम्। तथैव यस्तु जगत्त्रयं कालत्रयं सर्वज्ञरहितं जानाति तस्य जगत्त्रये कालत्रयेऽपि सर्वज्ञो नास्तीति वक्तुं युक्तं भवति, यस्तु जगत्त्रयं कालत्रयं न जानाति स सर्वस्वज्ञनिषेधं कथमपि न करोति। कस्मादिति चेत्—जगत्त्रयकालत्रयपरिज्ञानेन स्वयमेव सर्वज्ञत्वादिति।

अथोक्तमनुपलब्धेरिति हेतुवचनं तदप्ययुक्तम्। कस्मादिति चेत्—किं भवतामनुपलब्धिः, किं जगत्त्रयकालत्रयवर्त्तिपुरुषाणां वा? यदि भवतामनुपलब्धिस्तावता सर्वज्ञाभावो न सिध्यति, भवद्भिरनुपलभ्यमानानां परकीयचित्तवृत्तिपरमाण्वादिसूक्ष्मपदार्थानामिव। अथवा जगत्त्रयकालत्रयवर्त्तिपुरुषाणामनुलब्धिस्तत्कथं ज्ञातं भवद्भिः। ज्ञातं चेत्तर्हि भवन्त एव सर्वज्ञा इति पूर्वमेव भणितं तिष्ठति। इत्यादि हेतुदूषणं ज्ञातव्यम्। अथोक्तं खरविषाणवदिति दृष्टान्तवचनं तदप्यनुचितम्। खरे विषाणं नास्ति गवादौ तिष्ठतीत्यन्ताभावो नास्ति यथा तथा सर्वज्ञस्यापि नियतदेशकालादिष्वभावेऽपि सर्वथा नास्तित्वं न भवति इति दृष्टान्तदूषणं गतम्।

अथ मतम्—सर्वज्ञविषये बाधकप्रमाणं निराकृतं भद्भिस्तर्हि सर्वज्ञसद्भावसाधकं प्रमाणं किम्? इति पृष्टे प्रत्युत्तरमाह—कश्चित् पुरुषो धर्मी, सर्वज्ञो भवतीति साध्यते धर्मः, एवं धर्मिधर्मसमुदायेन पक्षवचनम्। कस्मादिति चेत् पूर्वोक्तप्रकारेण बाधकप्रमाणाभावादिति हेतुवचनम्। किंवत् स्वयमानुभूयमानसुखदुःखादिवदिति दृष्टान्तवचनम्। एवं सर्वज्ञसद्भावे पक्षहेतुदृष्टान्तरूपेण त्र्यङ्गमनुमानं विज्ञेयम्। अथवा द्वितीयमनुमानं कथ्यते—रामरावणादयः कालान्तरिता, मेर्वादयो देशान्तरिता, भूतादयः स्वभावान्तरिता, परचेतोवृत्तयः परमाण्वादयश्च सूक्ष्मपदार्था, धर्मिणः कस्यापि पुरुषविशेषस्य प्रत्यक्षा

भवन्तीति साध्यो धर्म इति धर्मिधर्मसमुदायेन पक्षवचनम् । कस्मादिति चेत्—अनुमानविषयत्वादिति हेतुवचनम् । किंवत् यद्यदनुमानविषयं तत्तत् कस्यापि प्रत्यक्षं भवति, यथाग्न्यादि, इत्यन्वयदृष्टान्तवचनम् । अनुमानेन विषयाश्चेति, इत्युपनयवचनम् । तस्मात् कस्यापि प्रत्यक्षा भवन्तीति निगमनवचनम् ।

इदानीं व्यतिरेकदृष्टान्तः कथ्यते—यन्न कस्यापि प्रत्यक्षं तदनुमानविषयमपि न भवति यथा खपुष्पादि, इति व्यतिरेकदृष्टान्तवचनम् । अनुमानविषयाश्चेति पुनरप्युपनयवचनम् । तस्मात् प्रत्यक्षा भवन्तीति पुनरपि निगमनवचनमिति । किन्त्वनुमानविषयत्वादित्ययं हेतुः सर्वज्ञस्वरूपे साध्ये सर्वप्रकारेण सम्भवति यतस्ततः कारणात्स्वरूपासिद्धभावासिद्धविशेषणाद्यसिद्धो न भवति । तथैव सर्वज्ञस्वरूपं स्वपक्षं विहाय सर्वज्ञाऽभावं विपक्षं न साधयति तेन कारणेन विरुद्धो न भवति । तथैव च यथा सर्वज्ञसद्भावे स्वपक्षे वर्त्तते तथा सर्वज्ञाभावेऽपि विपक्षेऽपि न वर्त्तते तेन कारणेनानैकान्तिको न भवति । अनैकान्तिकः कोऽर्थो व्यभिचारीति । तथैव प्रत्यक्षादिप्रमाणबाधितो न भवति । तथैव च प्रतिवादिनां प्रत्यसिद्धं सर्वज्ञसद्भावं साधयति तेन कारणेनाकिञ्चित्करोऽपि न भवति । एवमसिद्धविरुद्धानैकान्तिकाकिञ्चित्करहेतुदोषरहितत्वात्सर्वज्ञसद्भावं साधयत्येव । इत्युक्तप्रकारेण सर्वज्ञसद्भावे पक्षहेतुदृष्टान्तोपनयनिगमनरूपेण पञ्चाङ्गमनुमानं ज्ञातव्यमिति ।

किं च यथा लोचनहीनपुरुषस्यादर्शे विद्यमानेऽपि प्रतिबिम्बानां परिज्ञानं न भवति, तथा लोचनस्थानीयसर्वज्ञतागुणरहितपुरुषस्यादर्शस्थानीयवेदशास्त्रे कथितानां प्रतिबिम्बस्थानीयपरमाण्वाद्यनन्तसूक्ष्मपदार्थानां क्वापि काले परिज्ञानं न भवति । तथाचोक्तं "यस्य नास्ति स्वयं प्रज्ञा शास्त्रं तस्य करोति किम् । लोचनाभ्यां विहीनस्य दर्पणः किं करिष्यति ॥" इति संक्षेपेण सर्वज्ञसिद्धिरत्र बोद्धव्या । एवं पदस्थपिण्डस्थरूपस्थध्याने ध्येयभूतस्य सकलात्मनो जिनभट्टारकस्य व्याख्यानरूपेण गाथा गता ।

अथ सिद्धसदृशनिजपरमात्मतत्त्वपरमसमरसीभावलक्षणस्य रूपातीतनिश्चयध्यानस्य पारम्पर्येण कारणभूतं मुक्तिगतसिद्धभक्तिरूपं 'णमोसिद्धाणं' इति पदोच्चारणलक्षणं यत्पदस्थं ध्यानं तस्य ध्येयभूतं सिद्धपरमेष्ठिस्वरूपं कथयति ।

व्याख्या । 'णट्ठट्ठकम्मदेहो' शुभाशुभमनोवचनकायक्रियारूपस्य द्वैतशब्दाभिधेयकर्मकाण्डस्य निर्मूलनसमर्थेन स्वशुद्धात्मतत्वभावनोत्पन्नरागादिविकल्पोपाधिरहितपरमाल्हादैकलक्षणसुन्दरमनोहरानन्दस्यंदिनिःक्रियाद्वैतशब्दवाच्येन परमज्ञानकाण्डेन विनाशितज्ञानावरणाद्यष्टकर्मौदारिकादिपञ्चदेहत्वात् नष्टाष्टकर्मदेहः । 'लोयालोयस्स जाणओ दट्ठा' पूर्वोक्तज्ञानकाण्डभावनाफलभूतेन सकलविमलकेवलज्ञानदर्शनद्वयेन लोकालोकगतत्रिकालवर्त्तिसमस्तवस्तुसंबन्धिविशेषसामान्यस्वभावनामेकसमयज्ञायकदर्शकत्वात् लोकालोकस्य ज्ञाता द्रष्टा भवति । 'पुरिसायारो' निश्चयनयेनातीन्द्रियामूर्त्त परमचिदुच्छलननिर्भरशुद्धस्वभावेन निराकारोऽपि व्यवहारेण भूतपूर्वनयेन किञ्चिदूनचरमशरीराकारेण गतसिक्थमूषागर्भाकारवच्छायाप्रतिमावद्वा पुरुषाकारः । 'अप्पा' इत्युक्तलक्षण आत्मा किं भण्यते 'सिद्धो' अञ्जनसिद्धपादुकासिद्धगुटिकासिद्धखड्गसिद्धमायासिद्धादिलौकिकसिद्धविलक्षणः केवलज्ञानाद्यनन्तगुणव्यक्तिलक्षणः सिद्धो भण्यते । 'ज्झाएह लोयसिहरत्थो' तमित्थंभूतं सिद्धपरमेष्ठिनं लोकशिखरस्थं दृष्टश्रुतानुभूतपञ्चेन्द्रियभोगप्रभृतिसमस्तमनोरथरूपनानाविकल्पजालत्यागेन त्रिगुप्तिलक्षणरूपातीतध्याने स्थित्वा ध्यायत हे भव्या यूयमिति ॥५१॥ एवं निष्कलसिद्धपरमेष्ठिव्याख्यानेन गाथा गता ॥

अथ निरुपाधिशुद्धात्मभावनानुभूत्यविनाभूतनिश्चयपञ्चाचारलक्षणस्य निश्चयध्यानस्य परम्परया- कारणभूतं निश्चयव्यवहारपञ्चाचारपरिणताचार्यभक्तिरूपं 'णमो आयरियाणं' इति पदोच्चारणलक्षणं यत्पदस्थध्यानं तस्य ध्येयभूतमाचार्यपरमेष्ठिनं कथयति ।

'दंसणणाणपहाणे वीरियचारित्तवरतवायारे' सम्यग्दर्शनज्ञानप्रधाने वीर्यचारित्रवरतपश्चरणाचारेऽधिकरणभूते 'अप्पं परं च जुंजइ' आत्मानं परं शिष्यजनं च योऽसौ योजयति संबन्धं करोति 'सो आयरिओ मुणी झओ' स उक्तलक्षण आचार्यो मुनिस्तपोधनो ध्येयो भवति । तथा हि—भूतार्थनयविषयभूतः शुद्धसमयसारशब्दवाच्यो भावकर्मद्रव्यकर्मनोकर्मादिसमस्तपरद्रव्येभ्यो भिन्नः परमचैतन्यविलासलक्षणः स्वशुद्धात्मैवोपादेय इति रुचिरूपसम्यग्दर्शनं, तत्राचरणं परिणमनं निश्चयदर्शनाचारः ॥ तस्यैव शुद्धात्मनो निरुपाधिस्वसंवेदनलक्षणभेदज्ञानेन मिथ्यात्वरागादिपरभावेभ्यः पृथक्परिच्छेदनं सम्यक्ज्ञानं,

तत्राचरणं परिणमनं निश्चयज्ञानाचारः । तत्रैव रागादिविकल्पोपाधिरहितस्वाभाविकसुखास्वादेन निश्चलचित्तं वीतरागचारित्रं, तत्राचरणं परिणमनं निश्चयचारित्राचारः । समस्तपरद्रव्येच्छानिरोधेन तथैवानशनादिद्वादशतपश्चरणबहिरङ्गसहकारिकारणेन च स्वस्वरूपे प्रतपनं विजयनं निश्चयतपश्चरणं, तत्राचरणं परिणमनं निश्चयतपश्चरणाचारः । तस्यैव निश्चयचतुर्विधाचारस्य रक्षणार्थं स्वशक्त्यनवगूहनं निश्चयवीर्याचारः । इत्युक्तलक्षणनिश्चयपञ्चाचारे तथैव "छत्तीसगुणसमग्गे पंचविहाचारकरणसन्दरिसे । सिस्साणुग्गहकुसले धम्मायरिए सदा वंदे ॥" इति गाथाकथितक्रमेणाचाराराधनादिचरणशास्त्रविस्तीर्णबहिरङ्गसहकारिकारणभूते व्यवहारपञ्चाचारे च स्वं परं च योजयत्यनुष्ठानेन सम्बन्धं करोति स आचार्यो भवति । स च पदस्थध्याने ध्यातव्यः । इत्याचार्यपरमेष्ठिव्याख्यानेन सूत्रं गतम् ॥५२॥

अथ स्वशुद्धात्मनि शोभनमध्यायोऽभ्यासो निश्चयस्वाध्यायस्तल्लक्षणनिश्चयध्यानस्य पारम्पर्येण कारणभूतं भेदाभेदरत्नत्रयादितत्त्वोपदेशकं परमोपाध्यायभक्तिरूपं 'णमो उवज्झायाणं' इति पदोच्चारणलक्षणं यत् पदस्थध्यानं, तस्य ध्येयभूतमुपाध्यायमुनीश्वरं कथयति ।

व्याख्या ।—'जो रयणत्तयजुत्तो' योऽसौ बाह्याभ्यन्तररत्नत्रयानुष्ठानेन युक्तः परिणतः । 'णिच्चं धम्मोवएसणे णिरदो' षट्द्रव्यपञ्चास्तिकायसप्ततत्त्वनवपदार्थेषु मध्ये स्वशुद्धात्मद्रव्यं स्वशुद्धजीवास्तिकायं स्वशुद्धात्मतत्त्वं स्वशुद्धात्मपदार्थमेवोपादेयं शेषं च हेयं, तथैवोत्तमक्षमादिधर्मं च नित्यमुपदिशति योऽसौ स नित्यं धर्मोपदेशने निरतो भण्यते । 'सो उवझाओ अप्पा' स चेत्थम्भूतो आत्मा उपाध्याय इति । पुनरपि किं विशिष्टः ?—'जदिवरवसहो' पञ्चेन्द्रियविषयजयेन निजशुद्धात्मनि यत्नपराणां यतिवराणां मध्ये वृषभः प्रधानो यतिवरवृषभः । 'णमो तस्स' तस्मै द्रव्यभावरूपो नमो नमस्कारोऽस्तु । इत्युपाध्यायपरमेष्ठिव्याख्यानरूपेण गाथा गता ॥ ५३ ॥

अथ निश्चयरत्नत्रयात्मकनिश्चयध्यानस्य परम्परया कारणभूतं बाह्याभ्यन्तरमोक्षमार्गसाधकं परमसाधुभक्तिरूपं 'णमो लोए सव्वसाहूणं' इति पदोच्चारणजपध्यानलक्षणं यत् पदस्थध्यानं तस्य ध्येयभूतं साधुपरमेष्ठिस्वरूपं कथयति ।

व्याख्या ।—'साहू स मुणी' स मुनिः साधुर्भवति । यः किं करोति—

'जो हु साधयदि' यः कर्त्ता हु स्फुटं साधयति । किं 'चारित्त' चारित्रं कथम्भूतं 'दंसणणाणसमग्ग' वीतरागसम्यग्दर्शनज्ञानाभ्यां समग्रं परिपूर्णम् । पुनरपि कथम्भूतं 'मग्गं मोक्खस्स' मार्गभूतं कस्य मोक्षस्य । पुनश्च किं रूपं 'णिच्चसुद्धं' नित्यं सर्वकालं शुद्धं रागादिरहितम् । 'णमो तस्स' एवं गुणविशिष्टो यस्तस्मै साधवे नमो नमस्कारोऽस्त्विति । तथाहि—"उद्योतनमुद्योगो निर्वहणं साधनं च निस्तरणम् । दृगवगमचरणतपसामाख्याताराधना सद्भिः ॥" इत्यार्याकथितबहिरङ्गचतुर्विधाराधनाबलेन, तथैव "सम्मत्तं सण्णाणं सच्चारित्तं हि सत्तवो चेव । चउरो चिट्ठहि आदे तम्हा आदा हु मे सरणं ॥" इति गाथाकथिताभ्यन्तरनिश्चयचतुर्विधाराधनाबलेन च बाह्याभ्यन्तरमोक्षमार्गद्वितीयनामाभिधेयेन कृत्वा यः कर्त्ता वीतरागचारित्राविनाभूतं स्वशुद्धात्मानं साधयति भावयति स साधुर्भवति । तस्यैव सहजशुद्धसदानन्दैकानुभूतिलक्षणो भावनमस्कारस्तथा 'णमो लोए सव्वसाहूणं' द्रव्यनमस्कारश्च भवत्विति ॥५४॥

एवमुक्तप्रकारेण गाथापञ्चकेन मध्यमप्रतिपत्त्या पञ्चपरमेष्ठिस्वरूपं ज्ञातव्यम् । अथवा निश्चयेन "अरिहासिद्धायरियाउवज्झयासाहुपंचपरमेट्ठी । ते वि हु चिट्ठहि आदे तम्हा आदा हु मे सरणं ॥" इति गाथाकथितक्रमेण संक्षेपेन, तथैव विस्तरेण पञ्चपरमेष्ठिग्रन्थकथितक्रमेण, अतिविस्तारेण तु सिद्धचक्रादिदेवार्चनाविधिरूपमन्त्रवादसंबन्धिपञ्चनमस्कारग्रन्थे चेति । एवंगाथापञ्चकेन द्वितीयस्थलं गतम् ।

अथ तदेव ध्यानं विकल्पितनिश्चयेनाविकल्पितनिश्चयेन प्रकारान्तरेणोपसंहाररूपेण पुनरप्याह । तत्र प्रथमपादे ध्येयलक्षणं, द्वितीयपादे ध्यातृलक्षणं, तृतीयपादे ध्यानलक्षणं, चतुर्थपादेन नयविभागं कथयामीत्यभिप्रायं मनसि धृत्वा भगवान् सूत्रमिदं प्रतिपादयति ।

व्याख्या । 'तदा' तस्मिन् काले आहुर्ब्रुवन्ति 'तं तस्स णिच्चयं झाणं' तत्तस्य निश्चयध्यानमिति । यदा किं 'णिरीहवित्ती हवे जदा साहू' निरीहवृत्तिर्निस्पृहवृत्तिर्यदा साधुर्भवति । किं कुर्वन् 'जं किंचिवि चिंततो' यत् किमपि ध्येयवस्तुरूपेण वस्तु चिन्तयन्निति । किं कृत्वा पूर्वं 'लद्धूणय एयत्तं' तस्मिन् ध्येये लब्ध्वा किं ? एकत्वं एकाग्रचिन्तानिरोधनमिति । अथ विस्तारः यत् किञ्चिद् ध्येयमित्यनेन किमुक्तं भवति ? प्राथमिकापेक्षया सविकल्पावस्थायां

विषयकषायवञ्चनार्थं चित्तस्थिरीकरणार्थं पञ्चपरमेष्ठ्यादिपरद्रव्यमपि ध्येयं भवति। पश्चादभ्यासवशेन स्थिरीभूते चित्ते सति शुद्धबुद्धैकस्वभावनिजशुद्धात्मस्वरूपमेव ध्येयमित्युक्तं भवति। निस्पृहवचनेन पुनर्मिथ्यात्वं वेदत्रयं हास्यादिषट्कक्रोधादिचतुष्टयरूपचतुर्दशाऽभ्यन्तरपरिग्रहेण तथैव क्षेत्रवास्तुहिरण्यसुवर्णधनधान्यदासीदासकुप्यभाण्डाऽभिधानदशविधबहिरङ्गपरिग्रहेण च रहितं ध्यातृस्वरूपमुक्तं भवति। एकाग्रचिन्तानिरोधेन च पूर्वोक्तविविधध्येयवस्तुनि स्थिरत्वं निश्चलत्वं ध्यानलक्षणं भणितमिति। निश्चयशब्देन तु प्राथमिकापेक्षया व्यवहाररत्नत्रयानुकूलनिश्चयो ग्राह्यः। निष्पन्नयोगपुरुषापेक्षया तु शुद्धोपयोगलक्षणविवक्षितैकदेशशुद्धनिश्चयो ग्राह्यः। विशेषनिश्चयः पुनरग्रे वक्ष्यमाणस्तिष्ठतीति सूत्रार्थः ॥ ५५ ॥

अथ शुभाशुभमनोवचनकायनिरोधे कृते सत्यात्मनि स्थिरो भवति तदेव परमध्यानमित्युपदिशति।

व्याख्या। 'मा चिट्ठह मा जंपह मा चिंतह किंवि' नित्यनिरञ्जननिष्क्रियनिजशुद्धात्मानुभूतिप्रतिबन्धकं शुभाशुभचेष्टारूपं कायव्यापारं, तथैव शुभाशुभान्तर्बहिर्जल्परूपं वचनव्यापारं, तथैव शुभाशुभविकल्पजालरूपं चित्तव्यापारञ्च किमपि मा कुरुत हे विवेकिजनाः! 'जेण होइ थिरो' येन योगत्रयनिरोधेन स्थिरो भवति। स कः 'अप्पा' आत्मा। कथम्भूतः स्थिरो भवति 'अप्पम्मि रओ' सहजशुद्धज्ञानदर्शनस्वभावपरमात्मतत्त्वसम्यक्श्रद्धानज्ञानानुचरणरूपाभेदरत्नत्रयात्मकपरमसमाधिसमुद्भूतसर्वप्रदेशाल्हादजनकसुखास्वादपरिणतिसहिते निजात्मनि रतः परिणतस्तल्लीयमानस्तच्चित्तस्तन्मयो भवति। 'इणमेव परं हवे ज्झाणं' इदमेवात्मसुखरूपे तन्मयत्वं निश्चयेन परमुत्कृष्टं ध्यानं भवति।

तस्मिन् ध्याने स्थितानां यद्वीतरागपरमानन्दसुखं प्रतिभाति, तदेव निश्चयमोक्षमार्गस्वरूपम्। तच्च पर्यायनामान्तरेण किं किं भण्यते तदभिधीयते। तदेव शुद्धात्मस्वरूपं, तदेव परमात्मस्वरूपं, तदेवैकदेशव्यक्तिरूपविवक्षितैकदेशशुद्धनिश्चयेन स्वशुद्धात्मसंवित्तिसमुत्पन्नसुखामृतजलसरोवरे रागादिमलरहितत्वेन परमहंसस्वरूपम्। इदमेकदेशव्यक्तिरूपं शुद्धनयव्याख्यानमत्र परमात्मध्यानभावनानाममालायां यथासम्भवं सर्वत्र योजनीयमिति।

तदेव परब्रह्मस्वरूपं, तदेव परमविष्णुस्वरूपं, तदेव परमशिवस्वरूपं, तदेव

परमशुद्धस्वरूपं, तदेव परमनिजस्वरूपं, तदेव परमस्वात्मोपलब्धिलक्षणं सिद्धस्वरूपं, तदेव निरञ्जनस्वरूपं, तदेव निर्मलस्वरूपं, तदेव स्वसंवेदनज्ञानं, तदेव परमतत्त्वज्ञानं, तदेव शुद्धात्मदर्शनं, तदेव परमावस्थास्वरूपं, तदेव परमात्मनः दर्शनं, तदेव परमतत्त्वज्ञानं, तदेव शुद्धात्मदर्शनं, तदेव ध्येयभूतशुद्धपारिणामिकभावरूपं, तदेव ध्यानभावनास्वरूपं, तदेव शुद्धचारित्रं, तदेवान्तस्तत्त्वं, तदेव परमतत्त्वं, तदेव शुद्धात्मद्रव्यं, तदेव परमज्योतिः, सैव शुद्धात्मानुभूतिः, सैवात्मप्रतीतिः, सैवात्मसंवित्तिः, सैव स्वरूपोपलब्धिः, स एव नित्योपलब्धिः, स एव परमसमाधिः, स एव परमानन्दः, स एव नित्यानन्दः, स एव सहजानन्दः, स एव सदानन्दः, स एव शुद्धात्मपदार्थाध्ययनरूपः, स एव परमस्वाध्यायः, स एव निश्चयमोक्षोपायः, स एव चैकाग्रचिन्तानिरोधः, स एव परमबोधः, स एव शुद्धोपयोगः, स एव परमयोगः, स एव भूतार्थः, स एव परमार्थः, स एव निश्चयपञ्चाचारः, स एव समयसारः, स एवाध्यात्मसारः, तदेव समतादिनिश्चयषडावश्यकस्वरूपं, तदेवाभेदरत्नत्रयस्वरूपं, तदेव वीतरागसामायिकं, तदेव परमशरणोत्तममङ्गलं, तदेव केवलज्ञानोत्पत्तिकारणं, तदेव सकलकर्मक्षयकारणं, सैव निश्चयचतुर्विधाराधना, सैव परमात्मभावना, सैव शुद्धात्मभावनोत्पन्नसुखानुभूतिरूपपरमकला, सैव दिव्यकला, तदेव परमाद्वैतं, तदेव परमामृतपरमधर्मध्यानं, तदेव शुक्लध्यानं, तदेव रागादिविकल्पशून्यध्यानं, तदेव निष्कलध्यानं, तदेव परमस्वास्थ्यं, तदेव परमवीतरागत्वं, तदेव परमसाम्यं, तदेव परमैकत्वं, तदेव परमभेदज्ञानं, स एव परमसमरसीभावः इत्यादिसमस्तरागादिविकल्पोपाधिरहितपरमाल्हादैकसुखलक्षणध्यानरूपस्य निश्चयमोक्षमार्गस्य वाचकान्यन्यान्यपि पर्यायनामानि विज्ञेयानि भवन्ति परमात्मतत्त्वविद्भिरिति ॥ ५६ ॥

अतःपरं यद्यपि पूर्वं बहुधा भणितं ध्यातृपुरुषलक्षणं ध्यानसामग्री च तथापि चूलिकोपसंहाररूपेण पुनरप्याख्याति ।

व्याख्या । 'तवसुदवदवं चेदा ज्झाणरहधुरंधरो हवे जम्हा' तपश्रुतव्रतवानात्मा चेतयिता ध्यानरथस्य धुरन्धरो समर्थो भवति 'जम्हा' यस्मात् 'तम्हा तत्तियणिरदा तल्लद्धीए सदा होह' तस्मात् कारणात् तपश्रुतव्रतानां संबन्धेन यत्त्रितयं तत् त्रितये रता सर्वकाले भवत हे भव्याः ! किमर्थं ? तस्य ध्यानस्य

लब्धिस्तल्लब्धिस्तदर्थमिति । तथाहि—अनशनावमौदर्यवृत्तिपरिसंख्यानरस-परित्यागविविक्तशय्यासनकायक्लेशभेदेन बाह्यं षड्विधं, तथैव प्रायश्चित्तविनय-वैय्यावृत्यस्वाध्यायव्युत्सर्गध्यानभेदेनाभ्यन्तरमपि षड्विधं चेति द्वादशविधं तपः । तेनैव साध्यं शुद्धात्मस्वरूपे प्रतपमं विजयनं निश्चयतपश्च । तथैवाचा-राराधनादिद्रव्यश्रुतं, तदाधारेणोत्पन्नं निर्विकारस्वसंवेदनज्ञानरूपं भावश्रुतं च । तथैव च हिंसानृतस्तेयाब्रह्मपरिग्रहाणां द्रव्यभावरूपाणां परिहरणं व्रतपञ्चकं चेति । एवमुक्तलक्षणतपःश्रुतव्रतसहितो ध्याता पुरुषो भवति । इयमेव ध्यान-सामग्री चेति । तथाचोक्तं—"वैराग्यं तत्त्वविज्ञानं नैर्ग्रन्थ्यं समचित्तता । परीषहजयश्चेति पञ्चैते ध्यानहेतवः ॥"

भगवन्, ध्यानं तावन्मोक्षमार्गभूतम् । मोक्षार्थिना पुरुषेण पुण्यबन्धका-रणत्वाद्व्रतानि त्याज्यानि भवन्ति, भवद्भिः पुनर्ध्यानसामग्रीकारणानि तपःश्रु-तव्रतानि व्याख्यातानि, तत्कथं घटत इति । तत्रोत्तरं दीयते—व्रतान्येव केवला-नि त्याज्यान्येव न किन्तु पापबन्धकारणानि हिंसादिविकल्परूपाणि यान्यव्र-तानि तान्यपि त्याज्यानि । तथाचोक्तं पूज्यपादस्वामिभिः—"अपुण्यमव्रतैः पुण्यं व्रतैर्मोक्षस्तयोर्व्ययः । अव्रतानीव मोक्षार्थी व्रतान्यपि ततस्त्यजेत् ॥" किंत्वव्रतानि पूर्वं परित्यज्य ततश्च व्रतेषु तन्निष्ठो भूत्वा निर्विकल्पसमाधिरूपं परमात्मपदं प्राप्य पश्चादेकदेशव्रतान्यपि त्यजति । तदप्युक्तं तैरेव—"अव्रतानि परित्यज्य व्रतेषु परिनिष्ठितः । त्यजेत्तान्यपि संप्राप्य परमं पदमात्मनः ॥"

अयं तु विशेषः—व्यवहाररूपाणि यानि प्रसिद्धान्येकदेशव्रतानि तानि त्यक्तानि । यानि पुनः सर्वशुभाशुभनिवृत्तिरूपाणि निश्चयव्रतानि तानि त्रिगुप्ति-लक्षणस्वशुद्धात्मसंवित्तिरूपनिर्विकल्पध्याने स्वीकृतान्येव न च त्यक्तानि । प्रसिद्धमहाव्रतानि कथमेकदेशरूपाणि जातानि । इति चेत्तदुच्यते—जीवघा-तानिवृत्तौ सत्यामपि जीवरक्षणे प्रवृत्तिरस्ति । तथैवासत्यवचनपरिहारेऽपि सत्य-वचनप्रवृत्तिरस्ति । तथैव चादत्तादानपरिहारेऽपि दत्तादाने प्रवृत्तिरस्तीत्याद्येक-देशप्रवृत्त्यपेक्षया देशव्रतानि । तेषामेकदेशव्रतानां त्रिगुप्तिलक्षणनिर्विकल्पसमा-धिकाले त्यागः । न च समस्तशुभाशुभनिवृत्तिलक्षणस्य निश्चयव्रतस्येति । त्यागः कोऽर्थः । यथैव हिंसादिरूपाव्रतेषु निवृत्तिस्तथैकदेशव्रतेष्वपि । कस्मादिति चेत्—त्रिगुप्तावस्थायां प्रवृत्तिनिवृत्तिरूपविकल्पस्य स्वयमेवावकाशो नास्ति ।

अथवा वस्तुतस्तदेव निश्चयव्रतम् । कस्मात्—सर्वनिवृत्तित्वादिति । योऽपि घटिकाद्वयेन मोक्षं गतो भरतश्चक्री सोऽपि जिनदीक्षां गृहीत्वा विषयकषायनिवृत्तिरूपं क्षणमात्रं व्रतपरिणामं कृत्वा पश्चाच्छुद्धोपयोगत्वरूपरत्नत्रयात्मके निश्चयव्रताभिधाने वीतरागसामायिकसंज्ञे निर्विकल्पसमाधौ स्थित्वा केवलज्ञानं लब्धवानिति । परं किन्तु तस्य स्तोककालत्वाल्लोका व्रतपरिणामं न जानन्तीति । तदेव भरतस्य दीक्षाविधानं कथ्यते । हे भगवन् जिनदीक्षादानानन्तरं भरतचक्रिणः कियति काले केवलज्ञानं जातमिति श्रीवीरवर्द्धमानस्वामितीर्थकरपरमदेवसमवसरणमध्ये श्रेणिकमहाराजेन पृष्टे सति गौतमस्वामी आह । "पञ्चमुष्टिभिरुत्पाट्य त्रोट्यन् बन्धस्थितीन् कचान् । लोचानन्तरमेवापद्राजन् श्रेणिक केवलम् ॥"

अत्राह शिष्यः । अद्य काले ध्यानं नास्ति । कस्मादिति चेत्—उत्तमसंहननाभावाद्दशचतुर्दशपूर्वगतश्रुतज्ञानाभावाच्च । अत्र परिहारः । शुक्लध्यानं नास्ति धर्मध्यानमस्तीति । तथाचोक्तं मोक्षप्राभृते श्रीकुन्दकुन्दाचार्यदेवैः "भरहे दुस्समकाले धम्मज्झाणं हवेइ णाणिस्स । तं अप्पसहावठिए णहु मण्णइ सो दु अण्णाणी ॥ अज्जवि तिरयणसुद्धा अप्पा झाऊण लहइ इंदत्तं । लोयंतियदेवत्तं तच्छचुदा णिव्वुदिं जंति ॥" तथैव तत्त्वानुशासनग्रन्थे चोक्तं "अत्रेदानीं निषेधन्ति शुक्लध्यानं जिनोत्तमाः । धर्मध्यानं पुनः प्राहुः श्रेणीभ्यां प्राग्विवर्त्तिनाम् ॥" यथोक्तमुत्तमसंहननाभावात्तदुत्सर्गवचनम् । अपवादव्याख्यानेन पुनरुपशमक्षपकश्रेण्योः शुक्लध्यानं भवति, तच्चोत्तमसंहननेनैव । अपूर्वगुणस्थानादधस्तनेषु गुणस्थानेषु धर्मध्यानं, तच्चादिमत्रिकोत्तमसंहननाभावेऽप्यन्तिमत्रिकसंहननेनापि भवति । तदप्युक्तं तत्रैव तत्त्वानुशासने "यत्पुनर्वज्रकायस्य ध्यानमित्यागमे वचः । श्रेण्योर्ध्यानं प्रतीत्योक्तं तन्नोऽधस्तान्निषेधकम् ॥" यथोक्तं दशचतुर्दशपूर्वगतश्रुतज्ञानेन ध्यानं भवति तदप्युत्सर्गवचनम् । अपवादव्याख्यानेन पुनः पञ्चसमितित्रिगुप्तिप्रतिपादकसारभूतश्रुतेनापि ध्यानं भवति केवलज्ञानञ्च । यद्येवमपवादव्याख्यानं नास्ति तर्हि "तुसमासं घोसण्ती सिवभूदी केवली जादो" इत्यादिगन्धर्वाराधनादिभणितं व्याख्यानं कथं घटते ।

अथ मतं—पञ्चसमितित्रिगुप्तिप्रतिपादकं द्रव्यश्रुतिमिति जानाति । इदं

भावश्रुतं पुनःसर्वमस्ति । नैवं वक्तव्यम् । यदि पञ्चसमितित्रिगुप्तिप्रतिपादकं द्रव्यश्रुतं जानाति तर्हि 'मा रूसह मा तूसह' इत्येकं पदं किं न जानाति । तत एव ज्ञायतेऽष्टप्रवचनमातृप्रमाणमेव भावश्रुतं, द्रव्यश्रुतं पुनः किमपि नास्ति । इदन्तु व्याख्यानमस्माभिर्न कल्पितमेव । तच्चारित्रसारादिग्रन्थेष्वपि भणितमास्ते । तथाहि—अन्तर्मुहूर्त्तादूर्ध्वं ये केवलज्ञानमुत्पादयन्ति ते क्षीणकषायगुणस्थानवर्त्तिनो निर्ग्रन्थसंज्ञा ऋषयो भण्यन्ते । तेषां चोत्कर्षेण चतुर्दशपूर्वादिश्रुतं भवति, जघन्येन पुनः पञ्चसमितित्रिगुप्तिमात्रमेवेति ।

अथ मतं—मोक्षार्थं ध्यानं क्रियते न चाद्य काले मोक्षोऽस्ति; ध्यानेन किं प्रयोजनम् । नैवं—अद्य कालेऽपि परम्परया मोक्षोऽस्ति । कथमिति चेत् स्वशुद्धात्मभावनाबलेन संसारस्थितिं स्तोकां कृत्वा देवलोकं गच्छति, तस्मादागत्य मनुष्यभवे रत्नत्रयभावनां लब्ध्वा शीघ्रं मोक्षं गच्छतीति । येऽपि भरतसगररामपाण्डवादयो मोक्षं गतास्तेपि पूर्वभवेऽभेदरत्नत्रयभावनया संसारस्थितिं स्तोकां कृत्वा पश्चान्मोक्षं गताः । तद्भवे सर्वेषां मोक्षो भवतीति नियमो नास्ति । एवमुक्तप्रकारेण अल्पश्रुतेनापि ध्यानं भवतीति ज्ञात्वा किं कर्त्तव्यम्—"वधबन्धच्छेदादेर्द्वेषाद्रागाच्च परकलत्रादेः । आध्यानमपध्यानं शासति जिनशासने विशदाः ॥ संकल्पकल्पतरुसंश्रयणात्त्वदीयं चेतो निमज्जति मनोरथसागरेऽस्मिन् । तत्रार्थतस्तव चकास्ति न किं च नापि पक्षे परं भवति कल्मषसंश्रयस्य ॥ दौर्विध्यदग्धमनसोऽन्तरुपात्तभुक्तेश्चित्तं यथोल्लसति ते स्फुरितोत्तरङ्गम् । धाम्नि स्फुरेद्यदि तथा परमात्मसंज्ञे कौतस्कुती तव भवेद्विफला प्रसूतिः ॥ कं खिद कलुसिदभूतो कामभोगे हि मुच्छिदो जीवो । ण य भुंजंतो भोगे बन्धदि भावेण कम्माणि ॥" इत्याद्यपध्यानं त्यक्त्वा—"ममत्तिं परिवज्जामि णिममत्तिमुवट्ठिदो । आलंवणं च मे आदा अवसेसाइं वोसरे ॥ आदा क्खु मज्झ णाणे आदा मे दंसणे चरीत्ते य । आदा पच्चक्खाणे आदा मे संवरे जोगे ॥ एगो मे सस्सदो अप्पा णाणदंसणलक्खणो । सेसा मे वाहिरा भावा सव्वे संजोयलक्खणा ॥" इत्यादिसारपदानि गृहीत्वा च ध्यानं कर्त्तव्यमिति ।

अथ मोक्षविषये पुनरपि नयविचारः कथ्यते । तथाहि मोक्षस्तावत् बन्धपूर्वकः ॥ तथाचोक्तं "मुक्तश्चेत् प्राक्भवेद्बन्धो नो बन्धो मोचनं कथम् ।

अबन्धे मोचनं नैव मुञ्चेरर्थो निरर्थकः ॥'' बन्धश्च शुद्धनिश्चयनयेन नास्ति। तथा बन्धपूर्वको मोक्षोऽपि । यदि पुनः शुद्धनिश्चयेन बन्धो भवति तदा सर्वदैव बन्ध एव मोक्षो नास्ति । किंच—यथा शृङ्खलाबद्धपुरुषस्य बन्धच्छेदकारणभूतभावमोक्षस्थानीयं बन्धच्छेदकारणभूतं पौरुषं पुरुषस्वरूपं न भवति, तथैव शृङ्खलापुरुषयोर्यद्द्रव्यमोक्षस्थानीयं पृथक्करणं तदपि पुरुषस्वरूपं न भवति । किन्तु ताभ्यां भिन्नं यद्दृष्टं हस्तपादादिरूपं तदेव पुरुषस्वरूपम् । तथैव शुद्धोपयोगलक्षणं भावमोक्षस्वरूपं शुद्धनिश्चयेन जीवस्वरूपं न भवति, तथैव तेन साध्यं यज्जीवकर्मप्रदेशयोः पृथक्करणं द्रव्यमोक्षरूपं तदपि जीवस्वभावो न भवति । किन्तु ताभ्यां भिन्नं यदनन्तज्ञानादिगुणस्वभावं फलभूतं तदेव शुद्धजीवस्वरूपमिति । अयमत्रार्थः—यथा विवक्षितैकदेशशुद्धनिश्चयेन पूर्वं मोक्षमार्गो व्याख्यातस्तथा पर्यायमोक्षरूपो मोक्षोऽपि । न च शुद्धनिश्चयनयेनेति । यस्तु शुद्धद्रव्यशक्तिरूपः शुद्धपारिणामिकपरमभावलक्षणपरमनिश्चयमोक्षः स च पूर्वमेव जीवे तिष्ठतीदानीं भविष्यतीत्येवं न । स एव रागादिविकल्परहिते मोक्षकारणभूते ध्यानभावनापर्याये ध्येयो भवति । न च ध्यानभावनापर्यायरूपः । यदि पुनरेकान्तेन द्रव्यार्थिकनयेनापि स एव मोक्षकारणभूतो ध्यानभावनापर्यायो भण्यते तर्हि द्रव्यपर्यायरूपधर्मद्वयाधारभूतस्य जीवधर्मिणो मोक्षपर्याये जाते सति यथा ध्यानभावनापर्यायरूपेण विनाशो भवति, तथा ध्येयभूतस्य जीवस्य शुद्धपारिणामिकलक्षणभावद्रव्यरूपेणापि विनाशः प्राप्नोति । न च द्रव्यरूपेण विनाशोऽस्ति । ततः स्थितं शुद्धपारिणामिकभावेन बन्धमोक्षौ न भवत इति ।

अथात्मशब्दार्थः कथ्यते। अतधातुः सातत्यगमनेऽर्थे वर्त्तते । गमनशब्देनात्र ज्ञानं भण्यते 'सर्वे गत्यर्था ज्ञानार्था, इति वचनात् । तेन कारणेन यथासंभवं ज्ञानसुखादिगुणेषु आ समन्तात् अतति वर्त्तते यः स आत्मा भण्यते । अथवा शुभाशुभमनोवचनकायव्यापारैर्यथासम्भवं तीव्रमन्दादिरूपेण आ समन्तादतिवर्त्तते यः स आत्मा । अथवा उत्पादव्ययध्रौव्यैरासमन्तादतति वर्त्तते यः स आत्मा । किञ्च—यथैकोऽपि चन्द्रमा नानाजलघटेषु दृश्यते तथैकोऽपि जीवो नानाशरीरेषु तिष्ठतीति वदन्ति तत्तु न घटते । कस्मादिति चेत्—चन्द्रकिरणोपाधिवशेन घटस्थजलपुद्गला एव नानाचन्द्राकारेण परिणता, न चैकश्चन्द्रः ।

तत्र दृष्टान्तमाह—यथा देवदत्तमुखोपाधिवशेन नानादर्पणस्थपुद्गला एव नानामुखाकारेण परिणता, न चैकं देवदत्तमुखं नानारूपेण परिणतम् । परिणमतीति चेत्—तर्हि दर्पणस्थप्रतिबिम्बं चैतन्यं प्राप्नोतीति । न च तथा । किन्तु यद्येक एव जीवो भवति, तदैकजीवस्य सुखदुःखजीवितमरणादिके प्राप्ते तस्मिन्नेव क्षणे सर्वेषां जीवितमरणादिकं प्राप्नोति न च तथा दृश्यते ।

अथवा ये वदन्ति यथैऽकोपि समुद्रः क्वापि क्षारजलः क्वापि मिष्टजलस्तथैकोऽपि जीवः सर्वदेहेषु तिष्ठतीति । तदपि न घटते । कथमितिचेत्—जलराश्यपेक्षया तत्रैकत्वं, न च जलपुद्गलापेक्षया तत्रैकत्वम् । यदि जलपुद्गलापेक्षया भवत्येकत्वं तर्हि स्तोकजले गृहीते शेषजलं सहैव किन्नायाति । ततः स्थितं षोडशवर्णिकासुवर्णराशिवदनन्तज्ञानादिलक्षणं प्रत्येकं जीवराशिं प्रति न चैकजीवापेक्षयेति । अध्यात्मशब्दस्यार्थः कथ्यते । मिथ्यात्वरागादिसमस्तविकल्पजालरूपपरिहारेण स्वशुद्धात्मन्यधि यदनुष्ठानन्तदध्यात्ममिति । एवं ध्यानसामग्रीव्याख्यानोपसंहाररूपेण गाथा गता ॥ ५७ ॥

अथौद्धत्यपरिहारं कथयति ।

व्याख्या । "सोधयंतु" शुद्धं कुर्वन्तु । के कर्त्तारः ? "मुणिणाहा" मुनिनाथा मुनिप्रधानाः । किंविशिष्टाः ? "दोससंचयचुदा" निर्दोषपरमात्मनो विलक्षणा ये रागादिदोषास्तथैव च निर्दोषपरमात्मादितत्त्वपरिज्ञानविषये संशयविमोहविभ्रमास्तैश्च्युता रहिता दोषसंचयच्युताः । पुनरपि कथम्भूताः ? "सुदपुण्णा" वर्त्तमानपरमागमाभिधानद्रव्यश्रुतेन तथैव तदाधारोत्पन्ननिर्विकारस्वसंवेदनज्ञानरूपभावश्रुतेन च पूर्णाः समग्राः श्रुतपूर्णाः । कं शोधयन्तु ? "दव्वसंगहमिणं" शुद्धबुद्धैकस्वभावपरमात्मादिद्रव्याणां सङ्ग्रहो द्रव्यसङ्ग्रहस्तं द्रव्यसङ्ग्रहाभिधानं ग्रन्थमिमं प्रत्यक्षीभूतम् । किं विशिष्टं ? 'भणियं जं" भणितः प्रतिपादितो यो ग्रन्थः । केन कर्तृभूतेन ? "णेमिचंदमुणिणा" श्रीनेमिचन्द्र-सिद्धान्तिदेवाभिधानेन मुनिना सम्यग्दर्शनादिनिश्चयव्यवहाररूपपञ्चाचारोपेताचार्येण । कथम्भूतेन "तणुसुत्तधरेण" तनुश्रुतधरेण तनुश्रुतं स्तोकं श्रुतं तद्धरतीति तनुश्रुतधरस्तेन । इति क्रियाकारकसम्बन्धः । एवं ध्यानोपसंहारगाथात्रयेण, औद्धत्यपरिहारार्थं प्राकृतवृत्तेन च द्वितीयान्तराधिकारे तृतीयं स्थलं गतम् ॥ ५८ ॥

इत्यन्तराधिकारद्वयेन विंशतिगाथाभिर्मोक्षमार्गप्रतिपादकनामा तृतीयोऽधिकारः समाप्तः ।

अत्र ग्रन्थे 'विवक्षितस्य सन्धिर्भवति' इति वचनात्पदानां सन्धिनियमो नास्ति । वाक्यानि च स्तोकस्तोकानि कृतानि सुखबोधनार्थम् । तथैव लिङ्गवचनक्रियाकारकसम्बन्धसमासविशेषणवाक्यसमाप्त्यादिदूषणं तथा च शुद्धात्मादितत्त्वप्रतिपादनविषये विस्मृतिदूषणं च विद्वद्भिर्न ग्राह्यमिति ।

एवं पूर्वोक्तप्रकारेण "जीवमजीवं दब्वं" इत्यादिसप्तविंशतिगाथाभिः षट्द्रव्यपञ्चास्तिकायप्रतिपादकनामा प्रथमोऽधिकारः । तदनन्तरं "आसवबन्धण" इत्येकादशगाथाभिः सप्ततत्त्वनवपदार्थप्रतिपादकनामा द्वितीयोऽधिकारः । ततः परं "सम्मद्दंसण" इत्यादिविंशतिगाथाभिर्मोक्षमार्गप्रतिपादकनामा तृतीयोऽधिकारः ।

इत्यधिकारत्रयेनाष्टाधिकपञ्चाशत्सूत्रैः श्रीनेमिचन्द्रसिद्धान्तिदेवैर्विरचितस्य द्रव्यसंग्रहाभिधानग्रन्थस्य सम्बन्धिनी
श्रीब्रह्म-देवकृतवृत्तिः समाप्ता ॥

NOTES ON

IMPORTANT REFERENCES

Verse I. Page 2.

A. The Jinas and the Jineśvaras.

The epithet "Gaṇadhara" or the leader of the assembly was first applied to Gautama of Brahmapura who became a disciple of the twenty-fourth Tîrthaṅkara Mahâvîra. There were other Gaṇadharas after Gautama. Gaṇadharas are also called Jinas, or the victors and the Jineśvaras or Lords of Jinas are the Tîrthaṅkaras themselves.

Gautama was called a Gaṇadhara when he became a desciple of Mahâvîra after the latter had attained omniscience. The attainment of omniscience (Kevala Jñâna) is preceded by complete eradication of the four Ghâtiya Karmas, *viz.*, Jñânâvaraṇîya, Darśanâvaraṇiya, Mohanîya and Antarâya. There is no Âsrava or influx of Karmas. Consequently there is no voluntary physical motion and therefore no speech which is the result of the motion of tongue, lips, etc. The voice of silence, the letterless speech, the Divya-vâṇî which proceeds from the Arhat is due to the good and strong Karmic energy of the audience. Therefore there must be an individual among the audience so learned as to be capable of interpreting this voice of silence. There was no such person present in the court (Samavasaraṇa) of Mahâvîra when he attained omniscience. The Arch-angel of the first Empyrian then thought of the learned Brahmin Gautama of Brahmapura. He went to Gautama in the assumed form of a poor old Brahmin and asked him to explain to him the meaning of a Śloka. Gautama was quite perplexed when he heard the Śloka and being unable to understand its purport, proposed to go and discuss the meaning of it with Mahâvîra himself, the preceptor of that poor old Brahmin. With this object, he approached the court of Mahâvîra and at the sight of the Manastambha, the pillar at the entrance, his pride disappeared and he entered the court full of reverence and humility. It was then that the voice of silence was revealed to him and he discoursed upon it to the assembled audience and was called Gaṇadhara, the leader of the assembly. Such is the Digambar tradition about Gautama.

CHART No. VI.

The Tirthankaras are twenty-four in number and their names with some details about each will be found in the following table.*

No.	Name of Tirthankara.	Father.	Mother.	Complexion.	Emblem.	Birth-place.	Place of Nirvana.
1	Riṣabhadeva or Âdinâtha.	Nâbhi-râja.	Maru-devî.	Yellow or golden.	A bull.	Vinîta-nagara or Ayodhyâ.	Mount Aṣṭâpada or Kailâśa.
2	Ajita-nâtha ...	Jita-śatru.	Vijayâ-devî.	Do.	An elephant.	Ayodhyâ.	Mount Pârśvanâtha or Sameta-sikhara.
3	Sambhava-nâtha	Jitâri.	Senâ.	Do.	A horse.	Śrâvastî.	" "
4	Abhinandana-nâtha.	Saṃvara.	Siddhârthâ.	Do.	An ape.	Ayodhyâ.	" "
5	Sumati-nâtha ...	Megha-prabha.	Sumaṅgalâ or Maṅgalâ (Svetâmbara).	Do.	A red goose or curlew (क्रौञ्च)	"	" "
6	Padma-prabha ...	Dharaṇa or Śrîdhara (Svetâmbara)	Susîmâ.	Red.	A red lotus.	Kauśâmbî.	" "
7	Supârśva-nâtha.	Supratiṣṭha or Pratiṣṭha (Svetambara).	Prithivî.	Yellow or golden or green.	The Svastika Symbol (卐)	Bârâṇasi.	" "
8	Chandra-prabha	Mahâ-sena.	Lakṣmaṇâ.	White.	Crescent.	Chandra-purî.	" "
9	Puṣpa-danta or Suvidhi-nâtha.	Sugrîva.	Râmâ.	Do.	Crab or Dolphin or crocodile (मकर)	Kâkandî-nagara	" "
10	Śîtala-nâtha ...	Dridha-ratha	Sunandâ or Nandâ (Śvetâmbara).	Yellow or golden.	*Ficus Religiosa* or wishing tree or the Śrîvatsa figure (Svetâmbara).	Bhadrikâ-purî or Bhadilâ-puri (Svetâmbara).	" "
11	Śreyâṃsa-nâtha	Viṣṇu.	Viṣṇudrî or Viṣṇâ (Śvetâmbara).	Do.	A rhinoceros or Garuḍa (Svetâmbara).	Siṃha-purî.	" "

12	Vâsu pûjya ...	Vasu pûjya.	Vijayâ or Jayâ (Śvetâmbara).	Red.	A buffalo.	Champâ-purî	Champâ-purî
13	Vimala-nâtha ...	Kṛita-varman.	Suramyâ or Syâmâ (Śvetâmbara).	Yellow or golden.	A boar.	Kâmpilya-pura.	Mount Pârśvanâtha or Sameta-sîkhara.
14	Ananta-nâtha ...	Siṃha-sena.	Sarva-yaśâ or Suyaśâ (Śvetâmbara).	Do.	A bear or hawk (Śvetâmbara).	Ayodhyâ.	" "
15	Dharma-nâtha ...	Bhânu.	Suvratâ.	Do.	A club or thunderbolt (वज्रदण्ड)	Ratna-purî.	" "
16	Śânti-nâtha ...	Viśva-sena.	Achirâ.	Do.	A deer.	Hastinâ-pura.	" "
17	Kunthu-nâtha ...	Sûrya or Śûra (Svetâmbara).	Śrî-devî.	Do.	A he-goat.	"	" "
18	Ara-nâtha ...	Sudarśana.	Mitrâ or Devî (Svetâmbara).	Do.	A fish or Nandyâ-vartta diagram (Svetâmbara)	"	" "
19	Malli-nâtha (accord to the Svetâmbara sect a woman).	Kumbha.	Rakṣitâ or Prabhâvatî (Svetâmbara).	Yellow or golden or blue (Svetâmbara).	Water-pot.	Mithilâ-purî or Mathurâ (Svetâmbara).	" "
20	Muni-suvrata ...	Sumitra.	Padmâvatî.	Black.	A tortoise.	Kuśâgranagara or Râjagriha.	" "
21	Nami-nâtha ...	Vijaya.	Vaprâ or Viprâ (Svetâmbara).	Yellow or golden.	A blue lotus or Aśoka tree.	Mithilâpurî or Mathurâ (Svetâmbara).	" "
22	Nemi-nâtha ...	Samudra-vijaya	Śivâ-devî.	Black or black with inner tinge of red.	A conch-shell.	Śauripura or Dvârakâ.	Mount Girnâr
23	Pârśva-nâtha ...	Aśva-sena.	Vâmâ.	Blue.	A serpent.	Bârâṇasî.	Mount Pârśvanâtha or Sameta Sîkhara.
24	Mahâvîra or Vardhamâna.	Siddhârtha.	Priya-kâriṇi or Triśalâ (Śvetâmbara).	Yellow or golden.	A lion.	Kuṇḍapura or Kuṇḍagrâma.	Pâvâ-purî.

*Vide. The Heart of Jainism by Mrs. Sinclair Stevenson (Oxford University Press, 1915). Appendix II. Bühler—Indian Sect of the Jainas. Appendix by Burgess, page 66. J. L. Jaini—Outlines of Jainism (Cambridge University Press, 1916), page 6. D.P. Jaini's Tîrthaṅkara Chart (Central Jaina Publishing House, Arrah). Kalpa Sûtra and Nava Tatva by J. Stevenson, D. D. Also Proceedings of the A. S. Bengal No. X Dec. 1879 pp. 277-8.

B. *The Jaina Devas.*

The Devas or gods according to the Jainas are of four kinds Bhavana-bâsi (*i.e.*, those who live in Bhavana, the Lower World), Vyantara (*i.e.*, those who live in mountains, forests, etc.), Jyotiṣa (*i.e.*, those moving in the heavens) and Vaimânika (*i.e.*, those who live in the Vimâna, the Upper World.)[1] The Bhavanabâsi gods are divided into ten, the Vyantara gods into eight and the Jyotiṣa into five classes. Vaimânika gods are of two kinds Kalpopapanna and Kalpâtîta. Kalpopapanna are of twelve kinds.[2] The names of these sub-classes of gods will appear from the following table :—

---

[1] *Vide* :—

"देवाश्चतुर्णिकायाः ।"

[तत्वार्थाधिगमसूत्रम् । ४ । १ ।]

"भावनव्यन्तरज्योतिर्वैमानिकविभेदतः ।
देवाश्चतुर्णिकायाः स्युर्नामकर्मविशेषतः ॥"

[तत्वार्थसारः । २१३]

[2] "दशाष्टपंचद्वादशविकल्पाः कल्पोपपन्नपर्यन्ताः ।"

"भवनवासिनोऽसुरनागविद्युत्सुपर्णाग्निवातस्तनितोदधिद्वीपदिक्कुमाराः"

"व्यंतराः किन्नरकिंपुरुषमहोरगगन्धर्वयक्षराक्षसभूतपिशाचाः ।"

"ज्योतिष्काः सूर्याचन्द्रमसौ ग्रहनक्षत्रप्रकीर्णकतारकाश्च ।"

"वैमानिकाः कल्पोपपन्नाः कल्पातीताश्च ।"

"सौधर्मैशानसानत्कुमारमाहेन्द्रब्रह्मब्रह्मोत्तरलांतवकापिष्ठशुक्रमहाशुक्रशतारसहस्रारेष्वानतप्राणतयोरारणाच्युतयोर्नवसु ग्रैवेयकेषु विजयवैजयंतजयंतापराजितेषु सर्वार्थसिद्धौ च ।"

[तत्वार्थाधिगमसूत्रम् । ४ ॥ ३, १०, ११, १२, १६, १७, १९]

CHART No. VII.

DEVA.

Bhavana-bâsi.

1. Asura-kumâra.
2. Nâga-kumâra.
3. Vidyut-kumâra.
4. Suparṇa-kumâra.
5. Agni-kumâra.
6. Bâta-kumâra.
7. Stanita-kumâra.
8. Udadhi-kumâra.
9. Dvîpa-kumâra.
10. Dik-kumâra.

Vyantara.

1. Kinnara.
2. Kimpuruṣa.
3. Mahoraga.
4. Gandharva
5. Yakṣa
6. Râkṣasa.
7. Bhûta.
8. Piśâcha.

Jyotiṣa.

1. Sûrya.
2. Chandra.
3. Graha.
4. Nakṣatra.
5. Prakîrṇaka. Târakâ.

Vaimânika.

Kalpo-papanna.
There are sixteen Kalpas or spheres, *viz.*—

1. Saudharma.
2. Aiśâna.
3. Sânat-kumâra.
4. Mâhendra.
5. Brahma. }
6. Brahmottara. }
7. Lântava. }
8. Kâpistha. }
9. Śukra. }
10. Mahâ-śukra. }
11. Śatâra. }
12. Sahasrâra. }
13. Ânata.
14. Prâṇata.
15. Araṇa.
16. Achyuta.

[In these Kalpas there are twelve sets of Gods, the Kalpas bracketted together having one set only between them.]

Kalpâtîta.
[There are the following spheres in this division:— nine Graibeyaka, nine Anudiśa, Vijaya, Vaijayanta, Jayanta, Aparâjita and Sarvârtha-siddhi.]

All these gods are of various grades.* The highest among them are Indras who are possessed of superior powers and may be likened to kings in this world.[1] The next in order are Sâmânika gods who are to Indras as the preceptors are to kings.[2] The third grade consists of Trâyastrinśa gods who act for Indras as ministers and priests act for the benefit of kings.[3] Pârisada gods are next in order and are to Indras like friends and courtiers to kings.[4] Though the gods are not subject to injuries of any kind, yet to enhance their grandeur there is the fifth kind of gods known as Âtma-rakṣas who surround Indras like body-guards of kings.[5] The Lokapâla gods the sixth in order, are officers of Indras and control the different Lokas.[6] The Anîka gods are like soldiers of Indras.[7] The Prakîrṇaka gods are like the subjects[8] and Âbhiyogya gods the servants of Indras.[9] The Kilviṣaka gods being the tenth in grade cannot command the respect due to other gods belonging to the higher grades and these stand outside the circle of those of higher grades, like feudatories outside the kingdom of kings.[10]

Among the Vyantara and Jyotiṣa gods the classes known as Trâyastriṇśa and Loka-pâla are absent.[11]

There are a class of gods known as Laukàntika who reside in

* "इंद्रसामानिकत्रायस्त्रिंशपारिषदात्मरक्षलोकपालानीकप्रकीर्णकाभियोग्यकिल्विषिकाश्चैकशः ।"

[तत्वार्थाधिगमसूत्रम् ४ । ४ ।]

1 "परमैश्वर्यादिंद्रव्यपदेशः ।"

2 "तत्स्थानार्हत्वात् सामानिकाः ।"

3 "मन्त्रिपुरोहितस्थानीयास्त्रायस्त्रिंशाः ।"

4 "वयस्यपीठमर्दसदृशाः पारिषदाः ।"

5 "आत्मरक्षाः शिरोरक्षोपमाः ।"

6 "आरक्षकार्थचरसमा लोकपालाः ।"

7 "दंडस्थानीयान्यनीकानि ।"

8 "प्रकीर्णकाः पौरजनपदकल्पाः ।"

9 "आभियोग्याः दाससमानाः ।"

10 "अंत्यवासिस्थानीयाः किल्विषकाः ।"

[तत्वार्थराजवार्त्तिकम् । ४ । ४ । १—१० ।]

11 "त्रायस्त्रिंशलोकपालवर्ज्या व्यन्तरज्योतिष्काः । "

[तत्वार्थाधिगमसूत्रम् । ४ । ५ ।]

Brahma-loka (a sphere included in the Kalpas mentioned in the above table). These gods are of eight classes, *viz.*, Sârasvat, Âditya, Banhi, Aruṇa, Gardatoya, Tuṣita, Avyâvâdha, and Ariṣṭa.[1]

Verse 10. Page 30.

C. The Story of Dvîpâyana or Dvaipâyana.

We have quoted an extract from Yaśastilaka-champû (the reading of which however appears to be incorrect) in the footnote on page 30, a translation of which is as follows:

"During the wanderings of Lord Ariṣṭanemi he was asked by Nârâyaṇa Gaṇadharadeva on Urjayana Hill 'Lord! will this prosperous city of Dvârikâ be destroyed from any cause?' The Gaṇadhara said 'What is the necessity of such a thought?' But in spite of having spoken thus, he being pressed by Hari said 'After twelve years, the city will be burnt by Kumâra Dvaipâyana.' Hearing this, Dvaipâyana intending to make this prophecy false, took a vow and passing twelve years in the eastern country without noticing (that the period had not expired on account of) an additional month approached the city of Dvârikâ and sat at the gates with the intention of giving up his life. At that time being struck on the head by Mâtaṅga who was drunk became Agni-kumâra through rage and burnt the city."

The story of Dvîpâyana is thus narrated in Jaina Harivaṃśa Purâṇa by Jinasena. The Tirthaṅkar Neminâtha was on Girnar Hill, when Vasudeva, Baladeva, Kriṣṇa, etc., went to him and asked about the future state of the city of Dvârikâ. Neminâtha replied that after twelve years Dvârikâ will be burnt by Dvîpâyana who will get angry on account of the assault by drunken young men of the city. Dvîpâyana was the uncle of Baladeva. When he heard that it has been foretold that he himself will be instrumental in the destroyal of the city with the people in it he became an ascetic belonging to the Digambara sect of the Jainas and going away to the eastern country, began to practise penances. After the lapse of twelve years according to his calculation (though really the period was not over) he returned to the city of Dvârikâ and remained absorbed in meditation on a hill outside the city. In the meantime the young

[1] "ब्रह्मलोकालया लौकान्तिकाः ।"

"सारस्वतादित्यवह्न्यरुणगर्दतोयतुषिताव्याबाधारिष्टाश्च ।"

[तत्त्वार्थाधिगमसूत्रम् । ४ । २४—२५]

scions of Jadu race headed by Śâmba became drunk with wine and seeing Dvîpâyana in that posture said "This is that wretched Dvîpâyana who will destory Dvârikâ. Let us kill him." Saying this they began to throw stones at Dvîpâyana. Then Dvîpâyana became enraged and destroyed the city of Dvârikâ by fire. [See Canto 61, Harivaṃśa Purâṇa by Jinasena.]

The reader will notice the similarity of this story with that in the Mahâbhârata and Harivaṃśa of the Hindus where it is said that Dvârikâ was depopulated by the curse of the angry sage Durbâsâ who was ridiculed by the young Jadus headed by Śâmba. The members of the Jadu race drank wine and killed one another in a quarrel, arising from a trifling cause while they were under the influence of wine.

Verse 16. Page 48.

D. Sound.

Dr. Brajendranath Seal writes in his "Positive Sciences of the Ancient Hindus:" Sounds may be classed as "loud or faint, bass (thick) or treble (hollow), clang or articulate speech." In a letter to us Dr. Seal has written "This differs widely from the traditional explanations of Ghana as sound of metallic instruments and Suṣira (Sauṣira) as the sound of wind-instruments, etc." In page 48 we have followed the classification adopted by Akalaṅka Deva in Tattvârtha-râja-vârttika, Chapter V, Sûtra 24, Vârttikas 2—6. Dr. Seal is of opinion that Akalaṅka Deva has not interpreted the Sûtra of Umâsvâmi according to the earlier tradition. Dr. Seal writes "My interpretations are more primary than the traditional ones and are nearer to Umâsvâmi's meaning in this passage. The Amarkoṣa and the Râjavârttika (on Umâsvâmi) represent a later tradition."

Verse 17-18. Pages 52-56.

E. Dharma and Adharma Astikâyas.

In "Positive Sciences of the Ancient Hindus" by Dr. Brajendranath Seal, M.A., Ph.D., we find on page 93 the words "merit and demerit" used as equivalents for Dharma and Adharma. In a letter to us Dr. Seal writes that he had put down the words "Dharma and Adharma," but possibly his proof-reader thinking his retention of the Sanskrit terms to be a mere slip, put down what he thought to be their equivalents. This change escaped the notice of Dr. Seal when he hurried through the final proof.

Nothing could be farther from the idea conveyed by 'Dharma and Adharma' than 'merit and demerit.' In the aforesaid letter Dr. Seal writes "There is no English equivalent for the Jaina Dharmâstikâya or the Jaina Adharmâstikâya. (Merit and demerit are equivalents for Puṇya and Pâpa). Dharmâstikâya may be rendered as the cosmic principle which upholds (or simply conditions) *the order of simultaneous (or consentaneous) movements* in the world ("Sakrid-gati yugapad-vhâvi-gati"—Prabhâchandra) answering somewhat to Leibneitz's Pre-established harmony...........Dharmâstikâya is not simply the accompanying cause of movements—it is something more—it is the cause (or condition) of the *system of movements* the fact of an *order* in the movements of Jîva and Pudgala. This is my correction of the error."

Verse 48. Page 110.

F. Dhyâna.

The commentator Brahmadeva, in his explanation of this verse, has added a detailed account of Dhyâna, as recognised in Jainism. We give here an exposition of Dhyâna with quotations from a work named Jñânârṇava by Śubha-Chandra Âchârya in which this subject has been treated in an exhaustive manner.

Dhyâna (contemplation or meditation) is of four kinds, Ârta, Raudra, Dharma and Śukla. The first two give rise to pain while the last ones lead to the destruction of Karmas. Each of these four kinds of Dhyâna are again sub-divided into four classes.[1]

Ârta-dhyâna arises from the desire springing from Avidyâ (delusion) and is like the illusory belief of a person who has lost his way (and thinks the wrong way to be the right one).[2]

---

[1] " आर्त्तरौद्रविकल्पेन दुर्ध्यानं देहिनां द्विधा ।
द्विधा प्रशस्तमप्युक्तं धर्मशुक्लविकल्पतः ॥
स्यातां तत्रार्त्तरौद्रे द्वे दुर्ध्यानेऽत्यन्तदुःखदे ।
धर्मशुक्ले ततोऽन्ये द्वे कर्मनिर्मूलनक्षमे ॥
प्रत्येकं च चतुर्भेदैश्चतुष्टयमिदं मतम् ।
अनेकवस्तुसाधर्म्यवैधर्म्यालम्बनं यतः ॥"

[ज्ञानार्णवः । २५ ॥ २०—२२]

[2] " ऋते भवमथार्त्तं स्यादसद्ध्यानं शरीरिणाम्
दिङ्मोहान्मत्ततातुल्यमविद्यावासनावशात् ॥"

[ज्ञानार्णवः । २५ ॥ २३]

Ârta-dhyâna is of four kinds: (1) that arising from the loss of what is desirable, (2) that arising from avoidance of what is harmful, (3) that arising from sickness and (4) that arising from a desire to possess objects of enjoyment.[1]

Raudra-dhyâna is that which has reference to the external or internal activity of a being whose intention is cruel. Raudra-dhyâna is of four kinds: (1) that which arises from a delight in harming others, (2) that which arises from a delight in speaking a falsehood, (3) that which arises from a delight in theft and (4) that which arises from a delight in hoarding up and preserving things.[2]

Dharma-dhyâna arises when one controls his mind and desists from the enjoyment of worldly objects.

A person who being possessed of knowledge and indifferent to worldly objects is desirous of obtaining liberation, and being active to attain that end fixes his attention with an unruffled mind (is successful in having Dharma-dhyâna and) is praised by all.[3]

Dharma-dhyâna is of four kinds: Âjñâ-vichaya, Apâya-vichaya, Vipâka-vichaya and Saṃsthâna-vichaya.

Âjñâ-vichaya is the contemplation of the categories as laid down in the Jain scriptures according to the instruction of the

---

1 "अनिष्टयेागजन्माद्यं तथेष्टार्थात्ययात् परं।
रुक्प्रकोपात्तृतीयं स्यान्निदानात् तूर्यमङ्गिनाम् ॥"

[ज्ञानार्णवः । २५ ॥ २४]

2 " रुद्राशयभवं भीममपि रौद्रं चतुर्विधम् ।
कीर्त्यमानं विदान्त्वार्याः सर्वसत्वाभयप्रदाः ॥
रुद्रः क्रूराशयः प्राणी प्रणीतस्तत्वदर्शिभिः ।
रुद्रस्य कर्मभावेा वा रौद्रमित्यभिधीयते ॥
हिंसानन्दान् मृषानन्दाच्चौर्यात् संरक्षणात्तथा ।
प्रभवत्यङ्गिनां शश्वदपि राद्रं चतुर्विधम् ॥

[ज्ञानार्णवः । २६ ॥ १—३]

3 " अथ प्रशममालम्ब्य विधाय स्ववशं मनः ।
विरज्य कामभेागेषु धर्मध्यानं निरूपय ॥
ज्ञानवैराग्यसम्पन्नः संवृतात्मा स्थिराशयः ।
मुमुक्षुरुद्यमी शान्तेा धाता धीरः प्रशस्यते ॥"

[ज्ञानार्णवः । २७ ॥ १—३]

omniscient Jinas.[1] These should be believed and accepted on the authority of the words of the Jinas as they never speak what is false.[2]

Apâya-vichaya is the contemplation of means by which the Karmas are destroyed. It should be contemplated that persons are lost if they do not attain the three jewels, *viz.*, perfect faith, perfect knowledge and perfect conduct,[3] as laid down by the omniscient.

Vipâka-vichaya is the contemplation that creatures enjoy pleasure and pain as fruits of their Karmas,[4] and Samsthâna-vichaya is the contemplation of the arrangement of the universe.[5]

Śukla Dhyâna arises in a soul when it is void of action, beyond the influence of the senses and being meditative of itself is not conscious that it does so.[6]

---

1 "आज्ञापायविपाकानां क्रमशः संस्थितेस्तथा ।
विचयो यः पृथक् तद्धि धर्मध्यानं चतुर्विधम् ॥
वस्तुतत्वं स्वसिद्धान्तं प्रसिद्धं यत्र चिन्तयेत् ।
सर्वज्ञाज्ञाभियोगेन तदाज्ञाविचयो मतः ॥"

[ज्ञानार्णवः । ३३ ॥ ५—६]

2 सूक्ष्मं जिनेन्द्रवचनं हेतुभिर्यन्न हन्यते ।
आज्ञासिद्धं च तद् ग्राह्यं नान्यथावादिनो जिनाः ॥

[Verse quoted in Brahmadeva's commentary.]

3 "अपायविचयं ध्यानं तद्वदन्ति मनीषिणः ।
अपायः कर्मणां यत्र सोपायः स्मर्यते बुधैः ॥
श्रीमत्सर्वज्ञनिर्दिष्टं मार्गं रत्नत्रयात्मकम् ।
अनासाद्य भवारण्ये चिरं नष्टाः शरीरिणः ॥"

[ज्ञानार्णवः । ३४ ॥ १–२]

4 "स विपाक इति ज्ञेयो यः स्वकर्मफलोदयः ।
प्रतिक्षणसमुद्भूतश्चित्ररूपः शरीरिणाम् ॥
कर्मजातं फलं दत्ते विचित्रमिह देहिनाम् ।
आसाद्य नियतं नाम द्रव्यादिकचतुष्टयम् ॥"

[ज्ञानार्णवः । ३५ ॥ १–२]

5 "समस्तोऽयमहो लोकः केवलज्ञानगोचरः ।
तं व्यस्तं वा समस्तं वा स्वशक्त्या चिन्तयेद्यतिः ॥"

[ज्ञानार्णवः । ३५ ॥१८४]

6 "निष्क्रियं करणातीतं ध्यानधारणवर्जितम् ।
अन्तर्मुखं तु यच्चित्तं तच्छुक्लमिति पठ्यते ॥"

[ज्ञानार्णवः । ४२ ॥ ४]

Śukla Dhyâna is of four kinds: Prithaktva-vitarka-vîchâra, Ekatva-vitarka-vîchâra, Sûkṣmakriyâ-pratîpâti and Vyuparata-kriyâ-nivritti. In the first there is a transition of contemplation while in the second the contemplation is in the same state. In the third there is action of the body in a very subtle state while in the fourth the same is absent altogether.[1]

In Tattvârthâdhigama Sûtra we have a similar description of Dhyâna.[2]

The commentator Brahmadeva says that Dhyâna can also be divided in another manner into four classes, *viz.*, (1) Piṇḍastha, (2) Padastha, (3) Rûpastha and (4) Rûpâtîta.[3]

---

1 "सवितर्कं सवीचारं सपृथक्त्वं च कीर्त्तितम् ।
शुक्लमाद्यं द्वितीयं तु विपर्यस्तमतोऽ परम् ॥
सवितर्कमवीचारमेकत्वपदलाञ्छितम् ।
कीर्त्तितं मुनिभिः शुक्लं द्वितीयमतिनिर्मलम् ॥
सूक्ष्मक्रियाप्रतीपाति तृतीयं सार्थनामकम् ।
समुच्छिन्नक्रियं ध्यानं तुर्यमार्यैर्निवेदितम् ॥"

[ज्ञानार्णवः । ४२ ॥ ९–११]

2 *Vide* "आर्त्तरौद्रधर्म्यशुक्लानि ।"
"परे मोक्षहेतू ।"
"आर्त्तममनोज्ञस्य सम्प्रयोगे तद्विप्रयोगाय स्मृतिसमन्वाहारः ।"
"विपरीतं मनोज्ञस्य ।"
"वेदनायाश्च ।"
"निदानं च ।"
"हिंसानृतास्तेयविषयसंरक्षणेभ्यो रौद्रमविरतदेशविरतयोः ।"
"आज्ञापायविपाकसंस्थानविचयाय धर्म्यम् ।"
"पृथक्त्वैकत्ववितर्कसूक्ष्मक्रियाप्रतिपातिव्युपरतक्रियानिवर्त्तीनि ।"

[तत्वार्थाधिगमसूत्रम् । ९ । २८–३३, ३५, ३६, ३९.]

3 "पदस्थं मन्त्रवाक्यस्थं पिण्डस्थं स्वात्मचिन्तनम् ।
रूपस्थं सर्वचिद्रूपं रूपातीतं निरञ्जनम् ॥"

[Verse quoted in Brahmadeva's commentary.]

Compare also—

"पिण्डस्थं च पदस्थं च रूपस्थं रूपवर्जितम् ।
चतुर्द्धा ध्यानमाम्नातं भव्यराजीवभास्करैः ॥"

[ज्ञानार्णवः । ३६ ॥ १]

Piṇḍastha Dhyâna is the contemplation of oneself and has "five Dhâraṇâs, *i.e.*, fixing the mind on five things. They are (1) Pârthivî, (2) Âgneyî, (3) Mârutî ; (4) Vâruṇî and (5) Rûpavatî. The Yogin should imagine or place before his mind a vast ocean of milk, hushed and tranquil and without waves. He should then imagine a lotus with a thousand petals, as big as Jambudvîpa and shining like gold, to be situated in the midst of it, and the lotus to have a celestial pericarp like a mountain of gold. He should conceive a lofty throne resembling the autumnal moon to be placed in that pericarp and should imagine himself as sitting at ease on that throne, serene, without desire, or hatred and prepared to conquer his enemy the Karman. Thus ends the first Dhâraṇâ.[1]

The Yogin should then imagine a shining and beautiful lotus with sixteen petals jutting out, as existing in the hollow of his navel. He should contemplate the fourteen vowels (अ, आ, इ, ई, उ, ऊ, ऋ, ॠ, ऌ, ॡ, ए, ऐ, ओ, औ) and अं अः as marked on the sixteen petals and the great Mantra Arhaṃ with the dot over the line as shining on the pericarp. Then he should imagine a volume of smoke arising from the curvilinear *r* or *repha* of the Mantra, then

---

1 "पिण्डस्थं पञ्च विज्ञेया धारणा वीरवर्णिताः ।
संयमी यास्वसंमूढो जन्मपाशान्निकृन्तति ॥
पार्थिवी स्यात्तथाग्नेयी श्वसनावाथ वारुणी ।
तत्वरूपवती चेति विज्ञेयास्ता यथाक्रमम् ॥
तिर्यग्लोकसमं योगी स्मरति क्षीरसागरम् ।
निःशब्दं शान्तकल्लोलं हारनीहारसंनिभम् ॥
तस्य मध्ये सुनिर्माणं सहस्रदलमम्बुजम् ।
स्मरत्यमितभादीप्तं द्रुतहेमसमप्रभम् ॥
अभ्ज़रागसमुद्भूतं केसरालिविराजितम् ।
जम्बूद्वीपप्रमाणं च चित्तभ्रमररञ्जकम् ॥
स्वर्णाचलमयीं दिव्यां तत्र स्मरति कर्णिकाम्
स्फुरत्पिङ्गप्रभाजालपिशङ्गितदिगन्तराम् ॥
शरच्चन्द्रनिभं तस्यामुन्नतं हरिविष्टरम् ।
तत्रात्मानं सुखासीनं प्रशान्तमिति चिन्तयेत् ॥
रागद्वेषादिनिःशेषकलङ्कक्षपणक्षमम् ।
उद्युक्तं च भवोद्भूतकर्मसन्तानशासने ॥"

[ज्ञानार्णवः । ३६ ॥ २–९]

a succession of sparks, and then a continuous flame. The flame increasing in intensity burns the lotus which exists in the heart, upside downwards and which is the product of eight Karmas and has eight petals. He should then imagine fire in a triangular shape with the Svastika on its apex away from his body blown by the wind and burning brightly with a golden flame. The fire from the Mantra burns the body in the inside, and this fire from outside, and being in flames the body is reduced to ashes and also the lotus in the navel. Thus far we have the Âgneyi Dhâraṇâ.[1]

Then the man should imagine wind blowing with the violence of a tempest and scattering away the ashes, after which he should think of it as becoming still. This is the Mârutî Dhâraṇâ.[2]

---

1 "ततोऽसौ निश्चलाभ्यासात् कमलं नाभिमण्डले ।
स्मरत्यतिमनोहारि षोडशोन्नतपत्रकम् ॥
प्रतिपत्रसमासीनस्वरमालाविराजितम् ।
कर्णिकायां महामन्त्रं विस्फुरन्तं विचिन्तयेत् ॥
रेफरुद्धं कलाबिन्दुलाञ्छितं शून्यमक्षरम् ।
लसदिन्दुच्छटाकोटिकान्तिव्याप्तहरिन्मुखम् ॥
तस्य रेफाद्विनिर्यान्तीं शनैर्धूमशिखां स्मरेत् ।
स्फुलिङ्गसन्ततिं पश्चाज्ज्वालालीं तदनन्तरम् ॥
तेन ज्वालाकलापेन वर्द्धमानेन सन्ततम् ।
दहत्यविरतं धीरः पुण्डरीकं हृदि-स्थितम् ॥
तदष्टकर्मनिर्माणमष्टपत्रमधोमुखम् ।
दहत्येव महामन्त्रध्यानोत्थप्रबलोऽनलः ॥
ततो बहिः शरीरस्य त्रिकोणं वह्निमण्डलम् ।
स्मरेज्ज्वालाकलापेन ज्वलन्तमिव वाडवम् ॥
वह्निबीजसमाक्रान्तं पर्यन्ते स्वस्तिकाङ्कितम् ।
ऊर्द्ध्ववायुपुरोद्भूतं निर्धूमं काञ्चनप्रभम् ॥
अन्तर्दहति मन्त्रार्चिर्बहिर्वह्निपुरं पुरम् ।
धगद्धगितिविस्फूर्जज्ज्वालाप्रचयभासुरम् ॥
भस्मभावमसौ नीत्वा शरीरं तच्च पङ्कजम् ।
दाह्याभावात् स्वयं शान्तिं याति वह्निः शनैः शनैः ॥"
[ज्ञानार्णवः । ३६ ॥ १०—१९]

2 "विमानपथमापूर्य संचरन्तं समीरणम् ।
स्मरत्यविरतं योगी महावेगं महाबलम् ॥

Then he should contemplate a number of clouds pouring down rain in torrents accompanied by thunder and lightning. After that he should imagine a stream of water bearing the standard of Varuṇa, beautiful like the crescent of the moon and overflowing the sky. With this water, he should wash off, in imagination, all the ashes of his body. This is Vâruṇî Dhâraṇâ.[1]

Then he should contemplate himself to be in qualities like an all-knowing being free from the seven elements, sitting on the throne, adored by the gods possessing celestial excellences and shining like the full moon."[2]

Padastha Dhyâna is the contemplation by using certain words or letters. The efficacy of prayer, examples of which are given in

---

चालयन्तं सुरानीकं ध्वनन्तं त्रिदशालयम् ।
दारयन्तं घनव्रातं क्षोभयन्तं महार्णवम् ॥
व्रजन्तं भुवनाभोगे संचरन्तं हरिन्मुखे ।
विसर्पन्तं जगत्क्रीडे निविशन्तं धरातले ॥
उद्धूय तद्रजः शीघ्रं तेन प्रबलवायुना ।
ततः स्थिरीकृताभ्यासः समीरं शान्तिमानयेत् ॥"

[ज्ञानार्णवः । ३६ ॥ २०–२३ ।]

1 "वारुण्यां स हि पुण्यात्मा घनजालचितं नभः ।
इन्द्रायुधतडिद्गर्जच्चमत्काराकुलं स्मरेत् ॥
सुधाम्बुप्रभवैः सान्द्रैर्बिन्दुभिर्मौक्तिकोज्ज्वलैः ।
वर्षन्तं तं स्मरेद्धीरः स्थूलस्थूलैर्निरन्तरम् ॥
ततोऽर्धेन्दुसमं कान्तं पुरं वरुणलाञ्छितम् ।
ध्यायेत् सुधापयःपूरैः प्लावयन्तं नभस्तलम् ॥
तेनाचिन्त्यप्रभावेण दिव्यध्यानोत्थिताम्बुना ।
प्रक्षालयति निःशेषं तद्रजः कायसंभवम् ॥"

[ज्ञानार्णवः । ३६ ॥ २४–२७]

2 " सप्तधातुविनिर्मुक्तं पूर्णचन्द्रामलत्विषम् ।
सर्वज्ञकल्पमात्मानं ततः स्मरति संयमी ॥
मृगेन्द्रविष्टरारूढं दिव्यातिशयसंयुतम् ।
कल्याणमहिमोपेतं देवदैत्योरगार्चितम् ॥
विलीनाशेषकर्माणं स्फुरन्तमतिनिर्मलम् ।
स्वं ततः पुरुषाकारं स्वाङ्गगर्भगतं स्मरेत् ॥"

[ज्ञानार्णवः । ३६ ॥ २८–३०]

verse 49, Dravya-saṃgraha is laid down in connection with this kind of contemplation.[1]

"Rûpastha Dhyâna is contemplating the Lord Jina, sitting on a throne of jewel in the assembly of men who are desirous of salvation, surrounded by the twelve Gaṇadharas and the eight door-keepers, possessing infinite greatness, a store of infinite, virtues, of a celestial body, shining more brilliantly than a Koti of suns, fanned by excellent *chowries*, attended on by the gods, free from the eighteen blemishes, endowed with all the excellences and expounding the Dharma.

Rûpâtîta Dhyâna consists in contemplating the highest form of one's own soul, as immaterial, a store of virtues, and resembling the Siddhas between whom and himself there is no specific difference."

---

1 "पदान्यालम्ब्यपुण्यानि योगिभिर्यद्विधीयते ।
तत्पदस्थं मतं ध्यानं विचित्रनयपारगैः ॥"

[ज्ञानार्णवः । ३८ ॥ १]

CHART—No. VIII.

TABLE I.

Dhyâna.

- Ârta.
  - Iṣṭavi-yoga.
  - Aniṣṭa-saṃyoga.
  - Vyâdhi-pratîkâra.
  - Bhoga-nidâna.
- Raudra.
  - Hiṃsâ-nanda.
  - Mṛiṣâ-nanda.
  - Steyâ-nanda.
  - Viṣaya-saṃ-rakṣaṇânanda.
- Dharma.
  - Âjñâ-vichaya.
  - Apâya-vichaya.
  - Vipâka-vichaya.
  - Samsthâna-vichaya.
- Śukla.
  - Prithaktva-vitarka-vichâra.
  - Ekatva-vitarka-vichâra.
  - Sûkṣma-kriyâ-prati-pâti.
  - Vyuparata-kriyâ-nivritti.

TABLE II.

Dhyâna.

- Piṇḍastha.
  - Pârthivî Dhâraṇâ.
  - Agneyî Dhâraṇâ.
  - Mârutî Dhâraṇâ.
  - Vâruṇî Dhâraṇâ.
  - Rûpavatî Dhâraṇâ.
- Padastha.
- Rûpastha.
- Rûpâtîta.

ALPHABETICAL INDEX OF THE PRÂKRIT GÂTHÂS

[Figures within brackets indicate the number of verses].

L.

M.

N.

P.

R.

S.

T.

U.

V.

ALPHABETICAL INDEX OF THE SANSKRIT CHHÂYÂS

[Figures within brackets indicate the number of verses.]

M.

N.

P.

R.

S.

T.

U.

V.

Y.

ALPHABETICAL INDEX TO THE INTRODUCTION

GENERAL INDEX

A

P.

R.

S.

T.

This index is the work of Srikanta Kumari Devi, wife of Kumar Devendra Prasad.